Islam and Gender in Colonial Northeast Africa

Islam in Africa

VOLUME 21

The titles published in this series are listed at *brill.com/isaf*

Sittī 'Alawiyya al-Mīrġanī.
PIOLA CASELLI ARCHIVE IN ROME.

Islam and Gender in Colonial Northeast Africa

Sittī ʿAlawiyya, the Uncrowned Queen

By

Silvia Bruzzi

BRILL

LEIDEN | BOSTON

This work has been produced within the framework of the LabexMed Unit of Excellence—Social Sciences and Humanities at the heart of multidisciplinary research for the Mediterranean—which has the following reference: 10-LABX-0090. It has enjoyed the benefits of a state grant from the Agence Nationale de la Recherche for the Investissements d'Avenir A*MIDEX project, reference no. ANR-11-IDEX-0001-02.

Cover illustration: The Duke of the Abruzzi's travels in Abyssinia. The sceriffa Alaluja El Morgani (sic) pays homage to the Duke of the Abruzzi. Reparto Attualità: 1927. 07.05.1927. La sceriffa Alaluja o Alabuia El Morgani accompagnata dai rappresentanti della missione—campo medio, cod. foto: A00000394. Istituto Luce Cinecittà Historical Archive, Rome.

Library of Congress Cataloging-in-Publication Data

Names: Bruzzi, Silvia, author.
Title: Islam and gender in colonial northeast Africa : Sitti ʿAlawiyya, the uncrowned queen / by Silvia Bruzzi.
Description: Boston : Brill, 2018. | Series: Islam in Africa ; volume 21 | Includes bibliographical references and index.
Identifiers: LCCN 2017036394 (print) | LCCN 2017040548 (ebook) | ISBN 9789004356160 (E-book) | ISBN 9789004348004 (hardback : alk. paper)
Subjects: LCSH: Sufism—Africa, Northeast—History—20th century. | Islam—Africa, Northeast—History—20th century. | Women sufis—Africa, Northeast—History—20th century. | Women in Islam—Africa, Northeast—History—20th century. | al-Mirghani, ʿAlawiyya, 1892–1940.
Classification: LCC BP188.8.A3553 (ebook) | LCC BP188.8.A3553 B78 2018 (print) | DDC 297.40963—dc23
LC record available at https://lccn.loc.gov/2017036394

Typeface for the Latin, Greek, and Cyrillic scripts: "Brill". See and download: brill.com/brill-typeface.

ISSN 1570-3754
ISBN 978-90-04-34800-4 (hardback)
ISBN 978-90-04-35616-0 (e-book)

This book is printed on acid-free paper and produced in a sustainable manner.

To My Family

Contents

Acknowledgements XI
List of Illustrations XII
A Note on Transliteration and Dates XVI
Transliteration List XVII

Introduction 1
Sufism, Colonialism and Gender Dynamics 1
Sufism and the Female Body 7

1 **Islamic Renewal Movements, Colonial Occupation, and the Ḫatmiyya in the Red Sea Region** 12
Islam and the Idrīsī Tradition in Northeast Africa 12
The Establishment of the Ḫatmiyya in the Red Sea Region 19

2 **Sufis at the Crossroads: Regional Conflicts and Colonial Penetration** 25
The Ḫatmiyya up against the Sudanese Mahdī 25
A Marriage Alliance between the Mīrġanī and the Beni ʿAmer People 31
Sīdī Hāšim: Spy or *walī*? 36

3 **Islam, Gender and Leadership** 43
Female Heirs by Blood Alone: A Power Vacuum? 43
Women and Heresy in Sufi Centres 47
Embodying Religious Orthodoxy 53

4 **Fragmented, (In)Visible and (Un)Told Stories** 63
Looking for Muslim Women in Northeast African History 63
Regional Women's Centres of Empowerment and Religious Learning 70
Baraka, Itinerant Preaching and the Mobility of Pious Women 82

5 **Sufi Women's "Fantasy", Performances and Fashion** 88
Imagination and Desire in Women's Bodies 88
Women's *Fantasia* in Sufi Regional Centres 91
Visiting a Fashionable, Cosmopolitan Woman 102

6 **Growing Visibility in the Political Arena** 112
Women's Bodies, Photography, and Colonialism 112
Growing Popularity Broadcast through Visual Media 120
Visibility, Visuality and Power in Portraits of the *Šarīfa* 133

7 **Marvels, Charisma and Modernity** 140
Performed and Contested *Karāmāt* 140
Modern Enchantment: Colonial Technologies and Infrastructures 144
Mediating Conflicts 159

8 **Military Bodies: Askaris, Officials and "the Female Warrior"** 165
Religious Intermediaries and Regional Networks 165
Enlisting Askaris and Colonial Propaganda 175
The Defeat of Italy 183

9 **A Female Icon of Muslim "Emancipation" for the Conquest of Ethiopia (1936–1941)** 187
Building Mosques: Muslim Policies from Libya to Ethiopia 187
A Female Icon of Muslim "Emancipation" 189
The Mosques Built in Honour of Sittī ʿAlawiyya 193
Muslim Attitudes towards the Italian Occupation: From Collaboration to Agency 200

10 **Conclusion: Sufi Memories** 205
Women's Embodied Archives and Spirit Possession 205
Embodying Sittī ʿAlawiyya's Visit to Harar 212
Sufi Visions and Historical Imagination 217

Bibliography 223
Index 247

Acknowledgements

This book is the result of my research at Bologna University and the Centre for Middle Eastern and Islamic Studies (SMI, Bergen University) with the support of the Norwegian Research Council and the Institut des Mondes Africains (*IMAf*, Paris). Along the way, I have met inspiring scholars whom I would like to thank, in particular Irma Taddia, Uoldelul Chelati Dirar, Massimo Papa, Alessandro Gori, Nicola Melis, Adriana Piga, Jean-Louis Triaud, Bertrand Hirsch, Anne Bang, Sean O'Fahey, Knut Vikør, Anne Hugon, Elena Vezzadini and other colleagues who enriched me with their knowledge and advice on my long journey.

I owe a special vote of thanks to Rémi Dewière, who shared much of this work with me and who always supported me. Of course, thanks also go out to all my friends, especially Anna and Cristina, and my family—my mother, my father, Sara, Gabriele, Diana, and Viola—who put up with my frequent absences with affection.

I would also especially like to thank the Institut Émilie du Châtelet and its members, which awarded me a grant (GID-Région Île-de-France) to pursue my research on gender perspectives, and agreed to extend my contract after the birth of my daughter Anaïs. Thanks to the IEC, research and motherhood did not cause the conflict I had feared they might.

Finally, my sincere wishes go out to Giulio Regeni and to his family, who continue to call for the truth. He was a brilliant young researcher, a Gramscian scholar and a citizen of the world, a symbol of a generation that creates bridges by travelling and writing.

List of Illustrations

Figures

1 Sittī ʿAlawiyya's shrine xv
2 Inscription at Sittī ʿAlawiyya's shrine xv
3 Portrait of Sīdī Hāšim 37
4 Keren—Tahil feast funeral prayers for the death of Šayḫ Morgani (holy man) 42
5 The Keren mosque 42
6 Entrance to Sittī ʿAlawiyya's residence 60
7 Sittī ʿAlawiyya and Sīdī Ǧaʿfar al-Mīrġanī, late 1930 61
8 Sittī ʿAlawiyya, an Italian officer and Sīdī Ǧaʿfar al-Mīrġanī, late 1930 62
9 Sittī Fāṭima al-Mīrġanī 69
10 Red Cross nurses visit Sittī ʿAlawiyya (1936) 79
11 A Red Cross nurse, Sittī ʿAlawiyya, and a child (1936) 80
12 Red Cross nurses, a colonial officer and Sittī ʿAlawiyya (1936) 81
13 East Africa—Bilen Fantasy 90
14 Tripolitania, Gadames—Arabic fantasy 92
15 Keren—Women's fantasy for the death of Šayḫ Morgani (a holy man), (a) 93
16 Keren—Women's fantasy for the death of Šayḫ Morgani (a holy man), (b) 93
17 Arabic Fantasy at *Sceriffa Alauia*'s residence, (a) 99
18 Arabic Fantasy at *Sceriffa Alauia*'s residence, (b) 99
19 Waiting for the Arabic Fantasy at *Sceriffa Alauia*'s residence 100
20 Portrait of Sittī ʿAlawiyya 106
21 Sittī ʿAlawiyya and the Princess of Piemonte dressed in Red Cross uniform, with other Red Cross nurses (1936) 108
22 Sittī ʿAlawiyya and Renzo Martinelli at her residence in Hetumlo (1927) 109
23 Sittī ʿAlawiyya and Renzo Martinelli at her residence in Hetumlo (1927) (1930: 52) 110
24 *Sceriffa Alauia* and her followers 114
25 Said Giafer and his caliphs 114
26 The Duke of the Abruzzi's travels in Abyssinia. The *sceriffa Alaluja El Morgani* (sic) pays homage to the Duke of the Abruzzi 118

27 The Duke of the Abruzzi's travels in Abyssinia. The *sceriffa Alaluja El Morgani* (sic) pays homage to the Duke of the Abruzzi 119
28 Luce National Institute [1932–37], memories of the Duke of the Abruzzi during his travel in Abyssinia 123
29 A Muslim community welcome ceremony in honour of the Governor Ammiraglio De Feo in Massawa (08/12/1937), (a) 125
30 A Muslim community welcome ceremony in honour of the Governor Ammiraglio De Feo in Massawa (08/12/1937), (b) 126
31 A Muslim community welcome ceremony in honour of the Governor Ammiraglio De Feo in Massawa (08/12/1937), (c) 127
32 Giuseppe Caniglia's book 'La Sceriffa di Massaua' 131
33 Sittī ʿAlawiyya and Mussolini at Palazzo Venezia (Rome) in 1938 132
34 The uncrowned Queen of the Eritrean colony 136
35 ʿAd Šayḫ Mosque in Camcena [Camceua] 146
36 The new mosque in Tesseney (1930s) 146
37 The renovated mosque in Barentu (1930s) 147
38 The school and the mosque, Agordat 147
39 The mosque, Agordat (1930s) 148
40 The New Mosque, Keren (1930s) 148
41 Salvago Raggi School, Keren 149
42 Visit and inauguration of hydraulic works in Tesseney. Meeting with Morgani, 1928, (a) 153
43 Visit and inauguration of hydraulic works in Tesseney. Meeting with Morgani, 1928, (b) 154
44 Visit and inauguration of hydraulic works in Tesseney. Meeting with Morgani, 1928, (c) 154
45 Orthodox Church inauguration with the participation of all religious, civil and military authorities (Massawa, 2 Febrauary 1936) 155
46 Sayyid Ǧaʿfar pays homage to Governor Gasparini, Asmara (1924?) 158
47 The Governor donates a Flobert carbine to the son of the Commissioner Sayyid Ǧaʿfar al-Mīrġanī, Asmara 158
48 Portrait of Sittī ʿAlawiyya (around 1939) 163
49 Visit of East African notables in Rome, late 1930s 164
50 Italian East Africa. Morgani crosses subject regions to collect tributes 170
51 Sayyid Ǧaʿfar rides a camel 171
52 Letter from Sayyid Ǧaʿfar (Keren and Asmara) 173
53 Letter from Sayyid Ǧaʿfar (Keren and Agordat) 174

54 Sittī ʿAlawiyya's Mosque in Harar 211
55 Qaṣīda (poem) written at Sittī ʿAlawiyya's death 222

Maps

1 Red Sea region 18
2 Genealogy of the Mīrġanī family and its four main branches 24
3 Mediterranean and Red Sea region 139

FIGURE 1 *Sittī ʿAlawiyya's shrine.*
PHOTO BY SILVIA BRUZZI, HETUMLO 2009.

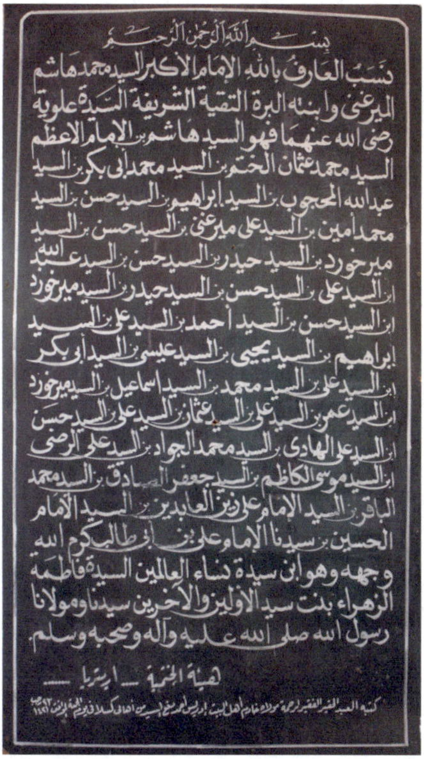

FIGURE 2
Inscription at Sittī ʿAlawiyya's shrine.
PHOTO BY SILVIA BRUZZI, HETUMLO 2009.

A Note on Transliteration and Dates

Words that are foreign to the English language are printed in italics (*šarīf, šarīfa, etc.*). Unless the English form is available, the names of places and people are written as they are usually spelt today in Latin script without diacritics. Noble Arabic titles used with reference to the Mīrġanī family such as Šayḫ, Sayyid, and Sīdī are employed interchangeably and printed in Roman script. The dates in this book are Common Era dates.

Transliteration List

ا	ā
ب	b
ة	-a
ت	t
ث	ṯ
ج	ǧ
ح	ḥ
خ	ḫ
د	d
ذ	ḏ
ر	r
ز	z
س	s
ش	š
ص	ṣ
ض	ḍ
ط	ṭ
ظ	ẓ
ع	ʿ
غ	ġ
ف	f
ق	q
ك	k
ل	l
م	m
ن	n
ه	h
و	w/ū
ي	y/ī
ء	ʾ
يّ	iyy
وّ	uww

Introduction

Sufism, Colonialism and Gender Dynamics

In 1938, a group of notables and dignitaries from East Africa and Libya were invited to Rome to celebrate the second anniversary of the foundation of the Italian Empire. Mussolini greeted them with a ceremony at Palazzo Venezia, in Rome. The national press reported enthusiastically on the event, which provided a fitting opportunity to show a consensus for Italian imperial policy in East Africa and the Mediterranean region. The official discourse stressed the policy of "emancipation" put in place by the Fascist government during the Second Italo-Ethiopian war in favour of "oppressed" Ethiopian Muslims; it lay at the heart of Italian propaganda during the occupation and was also widely used internationally to gain Muslim support in the Mediterranean region and the Middle East.[1] On this occasion, the Fascist propaganda stressed the presence of a woman as the representative of Eritrean Muslims—the so-called *Sceriffa Alauia el Morgani*—who declared her loyalty to Italy, and especially to Mussolini, who had claimed to be the "Sword of Islam", the protector of all Muslims, during his visit to Libya just one year earlier, in 1937.[2]

This political appeal to religious interests was strategically deployed not only by Italy but by all the colonial powers, especially as a part of the empire-building process in Africa; even in the context of the First World War, both the European powers and the Ottoman Empire had made increasingly active appeals to their pro-Islamic policies, their aim being on the one hand to seek a consensus in their African colonies, and on the other to promote the appointment of Muslim soldiers in colonial armies.[3]

From the 19th century on, Islamic revivalist movements crossed the Muslim world and spread into various regions of sub-Saharan Africa, at the same time as growing European penetration in the continent. In several cases, religious renewal was a response to the crisis triggered by the transition, and emerged as an alternative to the cultural hegemony of the European colonial powers. Among the main spokesmen for this religious renewal were the leaders

1 Sbacchi 1985: 163; Alvisini 2000: 4; Borruso 2001a: 57; Borruso 2001b: 1–45. See De Felice 1988; Wright 2005; Arielli 2010.

2 Borruso 1997: 40–41 and Figure 33. On Mussolini's ceremony in Libya, see Wright 2005.

3 With regard to British propaganda that claimed that it was a Muslim power during World War One, see Reynolds 2001: 605. For the French case, see, for example, Renard 2013 and Harrison 2003. On Islam and Empires see Motadel 2014.

 | DOI 10.1163/9789004356160_002

of the Islamic brotherhoods, some of whom led anti-colonial movements and appealed to Islamic precepts in order to justify the struggle against foreign occupation.[4] In other instances, members of the Sufi brotherhoods adopted a negotiating position, accommodated themselves to colonial rule, and actively participated in the ongoing modernization process. Depending on the specific context, the complex relationships between foreign domination and Islam were formulated in a variety of ways that had a decisive impact on political and social dynamics in Muslim African societies.[5] The colonial encounter inflamed the debate within Islamic circles from both a political and a theological point of view. It also involved controversies and conflicts relating to gender roles, raising the so-called "woman question",[6] and debates on women's religious leadership and female religious practices, which were accused of being backward and unorthodox.

Historians have discussed the socio-political dynamics that developed in various regions of Africa, especially in Francophone Africa during the colonial period,[7] extensively, but Northeast Africa and the former Italian colonial possessions remain largely underexplored.[8] This is especially the case with Eritrea and Ethiopia, where studies on Islam in general have experienced delays compared with what occurred in other areas of the continent.[9] The relationship between Islam and Italian colonialism, in particular, is still very much an open field of study.[10]

This work focuses specifically on one Islamic brotherhood, the Ḫatmiyya, in the cultural, religious and socio-political landscape of the time, and investigates in particular how it reacted and adjusted to the Italian occupation. My aim on the one hand is to bridge a gap that exists in studies of Islam in Eritrea and Ethiopia, in particular on the role played by this particular Sufi order during the Italian occupation, and on the other to make a contribution to our understanding of the broader gender dynamics that shaped the colonial encounter in the region. "A constitutive element of social relationships based on perceived differences between the sexes", and "a primary way of signify-

4 Peters 1979.

5 Robinson and Triaud 1997; Triaud 1995; Cruise O'Brien and Coulon 1988; Clancy-Smith 1994.

6 On this issue see Badran 2013.

7 Robinson 1999; Robinson 1988; Piga 2004.

8 However, there are important studies on Islam and Italian colonialism in Somalia and Libya: Battera 2001: 93–118; Battera 1998: 155–185; Baldinetti 2011: 408–436. See also Marongiu Buonaiuti 1982.

9 Gori 1995: 81–129; Gori 2006a: 72–94; Gori 2002, 2006b; Hussein Ahmed 2001; Hussein Ahmed 1992; Miran 2005: 177–215.

10 Taddia 2012.

ing relationships of power", is the gender paradigm that I have integrated into my analysis.[11] As Florence Rochefort has pointed out, the interplay between the political and religious spheres is crucial to the socio-cultural construction and organization of gender roles. Religions contribute towards the fostering of gender-based ideologies that are associated with cultural heritage and with political and moral values, as well as forms of authority and hierarchy. Women are more explicitly constrained by these dynamics, as "they are seen as embodying national, family and religious ideas, as well as the main agents for the transmission of values and the control of civil society by forms of male domination".[12]

Religious phenomena have contributed to questions being asked about a number of pivotal theoretical concepts in gender studies, including agency. Drawing from her ethnographic study of women's participation in Islamic movements, Saba Mahmood has suggested a different definition of agency "not as a synonym for resistance to relations of domination, but as a capacity for action that historically specific relations of subordination enable and create".[13]

The path I follow in this study travels through the clues and traces left by the principal representatives of the Ḫatmiyya Sufi order in Eritrea in general, but more particularly those left by Sittī ʿAlawiyya—*Sceriffa Alauia el Morgani*—the woman who achieved so much visibility in the Italian media during the celebrations of the second anniversary of the foundation of the Italian Empire in Rome in 1938. Throughout her life, this female member of the Mīrġanī family assumed a leading role in the Sufi order not only in Eritrea, but also on a trans-regional scale, which covered the entire period of the Italian occupation of Eritrea, *la colonia primogenita*. This was, in fact, a woman who achieved significant public visibility and exceptional political clout throughout the colonial period. In many ways, she was caught between two worlds: she was both a religious mentor and a political intermediary between the government and the local population, and as a representative of the Sufi order in Eritrea, she played both a socio-political and a religious role.

Sittī ʿAlawiyya was born in Massawa in 1892, two years after the creation of the colony, and died in Keren in 1940, on the eve of the famous and bloody 1941 Battle of Keren, which pitted the British and Italian armies against each other and marked a turning point in the liberation of Eritrea and Ethiopia, led by the British during the Second World War.

---

11 Scott 1986: 1067.

12 Rochefort 2007: 12–13.

13 Mahmood 2001: 202–236.

She was a member of the Mīrġanī family, whose members claimed to be descended from the Prophet and were recognized by the Italian colonial authorities as key Islamic leaders in Eritrea. After the death of her father in 1901, she inherited his role as representative of Ḫatmiyya, a transnational Islamic brotherhood that was—and still is—widespread in the Red Sea region, the Hejaz, Yemen, Egypt, Sudan and Eritrea. As representative and guardian of her father's shrine and mosque close to the port city of Massawa on the Eritrean side of the Red Sea, she became both a religious and a political authority. She was a shaykha, a point of reference for the Muslim population, the Italian authorities, who repeatedly sought her intermediation and intervention for the resolution of conflicts, and the believers who regularly visited her to seek her blessing and advice.

Sittī ʿAlawiyya is also one of those rare cases of a woman who emerged as an active agent of the Islamic renewal processes in the literature of twentieth-century Africa. African women, especially in majoritarian Muslim societies, tend to be marginal subjects, and it is only recently that they have earned more scholarly attention.[14] At the heart of this omission in the context of the colonial occupation lie a number of methodological issues, including the difficulties associated with accessing written sources. In many cases, the principal written sources of reference are kept in the colonial archives and reflect the experience of mainly male foreign authorities, from which African women emerge as silent or invisible parties. Their account expresses a point of view that pursues an orientalist discourse, tending to consider Muslim and "Oriental" societies as being segregated into two social spheres demarcated on the basis of gender. Even most ethnographic and sociological studies have long emphasized the division between the private and domestic space, which was reserved for women, and the public space, which was reserved for men. This Orientalist perspective relegated Muslim women into the shadows of history, to being a subject that was often omitted from narratives or only ever represented beneath the veiled dress of silent passivity.[15]

One of the first attempts to bridge this historiographical gap was made by Fatima Mernissi. By collecting the histories of women who have held political and public positions in the history of Islam, she stressed the lack of foundation for the assumption that Islam was incompatible with the political power of women. The disregard for these women of power has mainly been looked at in regional and area studies, and Mernissi therefore proposed more detailed historical research that especially penetrated regional memories.[16] As Lazreg has

14 Frede and Hill 2014: 131–165.

15 Nelson 1974: 551–563.

16 Mernissi 1977.

pointed out, there is a tendency in studies of women in majoritarian Muslim societies to attribute gender inequalities to religion, whereas by the adoption of a paradigm such as this, women are seen "as evolving in non-historical times". We agree with Lazreg when she claims that this assumption leads to the belief that Islam itself simultaneously represents the cause of and the solution to such discrimination. Gender relations are constructed under specific historical and socio-cultural circumstances that cannot be reduced to such a cultural simplification.[17]

A number of women emerged in 19th century Africa as leading political and religious mentors on the wave of Islamic renewal. In the apparently exceptional case in Nigeria of Nana Asma'u (1793–1864), the daughter of Shehu Usman dan Fodio, the founder of the Sokoto Caliphate, and a prolific author of written literature, a woman entered African historiography as a leading figure in the process of re-Islamization of the continent. An acknowledged scholar and teacher, she played a prominent role in the policy, education, and socio-religious reforms of her time. In addition to teaching students in her community, she created a network of itinerant women teachers known as *'yan taru* whom she herself instructed so as to impart her teachings to women in rural areas and remote regions. Once instructed in Nana Asma'u teachings, *'yan tarus* used her literary works as mnemonic lectures and texts for teaching women in their homes. Her verses not only described how to observe Islam in everyday religious practices such as clothing and prayers, but also offered details on the obligations of the pillars of Islam as well as attitudes and Sufi practices. By teaching women how to follow the Sunna and the Qur'an, Asma'u intended to educate families on how to practice "orthodox" Sufism.[18] Her example expressed the power of orally transmitted knowledge, the literary production of women, and everyday religious practices to lead socio-cultural changes.

The coming of colonial domination presented no opportunities for the empowerment of Muslim women, and brought no special improvements to their conditions in Africa. On the contrary, a number of studies have shown that colonial rule actually marginalized women from positions of power, which were eventually offered to men. Women's pre-colonial participation in political life tended to be generally ignored by the colonial authorities. The history of the Algerian saint and mystic Lalla Zaynab (1850?–1904) is impressive in this context due to its resemblance to that of Sittī 'Alawiyya. A descendent of the Prophet Muhammad, she was a pious woman, learned in Islamic sciences. After the death of her father, she succeeded him in his religious leadership, despite the fact that the colonial authorities had ignored her power and appointed

17 Lazreg 1988.

18 Boyd 1989; Boyd and Mack 2000, 1997.

her cousin as his successor as local religious leader. She devoted her life to the poor, students, travellers, and her father's religious disciples, and eventually acquired great popularity among European travellers and her disciples, who respected her and believed that she had been blessed with miracle-working powers.[19] Within the Tiǧānī Sufi communities in Mauritania, too, the presence of female spiritual guides (*muqaddamāt*) was observed as early as the 1820s, a situation that persisted throughout the 20th century. During the colonial period, women joined the Tiǧānī order, often against their husbands' and the colonial authorities' wishes, promoting its rapid spread in the region.[20] Another example of religious leadership from the 1940s is that of Sokhna Magat Diop, a *maraboute* of the Muridiyya, who succeeded her father as leader of a branch of the order as a *ḫalīfa*, participating actively in the order's religious and political issues. When her father died in 1940 with no male heirs, she became the leader and erected shrines (*qubba*) to her father that became a regional destination for pilgrimage (*magal*). Her position in the order was similar to that of women in pre-colonial Wolof monarchies, who had the right to succeed to the throne where there were no male heirs. She had a residence in Touba, a holy city and the burial place of the founder of the order, where she stayed on the occasion of religious ceremonies, like other dignitaries within the order. She did not enter the mosque or lead public prayers, however, instead praying at her residence, but her sense of discretion did not conflict with her power and active participation in socio-political life. Sokhna Magat Diop's charisma was related to her *baraka* as well as to her knowledge and the visions that allowed her to perform marvels (*karāmāt*).[21]

With the Islamic revival movement that spread from as early as the 19th century, and with the emergence of militant Sufi movements, we begin to find a number of studies of women who became socio-religious and political agents within charismatic Sufi movements. This process coincided and interacted with the colonial encounter, in which gender dynamics played a pivotal role. Although women's activities impacted socio-political changes by actively contributing to the process of Islamization, however, historical sources are sparse and fragmented.

19 Clancy-Smith 1992.

20 Frede and Hill 2014: 140–141; Frede 2014: 400–414. Hutson 1997, 1999, 2001, 2004.

21 Coulon and Reveyrand 1990: 9–10, 16.

Sufism and the Female Body

Most studies on cults of saints and Sufism in Northeast Africa have focused on intellectual and socio-political history. Scholars have drawn mainly from hagiographical sources and a study of the literature and intellectual production of Sufi masters to shed light on the biographical trajectories of leading Sufi personalities and their literary output and teachings, and their works have brought these religious and intellectual figures and their scholarly writings back from obscurity. Despite this noteworthy contribution, the biographical approach has still not yet been problematized, as has been the case with European historiography; there is still a tendency to concentrate on events and literary production through the prism of intellectual history, with a focus on Sufi poetry and literature to provide basically theological and socio-political understandings, and by adopting a predominantly literary—and disembodied—approach to texts. The intellectual output of Sufi masters was long opposed to a rather marginal "popular Islam", such as cults of saints and everyday religious practices.

It has been thanks to the contributions of anthropologists such as Pnina Werbner[22] that the everyday dimension of religiosity and the paradigm of embodiment has been integrated into the study of Sufism, overcoming such dichotomies as orthodox and popular Islam, and into written and oral traditions. More recently, the concept of embodiment—"the human experience of being in and with a body"[23]—has allowed the body to be thought as the site of holiness and charisma.

By analysing concepts of the body in biographies of saints and Sufi writings from North Africa and Asia between the late fifteenth and 19th centuries, Scott Kugle has shown us that the body has been at the heart of religious, cultural, and social experience in the Sufi intellectual tradition. Sufi scholars argue that Sufism cannot be understood through books, and that it can only be learned through direct contact with, and dedication to, a spiritual master. They believe that true understanding cannot be separated from direct experience and faith. Besides, both emotion and empathy play a pivotal role in the process of acquiring Sufi knowledge. This new focus on the body and the paradigm of embodiment have led to a consideration of the place of emotions and sensual experience in the charismatic power of Sufi masters.

In Ethiopia and beyond, hagiographic literature has tended to underrepresent women saints: instead, oral culture, embodiment, and everyday religious practices play a crucial role in the handing down of the memories

22 Werbner 2003; Werbner and Basu 1998.

23 Kugle 2007: 9. See also Bashir 2011.

of holy women.[24] The lack or scarcity of written sources on the subject should not, however, induce historians not to pursue their enquiries, but rather should stimulate a search for new sources and perspectives. As Rosenwein has observed, "emotional communities may coalesce around the memory of a charismatic figure; in that case, the myths about that figure are more important than any writings he or she may have produced".[25] In this work, the purpose of my focus on Sittī ʿAlawiyya—who is remembered as the "uncrowned queen" of colonial Eritrea—is not to produce a biographical narrative of a female saint, but to follow the traces she left behind in order to reconstruct the world in which she lived. Here, the imprint left by the body of her charismatic figure has been the driver of my historical research: from her memory, as crystallized at her shrines near the port town of Massawa and the mosques built in her honour in Ethiopia, passing by way of oral memories, colonial archives, and travel accounts to a series of portraits, photographs and newsreels that immortalized her charismatic body.

In order to integrate the role of emotion and affect into the historical process, I have both turned to "alternative" sources and reconsidered old ones from a new perspective, and my readings of literary output such as hagiographies, theological writings, and travel accounts and visual representations were then pursued by looking more deeply at the traces of emotion and sensuality that surround her and her family members alike, as well as their communities of loved ones.

Despite the visibility of Sittī ʿAlawiyya in the political sphere and her prominent socio-religious activities, the available written sources appear at first glance to be particularly tight-lipped. Unlike colonial documents on male members of the Ḫatmiyya, such as Sayyid Ǧaʿfar and Sayyid Hāšim al-Mīrġanī, on whom there is correspondence in Arabic with a direct translation into Italian, references to Sittī ʿAlawiyya in the colonial archives are merely marginal. Communication and personal relationships with Italians took place informally inside the *šarīfa*'s residence and do not seem to have been formalized in writing. In fact, even where there is reference to her letters and written correspondence, the original texts have not been collected in the archive, and even the Arabic and hagiographic sources of the Ḫatmiyya that are available on male members of the order do not deal with her. The only exception is a poem written on her death, a copy of which is conserved by a private individual in Keren (Figure 55). It therefore proved necessary to diversify the sources as much as possible, integrating and juxtaposing colonial archives with diaries,

24 Mecca 2009; Bruzzi 2011; Bruzzi and Zeleke 2015.

25 Rosenwein 2010: 13.

memoirs and travel literature on the one hand, and with photographic and oral information on the other. In the process of our search for clues about Sittī ʿAlawiyya, a multiplicity of constructions of the past and imaginaries emerged. We pursued our exploration of the ambiguities shaped around her "myth-biography" by resorting to diversified, fragmented sources: articles, newspapers, photographs, postcards, newsreels, poems, colonial documents, and oral stories told by her descendants and people who had known her or heard about her. These oral stories, handed down from generation to generation, portray a mythology of the past that has been incorporated into the present.[26] The deployment of heterogeneous sources, each with its own specific and related method of analysis, led to a depiction of a polyphonic historical text that is not always cohesive: as the book progresses, the reader will notice a progressive shift from a more classical historical approach to written archives, characterized by a detached "objective" and factual perspective, to a growing interest in juxtaposing histories and different temporalities. This process involves the introduction of the paradigm of embodiment, followed by the integration of oral narratives, and finally an acknowledgment of the different temporalities and a change in "the regime of historicity" (Hartog 2003). The body is first considered in its visual, imaginative, and narrative representations through an analysis of photographic archives, colonial accounts, newspapers, and travel literature. Holistically speaking, the body is viewed as a vehicle of history, and by the use of interviews and oral history methods it has been possible to juxtapose a variety of narratives around the memory of Sittī ʿAlawiyya's charismatic figure, and during this process the issue of inter-subjectivity gains an increasing amount of attention.

It proved necessary to diversify the historical sources, which led to an interpretative effort the results of which only rarely led to one single image of the Mīrġanī; more frequently, it brought out a series of discourses, representations, and imaginaries. Drawing from methods and perspectives taken from historical anthropology and micro-history, our "thick description" (Geertz) of fragmentary documents and traces of the hidden story of Sittī ʿAlawiyya meant we were able to shed light on the wider socio-cultural landscape in which she lived, and to explore the gender dynamics that shaped the religious and socio-political context of the Islamic renewal and the Italian colonial occupation in Northeast Africa.

Her charismatic personality, which is still designated by the Arabic epithet "*al-ḥarbiyya / al-lābisa ḥarbiyya*"—that is to say, "the warrior / she who dresses

26 An inspiring study on memory and oral history methods as well as on feminist theory on the subject can be found in Passerini 2003.

like a warrior"—is the red line for this study. My ambition is to offer a micro-history of the Eritrean plain (predominantly Muslim) during the colonial era, and I pursued it by following in the footsteps of Sittī ʿAlawiyya in her life trajectory, which runs throughout the colonial period (1890–1941).

The traces we discovered of her led us to look not only at the local communities of the order in Eritrea, which were mainly located around the cities of Massawa and Keren, but also at a supra-regional area that included the Red Sea, the Ethiopian hinterland, and the Mediterranean region. Our focus on the links between the Mediterranean and the Horn of Africa might be seen to be the result of the influence of a colonial discourse that saw (and sought) geo-political continuity between the two areas: on the eve of the declaration of the Colony of Eritrea, Pasquale Stanislao Mancini, who was the Italian Foreign Minister at the time, promoted the 1885 expedition to Massawa, declaring to the Chamber of Deputies that the key to the Mediterranean—that is to say, the real interests of Italian foreign policy at the time—was the Red Sea (Mancini, Camera dei Deputati, 1885); indeed, the idea and vision of a Mediterranean Africa were a feature of colonial and postcolonial Italian history for many years.[27] A careful historical analysis of the connections between these two regions allows us to gain an understanding of both the complexity and the continuities and the breakdowns of broader socio-political dynamics that traversed the region. In effect, the establishment of the transnational Ḫatmiyya brotherhood took place in the context of the Islamic revival and the spread of Islamic brotherhood networks on a global level during the colonial period. In particular, two main issues should be noted: the first is Italian colonial policy towards Islam in Northeast Africa, and the second is the role played by the Ḫatmiyya in the political, economical, and religious landscape of the time, accompanied by a study of how the order responded and adapted to the historical and political contexts of the Italian occupation. To this end, I have focused on the individual trajectories of the main representatives of the brotherhood in Eritrea, who were often related to the Mīrġanī family, and their roles in dealings with the Italian colonial administration. In particular, these issues are observed through the prism of the female representative of the order in Eritrea. While the available literature has attached great significance to secular feminist movements in the Southern Mediterranean, the activities of the female religious elite still appears to be largely unexplored. This book therefore aims to decipher this chapter in the history of the region from its transnational dimension, in which religious language played a pivotal role, from the Mediterranean to the Red Sea.

---

27 See Trento 2012.

The first part of the book reviews the origins of the order and its spread across Northeast Africa. The interweaving of the spread of the order and the parallel process of penetration by the colonial powers into the Red Sea region is explored, and new light is shed on the dynamics of accommodation between the colonial authorities and Sufi leaders in the context of regional conflicts. The death of Sittī ʿAlawiyya's father, who was an early, conflicting interlocutor for the colonial powers, then led to the controversial issue of women inheriting religious leadership through bloodlines, and the intervention by the colonial authorities to re-establish a patriarchal regime that would be able to secure the *pax colonial*. The second part of the book is devoted to an exploration of imagined, contested and performed feminine spaces of agency around Sittī ʿAlawiyya's popular authority, as well as the increasing presentation of her charismatic figure on the colonial stage. Her role as an intermediary, with that of other representatives of the order, is then reviewed in the context of regional policy and transregional conflicts from the Italian colonial wars in Libya to the second Italo-Ethiopian war. Finally, the memory of the past is considered in order to illustrate the heritage of the "Italian mosques" that were built in Ethiopia in her honour.

Oral history methods are employed together with written narratives and representations, and our historical gaze then shifts towards the co-existence of the various temporalities and experiences from the past that emerged from our juxtaposition of archival sources and oral stories. This shift becomes even more evident in the conclusion, where historical investigation is associated with ethnographic fieldwork and the historian's direct experience is intermingled with that of the subjects of the stories. Ethnographic experiences were looked at in order to cast a new light on written archives and oral stories. This perspective is influenced by Passerini's observations on the recent scholarship on biography, which has adopted an approach that admits the inter-subjectivity inherent in scholarly activity and has taken account of the subjectivity of the people whose lives have been narrated. The juxtaposition of a variety of stories and narratives about one single person did not always permit a dialogical account to be provided, however, due partly to the highly fragmentary nature of the available sources, but also to the different—and conflicting—experiences and narratives of the past. Inevitably this sometimes resulted in a multifaceted depiction of the reality on the ground, a consequence of an exploration of the process of construction of ambivalences that inevitably emerges whenever issues of subjectivity and intersubjectivity are employed in historical accounts.[28]

28 Passerini 2000: 413–416; Werbner 2016: 135–153.

CHAPTER 1

Islamic Renewal Movements, Colonial Occupation, and the Ḫatmiyya in the Red Sea Region

Islam and the Idrīsī Tradition in Northeast Africa

It is only in recent years that scholars have begun to study Islamic history in the Horn of Africa, and to transcend the old notion that Ethiopia was "an island of Christianity in the sea of Islam", which had led them to focus on a simplified relationship of rivalry and conflictuality with the Christian religion. As a result of this shift, recent studies have been able to illustrate the long social, political, and intellectual history of Islam in the region, as well as inter-religious encounters, with an emphasis on the co-existence and interactions that have shaped Ethiopian and Eritrean societies.[1]

The earliest contacts with the Red Sea coast of the African continent had already been established when Islam appeared and spread beyond the revolutionizing Hejaz societies of the region as a whole. In 615 AD, the persecutions that the newly-born Muslim community had suffered in Mecca led some, the *muhāǧirūn*, to seek exile in Axum, the Christian kingdom on the other side of the Red Sea. The Prophet's biographers, Ibn Isḥāq (706–761 AD) and Ibn Hišām (828–833 AD) recorded this first Muslim *hiǧra*, or migration, to Abyssinia; Ibn Hišām reported that on this occasion, the Prophet Muhammad ruled that Abyssinia would not be a land of *ǧihād*.[2] Historical records recount the presence of women among these first Muslim migrants from Arabia, such as Umm Ḥabība bint Abī Sufyān and Umm Salama bint Abī Umayya, who are numbered among the earliest disciples of the Prophet, and who returned to Arabia and married the Prophet after the deaths of their husbands.

In Ethiopian Islamic history, another well-known female personality is Batī Del Wämbära, the daughter of the Governor of Zaylaʿ, Imām Maḥfuz, and the wife of Imām Aḥmad ibn Ibrahīm al-Gāzī, also known as Grāñ. Batī Del Wämbära accompanied her husband on the *ǧihād* against the Christian

1 Hussein Ahmed 1992: 15–46; Hussein Ahmed 2006: 4–22; Hussein Ahmed 2009: 59; Ficquet, *forthcoming*.

2 On the first contacts with Islam and this Muslim *hiǧra* to Ethiopia, see: Trimingham 1952: 42–48; Cass 1965; Hussein Ahmad 1992: 15–46; Hussein Ahmad 2009.

 | DOI 10.1163/9789004356160_003

empire and became a symbol of the success of the holy war, actively participating in propagating the faith.[3]

At least until the 16th century, Islam would mostly spread peacefully, thanks to Arab traders and migrant communities along the trading routes from the Red Sea ports into the hinterland.[4] One branch of the Ethiopian community, the so-called Jabarti, claims that their conversion originated during this early period. The first Eritrean and Ethiopian groups to adopt Islam were in contact with Muslim traders and trade centres all along the caravan routes between the African hinterland and the Red Sea coast. In addition to the role played by the Muslim traders, artisans, and adventurers who travelled or migrated to the region, living in close touch with the natives and sometimes marrying local women, the expansion of Islam was promoted by the activities of Sufi scholars and Islamic brotherhoods, who played a pivotal role in spreading the new religion, while at the same time mediating with African cultures and beliefs. It seems that the Qādiriyya was the first Islamic brotherhood (*ṭarīqa*) to be introduced by immigrants from Yemenite Ḥaḍramawt to Massawa, Zaylaʿ, Mogadishu and other coastal centres. The *ṭarīqa* was also well established in Maghreb, Andalusia, Anatolia, Arabia, and Iraq, from where its founder, the Persian mystic ʿAbd al-Qādir al-Ǧīlānī (1078–1166), originally came. In the 15th century, Šarīf Abū Bakr ibn ʿAbd Allāh al-Aydarūs, who died in Aden in 1503 AD, introduced the Qādiriyya to Harar, which was the principal centre of Islamic learning in the Horn of Africa, and the order first became semi-official, and later the most widely spread *ṭarīqa* in the region.[5]

In Sudan, Islamization was initially marked by the activities of religious figures who were not affiliated with a particular order. These orders subsequently became active agents of Islamization, especially in the 16th century with the arrival of Qādiriyya and Šāḏiliyya, which were decentralized Sufi orders, and in the 18th and 19th centuries through the spread of centralized and semi-centralized orders such as the Sammāniyya, the Tiǧāniyya, the Ḫatmiyya, and the Idrīsiyya.[6] In Ethiopia and Eritrea, the influence of Sufi traditions and teachings from Sudan and Egypt was especially significant due to the intense activity of regional centres of Islamic learning, which spread and allowed the

3 Pankhurst 2009; Böll 2003; Chernetsov 2003.

4 Cerulli 1971: 115.

5 Trimingham 1952: 234.

6 Trimingham 1971: 1–104; Karrar 1992: 1–4. According to Karrar, the three stages of development of the Sufi orders (*khānaqāh, ṭarīqa* and *ṭāʾifa*) proposed by Trimingham do not apply to Sudan because the spread of Islam in this region was marked by two main stages: pre-*ṭarīqa* and *ṭarīqa*.

circulation of the ideas that were arriving from other regions of the Islamic world. Later on, beginning in the 19th century, Sufi orders actively participated in the Islamic renewal movement,[7] which was interwoven with the expansion of both the European powers and African regional powers such as Egypt, Zanzibar, and Ethiopia.

As the religious revival crossed the Islamic world, the colonial powers also expanded in Northeast Africa. In particular, following the opening of the Suez Canal in 1869, the Ottoman Empire, Great Britain, Italy, and France turned their attention to Northeast Africa within their own sphere of influence on the Red Sea. The Ethiopian Christian Empire progressively penetrated the Southern region, and incorporated new territories in the Horn of Africa.[8] From there, and from the Nile Valley to the Maghreb, Muslims were defeated and subjected to foreign domination, and Islamic revival movements acquired a political dimension. According to some interpretations, colonial and imperial penetration was perceived as a Christian violation of the integrity of *Dār al-Islām*, stimulating much debate within Islamic circles, and in some cases, Islam represented a reaction to this period of upheaval. In the early stages of colonial occupation, some Muslim elites, such as the leaders of the Islamic brotherhoods, became the principal spokespersons for religious renewal. Some led anti-colonial movements and developed a discourse based on Islamic principles to justify the struggle against foreign occupation, while others took on the role of intermediaries and negotiated with the colonial powers, actively participating in the ongoing "modernization" process.[9] The available historiography has pursued the study of these socio-political dynamics that developed in a number of African societies in Francophone and Islamic West Africa extensively, but less attention seems to have been dedicated to the former Italian colonies in Northeast Africa.[10]

In other regions of the African continent, colonial policies towards Islam were complex, and varied according to the specific context and case, but it is still

---

7 On Ethiopia, see Hussein Ahmed 2001.

8 Donham and Wendy 1986.

9 Battera 1998. Copious literature is available on the relations between Islam and Modernity. For an overview of the debate, see: Masud, Salvatore, and Van Bruinessen 2009. For a study focusing on the ideas of a number of contemporary modernist and liberal Muslim thinkers and their incorporation of modern Western ideas: Nettler, Mahmoud, and Cooper 1998.

10 See, in particular, the works written and edited by David Robinson and Jean-Louis Triaud: Robinson and Triaud 1997; Triaud and Robinson 2000; Robinson 2000; Triaud 1995. A study on Italian East Africa is provided on Somalia in Battera 1998: 155–185.

possible to identify a number of intervention strategies and general approaches that were pursued by the colonial powers. In several contexts, in fact, the colonial powers referred to the "Islamic orthodoxy/non-orthodoxy" dichotomy not only to justify their support for certain groups, but also to discourage or control Islamic and international attacks on the colonial establishment. France, for example, leant towards the promotion of the idea of a Black Islam (*Islam noir*) in its Western African colonies; this was an "unorthodox", highly localized form of Islam that would be marginalized from the pan-Islamic movements in North African and Middle Eastern countries. An early decree in 1857 authorized freedom of worship in Senegal, conferred prestige on a particular Muslim elite, ordered the use of Arabic in the government bureaucracy, and promoted the implementation of Islamic law at the expense of common law.[11]

While the French policy model developed predominantly in Mauritania and Senegal, the British approach towards Islam was shaped in Nigeria. Hitherto, the indirect rule system promoted by Lord Lugard had supported a strategic alliance between the traditional Islamic establishment and the colonial government. Although the colonial administration claimed to have a policy of non-interference on religious issues, it actually sought to adopt a diversified approach towards those classified as "good" and "bad" Muslims.[12] To this end, it evaluated various Muslim groups on the basis of their Islamic education and piety, also taking into account whether they were indigenous or foreign, as well as whether they posed a potential threat to the "religious orthodoxy" of the well-established "traditional" authority. According to Reynolds, the arguments put forward in *Christianity, Islam and the Negro Race* (1888),[13] which portrayed Islam as being suited to the nature and needs of African people, influenced the colonial policies of a number of British officials.

Although Christianity was generally considered to be superior to Islam, the colonial authorities were aware that proselytizing might lead to trouble in predominantly Muslim societies, while support for Islam, on the other hand, was a more advisable alternative when it came to spreading civilization among the

11 Piga 2004; Robinson 1988. According to Robinson, the French used the Senegalese-Mauritanian "laboratory", located along the border between "black" and "white" Africa to formulate policies and practices to apply in other regions. Robinson 1997 and Robinson and Triaud 1997: 155–180.

12 Reynolds 2001: 601–618.

13 Blyden 1888.

indigenous population and promoting trade. They therefore sought to do business with those local Muslim elites who were willing to negotiate.[14]

Indeed, some Islamic brotherhoods and their charismatic leaders held leadership positions during the foreign occupation. They were often favoured intermediaries for the colonial authorities, whose aim was to monitor and control religious and political unrest. At least from the 18th century, they played a pivotal role in the Sub-Saharan African process of re-Islamization, acquiring a socio-religious leadership role among those African societies that were suffering from political and economic unrest. During the Islamic renewal period of the 18th and 19th centuries, a number of charismatic personalities, organizations, and networks emerged, and showed that they shared a common missionary, educational, and militant attitude towards Islam. Their response to foreign penetration in *Dār al-Islām* led to various reactions, which were often ambivalent and in opposition to each other, even within the same organization or *ṭarīqa*. Phases of open resistance to, and conflict with, the colonial powers alternated with other moments of negotiation and mutual acknowledgement with the foreign establishment. In some ways, a complex relationship of surveillance and collaboration was established between the colonial and religious authorities during this period. Religious leaders adopted a number of different accommodation strategies and practices in their relations with the colonial establishments.[15] The most significant aspect of the "Islamic revival" in Northeast Africa was the emergence of reformed Sufi brotherhoods, which were noteworthy for their more militant and centralized organizational structures, together with an intensification of the activities of existing orders. The controversial terms "neo-Sufism" or "reformed Sufism" have been employed with reference to these religious movements. According to O'Fahey, the idea of neo-Sufism originated from colonial encounters with Islam and the associated "literature of surveillance" produced by colonial officials in the context of the occupation. Taking account of the resistance led by a number of Sufi scholars such as ʿAbd al-Qādir (1808–1883) of the Qādiriyya in Algeria, Sayyid Muḥammad ʿAbd Allāh Ḥasan (1899–1920) of the Ṣāliḥiyya in Somalia, and Aḥmad al-Šarīf al-Sanūsī in Libya[16] against the foreign occupation, colonial scholars and administrators developed conspiracy theories according to which reformist Sufi leaders were depicted as key figures in the constitution of pan-Islamic and fundamentalist organizations whose main aim was to undermine

14 Reynolds 2001: 602. The same idea was widespread in Italian colonial policy towards Islam in Northeast Africa: Marongiu Buonaiuti 1982: 103–107.

15 Robinson 2000; Robinson 1991.

16 Clancy-Smith 1994; Samatar 1992; Triaud 1995; Vikør 1995.

the colonial establishment and to "threaten the progress of civilization in Africa". This interpretation placed the emphasis on the political, rather than the theological and intellectual, dimension of the phenomenon, but Aḥmad Ibn Idrīs (1749/50–1837), who was one of the leading—and most popular—figures of the so-called neo-Sufi movement, was fundamentally a Muslim scholar and spiritual master (*muršid*), and not the founder of any order or political movement.[17] Rather, he sought to rouse religious spirit through teaching and education; indeed, his participation in *ǧihād* was by *daʿwa* ("invitation") and through litanies and prayers.[18]

He was born in Morocco, and studied at the Qarawiyyīn Mosque in Fez, where he was initiated into several orders and was mainly associated with *šāḏilī* teachings. In 1799, he left the Maghreb, where he was already a respected scholar, and travelled first to Mecca and later to Upper Egypt. In the Hejaz region, he acquired great influence, and attracted Muslim students from all over the Islamic world. His involvement in Muslim education was in line with the classical Sufi intellectual and spiritual tradition; indeed, like the traditional Sufi opposition to legalism and intellectualism, he was critical of theology and Islamic schools of law such as philosophy and *kalām*, and it was this approach that brought about his conflict with the Meccan *ʿulamāʾ*. In his view, knowledge was rooted in mystical experience: "included in the Qur'anic verses are hidden allusions to subtle meanings which are revealed to followers of the Way and which can be correlated with the intended esoteric meaning".[19] He believed that the mystical path led to direct communication with the Prophet and to knowledge of God, beyond the constraints of human authorities like *ʿulamāʾ*, or others such as religious or secular authorities. Although he shared a critical approach towards the school of law with the Wahhābiyya, their opinions on the Sufi classical tradition clearly diverged. Speaking about Ibn ʿAbd al-Wahhāb, Aḥmad Ibn Idrīs claimed: "We do not deny his merit. His intention was righteous in what he did. He eliminated innovations and unfortunate practices, but that mission was sullied by excess. He declared those Muslims who had a belief in anything other than God Most High to be unbelievers and moreover allowed them to be killed and their property to be seized without justification".[20] Furthermore, unlike the *wahhābis*, Aḥmad Ibn Idrīs recommended practical methods and disciplines based on centuries-old Sufi spiritual

17 O'Fahey and Radtke 1993: 52–87.

18 O'Fahey 1990: 23.

19 ʿĀkish, Munāẓara, 349 Abu Dahish, quoted from O'Fahey 1990: 196. Thomassen and Radtke 1993: 1–8, 42–117.

20 O'Fahey 1990: 105.

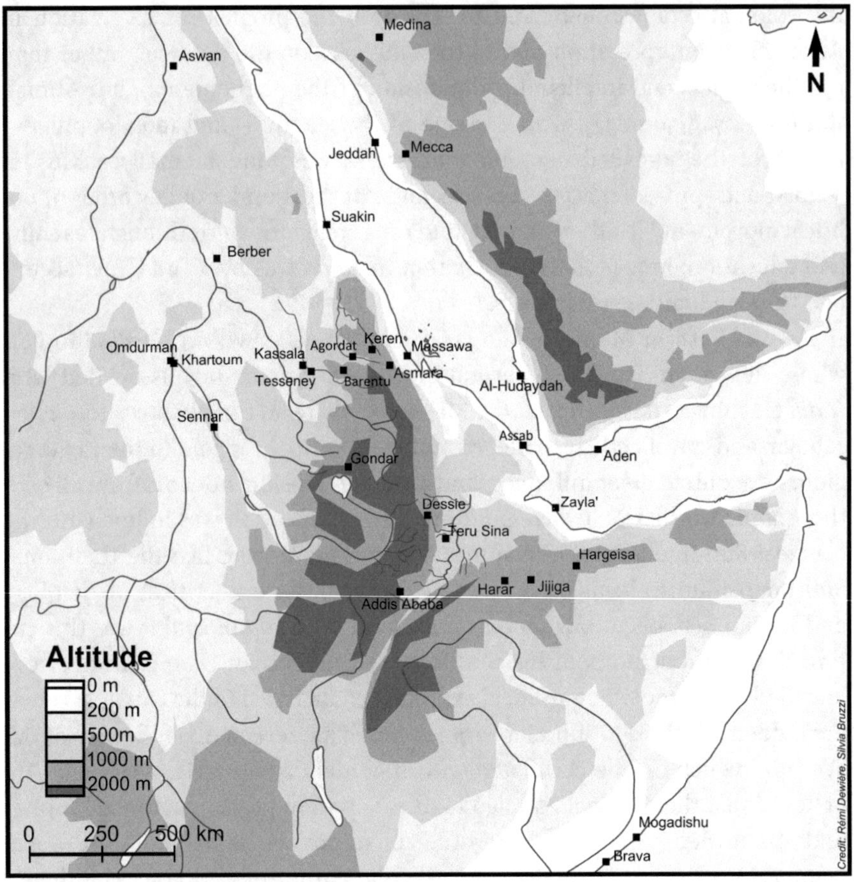

MAP 1 *Red Sea region.*

traditions. Among his points of references were classical masters such as Ibn al-Fāriḍ and Ibn al-ʿArabī.[21] As a Sufi shaykh, he urged his pupils to travel to Africa and proselytize Islam, but he created no order or institution around himself. It was only after his death that some of his disciples, such as Muḥammad b. ʿAlī al-Sanūsī (1787–1859), Ibrāhīm al-Rašīd (1817–74) and Muḥammad ʿUṯmān al-Mirġanī (1793–1852), established their own orders in Africa and his traditions and teachings became particularly influential for a number of the brotherhoods that were established in 19th century Northeast Africa, namely the Aḥmadiyya, Dandarawiyya, Rašīdiyya, Ṣāliḥiyya and Ḫatmiyya. The last of these, which lies at the heart of this study, was established in the Red Sea re-

21 O'Fahey 1990: 90–106.

gion by one of Aḥmad Ibn Idrīs's pupils, Muḥammad ʿUṯmān al-Mīrġanī, and his sons, across what are now Yemen, Eritrea, Sudan, Egypt, and Ethiopia.

The Establishment of the Ḫatmiyya in the Red Sea Region

The early socio-political and intellectual history of the Mīrġanī family and the Ḫatmiyya *ṭarīqa* begins with the establishment of the *ṭarīqa* in the framework of the Ottoman rule along the Red Sea region, and runs right through the process of regionalization of its leadership following the outbreak of the Mahdist War in Sudan and the subsequent gradual penetration into Sudan and Eritrea by the British and Italian colonial powers respectively.[22]

Muḥammad ʿUṯmān (1793–1852), the founder of the Ḫatmiyya Islamic brotherhood, was from the prestigious Mīrġanī family, whose members were historically granted the title of *ašrāf*, which was attributed to personalities who claimed to be, and were recognized as, descending from the Prophet. Especially in the Hejaz region, *ašrāf* generally enjoyed great respect and support from their followers, who would travel to visit them from all corners of the Muslim world. The origins of the family are uncertain. The folk origin of its name claims that its etymology was "the rich descendent of the Prophet", whereas according to Italian colonial accounts, the name derives from the Arabic verb *ġannā* (to sing), because the family would traditionally have been in charge of leading cantors during religious prayers in Mecca.[23] According to far more recent interpretations, the family name originated from a place named "Marghan" or "Murghan" in Ghōr, a mountainous area in what is today North-Central Afghanistan.[24] Hofheinz writes that:

> One of the five principal mountain massifs of Ghōr is called Zāmorgh; according to local legend, this is the mountain where mythical Sīmorgh, the "king of birds" (shā-e morghān) nurtured Zāl, the father of the greatest of all Iranian heroes, Rostam. In these mountains rises the river Morghāb, which flows north, passes through several settlements that bear its name, then waters the densely cultivated oasis of Marw, and finally seeps away into the black sands of the Qāra-Qum desert.

22 The early socio-political and intellectual history of the Mīrġanī family and the Ḫatmiyya *ṭarīqa* is reported in a rich historiographical literature. See, in particular, the works by Voll and O'Fahey: Voll 1969; O'Fahey 1990.

23 Odorizzi 1916: 18.

24 On the origins and genealogy of the family, see Hofheinz 1992: 9–27.

> Poetry aside, place names like "Marqan," "Morghān" or "Morghāb" abound in Khorāsān, and also occur elsewhere in Iran. It should be noted in this context that in Khorāsānī usage, "Morghāb" denotes any rivulet or spring with not much water in it.[25]

This origin might explain the family affiliation with the Ḥanafī School, which was dominant not only in the Ottoman Empire but also in India and Afghanistan, as well as the great influence the Naqšbandī tradition exercised on Muḥammad ʿUṯmān al-Mīrġanī's spiritual formation. For some reason, its members were popular among pilgrims from Central Asia, from where the Mīrġanī seemingly originated before one of their ancestors migrated to Mecca.[26] At the end of the 18th century, the grandfather of Muḥammad ʿUṯmān al-Mīrġanī, ʿAbd Allāh al-Maḥǧūb al-Mīrġanī, earned the reputation of the family by his writings and teachings; indeed, scholars from Maghreb to India, especially those connected with the Naqšbandī tradition, would come to visit him. He was erudite, a Sufi and scholar of *ḥadīṯ*, a member of the reformist circles of the Hejaz, who was in touch with both Muslim and foreign intellectuals. After he had been teaching in Mecca for years, political conflicts arose with certain *ʿulamāʾ* and he had to move to Ta'if with his family, but even after his death, the family was able to maintain its previous prestige. His nephew Muḥammad Yasīn, who was also a teacher, adopted and raised Muḥammad ʿUṯmān, who was orphaned after his father death.[27]

Muḥammad ʿUṯmān, who was also known by the epithet al-Ḫatm ("the Seal"), was born in Salama, a village close to Ta'if, in 1208/1793, and studied Islamic sciences such as the *ḥanafī fiqh, ḥadīṯ, tafsīr* and Arabic language and grammar in Mecca. His family included renowned Sufi scholars such as his father and grandfather. After learning the Qur'an by heart by the age of eleven, he became interested in Sufism and began to travel between Mecca, Medina, and Ta'if to meet popular shaykhs. He became affiliated with five orders: first the Naqšbandiyya and then the Qādiriyya, Šāḏiliyya, Ǧunaydiyya and Mīrġanīyya (the order that had been founded by his grandfather). According to his hagiographies, during this period of devotion and mystical practices, he received an order from the Prophet to establish his own *ṭarīqa*: the Ḫatmiyya, "the seal of all *ṭuruq*".[28] A turning point in his life came when he met Aḥmad Ibn Idrīs, his most influential teacher, whom he would follow until his death in 1837.

25 Hofheinz 1992: 17.

26 Hofheinz 1992: 19.

27 Voll 1969.

28 Grandin 1984: 139–155.

After spending four years with him, Aḥmad Ibn Idrīs sent Muḥammad ʿUṯmān to a region in the South-West of Keren, in present-day Eritrea. The local ruler, who saw his authority being threatened, attempted to poison al-Mīrġanī because of his success among the Jabarti community, and he had to leave and return to Mecca to join his master.[29] In 1813, Muḥammad ʿUṯmān followed Aḥmad to Upper Egypt, to the village of Zayniyya, near Luxor, where the master was very popular, and it was from there, in around 1815–16, that he made his second journey. He continued his religious peregrinations towards Sudan and the Red Sea coast on his own, notwithstanding Aḥmad Ibn Idrīs's reluctance. The master was concerned about the considerable problems involved in travelling there, but more importantly, he warned al-Mīrġanī that building a following might lead him to become absorbed with matters of "the world". The admiration of the people might poison him, and bring down a veil between "the seeker and God". Aḥmad devoted his vocation to being "a guide for the individual seeker", while Muḥammad ʿUṯmān manifested the ambition to establish a religious organization.[30] He pursued this enterprise by teaching and travelling extensively in Northern Sudan and along the Red Sea coast, in Nubia and Kordofan, among the Beja and in Suakin.[31] He appointed representatives and established marriage alliances with the families of local notables. In particular, during his second visit in Kordofan, he married Ruqayya bin Ǧallab from Bara, who came from the Hawwāra group. In 1819, he had a son by her in Bara, al-Ḥasan, who would later spread his father's order within Sudan. Later, he travelled to Suakin, and finally returned to the Hejaz, where his master was established at the time. In 1827–1828, conflicts arose with notables and *ʿulamāʾ* in Mecca, and Aḥmad Ibn Idrīs was forced to go into exile in Yemen, along with Muḥammad ʿUṯmān and his followers.[32] When the master died in 1837, a quarrel arose among his blood heirs and spiritual heirs, namely Aḥmad Ibn Idrīs's sons and his pupils Muḥammad ibn ʿAlī al-Sanūsī, Ibrāhīm al-Rašīd, and Muḥammad ʿUṯmān al-Mīrġanī regarding who should inherit the master's spiritual leadership. The rivalry between Muḥammad ʿUṯmān and Muḥammad ibn ʿAlī al-Sanūsī had already existed while their master was living, and Aḥmad had expressed his unhappiness with the situation, because his aim was unity, mutual assistance, and devotion.[33]

---

29 Thomassen and Radtke 1993: 42.

30 Thomassen and Radtke 1993: 45, 53.

31 O'Fahey 1990; Thomassen and Radtke 1993.

32 Grandin 1984: 47.

33 Thomassen and Radtke 1993: 46.

Ibrāhīm al-Rašīd, who had the support of Aḥmad Ibn Idrīs's family, left for Upper Egypt to avoid the dispute, but the declaration he issued in Mecca that he was the heir to the spiritual status (*maqām*) of his teacher and that he was identical to his master is probably what caused the Mīrġanī members and followers to accuse him of heresy in 1856–57. Al-Mīrġanī and al-Sanūsī went first to Mecca, where they established their orders and *zawāyā*. Al-Sanūsī then left the city because of conflicts that had arisen with local *ʿulamāʾ* and established his *zāwiyya* in Libya, where he attained notable popularity.[34] After the establishment of his order in the Hejaz, Muḥammad ʿUṯmān al-Mīrġanī appointed representatives (*ḫulafāʾ*, singular *ḫalīfa*) in a number of regions, and sent his sons, including Muḥammad Sirr al-Ḫatm (1814/15–1855), who lived as a *ḥadīṯ* teacher in Yemen until 1853–54 (when he returned to Mecca), and Ḥasan (1820–1869), who lived in Sudan, to propagate his order in other areas of the Red Sea.[35]

Because he was perceived as a foreign *ʿalīm* and Sufi (*walī*) able to perform *karāmāt* and was married to local women, Muḥammad ʿUṯmān had earned prestige and acquired followers in Sudanese society. In fact, being a foreigner married to indigenous women, he was integrated into local society but remained beyond its ethnic boundaries. Furthermore, the support he gained among teachers, religious people and *fuqahāʾ*—in other words among the key figures in Sudanese Islam—turned out to be crucial. It was from among this group that he appointed several of his representatives, but the success of the order in Sudan was due not only to his activity, but also to that of his son Ḥasan. The latter was the son of a Sudanese woman, and was therefore not a foreigner like his father, even though he had been educated by him in the Hejaz.[36] After travelling across the country, Ḥasan finally established a village called Ḫatmiyya, close to Kassala in Eastern Sudan, that would became the brotherhood's leading centre in the region.

The historical roots of the brotherhood in Sudan developed with the consent of the Ottoman-Egyptian authorities that ruled Sudan from 1821 to 1885. In the 1820s, the armies of Muḥammad ʿAlī, the Ottoman Governor of Egypt, had conquered the region and created an administrative zone that included much

34 On the Sanūsīyya see: Vikør 1995; Triaud 1995; Le Gall 1989: 91–106; Gazzini 2004.

35 According to Voll 1969: 247–248, Muḥammad Sirr al-Ḫatm was recognized as the representative of the order in Yemen and after his father's death as the head of the order. After him, no member of his family was established as the main leader. The dates I have used are those provided in Hofheinz 1992: 21.

36 Voll 1969: 126, 132–133.

of modern Sudan and Eritrea. The Ottoman Empire, which was making special efforts to strengthen its political and legal control over the Red Sea area, and was attempting to establish *ḥanafī* law as the only official interpretation of the *šarīʿa*, recognized the Mīrġanī as influential *ḥanafī* learned men not only in Sudan and Eritrea but also in Yemen, where a branch of the brotherhood was well established thanks to another son of Muḥammad ʿUṯmān, Muḥammad Sirr al-Ḫatm.[37]

Owing to the efforts of Ḥasan and his father, the Ḫatmiyya became particularly popular in Sudan among the Beja people, such as the recently Islamized groups of the Beni ʿAmer, Halanqa, and Habab, incorporating Sudanese religious practices and elites and enrolling a number of Sudanese *fuqahāʾ* as *ḫulafāʾ* into the order.[38] The *ṭarīqa* networks integrated previous regional religious centres into the more centralized structure of the order. This process of development was a common feature of the establishment of a number of 19th and 20th century Sufi orders, such as the Ḫatmiyya and the Sanūsiyya, which were both supported by the Ottoman occupying powers while they were establishing their religious centres in Northeast Africa.

After the death of Muḥammad ʿUṯmān in 1852, his *ṭarīqa* commenced a process of regionalization. While the Ḫatmiyya did not became a mass movement in Hejaz and Egypt, where it tended towards fragmentation, its main centres of influence were gradually created in Sudan and Eritrea.[39] In Sudan, the order supported the centralized, "orthodox" Islam for which the government had expressed a preference, and collaborated with the Ottoman-Egyptian rulers, who tolerated and subsidized its religious centres and exempted the Ḫatmī shaykhs from taxation. Relations with the government were not always cordial, however, especially for a few years immediately following Sayyid Ḥasan's death, when Ḫatmī agents were arrested and their privileges temporarily abolished.[40]

The family and principal agents of the order recognized Sayyid Ḥasan's son Sayyid Muḥammad ʿUṯmān II as his successor, and it was he who had to face a number of challenges, first of all the uprising by the Mahdiyya.

---

37 Melis 2012: 115.

38 Voll 1969: 187.

39 Voll 1969: 254.

40 Warburg 2013: 212–213.

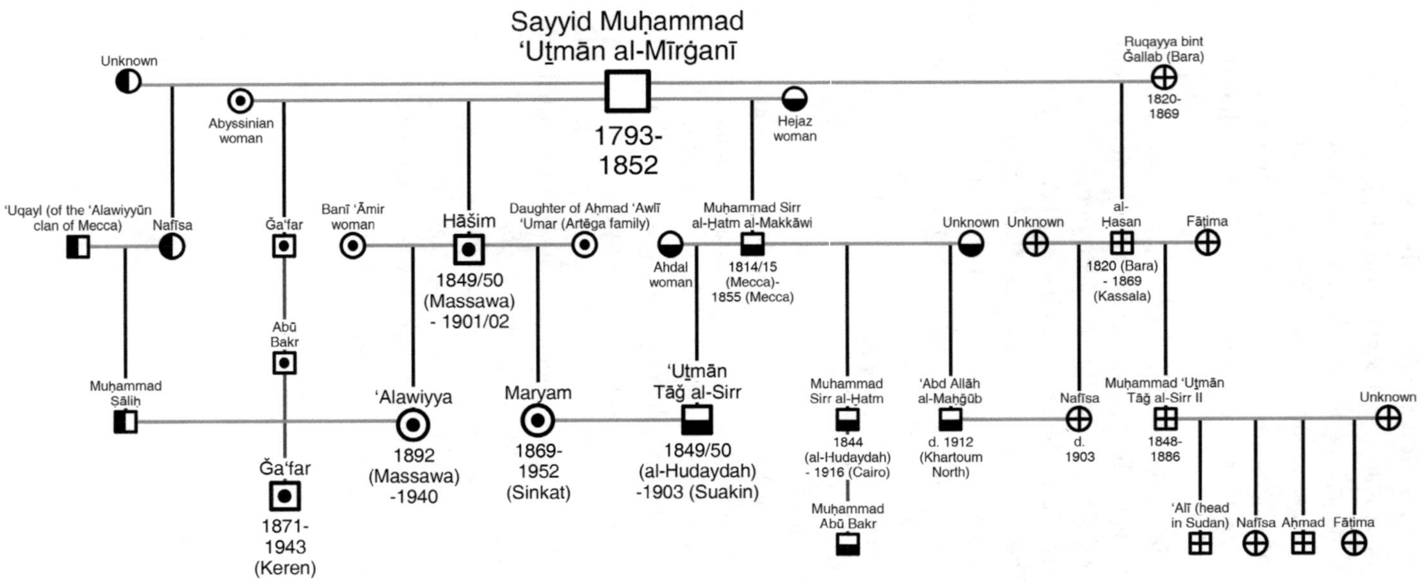

MAP 2 *Genealogy of the Mīrġanī family and its four main branches.*
The circles represent women and the squares represent men. The vertical lines represent filiation kinship and the horizontal lines matrimonial kinship.

CHAPTER 2

Sufis at the Crossroads: Regional Conflicts and Colonial Penetration

The Ḫatmiyya up against the Sudanese Mahdī

During the 1870s, discontent intensified with the Ottoman-Egyptian administration, which employed a number of non-Muslim and European administrators to rule its Sudanese territories who were seen by many as corrupt and oppressive. The policy to abolish slavery and the slave trade was also causing unrest among the powerful, wealthy elites involved in the trade. Growing apocalyptic expectations among Muslims became fertile territory for the emergence of the Islamic millenarianism of the Mahdiyya under the leadership of Muḥammad Aḥmad, a charismatic religious teacher with a reputation for piety.[1] Aḥmad preached that the Ottoman-Egyptian administrators were non-believers, impious and oppressive, and called on Muslims to fight against them. The Sudanese Mahdiyya was a mass religious movement that called for a revolt against oppression by "foreigners and non-believers".[2] Corruption in Sudanese society was expressed in the form of the spread of foreign influences and practices such as prostitution, gambling, tobacco, alcohol, and music. The Egyptian Ottoman rulers were accused of being foreigners and infidels who "disobeyed the command of His messenger and his Prophet, … ruled in a manner not in accord with what God has sent, … altered the Sharia of our master, Muhammad, the messenger of God, and … blasphemed against the faith of God".[3] The government was accused of not acting respectfully towards religious prescriptions because it had Christian employees in the administration (such as the British army officer and administrator Gordon) and because of their habit of drinking alcohol and consorting with prostitutes in public.

The Mahdiyya also targeted Sudanese customs in general, and the conduct of women in particular. Muḥammad Aḥmad prohibited lavish expenditure on weddings, the wearing of amulets, and wailing by women at funerals. He forbade women from going to markets or being unveiled in public; he had already

1 Voll 2000: 153–167; Holt 1958; Warburg 2003.

2 There is very extensive literature available on the Mahdi revolution. See, for example: Abu Shouk 1999: 133–168. On the Sudanese Mahdiyya, see also: Searcy 2010 and Kramer 2010.

3 Cit. in Esposito 1998: 41.

 | DOI 10.1163/9789004356160_004

had a dispute on this topic with one of his teachers who had admitted women into Sufi sessions even before the revolt.[4]

The privileges enjoyed by the Ḫatmiyya in the administration caused tensions with other groups and led to its taking the side of the government. Competition among religious leaders also added to the conflict;[5] the historical rivalry between the Ḫatmiyya and the Mahdiyya is a well-known example of this. When in June 1881 Muḥammad Aḥmad proclaimed that he would be the next Mahdī and declared his *ǧihād* against the Ottoman-Egyptian administration, Sayyid Muḥammad ʿUṯmān II (1848–1886) denounced the Mahdi as an impostor. As soon as the Mahdist revolution gained support in the west and began to spread to Eastern Sudan, the Mīrġanī family took on a leading role in support of the anti-Mahdist party. The Mahdist offensive in the region, where the Ḫatmiyya was well-established, was under the leadership of ʿUṯmān Diqna (c. 1840–1926), a descendent of a merchant family from Suakin, who had joined the Mahdist revolution against the government before the fall of El Obeid in 1883. In May 1883, the Mahdī sent him to foment the revolt among the Beja people in the Red Sea province. The Ḫatmiyya, which viewed the Mahdī's *ǧihād* as sedition (*fitna*), opposed the Mahdiyya from both a theological and military standpoint.[6]

Sayyid Muḥammad ʿUṯmān II declined the Mahdī's offer to become one of his *ḫulafāʾ*, and assisted with the recruitment of anti-Mahdist forces in Eastern Sudan. Between 1883 and 1884, he travelled to Kassala, Sinkat, Suakin, and Massawa to convince tribal leaders to support the government against the revolt. In contrast with the demands of the Mahdiyya's religious leadership, the Ḫatmiyya claimed that its shaykhs belonged to the ranks of the "pole of poles" and that it was the "seal of the representation of Muhammad" based on the direct approval of the Prophet. Because of the growing threat from the Mahdiyya, Sayyid Muḥammad ʿUṯmān II fled via Massawa to Suakin with his son ʿAlī al-Mīrġanī in June 1884, from where they were able to reach Egypt, which had become the centre of their anti-Mahdist propaganda.[7] Later, after Muḥammad ʿUṯmān II's death in 1886, ʿUṯmān Tāǧ al-Sirr, son of Muḥammad Sirr al-Ḫatm, and Sittī Maryam, daughter of Hāšim al-Mīrġanī, became the leading representatives of the family in Eastern Sudan and continued to support the anti-Mahdist party from their residence in Suakin. Apart from Sittī Maryam, other women from the family played a pivotal role during the conflict,

4 Voll 1969: 156.

5 Voll 1969: 299.

6 Voll 1969: 273; Daly 2012: 108–110.

7 Warburg 2013: 212–213.

such as Nāfisa and Fāṭima, who were, it was claimed, "the mother and daughter" of Muḥammad 'Uṯmān al-Mīrġanī, and who were living in Shendi during the Mahdiyya, but unfortunately only fragmentary records remain of their involvement.[8]

The government was aware of the religious dimensions of the Mahdī revolt and attempted to counterbalance it with other religious authorities, from the al-Azhar *'ulamā'* to the representatives of the Mīrġanī family. In 1883, the *khedive* asked Muḥammad Sirr al-Ḫatm, who was living in Cairo at the time, to visit Sudan. His visit to the country had a positive impact, but it was limited to Suakin and the coast, where there was already support for the government, while the Mahdī's influence continued to prevail in the hinterland.[9] In Eastern Sudan, Mīrġanī *ḫulafā'* succeeded in transmitting reliable information to the British to assist their fight against the Mahdiyya, and in Shendi, Muḥammad 'Uṯmān II's family represented a focal point for opposition to the revolt, and they were viewed by the British as a tool for helping them with pacification of the region. During the Mahdī siege in Kassala from November 1883 to the summer of 1885, Muḥammad 'Uṯmān II was the centre of gravity for the defence of the city until it fell under the control of the Mahdist forces. Fearing that he would be captured, he finally escaped from Kassala, and some months later his cousin Sīdī Bakrī also wrote to the government to communicate his intention to leave if it did not lend its support to the defence of the city. He remained there until he was seriously wounded, but finally had to leave for the Hejaz, where he died.[10]

During the Mahdist war, the Ḫatmiyya faced a period of fragmentation in its leadership, and it was only when the Mahdist state was defeated under the aegis of the Anglo-Egyptian armies in 1898 and the British established the Anglo-Egyptian condominium (1899–1955) that Sayyid 'Alī al-Mīrġanī appeared as head of the order and became the most important point of reference in Sudan. During the Condominium, the British wished to reward the family for their support during the war, and Sayyid 'Alī became the only Sudanese to receive a British decoration before the First World War when he was awarded the CMG by Queen Victoria in 1900. In Kassala, meanwhile, the order's main mosque, which had been destroyed by the Mahdiyya, was rebuilt with government funds, and the subsidy the Mīrġanī family had continued to receive

8 Voll 1969: 234 (footnote no. 150). See also Figure 9. Sittī Fāṭima al-Mīrġanī portrait.

9 Voll 1969: 273–302.

10 Voll 1969: 283.

during their exile in Egypt was also paid to them throughout the time of the Anglo-Egyptian Condominium in Sudan.[11]

This fragmentation of the Mīrġanī leadership during the Mahdiyya led to the establishment of at least two regional centres on the African Red Sea coast, in the Sudanese port of Suakin and in the Eritrean port of Massawa, where Sittī Maryam, Muḥammad ʿUṯmān Tāǧ al-Sirr (1849/50–1903), and Sayyid Hāšim (1849/50–1901) established their main residences.

According to Mīrġanī oral sources, Sayyid Hāšim b. Muḥammad ʿUṯmān b. Muḥammad Abī Bakr al-Mīrġanī, the youngest son of the founder of the order, was born in the Eritrean-Ethiopian region, while others sources report that he was born in Mecca.[12] In any event, we know that it was an unknown Abyssinian woman—from ʿAbabda, according to Voll—who gave birth to him in 1849–50. He was raised in Mecca until around 1860, when he left for Eritrea. He established a regional centre of the *ṭarīqa* in Massawa, which at that time was under Ottoman rule. Because he was only eleven at the time, it is probable that he did not take on a leadership role immediately, but it is still likely that he served as a regional focal point for the order in the area. It was not unusual for members of the Mīrġanī family to take an active role in the leadership of the order at an early age: for example, Sayyid ʿAlī ibn Muḥammad ʿUṯmān II, who was born around 1878, is mentioned in British dispatches in 1887–88 as having met with tribesmen on behalf of the government.[13] Similarly, as we will see, Sayyid Bakrī in Keren was reported in Italian records as a religious intermediary in conflict resolution, in spite of his youth.

When Sayyid Hāšim was not yet twenty years old, he asked for the hand in marriage of the daughter of Aḥmad ʿAwlī ʿUmar, a wealthy trader from Suakin and a member of the Artega aristocracy that controlled the main trade traffic in the port. Muḥammad ʿUṯmān had already initiated Aḥmad ʿAwlī ʿUmar into the order in around 1820, and in later years Sayyid Ḥasan had maintained correspondence with him and arranged an alliance with his brother Hāšim by marriage in order to increase the authority of the order among the Artega and Beja population in Suakin.

Sayyid Hāšim stayed in the port city for a brief period before returning to his residence near Massawa. It seems that his visit only lasted long enough for him to consummate his marriage and ensure the families' alliance with the birth

11 Warburg 2003: 62–63.

12 Hofheinz 1992: 25; Grandin 1988: 122–128; O'Fahey 1994: 208–9; Miran 2014 and 2009: 179–191, 200, 211, 239.

13 Trimingham 1952: 245; Voll 1969: 248.

of his heir Maryam in 1868.[14] Marriage alliances with influential local families were a very important strategy used by the Mīrġanī family and their order to cement their presence in the region, and another marriage took place several years later to confirm their close relationship with the Artega elites between Sayyid Hāšim's daughter Maryam and his nephew Muḥammad ʿUṯmān Tāǧ al-Sirr (1849/50–1903),[15] who was the son of Muḥammad Sirr al-Ḫatm al-Mīrġanī (1814/15–1855) and a woman from the well-known al-Ahdal family from Zabid, which was an important family of *sayyids* in Yemen.[16]

Muḥammad ʿUṯmān Tāǧ al-Sirr was born in 1849–50 in al-Hudayda in Yemen, where he studied under the supervision of his grandfather and became a renowned *ʿalīm* in Arabic language and grammar before moving to Bafda, in the Habab region in Northeast Eritrea. He lived in Eritrea until 1867–8 and then in Suakin, with his wife Maryam bt. Hāšim al-Mīrġanī, until his death.[17] He was a popular and highly-respected personality in the region, not only for his writings but also for his charismatic personality.[18] As we have seen, with the outbreak of the Mahdist revolt (1881–1889), the Mīrġanī family took a political position in support of the government both religiously and militarily. According to ʿUṯmān Diqna, the Mahdī's representative in Eastern Sudan, the Mīrġanīs' influence was the main reason behind the Mahdist opposition in the area.[19] During the Mahdiyya, the prestige of Sayyid Tāǧ al-Sirr and Šarīfa Maryam, assisted by the former's reputation for sanctity, gave them a role in the resistance against the Mahdist forces in Suakin. The city became a place of refuge for the anti-Mahdist party and never fell into the hands of the Anṣār, the followers of the Mahdī, in part thanks to the Mīrġanīs' commitment. Indeed, when the Mahdiyya was defeated and the Anglo-Egyptian condominium was established under Sudan in 1898, their support for negotiations with the local population was rewarded with a substantial pension.[20] A number of stories of miracles (*karāmāt*, singular *karāma*) celebrate Tāǧ al-Sirr's spiritual authority and are reported in his hagiographies. They confirm his active role against the Mahdiyya and record his charismatic figure as a visionary. One in particular states that when ʿUṯmān Diqna laid siege to Suakin, Tāǧ al-Sirr said that "he would not enter Suakin dead or alive". With the fall of Tukar and Sinkat, Egyptian control was reduced

14 Grandin 1988: 123.

15 Grandin 1988: 124. The marriage remained childless.

16 See Voll 2014; Bang 2003: 63.

17 Hofheinz 1992: 21; Grandin 1988: 124; O'Fahey 1994: 201.

18 On his literary production see O'Fahey 1994: 202–203.

19 Voll 1969: 299.

20 Grandin 1988: 124.

to Suakin, but the city never fell to ʿUṯmān Diqna's offensive during the entire Mahdist war, and in fact, the British never abandoned the city, which became an anti-Mahdist fortress thanks to Mīrġanī's support, as celebrated in the *karāmāt* stories about Tāǧ al-Sirr. Indeed, it was not only during the Mahdiyya that ʿUṯmān Diqna could not enter the city: he was not able to do so even after his death. According to a *karāma* story, when the British authorities wanted to move the remains of ʿUṯmān Diqna to his home town of Suakin, the train broke down, and he was finally buried in Arkwit.[21]

The available records of the activities of Sittī Maryam's father, Sayyid Hāšim, up to the time of the Italian occupation of the Red Sea ports are scarce. In February 1885, when Italian troops under the command of General Tancredi Saletta occupied Massawa, Sīdī Hāšim was in the town with his brother-in-law Muḥammad ʿUṯmān b. Muḥammad Sirr al-Ḫatm, who had retreated there to escape from the Mahdist advance. The Mahdiyya was gaining ground at the time following successful battles in Eastern Sudan, which they fought using guerrilla tactics. Following the fall of Tukar, Sīdī Hāšim's daughter Sittī Maryam and some of her followers were imprisoned by the Anṣār in February 1884, and they were only released when an Anglo-Egyptian expedition from Suakin defeated the Mahdists and occupied the region in 1891.[22]

The British supported the Italian occupation of Eritrea after the first Italian settlements in the area had been established in 1882 around the port of Assab. In particular, they encouraged Italy to expand into Massawa in the hope that the Italian colonial army would help hold the Mahdiyya back, and very shortly thereafter, the Italians led a number of battles against the Anṣār with the vital support of local soldiers; in fact, the anti-Mahdist resistance included contingents of African soldiers enlisted from peoples who were partly affiliated with the Ḫatmiyya,[23] among whom were the Beni ʿAmer, who openly opposed the Mahdiyya and finally opted to side with the Italian army.

21 This is reported in a copy of the *manāqib* of Muḥammad ʿUṯmān Tāǧ al-Sirr, known as *Sirr al-Sirr fi manāqib Tāǧ al-Sirr*, compiled by ʿAli Hāšim ʿAli al-Ḥanafī, 1995. A copy was donated to me by Aḥmad al-Mīrġanī in Cairo in 2009. Another *manāqib* is available in the Italian colonial archives in Rome: Archivio Storico Diplomatico del Ministero degli Affari Esteri (ASDMAE), Archivio Eritrea (AE), Pacco 1044/8 "Agiografia di Tajj-as sir".

22 Warburg 2013.

23 Voll 1969: 281–282; Fiaschi 1896: 28.

A Marriage Alliance between the Mīrġanī and the Beni ʿAmer People

In May 1885, some months after the arrival of the Italian troops in Massawa, the Mahdists occupied and plundered Kassala, which lay close to the main centre of the Ḫatmiyya, and destroyed Sayyid Ḥasan al-Mīrġanī's shrine and mosque there. From this moment, Suakin became a base from which numerous attacks against the Anṣār were launched, with the support of the British.[24]

The British welcomed the Italian occupation of Eritrea during this period because they needed support in order to arrest the progress of the Mahdiyya in Sudan and French colonial penetration into the Red Sea region. Additionally, from 1880 to 1890, the Beni ʿAmer people, who inhabited the northern part of the Eritrean lowlands on the Sudanese border and the area near the coast of Massawa and Arkiko, suffered from political unrest and internal conflicts.[25] The refusal of certain groups, who were principally affiliated with the Ḫatmiyya in Kassala, to join the Mahdiyya was the reason behind the Mahdist devastation of the Gash-Barka and Anseba valleys, which were a part of the Beni ʿAmer's seasonal grazing lands, between 1885 and 1893. A delegation from the Beni ʿAmer despatched a request to the Italian authorities for protection, which led to a political collaboration agreement. Their arrival in Massawa in 1888 was reported in colonial newspapers in colourful terms that evoked the image of the biblical visit of the Magi. The Beni ʿAmer established a large tribe of around forty to fifty thousand members on the borders with the Keren, Kassala, and Habab territories. Something then happened that caused unrest and internal conflict; there was a bitter struggle, the people were in danger of losing their unity. Italian intervention supported a peace between Mohammed El Fil and ʿAli Hossen (sic), whose two families were challenging for leadership, with the aim of reuniting the scattered parties and bringing the Beni ʿAmer's socio-political power into line with colonial policy. The main purpose behind co-opting the Beni ʿAmer was to use them to protect caravans on the Keren-Kassala route in general, and in trade with Sudan in particular, and they were also viewed as an additional opponent of the Abyssinians. According to early colonial reports, the Beni ʿAmer's "friendly power" would be conquered "cheaply and with little effort".[26]

---

24 Karrar 1992: 100. A group portrait of Muḥammad ʿUṯmān b. Muḥammad Sirr al-Ḫatm with the colonial army is available in Goglia 1989: 80.

25 Morin 2003: 527–529.

26 Newspaper article "Da unirsi alla lettera del Comando superiore in Africa" dated 11 November 1888, transmitted by the War Ministry by a letter dated 23 November 1888,

The collaboration with the Italian authorities would secure the interests of traders along the Sudanese-Eritrean border along the Keren-Kassala route, where both the Beni ʿAmer and the Ḫatmiyya were established. It is difficult to determine whether Sīdī Hāšim played any kind of role as an intermediary in suppressing the internal conflict among the Beni ʿAmer and establishing their relationship with the colonial authorities. We can only speculate on what actually took place, but we do know that he visited Western Eritrea during this period, where he married a woman from a Beni ʿAmer family, according to oral accounts, probably from Agordat, which was the city of the Diglal, the principal local authority.[27] Their marriage resulted in the birth during this period (in 1892–93), of Šarīfa ʿAlawiyya, who would later assume a leading role among the Muslim population of the Eritrean lowlands. These years were crucial for the successful struggle against the Mahdiyya, thanks in part to the involvement of the Beni ʿAmer people, who fought side by side with the British and Italian armies. In February 1891, an Anglo-Egyptian expedition captured ʿUṯmān Diqna's headquarters near Tokar, and other later battles were led by the Italian army and African warriors in Eastern Eritrea. In particular, the Italian army fought a number of battles against the Mahdists around Agordat. In June 1890, the first Battle of Agordat took place as a consequence of Mahdist raids and reprisals against the Beni ʿAmer, who had just signed their collaboration agreement with Italy. In December 1893, a Mahdist expedition into Eritrean territory was defeated at the Second Battle of Agordat, which was the prelude to an Italian offensive against Kassala, the main centre of the Ḫatmiyya order, which fell in July.[28]

The first phase of the Second Battle of Agordat was fought using information rather than weapons:[29] information was provided to the Italian and British armies by the Mīrġanī family and the *ḫulafāʾ* of the order throughout the conflict against the Mahdiyya,[30] and their support was rewarded with religious respect from their followers, which contributed towards the victory

Archivio Storico Diplomatico del Ministero degli Affari Esteri (ASDMAE), Archivio Eritrea (AE), 1886–1912, Pacco 43 (Morgani-Adigrat—Varie Eritrea), Fasc. 1 Morgani (1886–1911).

27 Interview with Aḥmad al-Mīrġanī, a descendant of Šarīfa ʿAlawiyya and nephew of Ǧaʿfar al-Mīrġanī on May 2009 in Cairo.

28 Holt 1958: 110.

29 Scardigli 1996: 116–118.

30 Letters containing information for the Italian authorities are available at Archivio Storico Diplomatico del Ministero degli Affari Esteri (ASDMAE), Archivio Eritrea (AE), 1886–1912, Pacco 43 (Morgani-Adigrat—Varie Eritrea), Fasc. 1 Morgani (1886–1911). See in particular: letter from the Mahdist Emir in Kassala and letters of information from the "Morgani", 1892, Archivio Storico Diplomatico del Ministero degli Affari Esteri (ASDMAE), Archivio

in the war against the Mahdiyya. This reward was manifested after the "liberation" of Kassala, when both Christian and Muslim African soldiers, whose military efforts had been pivotal to the struggle, honoured the ruins of the Ḫatmiyya mosque, which had been destroyed by the Mahdists during the occupation, with pious visits.[31] The Mīrġanī had been important intermediaries between the Italian and British Governments and local rulers during the conflict, while the *ḫulafā'* of the Ḫatmiyya acted as informers on events taking place in a number of regions. Mahdist leaders also often resorted to representatives of the Ḫatmiyya to communicate with the government, and their prestige remained high, despite the persecution they suffered in the territories that lay under Mahdiyya control.[32] On the other side, the participation of the Beni ʿAmer, who fought side by side with the Italian army, was remarkable. The Beni ʿAmer people were divided into branches (*badana*) bounded by a common descent called Amer. According to an oral tradition, this common ancestor was a holy man, the son of a Ja'ali man and a Bellou woman, who "sprang from the ground". Various governments in the region (first Egyptian, and then Italian and British) included heterogeneous groups under the Beni ʿAmer label for administrative reasons who, under the paramount chief of the Beni ʿAmer, known by his traditional title of Diglal, were submitted to taxation. This chieftainship is said to have emerged in the 16th century, when the Diglal was a vassal of the Funj dynasty in Sudan. The symbol of his rank was a two-cornered hat (called the *mgren*), which originated from the Funj, whose rulers possessed the same regalia. The Ottoman and Egyptian regimes in Sudan and Eastern Eritrea extended his sovereignty to other peoples in the Beni ʿAmer area, thereby including a number of different groups under Beni ʿAmer rule, all of which were divided into a small ruling aristocracy, the Nabtab, and a caste of serfs known as the Tigré, who were not considered to be "sons of Amer", but rather slaves belonging to Beni ʿAmer masters. As a result of wars and raids, slavery co-existed side by side with serfdom, and nothwithstanding its formal abolition, many ex-slaves and descendants of slaves remained dependent on their masters in a condition of serfdom or slavery. In the following years of colonial rule, the Italian Government purposely weakened the master-serf dependence by the abolition of feudal dues. During colonial rule, new careers, such as enrollement in the colonial army or service in the police, were opened up to serfs. On the other hand, the Italian authorities also sought to back up the

---

Eritrea (AE), 1886–1912, Pacco 43 (Morgani-Adigrat—Varie Eritrea), Fasc. 1 Morgani (1886–1911).

31 Fiaschi 1896: 28.

32 Voll 1969: 309.

authority of the Diglal by supplying him with arms and armed escorts in order to guarantee the collection of taxes.[33] The Beni ʿAmer people, like the ʿAfar and Hadendowa, had no problem with collaborating with the Italians; they perceived colonialism as a phenomenon that was committed to the maintenance of order and the development of trade, they lived in areas that were environmentally unsuited to colonial settlers, and they experienced less unrest than did the Tigrinya people, who lived in the highland areas, which were where the Italians were mostly established.[34]

The Eritrean-Sudanese region was facing a period of crisis characterized on the one hand by growing internal fragmentation within the political and religious leadership and on the other by increasing infiltration by the European colonial powers. The Mahdist uprising (1882–1885) in Sudan undermined the Ottoman-Egyptian establishment that had ruled a large area of what is now Sudan and Eritrea (1820/21–1885), and provided the Anglo-Egyptian and Italian armies with further justification for gradually penetrating from the Red Sea coast into the hinterland to face the Mahdist "threat". The end of Ottoman-Egyptian rule and the subsequent Mahdist defeats resulted in the Anglo-Egyptian occupation of Sudan (1899–1956) and the Italian colonial occupation of Eritrea (1885–1941). The Ḫatmiyya secured a leading role in the fight against the Mahdiyya during the conflict, and they finally gave way to the British and Italian occupations of Sudan and Eritrea. In Italian reports, the rhetoric on the religious and political rivalry between the Mahdiyya and the Ḫatmiyya was used in order to lend legitimacy to the Ḫatmiyya's religious authority, and was a leitmotif throughout the colonial occupation to explain the support colonial policy gave the order, not only in Sudan but also in Eritrea. In an interview with an Italian traveller in the 1930s, Sīdī Hāšim's daughter ʿAlawiyya is reported to have stressed the positive impact of the Ḫatmiyya among the Beni ʿAmer affiliated with her order, which formed a solid bulwark against the spread of the Mahdī's "deleterious dissident movement" in Eritrea. The Mahdī is described as a "fanatical iconoclast who did not shrink even after the massacre of women and children". His numerous followers—who were explicitly accused of being "traitors to the Islamic religion"—troubled the government and the population alike. The religious and moral role of the Ḫatmiyya, on the other hand, was always to preach "truth and unity", and to open people's eyes so that they would not commit the same "blunder" as the Mahdī. This is the same discourse that was promoted by the colonial authorities, which stressed the Ḫatmiyya's con-

33 Nadel 1945: 51–84. See also Archivio Storico Diplomatico del Ministero degli Affari Esteri (ASDMAE), Archivio Eritrea (AE), Pacco 23, Fasc. 7 Beni Amer (1898, 1897, 1890).

34 Negash 1986: 47.

servative function of maintaining order: in other words, of stopping the spread of the Mahdists' "disordered movement, which conflicted with its proclaimed Islamic function" and with the "good moral principles" that the Ḫatmiyya, in contrast, promoted in the colony.[35] In fact, even after the Mahdists' defeat, Italian colonial policy would be to favour the Ḫatmiyya order—both economically and politically—in order to prevent the emergence of other dissident religious movements that might threaten the *pax colonial*.

The Italians' victory at the Battle of Agordat inspired General Baratieri to press on with Italian occupation as far as Kassala in July 1894, beyond the area allocated to Italian influence.[36] Italian expansion into the hinterland came to a gradual halt, however, due to the Batha Hagos' revolt in Akkele Guzay in 1894 and the subsequent Battle of Adwa in 1896, which finally put an end to Italian military penetration in East Africa.[37] Italy decided that it was too burdensome to maintain its occupation of Kassala, and in December 1897 it returned it to the British, who by that stage had gained control of Sudan. With hindsight, this was seen as a strategic error by Ferdinando Martini, who was Governor of the colony from 1897 to 1907, and as an excessively hasty political decision that in the subsequent years of the occupation was described as a "fatal error" with significant economic consequences that were perceptible throughout the period of colonial rule.[38] The decision certainly had a huge impact on the Italian project to make the city a centre for collecting Sudanese products that would be sent on to Massawa via Keren.[39] Immediately following the transfer of Kassala to the British, Martini was appointed to be the First Civil Governor of the Colony, and he began a project of pacification and reduction of troop numbers and salaries.[40] He also designed the main guidelines for a policy for Muslim leadership in Eritrea that would enable religious turmoil to be controlled and migration along the frontier with Sudan to be stabilized. The plan,

35 Caniglia 1940. In this book, Caniglia reports on an interview with the *šarīfa* in Massawa, through which he passed on his way back from his trip in Somalia and Harar. He visited the *šarīfa* on the advice of Governor Daodiace. As Caniglia explains in his introduction, his book was published under the aegis of the National Fascist Trade Union (*Sindacato nazionale fascista*) of Writers and Authors, the Ministry of Popular Culture, and the Ministry of Italian Africa after one of the first literary journeys into Italian East Africa. It was designed by the poet Marinetti and approved by Mussolini.

36 On the issue of Kassala, see Serra 1966: 526–563; Censoni 1941; Zaghi 1940: 412–464; Giglio 1950: 401–436.

37 Scardigli 1996: 125.

38 Omedeo, Peglion and Valenti 1913: 19. Cit. taken from Zaccaria 2005: 311.

39 Zaccaria 2005: 311.

40 Scardigli 1996: 169, 175.

which called for support for the establishment of a branch of the Ḫatmiyya inside the borders of Eritrea, was considered to be a key factor for preservation of the *pax colonial* among Muslims.[41]

Sīdī Hāšim: Spy or *walī*?

During the Mahdiyya, a number of representatives and followers of the Ḫatmiyya left Sudan for Hejaz and Egypt, some of whom passed through Eastern Eritrea and collaborated with the British and Italian armies by providing information on the struggle against the Mahdiyya. When the Italian armies occupied the Eritrean coast, they asked Sīdī Hāšim to remain in Massawa and attempted to co-opt him into directing religious issues within the Muslim community, promising him a salary that he mentioned in several letters, including one addressed to the King of Italy in person[42] He was then carefully monitored so that his role in the colony could be properly understood. At first, however, colonial officials failed to comprehend his religious role, and asked him to become a *muftī*, a proposal he immediately turned down. They then attempted to clarify his religious role in the community, and realized that he was not the leader of the Muslim community in the port, as they had thought, but rather a person whom people in the region "venerated" as a descendant of the Prophet.[43] These personalities—as a colonial officer observed—did not accept public appointments: they lived on offerings from believers. In Sīdī Hāšim's case, when his followers had struck a good bargain, they would bring

41 Romandini 1984: 127–131. For a historiographical overview of this issue see Miran 2005: 177–215.

42 Sīdī Hāšim's letter in which he writes of his first agreements with the Italians, and in particular of his meeting with General Genè (November 1900). Genè had apparently asked him to remain in Eritrea and not to continue on to Cairo as he had intended to. To this end, he promised him a fixed salary if he helped the Italians "with matters relating to the country". Contrary to these agreements, the government had not yet given him anything, in spite of the letter of complaint he had already presented to the King of Italy. Archivio Storico Diplomatico del Ministero degli Affari Esteri (ASDMAE), Archivio Eritrea (AE), 1880–1917, Pacco 1022 (Missioni Politiche—Varie—El Morgani) Fasc. 10 Famiglia El Morgani, 1895–1917.

43 Miran (2009: 183, 320 no. 70) suggests that in 1910s, the Mīrġanī family began to appoint whoever was delegated by the Italian Government as *muftī* or *qāḍī* of Massawa as *ḫalīfat al-ḫulafāʾ*.

FIGURE 3 *Portrait of Sīdī Hāšim.*
ḪATMIYYA PRIVATE COLLECTION, ASMARA.

him gifts as a sign of their gratitude.[44] The colonial gaze did not take the socio-religious dimension of African subjects into consideration, however, and figures like Sayyid Hāšim were simply described as exploitative individuals who used confidence tricks to "extort" money and goods from believers. The reality, however, was that spiritual guides—or "holy men", to use the colonial jargon—played a crucial socio-religious role in these times, and were highly-respected points of reference during an historical era characterized by socio-political upheavals. The Sufi and Islamic brotherhoods that gained followers during the 19th and 20th centuries became a resource for confronting socio-political crises across the region.

As was the case with the trading community of Benadir, troubles, disease, and economic crises were viewed as the consequences of a moral decline within the Muslim community.[45] Curing the soul was intertwined not only with religious teachings, but also with the treatment of diseases, as reported in stories of miracles performed by the Mīrġanī family, such as one that tells of Muḥammad 'Uṯmān II restoring a woman's sight.[46] Sayyid Hāšim also carried out healing practices in Massawa,[47] and performed so-called "exorcisms" during this period to heal members of the local population, who rewarded him with offerings. The colonial use of the term "exorcism" to refer to Sīdī Hāšim's spiritual practices is misleading, however: from a theological point of view, it would be more correct to speak of traditional Islamic medicine. These practices are not described in detail, but we might suppose that Sīdī Hāšim used Islamic treatments such as self-help therapy through prayer. Among the collections of Ḫatmiyya writings, we find one of these prayers in particular, *al-ṣalāt al-kašfiyya*, which was written by Muḥammad 'Uṯmān Tāǧ al-Sirr (d. 1903), the husband of Sittī Maryam, Sīdī Hāšim's daughter, and is aimed "at bringing relief from any kind of sorrow".[48]

44 Regio esercito italiano, Comando superiore in Africa al Ministero degli Affari Esteri, 16 gennaio 1887. Archivio Storico Diplomatico del Ministero degli Affari Esteri (ASDMAE), Archivio Eritrea (AE), Pacco 43 (Morgani-Adigrat—Varie Eritrea), Fasc. 1 Morgani (1886–1911). On this topic, see Bruzzi 2012a.

45 Reese 1999: 169–192.

46 Karrar 1992: 92.

47 "As Muslims put illness down to the influence of evil spirits, sick people generally turn to Morgani [Sīdī Hāšim] to be exorcised and, of course, they reward his work with gifts. These are given in proportion to the financial situation of the sick person himself …", Regio esercito italiano, 16 gennaio 1887. Archivio Storico Diplomatico del Ministero degli Affari Esteri (ASDMAE), Archivio Eritrea (AE), 1886–1912, Pacco 43 (Morgani-Adigrat—Varie Eritrea), Fasc. 1 Morgani (1886–1911).

48 Archivio Storico Diplomatico del Ministero degli Affari Esteri (ASDMAE), Archivio Eritrea (AE), pacco 1044/8. See O'Fahey, Hofheinz and Radtke 1994: 203. On *al-ṣalāt al-kašfiyya*

Popular belief in the existence of *ǧinn*, invisible spirits that were able to penetrate the lives and bodies of human beings and cause illness, was widespread in Arab and Muslim society. A number of Sufi shaykhs gained popularity due to their miraculous capacity to restore people troubled by the influence of *ǧinn* to good health. One example of this phenomenon was a contemporary of Sīdī Hāšim, Šayḫ Uways (1847–1909), who was a shaykh from the Qādiriyya Islamic brotherhood in Somalia, and a leading religious personality of the time.[49] We know that Sufi shaykhs were a source of not only social and economic resources, but also knowledge of spiritual medicine and healing practices, and this use of *ṭibb* ("medicine") contributed towards creating confidence in them and reinforcing their charisma.[50] Believers would visit Sufi saints and shrines because it was believed that they possessed *baraka*, a "beneficent force of divine origin, which causes superabundance in the physical sphere and prosperity and happiness within the psychic order".[51] The more *baraka* a shaykh was invested with, the more powerful his blessings were considered to be, with the result that he would achieve increased prestige among his followers. Cruise O'Brien made the point that *baraka* could be identified with the idea of health and power, applying the concept of health in a holistic sense.[52] Indeed, Sufi saints have often been regarded as being central to religious life as both political leaders and moral models, and the physical bodies of saints have been seen as the very repository of sacred power.[53] They were respected as Friends of God (*awliyā' allah*) who were able to teach people by their example in everyday life. As social and religious focal points for regional *ziyāra*, the residences of Muslim shaykhs were both destinations for believers and a place of treatment for the sick and troubled. The so-called *ziyāra* is a popular practice in Muslim societies that means a pious visit to living or dead saints. Despite theological critics who targeted this practice, people used to make *ziyāra* to visit Sufi shaykhs and leading Islamic personalities because they were believed to possess *baraka*. Through *ziyāra*, believers hope to get blessings, as well as relief, teachings, or answers to their questions. Saints' residences, or their shrines after they died, often became the centre of regional cults where gatherings and

---

composed by Muḥammad 'Uṯmān Tāǧ al-Sirr that is aimed "to bring relief from any sorrow" see Hofheinz 1992: 21.

49 Samatar 1992.

50 Last 1988: 185.

51 Colin 1986: 1032.

52 O'Brien 1988: 4.

53 Saints' physical bodies and images of them have been the focus of extensive Sufi literature. The body is often treated as a site of sacred power. The embodiment concept was used to study Sufi saints and cults in Werbner and Basu 1998. Kugle (2007) explored the concept of embodiment, and placed the body at the centre of Sufi phenomenology.

religious practices were performed. Attendance at these gatherings was considered to be therapeutic for the resolution of personal problems. Charitable work was especially promoted at Sufi shrines, and Muslim communities gathered around Sufi shaykhs to learn from their example and their acts of generosity and insight. This was also the case with Sīdī Hāšim's residence in Hetumlo, near the Eritrean port of Massawa, which was a crossroads for a variety of actors. Even colonial officials turned to the Sayyid to seek help, but with an obviously different, purely political, goal inspired initially by the fight against the Mahdiyya, and later by a desire to curb the religious troubles in the Sahel. They also decided to grant him a monthly salary in place of the payments in kind he had occasionally received from the Egyptian Government. Early contacts with Sīdī Hāšim were not, however, particularly satisfying for the colonial officials, who were critical of him and frustrated by his "laziness". There were widespread rumours about his lack of morality, fuelled by accusations from his rivals that he drank alcohol. His supporters countered by emphasizing that he was a holy man.[54] These accounts of his drunkenness might also be seen as the classic Sufi metaphor for spiritual experiences and states of ecstasy as he experienced intoxication with the Love of God. According to Sufi beliefs, the Sufi "remains and yet is separate", in the sense that his external appearance remains with human beings, while his internal appearance is separate and with the Truth.[55] Oral accounts relating to Sīdī Hāšim support this idea, and claim that while his body was asleep, his soul was in Mecca.[56] On the other hand, rivalries among religious authorities were especially bitter in Massawa at the time; they were expressed on theological as well as moral grounds, and called both the morality and authority of adversaries into question. Even Sīdī Hāšim, after he had refused the office of *muftī* in Massawa that had been offered to him by the colonial authorities, attempted to dissuade the Italians from appointing the son of the previous *muftī*, Muḥammad Nūr Sirāǧ, because he was too young and inexperienced and not at a sufficiently high level to take on this important task. Instead, he suggested that Muḥammad Nūr Sirāǧ be appointed as shaykh of the mosque and paid a monthly salary,[57] claiming that

54 Regio esercito italiano, Comando superiore in Africa al Ministero degli Affari Esteri, 16 gennaio 1887. Archivio Storico Diplomatico del Ministero degli Affari Esteri (ASDMAE), Archivio Eritrea (AE), 1886–1912, Pacco 43 (Morgani-Adigrat—Varie Eritrea), Fasc. 1 Morgani (1886–1911). Martinelli 1930: 56.

55 Ventura 1990: 70.

56 Interview with Hāšim Muḥammad ʿAlī Blenai, 102 years of age, a follower of the Ḫatmiyya, on March 2009 in Massawa.

57 Lettera del Morgani al Comm. Martini, Governatore della Colonia Eritrea, 23 gennaio 1901. Archivio Storico Diplomatico del Ministero degli Affari Esteri (ASDMAE), Archivio Eritrea

local dignitaries in Massawa had made the proposal without his knowledge, and against his will. His advice was that the previous Egyptian religious policy should be continued, and that a highly learned *qāḍī* and *muftī* from Cairo or Beirut should be invited to Eritrea. He also warned colonial officials of the danger to the Government represented by the Habab shaykh, Osman Kantibai, who was accused of inciting the people against the Italians and of threatening the peace, and suggested that he be imprisoned in order to resolve the ongoing conflict among the Habab. The region was under attack from a series of internal conflicts and the fragmentation of its leadership, and Sīdī Hāšim supported a situation of stability, acting as an intermediary by transmitting information from local to colonial authorities and vice versa.[58]

In 1898, as a part of the policy to pacify the colony, Governor Ferdinando Martini sought to transfer Sīdī Hāšim's residence from Massawa to Keren. His aim was to stabilize the Eastern Eritrean border with Sudan and to limit the influence of other shaykhs who opposed Italy, but Sīdī Hāšim did not offer his services to the Italian authorities, claiming that he was suffering from health issues, and so the Governor fell back on funding the Friday mosque in Keren (Figure 4). When he died some years later, the government once again sought to use his holy body to establish a Muslim centre of devotion inside Eritrea. The colonial authorities' attempt to transfer his shrines to Keren met with bitter popular resistance from the Muslim community in Massawa, however, and Governor Martini had to limit Italian action to a contribution to the funding of his shrine in Hetumlo, near Massawa and the construction of a mosque in Keren. It was, therefore, the First Governor of the Colony of Eritrea, Martini, who inaugurated a "Muslim policy" entailing the construction and renovation of mosques.[59] This policy of funding the building and renovation of mosques and Islamic schools was pursued by colonial authorities elsewhere in Africa,[60] and the colonial "Muslim policy" that had been launched in the early colonial period in Italian East Africa was to become increasingly structured in the 1930s (Figures 4, 5 and 36–40).

(AE), 1880–1917, Pacco 1022 (Missioni Politiche—Varie—El Morgani), Fasc. 10 Famiglia El Morgani, 1895–1917.

58 Lettera del Morgani al Comm. Martini, Governatore della Colonia Eritrea, 1 aprile 1901, Archivio Storico Diplomatico del Ministero degli Affari Esteri (ASDMAE), Archivio Eritrea (AE), 1880–1917, Pacco 1022 (Missioni Politiche—Varie—El Morgani), Fasc. 10 Famiglia El Morgani, 1895–1917.

59 Romandini 1984; Miran 2009: 176–186. See also Miran 2014.

60 Cantone 2012.

FIGURE 4 *Keren—Tahil feast funeral prayers for the death of Šayḫ Morgani (holy man).*
POSTCARD, GIORGIO ZAFIRACHI, MASSAWA. PERSONAL COLLECTION.

FIGURE 5 *The Keren mosque.*
SECTION 1 (EX ARMADI), ERITREA, E6B, CULTO MUSULMANO III 17. ISIAO ARCHIVE, ROME.

CHAPTER 3

Islam, Gender and Leadership

Female Heirs by Blood Alone: A Power Vacuum?

As Cynthia Nelson observed as early as 1974, Middle Eastern societies—and we also include Muslim Africa here—have long been presented as being segregated into "two social worlds marked out by the nature of the two sexes". These two social worlds "are by definition characterized as being private (the women's) and public (the men's). The former world is invariably described as domestic, narrow and restricted, whereas the latter is described as political, broad and expansive". Inherent in this assumption is the assertion that "the concern of women is the domestic and not the political".[1] This dichotomy was deeply rooted in colonial policies: colonial officers deemed authority and power to be limited to the male world, especially in Muslim societies. Contrary to this assumption, however, women historically expressed their agency in the social and political spheres, despite the dominant patriarchal establishment, and some even attained power: stories of the "forgotten queens of Islam" still survive today.[2]

How was authority exercised, accepted, reconfigured, and challenged in relation to gender and Islam in African contexts?[3] Gender inequalities are usually attributed to Islam's presumed influence on the lives of women and men in Northeast Africa, as well as in the Middle East. Trimingham has claimed that in Ethiopia, "the effect of Islam upon the position of women varies according to the depth of the Islamization. In general, the greater the hold of orthodox institutions the lower becomes the status of women".[4] While on the one hand the notion of "Islamic orthodoxy" is highly controversial, on the other, gender relations were established within complex historical circumstances and socio-cultural contexts that cannot be reduced to a merely cultural explanation. The colonial setting offers us a good example of this phenomenon: far from representing an opportunity for the emancipation of women, colonialism led to no improvements in their condition in Africa. Consuetudinary laws were

1 Nelson and Abu-Lughod 2007: 74. This article was also published in Nelson 1974: 551–563.
2 Mernissi 1977.
3 This issue has mainly been considered in West Africa in Frede and Hill 2014: 131–165.
4 Trimingham 1952: 227. For a criticism of this deep-rooted assumption in the MENA region, see Lazreg 1988.

 | DOI 10.1163/9789004356160_005

usually fixed and based on male advisors and intermediaries, and the practice was to marginalize African women in the political sphere.[5] This marginalization of female subjects in the colonies affected women from the motherland as well: the Italian colonial experience in Eritrea was predominantly a male enterprise from which Italian women were mostly excluded, especially from any position of power,[6] and the Italian authorities extended their underlying patriarchal philosophy, which held that women should have no access to any official position of power, to their colony.

When Sayyid Hāšim died in Massawa, he left only his two daughters—Sittī Maryam, who was 34 and childless, and Sittī ʿAlawiyya, who was only 10 at the time—as his heirs. In Suakin, Sittī Maryam was widowed just one year later, and was now the family's only representative in the city and among the Beja people, becoming the *ḫalīfa* of the order thanks to her prestige and influence among the Hadendowa and Beni ʿAmer people in the area.[7] In Eritrea, the Italian authorities underestimated the position that women could attain in Muslim societies and ignored Sittī ʿAlawiyya's authority for a while, at least until the 1910s, when she began to emerge openly as a leading religious figure. A double standard applied to female subjects in the colony at the time, so that while a female authority such as Sittī ʿAlawiyya was not even taken into account, a policy of controlling Eritrean women bodies was implemented in Massawa. Prostitutes were widely used by in the colonial army, and the colonial authorities were worried about the spread of disease among the troops. In 1903, the Regional Commissioner published a call for indigenous prostitution to be controlled: prostitutes had to be identified by the local authorities and had to wear an identification tag on their arms and necks.[8] In this period, the main interest in women in colonial policy was related to Eritrean prostitution, while their political and religious authority was totally ignored.

Conversely, according to the colonial view, there was a risk that the death of Sayyid Hāšim, the only male representative of the Mīrġanī holy family, would lead to a dangerous and destabilizing religious leadership vacuum in the colony, and so the colonial authorities called on another male Mīrġanī representative in Eritrea, Sayyid Ǧaʿfar al-Mīrġanī (1871–1943), a nephew of Sayyid Hāšim,

---

5 Bergstrom 2002: 6; Sheldon 2005: 295; Cooper 1998: 21–37.

6 Stefani 2007.

7 Grandin 1988: 124.

8 Governo dell'Eritrea, Commissariato Regionale di Massaua. Bando del 12 luglio 1903. Archivio Storico Diplomatico del Ministero degli Affari Esteri (ASDMAE), Archivio Eritrea (AE), Pacco 141, Fasc. 7, 1903 Esercizi pubblici. Prostituzione.

who until then had been living in Kassala, in Anglo-Egyptian Sudan. Regional Commissioner Pollera suggested he be given a monthly salary of 500 Lire, which was more than that the British had guaranteed the Mīrġanī in Kassala. The purpose of Sayyid Ǧaʿfar's time in Eritrea was to control and prevent the exodus of Eritreans to Sudan, as well as to combat the influence of other charismatic Muslim figures in the colony, such as the ʿAd Šayḫ in the Sahel. Colonial policy was intended to confine the population of the Barka region within colonial borders and to counterbalance the power exercised by other socio-religious Islamic authorities beyond them. After a short stay in Massawa, Sayyid Ǧaʿfar finally accepted this proposal and established his residence in Keren with his family.[9] According to the observations of Governor Martini, the presence of Sīdī Ǧaʿfar in the city ended up by contributing "to the formation of an Islamic sphere of influence within the colonial borders, mobilizing a large number of Muslims around an official representative of the branch of the Ḫatmiyya in Eritrea".[10]

However, his presence in Keren, which had been so intensely desired by the Italian authorities, led to a series of internal conflicts within the Ḫatmiyya with Sittī ʿAlawiyya, the daughter of Sīdī Hāšim, who had hitherto been living in Massawa near her father's shrines and mosque. The early conflicts between the two emerged from colonial correspondence after 1908, when the *šarīfa*—who had married another member of the family, *šarīf* Muḥammad Ṣāliḥ al-Mīrġanī, two years earlier—demanded a permanent residence in Keren from the Italian government.[11] She also asked for the same treatment that had been offered to Sīdī Ǧaʿfar, namely participation in the religious life of the city and a monthly allowance.[12] From the time she arrived in Keren, a series of conflicts arose, the first of which took place in September, when the

9 Colonia Eritrea, Commissariato Regionale di Cheren, 3 marzo 1910. Archivio Storico Diplomatico del Ministero degli Affari Esteri (ASDMAE), Archivio Eritrea (AE), 1886–1912 Pacco 43 (Morgani-Adigrat—Varie Eritrea), Fasc. 1 Morgani (1886–1911). Bruzzi 2006: 437–438; Romandini 1985: 57–72; Romandini 1984: 127–131. On the conflict with ʿAd Šayḫ in the Sahel, Miran 2005: 199; on the desertion of the Habab, see Lenci 1999; Pollera 1935: 286–287.

10 Miran 2005: 198; Mondaini 1927: 145.

11 Governo dell'Eritrea, Direzione degli Affari Civili, Telegramma, 22 febbraio 1908. Archivio Storico Diplomatico del Ministero degli Affari Esteri (ASDMAE), Archivio Eritrea (AE), 1886–1912, Pacco 43 (Morgani-Adigrat—Varie Eritrea), Fasc. 1 Morgani (1886–1911).

12 Colonia Eritrea, Commissariato Regionale di Cheren, 23 febbraio 1908. Archivio Storico Diplomatico del Ministero degli Affari Esteri (ASDMAE), Archivio Eritrea (AE), 1886–1912, Pacco 43 (Morgani-Adigrat—Varie Eritrea), Fasc. 1 Morgani (1886–1911).

šarīfa's husband, *šarīf* Muḥammad Ṣāliḥ al-Mīrġanī, and Sayyid Ǧaʿfar went to the Keren mosque armed for a fight that was only avoided because they were eventually disarmed. Initially, the colonial authorities explored the possibility of moving Sayyid Ǧaʿfar's residence out of Keren, but they were worried about a possible power vacuum that might lead Muslims to turn to the member of the Ḫatmiyya in Kassala, in Sudan. The authority of the *šarīfa* was considered to be too weak because—they thought—as a woman she could not appoint *ḫulafāʾ* or representatives of the order in Eritrea.

Sīdī Ǧaʿfar's residence in Keren was confirmed, but the government officials asked him to appoint favoured representatives from Eritrea to replace some of his own, who were mainly Sudanese.[13] The issue of the appointment of representatives of the brotherhood is especially relevant, since it was in colonial times that the organizational structure of the order became established in the territory through these actors. There were three hierarchical levels of representative in the Ḫatmiyya, of which the highest was *ḫalīfat al-ḫulafāʾ* and the lowest the ordinary *ḫalīfa*. The intermediate level was the *ḫalīfa muqaddam al-ḥaḍra*, who was called on to begin prayers, usually after a reading of the *Mawlid*, which commenced the *ḥaḍra*, the collective supererogatory ritual. In November 1909, Sīdī Ǧaʿfar's appointement of *ḫalīfa muqaddam al-ḥaḍra* in Massawa led to protests from Sīdī Hāšim's former representatives, who asked Sittī ʿAlawiyya to file a complaint with the colonial officials. In effect, this appointment was an expression of Sīdī Ǧaʿfar's interference in Sittī ʿAlawiyya's father's *zāwiya*, and represented a real affront to her authority and other related religious dignitaries.[14] Once again, the colonial authorities asked her to acknowledge her relative's leadership of the order, as he had been expressly appointed and invited to Eritrea by the government, but their attempt at reaching a conciliation was extremely harsh, as the Commissioner of Massawa reported: "I did my best to explain to the *Sceriffa* how things are, and tried to make her understand that in the end, as a women, she should not interfere in religious

---

13 Colonia Eritrea, Commissariato Regionale di Cheren, 3 marzo 1910. Archivio Storico Diplomatico del Ministero degli Affari Esteri (ASDMAE), Archivio Eritrea (AE), 1886–1912, Pacco 43 (Morgani-Adigrat—Varie Eritrea), Fasc. 1 Morgani (1886–1911); Colonia Eritrea, Commissariato Regionale di Cheren, 9 agosto 1910. Archivio Storico Diplomatico del Ministero degli Affari Esteri (ASDMAE), Archivio Eritrea (AE), 1886–1912, Pacco 43 (Morgani-Adigrat—Varie Eritrea), Fasc. 1 Morgani (1886–1911); Keren 17 agosto 1910. Archivio Storico Diplomatico del Ministero degli Affari Esteri (ASDMAE), Archivio Eritrea (AE), 1886–1912, Pacco 43 (Morgani-Adigrat—Varie Eritrea), Fasc. 1 Morgani (1886–1911).

14 Colonia Eritrea, Commissariato Regionale di Massaua, 24 agosto 1910. Archivio Storico Diplomatico del Ministero degli Affari Esteri (ASDMAE), Archivio Eritrea (AE), 1886–1912 Pacco 43 (Morgani-Adigrat—Varie Eritrea), Fasc. 1 Morgani (1886–1911).

matters, and should leave the broadest freedom relating to this and all other responsibilities to the head of Morgania, Giaffar El Morgani. But this woman is obstinate in her claims, and while reluctantly recognizing her nephew as the Eritrean head of the Islam religion, she argues that with regard to the mosque where her father is buried, no one can or must be involved except her. Regarding the newly-elected *ḫalīfat al-ḥaḍra*, who has recently been appointed by the Morgani in Massawa in the person of Hamed Abdalla Hamedi, she told me that she would rather allow her throat to be cut than allow him to set foot in her mosque. I have tried every means to make this woman see reason, but I was not able to persuade her."[15] Given the intransigence of the *šarīfa*, the colonial authorities ordered Sīdī Ǧaʿfar's *ḫalīfat al-ḥaḍra* not to enter Sīdī Hāšim's mosque. The rivalry between the two Mīrġanī remained an open issue, however, and led to concern in the colony. The battle for leadership of the order and the related issue of the appointment of *ḫulafāʾ* was not resolved, and the *šarīfa*'s influence continued to grow, arousing the envy of her relative until 1917, when open conflict broke out once more.

Women and Heresy in Sufi Centres

"Men (are) Muslims and women pagans", affirmed Trimingham in his influential work on Islam in Africa. Everywhere, men would be "more deeply involved in Islam whereas women's participation is marginal, for Islam provided women little scope for ritual participation".[16] It is worth noting that classic works on Islam in Africa such as Trimingham's tended to replicate the discourse that a section of the male Muslim community historically sought to delegitimize the religious authority of women in Islamic societies. There is a tendency for women to be presented as the guardians of pre-Islamic religious traditions, and they are often associated with certain practices that are considered to be "unorthodox", such as rites of possession and ecstatic practices. One example of this in Northeast Africa is the *zār-ḥaḍra* ritual, which was a target of criticism from legalists.[17] Holy places or the residences of living saints became popular places where women could practise parallel, and often separate, rituals, which earned them praise or condemnation from legalists. Indeed, women's

15 Colonia Eritrea, Commissariato Regionale di Cheren, 20 ottobre 1910. Archivio Storico Diplomatico del Ministero degli Affari Esteri (ASDMAE), Archivio Eritrea (AE), 1886–1912 Pacco 43 (Morgani-Adigrat—Varie Eritrea), Fasc. 1 Morgani (1886–1911).

16 Trimingham 1980: 46–47.

17 This section is a revision and reworking of my contribution in Bruzzi and Zeleke 2015.

morality and their religious practices became the target of a broader socio-political conflict: it has been seen, for example, how widespread criticism by medieval Muslim writers of women's responsibility for inter-faith celebrations at holy shrines was a discourse designed to "denigrate these practices and discourage women and men from participating in them".[18]

In the Maghreb, visits to sanctuaries have been interpreted as being one of the rare cases in which women were not in a subordinate position. Within these sanctuaries, women were able to create an exclusively female collective endeavour, a "therapeutic network of communication among them". Their gatherings stimulated their "energies against their discontent and allowed them to bathe in an intrinsically female community of soothers, supporters, and advisors". Shrines may therefore be viewed as "an informal women's association".[19] Within Sufi orders, women were able to conduct forms of protest, albeit controlled, against the more oppressive religious practices applied to them, which were eventually supported by *ʿulamāʾ*. According to Coulon, reform and legalist movements insist on gender distinction, whereas Sufism offers a number of possibilities for women to attain *baraka*, which is crucial for breaking down the dichotomy between public and private that segregates women in a state of subordination.[20]

Sufi contributions to women's empowerment in Islamic societies relate to specific historical contexts and discourses, however. Criticism and speeches from the Sufi orders shift constantly, in accordance with socio-political settings. Following Sittī ʿAlawiyya decision to move her residence to Keren, a series of conflicts arose within the community. Contrary to colonial expectations, she quickly emerged as a prominent political and religious mentor in the region. Her religious authority became progressively more popular, and the colonial authorities were soon forced to state that one of the leading religious figures among Muslims in the Eritrean lowlands was a woman. They reported on the effectiveness of her interventions as a mediator in resolving conflicts among the local people and between them and the Government. Her growing popularity in the colonial era, which lasted for her entire lifetime, began to challenge the authority of the Mīrġanī representative who had been appointed by the colonial authorities and his entourage: as Commissioner Fioccardi reported, her residence was visited far more frequently as a religious centre than

18 Cuffel 2005: 401.
19 Mernissi 1977: 104–105.
20 Constantin 1998: 39; Coulon 1988.

was that of her nephew Sayyid Ǧaʿfar in Keren.[21] Their rivalry generated numerous conflicts, and the colonial authorities warned that the situation might give rise to a split within the Ḫatmiyya in Eritrea. As a consequence of this, they began interfering in the challenge for leadership of the order, and forced *šarīfa* ʿAlawiyya to recognize Sayyid Ǧaʿfar officially as the "leader of Islam in Eritrea". In their view, despite the great respect she enjoyed in the country, she could not have access to a political role as a woman because Islamic tradition did not allow it. In particular, the colonial authorities forbade her to appoint new representatives of the *ṭarīqa*, as they considered this to be a traditional role reserved to male representatives alone. The appointment of *ḫulafāʾ* is an interesting case in point, as a discrepancy emerged between the colonial assumption (based on local male informants such as Sayyid Ǧaʿfar and his entourage) and the *šarīfa*'s subsequent conduct: colonial data suggest that she began appointing her *ḫulafāʾ* in Eritrea personally, despite having been forbidden to do so. This was denounced by Sayyid Ǧaʿfar, and was also heavily criticized by the Italian authorities.[22] It is interesting to note how the colonial rulers perceived the establishment of a patriarchal system within Muslim societies as being necessary in order to guarantee the *pax colonial*. In fact, the colonial discourse, which was similar to that of her Muslim rivals, was that female leadership might cause trouble in the Colony. A colonial report of a clash in Keren highlights the criticisms being made against Sittī ʿAlawiyya's role as a female religious leader. In 1917, one of Sayyid Ǧaʿfar's *ḫulafāʾ*—the *imām* of the Keren mosque—read an indictment of women and their supposed misconduct in the Muslim community to a male audience attending Friday prayers at the main mosque.[23] This event, which led to serious conflict, illustrates the discourses that were being mobilized at that time, in this specific context to challenge women's leadership in accordance with "Islamic orthodoxy". They

21 Colonia Eritrea, Commissariato di Cheren, Riservato-Urgente, Al Signor Reggente il Governo della Colonia. 'Oggetto: Grave dissidio seguito da ingiurie tra Morgani e Sceriffa', Cheren, 6 settembre 1917. Archivio Storico Diplomatico del Ministero degli Affari Esteri (ASDMAE), Archivio Eritrea (AE), 1880–1917, Pacco 1022 (Missioni Politiche—Varie—El Morgani), Fasc. 10 Famiglia El Morgani, 1895–1917.

22 Telegramma espresso di servizio, Commissariato Regionale di Cheren, 4 settembre 1917. Archivio Storico Diplomatico del Ministero degli Affari Esteri (ASDMAE), Archivio Eritrea (AE), 1880–1917, Pacco 1022 (Missioni Politiche—Varie—El Morgani), Fasc. 10 Famiglia El Morgani, 1895–1917.

23 Handwritten letter in Arabic with an attached Italian translation, 5 September 1917. Archivio Storico Diplomatico del Ministero degli Affari Esteri (ASDMAE), Archivio Eritrea (AE), 1880–1917, Pacco 1022 (Missioni Politiche—Varie—El Morgani), Fasc. 10 Famiglia El Morgani, 1895–1917.

included a list of suggestions and obligations prescribed by the Qur'an for the conduct of women. Sittī ʿAlawiyya's name is never mentioned in the text—the criticisms were addressed to women in general—but it was clear that she was the main target. The text was an attempt to use a religious argument to assert the claim that women's authority had to be seen as unlawful. The broader criticism was that it represented a *bidʿa*, or innovation, a practice for which there was no precedent at the time of the Prophet, and which was considered to be the opposite of Sunna. According to the text, this innovation was prohibited. Accusations of violations of *šarīʿa* and "orthodoxy" have been a leitmotiv throughout Islamic history whenever a woman has attained a high position.[24] In particular, the text warns Muslims that they would be moving away from the right path if they were to follow women's "heresy", which in this case consisted in the growing power of women at the expense of Sayyid Ǧaʿfar, who was the male representative of the *ṭarīqa*. According to the indictment, the authority of a woman should be treated as being essentially inferior to that of a man. The accusation was especially directed at certain Islamic religious services led by women, which the text declares to be illegal and "heretical" on the basis of some *ḥadīṯ* and the Qur'an. For example, it was claimed that a woman cannot appoint *ḫulafāʾ*, that she should be veiled and that she cannot receive people who are not known to her. All these accusations implicitly criticized Sittī ʿAlawiyya's way of life and conduct, as well as accusing her supporters of being unbelievers who subscribed to her heresy.[25] They stressed that women cannot compare themselves to men, and that they should be separate, according to God's will. They also argued that people cannot be ruled by a woman: "Oh believers (men and women), have you ever heard before that from the time of our Lord Mohammad until now a faithful and noble woman has gathered people together, appointed Caliphs and become an *imām*? Is it allowed in the book (the Qur'an) or the Sunna for women to organize religious meetings with unknown men? Are those who follow the Book and Sunna permitted to accept a caliphate or *ṭarīqa* (rule of life) from a woman? No, this is not allowed by either the book or the Sunna!" According to the *imām* of the mosque, a woman—namely the *šarīfa*—could not be an *imām*, a guide for prayer groups. He also claimed that it was unlawful for a woman to appoint *ḫulafāʾ* of the *ṭarīqa*.

---

24 Mernissi 1992.

25 Telegramma espresso di servizio, Commissariato Regionale di Cheren, 2 settembre 1917. Archivio Storico Diplomatico del Ministero degli Affari Esteri (ASDMAE), Archivio Eritrea (AE), 1880–1917, Pacco 1022 (Missioni Politiche—Varie—El Morgani), Fasc. 10 Famiglia El Morgani, 1895–1917.

Finally, this attack on women's leadership turned into an insult against women in general: "a woman's Imamate has no value because women lack intelligence and religion". Socio-political activities by women were also banned, the argument being that they could not take part in arbitrations or wars. Finally, it was argued that "even after ablutions, a woman is not pure, education is forbidden to her and she can never be a perfect being".

The main accusation, and one of the crucial points of the challenge, related to Sittī ʿAlawiyya's appointment of the *ḫulafāʾ* of the order: this was within the exclusive jurisdiction of the leader of the *ṭarīqa*, and was the focal point of their leadership challenge. Other aspects that were also especially criticized and called into question related to women taking on public roles; it conflicted with Sunna and "Islamic orthodoxy", which provided for a form of segregation for women. According to this charge, Muslims should avoid seeing women who are not a member of their families. This was an indirect criticism aimed at all the male followers who used to visit Sittī ʿAlawiyya's residence. The text appeals to "brothers to avoid seeing women, … to avoid adultery" and to sisters to "… avoid seeing men … to avoid adultery: not to show your beauty except to your husbands, fathers, sons, parents-in-law, and grandsons (…) not to let your footsteps be heard, not to draw people's attention to your beauty (…) If you (men) ask them (women) something, ask it through a curtain. It will be better for your and their purity of heart."[26] Social pressures and the threat of sexuality were especially relevant in Sittī ʿAlawiyya's case because the extreme kindness she showed to the colonial officials who visited her was not well thought of by the local population. More generally, African women who had entered into visible relationships with colonial officers were heavily stigmatized.[27] Through this accusation, the public visibility of women's bodies was questioned by the use of the Islamic prohibition against women's exposing their beauty to the view of strangers: namely, to a man who was not a relative. It was an attempt

26 Handwritten letter in Arabic with an attached Italian translation, 5 September 1917. Archivio Storico Diplomatico del Ministero degli Affari Esteri (ASDMAE), Archivio Eritrea (AE), 1880–1917, Pacco 1022 (Missioni Politiche—Varie—El Morgani), Fasc. 10 Famiglia El Morgani, 1895–1917.

27 Colonia Eritrea, Commissariato Regionale di Massawa, 12 febbraio 1910. Archivio Storico Diplomatico del Ministero degli Affari Esteri (ASDMAE), Archivio Eritrea (AE), 1886–1912, Pacco 43 (Morgani-Adigrat—Varie Eritrea), Fasc. 1 Morgani (1886–1911); Colonia Eritrea, Commissariato Regionale del Barca, 2 marzo 1910. Archivio Storico Diplomatico del Ministero degli Affari Esteri (ASDMAE), Archivio Eritrea (AE), 1886–1912, Pacco 43 (Morgani-Adigrat—Varie Eritrea), Fasc. 1 Morgani (1886–1911). Eritrean women who stayed with the "enemy" were socially stigmatised in colonial Eritrea (Barrera 1996: 57).

to limit her religious influence, because at the time Sittī ʿAlawiyya received numerous visitors at her residence in Keren: many people went to her in *ziyāra*, as they believed she held *baraka*.

The main issue at stake here was the Imamate, the "supreme leadership" of a Muslim community. The accusation claimed that a woman was not allowed to be an *imām*, who was a person who led prayers. It was emphasized that this was a role she could not play in a mosque, and that only a man—and by implication that man was Sayyid Ǧaʿfar—could. According to a *ḥadīth*, the Imāmate could only be forfeited by apostasy or by neglect of the Imām's duty to provide for communal prayers.[28] It was a duty that Sittī ʿAlawiyya could not assume, according to the accusation, because she was a woman. The issue of women's imamates and their access to mosques has often been associated with disorder and shame. Ibn Al-Ǧawzī quotes a *ḥadīṯ* that states: "If a woman is afraid of creating disorder in men's minds, it is better for her to pray at home".[29] The accusation made against the *šarīfa* for taking on the role of an *imām* can be understood in the context of this debate. Women were not permitted to lead prayers in the mosque, but this was not the point at issue here, as the gatherings and prayer groups were held at her residence, and not in the mosque; besides, she led superogatory, and not obligatory, prayers.

It is interesting to note that the Keren mosque where Muslims gathered and prayed, and where the criticisms of Sittī ʿAlawiyya were mobilized, had been built by the Italian authorities. It was a mainly male space, and women were banned from it. At the time, the leadership of Sīdī Ǧaʿfar as the male representative of the Eritrean branch of the Ḫatmiyya had been established, and was undoubtedly supported during this period by the colonial authorities, who were, in fact, allied with the Muslim elite, whom they attempted to co-opt as they sought to limit Sittī ʿAlawiyya's influence. Her response to her rivals' arguments stressed the Imamate esoteric doctrine. According to colonial sources, in fact, she claimed that she was superior (and consequently more suitable as a religious leader) to her relative because she was closer to the Prophet than he was:[30] "the eternal reality of the Imamate, now commonly termed *walāya* (the quality of a *walī*, a "friend of God"), is defined as the esoteric aspect of

28 Madelung 1971.

29 Ibn Al-Ǧawzī 1981, cit. in Mernissi 1992: 109–112.

30 Telegramma espresso di servizio, Commissariato Regionale di Cheren, 2 settembre 1917. Archivio Storico Diplomatico del Ministero degli Affari Esteri (ASDMAE), Archivio Eritrea (AE), 1880–1917, Pacco 1022 (Missioni Politiche—Varie—El Morgani), Fasc. 10, Famiglia El Morgani, 1895–1917.

prophecy".[31] When the criticisms levelled against her used arguments based on gender discrimination, she countered by stressing that she belonged to the category of the *walī* and that the emphasis should not be on her sex.

Embodying Religious Orthodoxy

The Sufi emphasis on religious interpretations that sidestep gender discrimination has been observed in a number of different contexts. In West Africa, the religious authority of women who are appointed as spiritual guides, as in the case of the *muqaddamat tiǧānī*, is based on the embodiment and interiority conventionally associated with pious women. Their domestic spaces become "internal public spaces" in which disciples assemble to learn about and discuss religion and other matters, and from which they influence "external public spaces".[32] Like Marabout women, who developed their authority within the framework of esoteric Sufi knowledge, Sufi women in Eritrea and Ethiopia adopted a variety of mechanisms for resisting those who objected to their authority and for retaining their powers as the custodians of shrines. These strategies ranged from embodying Sufi knowledge and spiritual traditions to establishing their own networks with Sufi scholars and the government.[33]

Sittī ʿAlawiyya was furious when she was told what had happened at the Keren mosque, and summoned some of those who had attended the Friday prayers at the mosque to her residence, including the *ḫalīfa* who had read the document against her. She reviled the *ḫalīfa* and railed against her nephew, declaring that he understood nothing and only thought about food, adding that she was more important than him because she was "closer to the Prophet". She then prepared another document to contradict the one that had been read out.[34] Based on their family's genealogy, it read, she was "closer to the Prophet" than her nephew: the founder of the order was Sittī ʿAlawiyya's grandfather and Sīdī Ǧaʿfar's great-grandfather.

As the colonial officer Fioccardi observed: "The Sceriffa, who is very smart, has long enjoyed a standard of living that is especially attractive to Europeans;

---

31 Madelung 1971.

32 Hill 2010: 375–412. On the notion of "internal public spaces" see Cooper 1997: 195–222.

33 Gemmeke 2009: 128–147; Bruzzi and Zeleke 2015: 37–67.

34 Telegramma espresso di servizio, Commissariato Regionale di Cheren, 2 settembre 1917. Archivio Storico Diplomatico del Ministero degli Affari Esteri (ASDMAE), Archivio Eritrea (AE), 1880–1917, Pacco 1022 (Missioni Politiche—Varie—El Morgani), Fasc. 10 Famiglia El Morgani, 1895–1917.

her attitude is that of a great lady who follows the precepts of the Quran and all matters relating to her action as a descendant of the Morgani, and she claims prerogatives that the Quran only grants to men. It came to the point where calling her "Lady" (meaning woman) is the greatest offence that can be committed against her".[35] Sittī ʿAlawiyya unlike Sīdī Ǧaʿfar, was recognized as a *walī*, and she stressed the point that attention should not be drawn to her sex.

It has often been recalled on the subject of the sex of *walī* that according to Al-Huǧwīrī (d. 1073), like Al-Ġazālī, travellers along the path of God are always men, while women are obstacles to men's spiritual life, although it is also clear that belonging to one sex or the other is not a barrier to the inspiration and grace of God; rather, it is said that pious women are "men sent in the form of a woman".[36] The famous Sufi master Farīd al-Dīn ʿAṭṭār, speaking of mystic Rābiʿa al-ʿAdawiyya (d. 801), recalled a *ḥadīṯ* of the Prophet that says: "Do not look outside a person, but take into account his good deeds and good will", which, for ʿAṭṭār, would apply to "any woman whose devotions and worship are approved at the court of the Most High Lord; we should not say that she is a woman".[37] This is very significant in historical sources because holy women frequently appear to be invisible because their traces have been masculinized.[38] Moroccan hagiographic texts from the 16th and 17th centuries have testified to a process of masculinizing the appearance of holy women along the path to female sainthood, such as by wearing a beard like a man or holding the *murūʾa*, both of which are archetypal masculine qualities of Arab men. These are examples of a model of sainthood for a woman who rejects a traditional role and pursues a process of "defeminization" along her spiritual path. On the other side stands a different model, one who symbolizes the "ideal" woman, attached to family institutions and educated within family networks. Her role is that of a mother or wife who hands down her knowledge within the domestic

35 Colonia Eritrea, Commissariato di Cheren, Riservato-Urgente, Al Signor Reggente il Governo della Colonia. Oggetto: Grave dissidio seguito da ingiurie tra Morgani e Scerifa, Cheren, 6 settembre 1917, Archivio Storico Diplomatico del Ministero degli Affari Esteri (ASDMAE), Archivio Eritrea (AE), 1880–1917, Pacco 1022 (Missioni Politiche—Varie—El Morgani), Fasc. 10 Famiglia El Morgani, 1895–1917. This letter was written in the context of the dispute that had arisen between the two Mīrġanī.

36 Hoffman 1996: 254–260, cit. in Boissevain 2006: 20.

37 Farīd al-Dīn ʿAṭṭār 1976: 82.

38 A suggestion provided to me by S. O'Fahey regarding oral sources in Karrar 1992. In this book, according to what O'Fahey told me, the author used several female informers, but they were described as men in the text.

space.[39] The cases of the two Mīrġanī sisters are fitting manifestations of these different models, the former being well represented by Sittī ʿAlawiyya, and Sittī Maryam being a representative of the latter. Certain general characteristics recur in historical sources as belonging to female Sufi saints. Some showed an extremely high level of asceticism, which led them to command great respect in their community and a degree of freedom that went far beyond the restrictions of Islamic law that applied to women, while others chose celibacy, thereby acquiring more liberty and autonomy and rejecting male tutorship and the "burden" of marriage. It is recorded that they avoided sexual relations even if they were married, and non-procreation was a typical feature of holy women.[40] They also used to deny their female nature through biological evidence such as amenorrhea: by halting their menstrual cycle, they eliminated the reason women were held to be impure, the most evident physical stigma associated with them under Islamic law. Their final characteristic was mystical love, which is the real goal of the Sufi spiritual path. According to other authors, women were able to be recognized as saints and impose their leadership within Sufi brotherhoods thanks to their *baraka* (blessing), knowledge, and purity and their image as ideal women.[41]

Because Sittī ʿAlawiyya's leadership had been called into question in the context of gender discrimination within an "orthodox" Islamic discourse, she entered the debate with a reply in the same vein: in response to this attempt to undermine her leadership, she gradually began to assert more authority by embodying "orthodox" Islamic practices. In particular, she wore special trousers beneath her traditional dress and a *ḥiǧāb* that covered her hair, ears and chin. This practice of covering herself was instrumental to her empowerment and to allowing her to take on a public and political role in the colony as a Muslim authority.[42]

The way Sufi shaykhs dressed is very meaningful. In some cases, it might be viewed as a further expression of the unity of believers, the principle of the *tawḥīd*. For example, the use of both Christian and Islamic symbols expresses the inter-religious dimension of the Sufi practices that were popular in Ethiopia. There is one photograph—the most widespread portrait of her that can be found in Ethiopia and Eritrea, in fact—in which Sittī ʿAlawiyya

39 Boissevain 2006: 21. On the process of masculinizing the appearance of holy women and the defeminization process, see Mediano (1995: 394) and Elias (1988: 211) cit. in Boissevain 2006: 21.

40 Boissevain 2006: 21; Scattolin 1993: 3–26. See also Schimmel 2003.

41 Gemmeke 2009: 128–147; Coulon 1988.

42 Interview with Aḥmad al-Mīrġanī on May 2009 in Cairo.

is portrayed wearing highly representative clothing, and this same image was used in a book about her published in Italy during the Fascist era (Figure 32).[43] In it, Sittī ʿAlawiyya is wearing a special veil that she also used to wear during official events organized by the Italian colonial authorities in the country. It is a special *ḥiǧāb*, one that reminds us of the veils worn by Christian nuns, and in fact it recalls both Christian and Islamic symbols and values. As Sirhindī, a Naqšbandī Master, has affirmed: "*ṭarīqa* (the mystical way) and the *šarīʿa* (the Islamic way that designates rules and regulations governing the lives of Muslims) are identical. They do not differ by even the thickness of a hair. Everything that is in opposition to (Islamic) Law must be rejected, and every belief that conflicts with it is heresy. The perfect being looks for the Truth by holding himself to the Law".[44]

Sittī ʿAlawiyya emphasized this notion, and promoted the strict observation of the Islamic obligations claimed by her rivals regarding the covering of women's bodies by wearing this particular veil. By expressing an "Islamic orthodoxy" rigour in her clothing, she defended her public role (and visibility) as—for example—a political mediator between the local people and the colonial authorities. By wearing a veil that recalls those used by Christian nuns, the *šarīfa* also seems to be appealing to Christian believers such as the Italian colonial authorities, thereby accomplishing her mission to "call" (*daʿwa*) people to the truth.[45] In fact, her residence was a destination not only for Muslims but also for Christians, who included European travellers, colonial settlers, and the Italian authorities. A Mīrġanī family oral tradition reports that when the Italian authorities invited her to visit the Christian cathedral in Asmara, they asked her to sit on a throne and told her she was *Santa Alawiyya* (Saint ʿAlawiyya). There was no distinction between Muslims and Christians in her family's tradition, and a number of her followers were *ascari* (colonial soldiers) or worked for the Government, but also looked on her as their leader. Throughout the colonial era, her influence in the social and political lives of both Muslims and Christians became increasingly important in the colony. Her public role was that of a mediator in conflict resolution as well as a socio-religious focal point. These days, she is remembered in Eritrea as a "queen without a crown", and in fact her leadership throughout the colonial occupation was informal but effective.[46]

43 Caniglia 1940.
44 Ventura 1990.
45 Ventura 1990.
46 Interview with Aḥmad al-Mīrġanī on May 2009 in Cairo.

While Sittī ʿAlawiyya's Imamate was repeatedly challenged by the Muslim and Sudanese elites associated with Sayyid Ǧaʿfar al-Mīrġanī, her sister *šarīfa* Maryam's religious authority was not: she was recognized as a *ḫalīfa*, and according to Grandin's oral sources, nobody contested her position as *ḫalīfa* because she had been personally appointed by her father, who claimed that of the ten men of the Mīrġanī, she was worth nine, and he was the tenth.[47] Incidentally, she never contested the authority of Sayyid ʿAlī al-Mīrġanī in Sudan, while Sittī ʿAlawiyya was highly critical of Sayyid Ǧaʿfar in Eritrea and expressly challenged his religious leadership. In any event, the issue of the legitimization of the religious leadership of the order in Eritrea remained unresolved,[48] and the rivalry between Sittī ʿAlawiyya and Sayyid Ǧaʿfar continued without a victor, as they both remained privileged points of reference for the colonial authorities. As we will see, they both continued to appear in colonial reports and the Italian media, appearing at colonial ceremonies as representatives of the Eritrean Muslim community.

They also both continued to receive a salary from the government, but were at the heart of plots and troubles among their followers, who aligned into two separate armed parties, one against the other.[49] In Keren, the conflict between the two factions came to a boil during this period. Internal rivalries within brotherhoods tended to replicate the lines of social conflict, and so the discord between the two parties can be interpreted as the tip of the iceberg of a wider conflict between the two opposing factions, which was particularly worrying because they were armed. The colonial authorities had been concerned about this conflict in Keren since 1908, but in 1919, the *šarīfa* finally left Eritrea to live at her sister Sittī Maryam's residence in Suakin, where she remained until 1923, when she returned to the colony.[50] The reasons behind her departure were connected with external pressures and increasing criticism from both the colonial and Muslim authorities and other local factions that opposed her authority in the colony.[51] These years also saw a period of discord within her

47 Grandin 1988: 128.

48 Interview with Aḥmad al-Mīrġanī on May 2009 in Cairo.

49 Colonia Eritrea, Commissariato di Cheren, Riservato-Urgente, Al Signor Reggente il Governo della Colonia. Oggetto: Grave dissidio seguito da ingiurie tra Morgani e Scerifa, Cheren, 6 settembre 1917. Archivio Storico Diplomatico del Ministero degli Affari Esteri (ASDMAE), Archivio Eritrea (AE), 1880–1917, Pacco 1022 (Missioni Politiche—Varie—El Morgani), Fasc. 10 Famiglia El Morgani, 1895–1917.

50 Miran 2005: 200.

51 These were the years of the First World War. In the course of the Italy-Turkish war of 1911–12, Sīdī Ǧaʿfar supported the Italians, and exhorted the Eritrean askaris to enter the

own family: in 1918, she divorced her cousin and husband Muḥammad Ṣāliḥ al-Mīrġanī, who was son of Nāfisa (Sīdī Hāšim's sister) and Sayyid 'Uqayl, a member of the 'Ālawiyyūn clan of Mecca.[52] According to oral sources, after her time in Port Sudan and Suakin, from where she resisted Sīdī Ǧa'far's activities, she returned to Eritrea and set up her residence near the port, close to her father's shrine and mosque in Hetumlo, but would travel to Asmara for several months every year.[53]

From an internal point of view, it is possible that the conflict between the two Mīrġanī was an expression of latent competition between foreign interests, mostly Sudanese, and Eritreans, including those with ties to the Massawa elite. According to the colonial authorities, Sīdī Ǧa'far was under the influence of his *ḫulafā'*, who were mostly foreigners, especially Sudanese, and rarely Eritreans. It is also worth noting that his shrines are in Kassala, and not in Eritrea, while Sittī 'Alawiyya's are in Hetumlo, where it is always claimed she lived throughout her entire life.

From a gender perspective, the infiltration and *fitna* that subsequently emerged within the Muslim community seem to have contributed towards a tightening up of Islamic practices, as seen from the use of *ḥiǧāb*. The portraits of Sittī Fāṭima al-Mīrġanī in 1903 (Figure 9) and of Sittī 'Alawiyya in the 1920s (Figure 24), show that their veils covered only their hair. This second portrait of Sittī 'Alawiyya has been thought not to be authentic because the *šarīfa* is shown wearing a veil that does not properly cover her face, and in fact, one of the accusations made against her in 1917 was that she did not cover herself in the presence of unknown men.

To safeguard their authority and protect themselves from criticism from their elite Islamic rivals, the Mīrġanī sisters adopted an exemplary expression of a general trend in the region: they began to cover themselves, and resorted to purdah. While Sittī 'Alawiyya limited herself to using a *ḥiǧāb* that covered her chin and neck, Sittī Maryam also imposed physical segregation. Again, the practice of purdah had multiple meanings, and became a highly-politicized symbol of identity.

Italy-Libya conflict against the Turkish infidels, as did Sittī 'Alawiyya's who sent a letter to the resident Mīrġanī in Alessandria, Egypt, to promote the good treatment reserved to Eritrean Muslims. It is noteworthy that the return of Sittī 'Alawiyya to the colony was in 1923, the year in which the Treaty of Losanne was signed, in which the Ottoman Empire abandoned all its claims and officially recognized Italian sovereignty over the territories it had lost duing the conflict. On this issue, see chapter 8.

52 These speculations are based on a family tree provided by Hofheinz 1992: 26.

53 3 January 1936, memories of Elena Pesenti in De Carli 2016.

While the literature on other African regions looked at the crucial role played by European women and their involvement in the sexual politics of imperialism, the Italian colonial paradigm was predominantly masculine, although this did change during the Fascist era, when the participation of women in colonial life and the creation of the Empire was more widely acknowledged. As Lombardi-Diop noted, in the mid-1930s, the growing militarization of women allowed the creation of a new model of female subjectivity, the so-called *cittadina* (female citizen), who was able to push the boundaries of class outwards and to serve as a national model.[54] In my opinion, this acknowledgment of the public role of women in the building of the Empire explains the change that took place in the attitude towards the political role of the *šarīfa* during the Italian Fascist era. As we will see, in the 1930s, Sittī ʿAlawiyya became a leading figure, and officially acquired high visibility. From the informal authority that had prevailed during the liberal era, she moved to an official public position during Fascism. The duality between public and private was abolished by the Fascist regime, and female militancy came to be promoted in the constitution of the nation and the empire. Fascism gave Italy a "warrior uniform" that led to an invitation to women for civil deployment, and to a widening of the family to embrace the national community, with the need to be prepared for a hypothetical war. Mussolini made explicit reference to women's involvement in the defence and resistance of the nation with the same spirit of devotion and sacrifice as the fighters as early as 1925.[55] The outbreak of the Italo-Ethiopian conflict in October 1935 emphasized this new trait of women as Fascist collaborators and propagandists for the regime.[56] Along these lines, in the period between 1937 and 1939, the Italian government developed a series of measures to prepare women for "the tasks and demands of life in the lands of Italian Africa".[57] The image of female militancy, of *cittadine* of the Empire—"kind, but strong and firm"—gained widespread visibility, and was also promoted through the production of new female travel literature on the East African Empire.[58]

---

54 Lombardi-Diop 2005: 146. See also Clancy-Smith and Gouda 1998; Grewal 1996.

55 Law no. 1699 of 14.12.1931, *Disciplina di Guerra*, cit. in Fraddosio 1989: 117.

56 Fraddosio 1989: 117.

57 PNF, Foglio di disposizioni no. 853, 8 August 1937. Cit. in Fraddosio 1989: 134.

58 See Hopkins 2010 and for example, Felter Sartori 1940, Di Augusta Perricone 1930 and 1935.

FIGURE 6 *Entrance to Sittī ʿAlawiyya's residence.*
PHOTO BY SILVIA BRUZZI, KEREN 2004.

FIGURE 7 *Sittī ʿAlawiyya and Sīdī Ǧaʿfar al-Mīrġanī, late 1930.*
PHOTOGRAPHER UNKNOWN, PRIVATE ARCHIVE IN ASMARA.

FIGURE 8 *Sittī ʿAlawiyya, an Italian officer and Sīdī Ǧaʿfar al-Mīrġanī, late 1930.*
PHOTOGRAPHER UNKNOWN, PRIVATE ARCHIVE IN ASMARA.

CHAPTER 4

Fragmented, (In)Visible and (Un)Told Stories

Looking for Muslim Women in Northeast African History

Finding Muslim women in the long history of the region is akin to searching in the dark. Although there may be traces of them crystallized in sites of memories, their stories have mainly been handed down through social memory, and only rarely in written literature. Despite this, however, a few prominent personalities did attain popularity and visibility in the Horn of Africa. They seem to have played particularly significant roles in Sufi orders, in which, at least from the late 19th century on, we find remarkable traces of pious and holy women, but it remains an undeniable fact that Northeast African histories of Islam and colonialism are more noteworthy for the marginalization of female protagonists: the history of African women has often been overlooked, but studies on Muslim women are even scarcer.[1] Both colonial and Arabic sources have mostly been written through a predominantly masculine gaze that overshadows the agency of women: for example, even though there is an abundance of literature on Sufism in Sub-Saharan Africa, women only figure in it here and there. Unlike their male counterparts, the life histories of Sufi women are rarely reported in hagiographies; in fact, it is difficult even to find their names, because they are not included in the genealogies of Islamic brotherhoods, and even where they do appear, their status as wives, mothers, or daughters of a shaykh is often the only form of identification available. In some instances, a process of masculinizing traces of them prevents us from shedding light on their presence as historical agents. In addition to this, the opportunity to remain invisible, unseen, and unknown proved to be the preferable alternative to facing criticism and to attacks on women's actions.[2] Briefly put, historians must face significant challenges brought about by the paucity and fragmented

1 Moosa 2003: 286–293; Jean Hay 1988: 431–417.

2 As Sartori pointed out the identity of Harari women saints may be kept hidden, as the living friends themselves often do in order to avoid the distractions of the mundane world. Nevertheless, many names of women saints are well-known and may be associated with special virtues: for instance, traditionally a *ziyāra* at the shrine of Ay Abida, considered the "mother" of the city, facilitates marriage; Ay Imaju brings new clothes and bread; for fertility, it is common to make a pilgrimage to Ummi Koda, the mother of ʿAbd al-Qādir al-Ǧīlānī (see Sartori 2013).

 | DOI 10.1163/9789004356160_006

nature of written sources and an apparent lack of visible signs in colonial archives and Arabic texts. They need to make an express effort to discover new, and irregular, sources that can fill the gaps in the available literature and enable the pursuit of a more detailed account of the rare signs that are available.

The apparent invisibility of women in historical narratives has been interpreted as proof of their disempowerment in Muslim societies,[3] but despite this, as Coulon has pointed out, women have been able to participate in Islam in their own way by manipulating and making accommodations according to their needs. In order to be able to face up to the limitations that have been imposed to them, they have developed a series of strategies to subvert their prescribed social roles and to adapt them to suit on their own requirements. Their agency is persistent "even if their practices are informal, hidden, or parallel, or heterodox". As Coulon has pointed out, in spite of the apparent invisibility of women, it would be a mistake to leave them in the dark merely because we are not able to shine a light on their stories.[4]

A number of pious women became popular icons in Ethiopia in the earliest days of Islam because they were among the first to become Muslims. The best-known example of this is a slave, Umm Ayman (Barakah, *raḍī Allāhu ʿanhā*), the Prophet's Abyssinian nurse, whom he looked on as his second mother. Although they were from Arabia, Umm Ḥabība bint Abī Sufyān and Umm Salama bint Abī Umayya fled with the first Muslims who took part in the migration to Abyssinia, and are considered to be among the first of the Prophet's disciples. After the deaths of their husbands, they married the Prophet and returned to Arabia, where they told of the wonders of Aksum. They are viewed among Jabarti communities as models for Ethiopian women. Another personality from a few centuries later who is remembered in the history of Ethiopia is Batī Del Wämbära, daughter of the *amīr* of Zaylaʿ, Maḥfuz, and wife of *imām* Aḥmad ibn Ibrahīm al-Ǧāzī. Powerful and ready to die for her faith, she succeeded in negotiating the release of Muslims leaders who had been captured by Christians in Harar. She was a symbol of success in the "holy war".[5]

Only fragmentary sources are available on the agency of the ruling women's elite in political intrigue. During the first decade of the twentieth century,

---

3 An interesting revision of this scholarly assumption is available in Stockereiter's recent works (2015). Drawing from Islamic courts records, Stockereiter sheds light on the status and agency of women in colonial Zanzibar. She re-examines previous assumptions on the status of Muslim women on the Swahili coast by illustrating how Muslim judges frequently supported the rights of women, ex-slaves, and other marginalized groups.

4 Coulon 1988: 115–116.

5 Pankhurst 2009; Böll 2003: 505; Chernetsov 2003.

the ʿAfar region was marked by a long war of succession called the Sangerra, which saw the various pretenders to the throne of Sultan Muhammad Hanfare "Illalta" (1861–1902) engage in bloody conflicts.[6] The Italian colonial authorities occupying the port of Assab were concerned about conflicts among dignitaries in Assab and Awsa relating to the activities of *šarīfa* Amina, wife of Shaykh ʿAbd al-Raḥmān and daughter of the Sultan Muhammad Hanfare. In 1907, Amina escaped from Assab to Awsa against her husband's will, and finally found protection from Degiac Omar there after she had made an attempt on the life of Zahara, who was another wife of her husband ʿAbd al-Raḥmān and who had given birth to the shaykh's only male heir in Massawa in 1899. Rumours were circulating at the time that in order to maintain his dignity, the shaykh—who was about 70 years old—recognized this long-awaited heir even though he was not the heir apparent. His growing preference for this son led the shaykh to abandon all his other spouses, including *šarīfa* Amina, who had been living at his main residence since 1885. Abandoned, and deprived of her servants, who were given to his favourite wife, Zahara, Amina tried to kill her rival and then unexpectedly left the marital home in Assab and returned to her father's house, taking slaves, servants, and camels with her. Her husband asked the Italian authorities in Assab to intervene, claiming that she had left with property that belonged to him, including livestock.[7]

What makes this fragmentary story particularly interesting is that it provides an exceptional glimpse into the agency of Muslim women and their mobility in colonial societies. The marriages, alliances, and conflicts of women from the elites had crucial political consequences, but the women who permitted marriage alliances to be formed between African families and Muslim traders and holy men are often anonymous figures who have remained in the shadows despite their crucial social role; their marriages are only viewed as being responsible for the change from a matrilineal to a patrilineal society in the context of the Islamization of the continent. Matriliny and Islam are considered to be mutually exclusive, and so the Islamization of the African continent tends to be presented as a transformative agent for patriliny, virilocality and patriarchy. This long-held assumption is not true of the whole of Africa, however, and it was possible for Islam and matriliny to co-exist in some cases.[8]

---

6 Soulé and Piguet 2009: 253.

7 Colonia Eritrea, Assab, 22 aprile 1907 and Asmara 18 maggio 1907. Archivio Storico Diplomatico del Ministero degli Affari Esteri (ASDMAE), Archivio Eritrea (AE), Pacco 497, Fasc. 1 Capi indigeni: nomine, revoche, Ramadan, Mascal. On Muhammad Hanfare, see Soulé 2005.

8 Bonate 2006: 139–140, 154–156.

In Northeast Africa, the Beja people, such as the Beni ʿAmer, gradually adopted Islam as a result of infiltration by Arab traders, holy men, and adventurers, who took Beja wives and settled among them.[9] In Beni ʿAmer territories, matrilocality was related to social status rather than religious belonging: in effect, notwithstanding a shared Muslim faith, there were differences in marriage customs in the colonial period depending on whether masters or serfs were involved. Among the (minority) aristocratic class, a bride moved into her husband's house on marriage, while among the Tigré serf class, a husband lived with his wife's parents until she had borne two children, after which it was the wife who decided where to live.[10] Conti Rossini has stressed not only Beni ʿAmer women's agency within family roles and social organizations, such as matrilocality, but also their special inheritance and divorce rights.[11] This was the background from which Sittī ʿAlawiyya, daughter of Sīdī Hāšim, came, as her mother was of Beni ʿAmer origin, and the Mīrġanī, from whom her father was descended, had contributed to the Islamization process in the Red Sea region during the 19th century, in part as a result of this type of marriage alliance. Like other *ašrāf* and holy families, men married local women while maintaining endogamy for women from within their group.[12] This did not necessarily lead to the disempowerment of women, however.

In Northeast African Muslim families, some women were able to acquire a leading socio-educational role by teaching the faith and handing down Muslim values. Here, too, there are fragmentary, and apparently exceptional, stories of socio-religious and educational activities on the part of women in East Africa, including Mwana Kupona (c. 1810–1860), a Swahili language poet who lived in Mombasa. She was the author of the *utendi wa Mwana Kupona*, a famous, and unique, classical Swahili epic that she dedicated to her daughter, principally in order to offer her advice on relationships between wives and husbands within Islam's ethical framework.[13] During *ziyāra* ceremonies in Mozambique, female and male *ḫulafāʾ* alike received donations from the followers of pious women

9 This lead them to adopt fictitious Arab lineages and—according to Trimingham (1952: 156)—to the change from a matriarchal to a patriarchal social structure.

10 Nadel 1945: 80. According to an oral tradition reported by Nadel (1945: 51–65), the Beni ʿAmer people originated from a common descendent, Amer—the son of a holy man of Ja'ali origin and a Bellou woman—to whom they owe their name. See also Paul 1954: 82–83. The Ja'ali people lived between the confluence of the Atbara and the Sabaloka Gorge, and from the sixteenth century until the Turco-Egyptian conquest formed a tribal kingdom dominated by a royal clan known as the Sa'dab (Holt and Daly 1979: 4).

11 Conti Rossini 1916: 730–736.

12 Pollera 1935: 204–205.

13 Topan 2004: 213–227.

such as Fatima Amur, Saquina of the Qādiriyya Bagdade, and Abuba Hafish of the Šāḏiliyya Madaniyya, who were heads of Sufi orders, and their shrines were regularly visited during the annual *ziyāra*.[14] In Harar, where the role of women in teaching and handing down Islamic learning is well-known and recognized, a recent study has shed light on the forgotten figure of a Harari scholar, Ay Amatullāh (1851–1893), the daughter of the *qāḍī* of Harar, ʿAbd al-Raḥmān bin Muḥammad, and Umma Ḫalima. She was a *zāhid*, a pious woman, who was not interested in worldly goods, and had been given the title of *kabīr*, which was normally granted to learned men. Ay Amatullāh studied with the same teachers as her brothers, thereby receiving a high level of education, and she became one of the pre-eminent scholars of her time. She studied Arabic grammar, the Qur'an, the *Ḥadīṯ* Exegesis, and Islamic law, and became a *faqīh*. Her brothers, who were *qāḍī*, would ask her for advice on religious issues, and to all intents and purposes she was a teacher of men and women alike. It was not common at the time for women to be highly educated, and it was only in the rare cases in which a member of their family was a *kabīr*, as with Ay Amatullāh, that higher education became available to them;[15] education within the family network represented a privilege for women. In 19th century Somalia, Šayḫ al-Zaylai taught groups of women known as *muridāt*, among whom was his daughter Šayḫ Fatima, who became an influential religious figure.[16] On the coast of Benadir, there was Mana Siti Habib Jamaluddin (1804–1921), who lived in Brava. Popularly known as Dada Masiti ("Grandmother" Masiti), she was a scholar, a poet, and a mystic, and a yearly *ziyāra* to her shrine is still held in Somalia today. She was a member of the Al-Ahdal clan, of *ašrāf* origin, and was therefore considered to be a descendent of the Prophet. When she was just six years old, she was kidnapped, taken to Zanzibar, and sold as a slave. Some years later, she was recognized by relatives or friends of her parents, who initiated her into Sufism and took her back to Brava. Here, after intensive study of religion and Sufi practices, she became popular as a poet and for her *baraka*, which allowed her to perform miracles (*karāmāt*). Her poems deal with Islamic law and mystical Sufi issues, and are memorized in Brava, especially by women in Somalia and from the diaspora. This oral literature hands down Islamic and Sufi teachings associated with the purity of the soul (*nafs*), expressing a deep desire for unity with the divine and revealing the vain desires of this world.[17]

14 Bonate 2006: 150.

15 Muna Abubeker Ibrāhīm 2007. On Sufi women and gender issues in Harar context, see also Gibb 1997, 1999, 2000.

16 Martin 1992: 14–15.

17 Dunbar 2000: 404; Kassim 1995: 21–37; Kassim 2002: 110.

In around 1920, Šayḫa Mtumwa bt. ʿAli b. Yusuf (d. 1958) received an *iǧāza* in Zanzibar and introduced the Qādiriyya to Malawi, where she began to teach the *ṭarīqa* ("the way"), *ḏikr* and Sufi rituals, especially to women.[18]

In Ethiopia, more particularly in Arsi, Sittī Momina (d. 1929)—another holy woman who was a contemporary of Dada Masiti—became popular for her spiritual practices and healing powers. Her shrine in Faraqasa became a place of worship for Muslims and Christian visitors from across the region, and was famous for being a place of religious co-existence, where pilgrims would join together to recite *ḏikr* that Sittī Momina had composed. Participation in these communal prayers is still considered to help solve all kinds of personal problems today.[19]

A number of women also attained great popularity in the Ḫatmiyya Islamic brotherhood. Rare traces report the cases of Fāṭima and Nāfisa, the mother and daughter of Muḥammad ʿUṯmān, son of Ḥasan, who lived in Shendi during the Mahdiyya, but it is difficult to identify them in the family genealogy.[20] We have a photograph of Fāṭima, but unfortunately we have nothing more than this one image (Figure 9).[21]

During the colonial occupation of the region, two charismatic members of the Mīrġanī family of Beja origin, sisters Sittī Maryam (1870/1–1952) and Sittī ʿAlawiyya (1892–93/1940), became popular on the Red Sea coast, in Sudan and Eritrea respectively. Contemporaries of Dada Masiti and Sittī Momina, they were the granddaughters of Muḥammad ʿUṯmān al-Mīrġanī, the founder of the Ḫatmiyya, whose main religious centre was located near Kassala. They are mentioned in several instances in the two Red Sea ports where they lived their entire lives: Suakin, in Sudan, and Massawa, in what is now Eritrea. As representatives of the brotherhood, they were points of reference for various actors who asked them for advice or to intervene to solve issues and conflicts in the years between the two World Wars. Their residences were considered to be bastions of Islam, places of rest and peace, and regional destinations for *ziyārāt*, and visitors converged there for personal, political, and religious

---

18 Kitula 2001: 87–96; Constantin 1987: 87; Greenstein 1976–77: 32–33.

19 Ishihara 2010: 81–89; Ishihara 2013: 91; Gemechu 2007.

20 Voll 1969: 234; Hofheinz 1992: 22–23, or it might possibly have been Fāṭima bt. Al-Ḥasan, wife of M. Bakrī, see Hofheinz 1992: 24.

21 I would like to thank Prof. Irma Taddia for sending a copy to me. Unfortunately I had no access to a pious book that contains short but interesting, quick portraits of Šarīfa ʿAlawiyya and her sister Maryam as well as Fāṭima and Nāfisa: Sarrāj, Muḥammad ibn ʿAbd al-Majīd. 1955. *Al-Manāhiǧ al-ʿalīya fī taraǧim al-sāda al-Mīrġanīya*. Khartoum: Maṭbaʿat al-Nahḍa al-Sūdāniyya.

FIGURE 9 *Sittī Fāṭima al-Mīrġanī.*
SAVILE, ROBERT VESEY COLLECTION. DURHAM UNIVERSITY LIBRARY, ARCHIVES AND SPECIAL COLLECTIONS, SAD.7/3/1–240—1901, 1902 MAY–1904 MAR.

reasons. Popular for their *baraka* and the support they offered their visitors, they played an active role in teaching and spreading Islam and *ṭarīqa*, especially to women.[22]

Throughout their lives, all these women became popular for their *baraka* and their ability to perform *karāmāt*, as was the case with the pious *ašrāf* who were popular in other Muslim societies, and just like with their homes when they were alive, their shrines remain destinations for *ziyārāt* for believers looking for "medicine" for their souls. While they may be among the most popular Sufi women in Northeast Africa, they should not be viewed as exceptional cases; rather, they represent the best-known examples of a broader phenomenon. Other women acquired comparable status in the area, as proved by the female names given to a number of shrines and mosques in Harar, which is one of the most important centres of Islamic learning in the Horn of Africa. Today, their historical memories are preserved in oral literature, or crystallized at sites of memory such as holy shrines and mosques: for example, Sittī Maryam's shrine (*maqām*) in Sinkat is a centre of female worship, and on the occasion of her *ḥawliyya*, women gather there to practice a collective, and exclusively feminine, *ḏikr*, sometimes combined with dancing.[23]

Regional Women's Centres of Empowerment and Religious Learning

On the wave of Islamic renewal, charismatic female figures emerged as points of reference and became popular for their learning and piety during a period that was seen to be one of moral decay. The embodiment of pious women as Muslim female models caused the boundaries between teachers, educators, and religious leader to twist and bend. Communities and solidarity networks such as charities and informal institutions were often established around these personalities, and the transmission of knowledge was expressed within these Muslim centres of worship with a special emphasis on embodied knowledge and oral practices such as dance, music, song, and poetry—a variety of cultural expressions that had a combined devotional, therapeutic, and entertainment dimension.

According to Constantin, colonialism and Islam both participated in the imposition of socio-political hierarchies and laws that discriminated against

22 On Sittī Maryam, see Grandin 1984, 1988. For a genealogy of the Mīrġanī family, see Hofheinz 1992: 9–27.

23 Cifuentes 2008: 52.

women in Northeast Africa. Political power and prestige were perceived as a male preserve in both the colonial administration and educational policies. In Sufi orders, on the other hand, women were able to perform certain roles and activities that were not explicitly forbidden by the Qur'an. As networking agents across generations, and as vectors of socialization and reproduction within African societies, women found a space within which they could bring about social changes in the Sufi movements in East Africa.[24]

During the time of colonial rule along the African Red Sea coast, "exceptional normal" (Grendi 1994) women—Sittī Maryam and Sittī ʿAlawiyya—began their charismatic "careers" as the guardians of shrines. When colonial troops occupied the Eritrean port, the representative of the Ḫatmiyya *ṭarīqa* there was their father, Sayyid Hāšim al-Mīrghanī (Massawa, b. 1849–50/1901–2). As we have seen, after the defeat of the Mahdiyya in Sudan, the Italian authorities tried—with only very limited success—to persuade Sayyid Hāšim to act as a local mediator for controlling the Muslim population of Eritrea, where he had influence as the representative of the order. At the time, he was a religious mentor especially well-regarded by locals, who would visit him for social, religious, and medical reasons during a period characterized by political and social instability.[25] When he died in Massawa, Sittī ʿAlawiyya and Sittī Maryam were 10 and 34 years old respectively. Sittī Maryam's husband, Sayyid ʿUṯmān Tağ al-Sirr, a highly-respected Sufi scholar and holy man, as well as a leading figure in combating the Sudanese Mahdiyya, died in Suakin just a year later.[26] The places where both men were buried—next to their homes—continued to be popular destinations for regional *ziyārāt*. The two Mīrġanī sisters became the guardians of these places and inherited the *baraka* through kinship. In addition to their status as heirs by blood, their authority was supported by their Sufi knowledge, which was the key to the success and popularity of a shaykh. Erudition or literacy in a pre-eminently oral society is associated with knowledge of the Qur'an and poetry, *ḏikr*, or other mystical practices. This knowledge is often self-taught, which helps create an aura of charisma around a shaykh.[27] Šarīfa Maryam, who was raised by her maternal grandfather and her mother, was educated in the *ḫalwa* (Sudanese religious school) that her paternal grandfather, the founder of the Ḫatmiyya, had established next to his mosque in Suakin. She studied the Qur'an under the direction of a woman whom Sayyid ʿUṯmān al-Mīrġanī had trained especially for female religious education, which

24 Constantin 1998: 31–40.

25 Bruzzi 2013: 63.

26 Grandin 1988: 124.

27 Cruise O'Brien and Coulon 1988: 4, 15.

was unusual in the region at that time. She undertook a part of her studies under the supervision of her husband, ʿUṯmān Taǧ al-Sirr, who was himself a famous scholar.[28] Šarīfa ʿAlawiyya, on the other hand, was raised and educated by her father, but we do not know very much more about her training. Her father died while she was still young, and she pursued most of her studies, which were based on the Qur'an, *ḥadīṯ*, and her family's literary output, at home,[29] but it is also possible that when she had to stay at her sister's home in Suakin in around 1919, she had the opportunity to deepen her Sufi learning there, too.[30] In Sudan, Šarīfa Maryam played an important role in the teaching of Islam, and especially the *ṭarīqa*, to women, who were not able to participate in the order's *ḏikr* sessions because they were for men only. Instead, Maryam used to lead exclusively female prayer groups during which she recited *Ratib* and *Mawlid* composed by her grandfather. Remembered for her commitment to women's education in the study of *fiqh, ḥadīṯ*, and the Qur'an, Šarīfa Maryam built other *ḫalwa* of the Ḫatmiyya for women in Suakin and in Sinkat. As in other cases we have reported above, Muslim women were not trained within the colonial educational framework, but rather by religious training under the supervision of Sufi masters, either women or within their own family networks. The two Mīrġanī sisters assumed the role of representatives of the *ṭarīqa* among the Beja people, from whom they were descended through their mothers: Hadendowa in the case of Sittī Maryam, and Beni ʿAmer in the case of Sittī ʿAlawiyya. Within the framework of their relations with the colonial authorities, they interacted and negotiated with the British and Italian authorities. In the Sudanese port of Suakin, Šarīfa Maryam was on good terms with the British, who requested her intervention to solve conflicts that had arisen in the country, for example regarding the selection of the shaykh of the Habab in 1937 and the dispute between the Beni ʿAmer and the Hadendowa in the final years of the Second World War. In a similar vein, the Italian authorities asked Šarīfa ʿAlawiyya to intervene in Massawa on several occasions, notably—as we will see—during the wars in Libya and Ethiopia. Despite their similar attitudes towards colonial rule, they had very different personalities. Sittī Maryam was merciful and modest; she avoided public ceremonies and took no important decisions without consulting her nephew, Sayyid ʿAlī al-Mīrġanī, who was the acknowledged leader of the *ṭarīqa* in Sudan at the time. She wore simple, modest white clothing that offered a mere glimpse of one part of her face. She welcomed visitors but said very little, and simply listened to the many people of

28 Grandin 1988: 122–128.

29 Caniglia 1940; Martinelli 1930.

30 She left the colony in around 1919 to stay at her sister's home in Suakin (Massara 1921).

different origins from all regions of Sudan who turned to her for consultation.[31] Sittī ʿAlawiyya, on the other hand, was popular for her eclectic, valiant and combative personality. She accepted public honours and had no hesitation in reaching decisions independently, without taking her nephew Sīdī Ǧaʿfar, who was recognized by the Italian authorities—against her will—as the "leader of Islam in Eritrea", into account.[32]

During the colonial occupation, based in their homes, which were considered to be strongholds of Islam and places of refuge and peace, Sittī Maryam and Sittī ʿAlawiyya adopted a militant stance, leading what might be termed a social *ǧihād* in line with Islamic reformist movements and the need to engage in imposing what is good and forbidding what is reprehensible.[33] In Eritrea, because she lived close to her father's shrine in Hetumlo, near the Eritrean port, Sittī ʿAlawiyya quickly assumed a leading role as custodian of the shrine in the area, a role traditionally played by a Sufi who is often a descendent of the "saint". In this way, even after her father had died, his home continued to be a focal point for social and religious networks.

It is not sure whether or not the name ʿAlawiyya was an intentional reference to the ʿAlawiyya *ṭarīqa*, which was a Sufi order based in Hadhramawt that had spread across the Indian Ocean with the Hadhrami diaspora.[34] The Mīrġanī were historically connected and in contact with the ʿAlawiyya *ṭarīqa*, and Sittī ʿAlawiyya's brother-in-law, Muḥammad ʿUṯmān Tāǧ al-Sirr, Sittī Maryam's husband, was the son of a woman from the famous al-Ahdal family of Zabid, an important family of sayyids in Yemen that had long-standing relations with ʿAlawīs. There were also other marriage alliances that may support the idea of a Mīrġanī-ʿAlawīs network: for example, in 1909, Sittī ʿAlawiyya married her cousin Muḥammad Ṣāliḥ, who was the son of Nāfisa (Sīdī Hāšim's sister) and Sayyid ʿUqayl, a member of the ʿAlawiyyun clan of Mecca.[35]

Her titles tell us more about her roles, which differ according to who the interlocutors were, and about the myths that built up around her. Colonial reports identify her by the Italian term *sceriffa* (which corresponds to the female version of the English word "sheriff"), which recalls the idea of a legal official with responsibility for an area, with political and administrative duties. In fact, as far as the colonial occupation was concerned, she also played a secular role

31 Grandin 1988: 126.

32 Bruzzi 2006; Interview with Aḥmad al-Mīrġanī on May 2009 in Cairo. Grandin 1988: 126.

33 On the importance of social *ǧihād*, see Melis 2006: 44.

34 On these Sufi family networks in East Africa, see Bang 2003: 39, especially on the al-Ahdal family of Zabīd.

35 These speculations are based on the family tree provided by Hofheinz 1992: 26.

as an intermediary between the local people and the Italian authorities. The term was, however, an imprecise translation of her Arabic title *šarīfa*, which was also adopted by the Italian press (as well as being used in colonial reports). Muslim notables who claimed to be descended from the Prophet used the term to evoke the prestige of their genealogy and in fact, like her relatives who led the Ḫatmiyya order, she did claim to be a descendant of the Prophet. Other Italian sources, such as Italian newsreels and travel literature, expressly used the word *Santona* ("holy woman") to depict her charisma. Sainthood in Islam was comparable to the status of *insān al-kāmil* (a perfect human being) or *walī* (friend of God). Piety, mercy, purity, gnosis, and self-restraint are among the characteristics that denote a *walī*. A *walī*'s acts and teachings were mainly dealt with in Sufi literature, and the terms "saint" and "Sufi mystic" are often used interchangeably. A saint is not necessarily a Sufi mystic, however, as was the case of personalities from the Qur'an like the Prophet's mother Amina and his daughter Fāṭima, or other leading religious figures in Islamic history. Moreover, a definition of saintly status is complex and controversial because in Sunni Islam it is established informally by local and popular recognition. Some scholars prefer to underline the difference between the Muslim and Sufi definitions, especially where one is dealing with the issue of cults of saints. As Reeves has pointed out, even though the Muslim saint cult and Sufi sects are two historically related topics, cults of saints potentially involved a broader section of the population than did Sufi sects in some cases. Moreover while Muslim saints have often been initiated in one or more Sufi sects, their followers could belong to any of them.[36]

The oral sources that are widespread across what are now Eritrea, Ethiopia and Egypt used the Arabic title *sittī*, which is an abbreviation of *sayyidatī*, "my lady", when referring to the *sceriffa*. This title is widely used not only in the Maghreb but also in Northeast Africa to refer to holy women and *Šayḫāt*. In Djibouti and North Somalia, its plural, *sittāt*, is used to describe sessions of prayers led by groups of women. These same sessions are known in other parts of Somalia along the Juba river as *Nabi-ammaan*.[37] Sittī ʿAlawiyya also used to lead prayer sessions for her African and foreign visitors at her home, and at sunset in particular, she would recite her ancestors' writings, such as *Maǧmūʿ al-awrād al-kabīr*, which were widely used in Sudan.[38] Her home, which was close to Massawa, a terminal port for Muslim pilgrims travelling

36 Reeves 1995: 307.

37 Lidwien, 1996; Declich 1996, 2000.

38 Caniglia (1940: 35) recalls three writings she used to recite: "El Macrat (the sunset prayer), El Aurad (the special prayer of her ancestor), and El Iscia (the 8 o'clock prayer)". *Maǧmūʿ*

to Mecca from Africa and an important trade centre, was a place of *ziyāra*, pious visits, in which Muslim and Christian communities both participated. In fact, as was the case with other Sufi centres and shrines in the region such as that of her contemporary Sittī Momina, her visitors were not only Muslims. During the early stages of the Italian occupation, the Mīrġanī shrine and mosque in Kassala were reported to be a place of convergence for Christian and Muslim men and women alike. The shrines were historically a pilgrimage destination for people from a variety of social, religious, and cultural backgrounds.[39] In Ethiopia, pilgrimages to shrines in their capacity as holy places for meetings between monotheistic and African religions brought a number of local cults together in the same place. Some of these shrines are located along the main pilgrimage route, where trade and cultural relationships intertwined, as was the case with Kassala and Massawa. The Eritrean port took Christian pilgrims from Ethiopia to Sinai, across the Nile Valley and Egypt or the Red Sea. Pilgrimages to Jerusalem opened up the main channel for cultural exchanges between Ethiopia and the Mediterranean world.[40] In addition, the route for African Muslims travelling to Mecca across the Red Sea passed by way of Massawa. Sittī ʿAlawiyya's house was located at this crossroads for pilgrims heading for the holy cities and was also a destination for pilgrims in its own right. She had a guesthouse annexed to her own residence so that she could welcome pilgrims, who might even stay for several weeks. As Caniglia noted, visitors lived "with the Sceriffa in such heartfelt and friendly intimacy that they even grant her the respect she deserves by asking for permission to leave her home to return to their own. This she grants, at times adding various gifts for personalities of note. The door of her home is closed to no one, and no one leaves it disappointed".[41]

The two sisters' residences were popular Mīrġanī destinations for visits or pilgrimages at the time, situated as they were at a crossroads of transnational routes and, significantly, near railway stations. Šarīfa Maryam's fame drew many visitors to Suakin, the port city where she resided in the winter, and to Sinkat, where she lived in the summer, or to Jubayt, a small town on the railway line where she owned two houses, and where she built a mosque in 1918. She

---

al-awrād al-kabīr was a collection of *awrād* compiled by Muḥammad al-Ḥasan that was particularly popular in Sudan. See O'Fahey, Hofheinz and Radtke 1994: 192.

39 Fiaschi 1896: 28. This inter-religious dimension is still observed in a number of Ethiopian shrines led by women today, such as those of Tiru Sina in Wollo and Sittī Momina in Arsi. See the ethnographies by Ishihara and Zeleke.

40 Gascon and Hirsch 1992.

41 Caniglia 1940: 36–37.

practiced purdah, and welcomed male visitors from behind a curtain without ever showing herself, simply listening, and speaking very little.[42]

Sittī ʿAlawiyya, on the other hand, lived in Hetumlo, near Massawa, during the winter months and in Keren in the warmer summer months. These two cities lay on the caravan route from the Red Sea port to Kassala, the main centre of Ḫatmiyya, in Sudan. Massawa was then a bustling cosmopolitan and multiethnic Red Sea port at the crossroads of long-distance and regional trade where traders and the urban class played a central role. It was a port city with a strong Islamic identity that quickly began to prosper and thrive after the opening of the Suez Canal in 1896, and was a lucrative destination for merchants, commercial agents, brokers, financiers, fishermen, and pearl traders, as well as for slave traders, not just from Europe but also from Hejaz, Egypt, and India. The suburbs of Massawa, Hergigo, Emkullu, and Hetumlo, where the Brotherhood enjoyed particular success, were the main departure points for caravans heading inland. The *šarīfa*'s residence was in Hetumlo, one of these suburbs, which was of great importance because of the water supply it provided to the city every day. There was a weekly market there, and it was also an important caravan station thanks to its wells, which supplied water to convoys.[43] The *šarīfa*'s residence was at the heart of this centre, with its vital sources of water, which was notoriously scarce in the region and a potential bone of contention and conflict. A state of peace around these sources was crucial for ensuring the social stability that the Mīrġanī generally showed they wished to maintain in the region. As with Hetumlo, the suburbs of Massawa were centres of mediation where transport networks, businesses, and products from the hinterland and the coast all converged. These places were inhabited by various types of population, from nomadic herders and traders to rich urban households, who were linked to each other in a common space by different kinds of bonds. There had been a large Sudanese community near Sittī ʿAlawiyya's house since 1890, and a number of families from Kassala lived under her father's protection in Ḫatmiyya, a suburb of Massawa.[44] In a social milieu in which socio-economic relationships were constantly being negotiated, and where disputes and competition for access to resources and port facilities were particularly bitter, Sittī ʿAlawiyya's residence occupied a central position for maintaining social stability and what the Italians considered to be "public order". People came to her for different reasons: for example, to seek material and financial aid from her to fund their marriages. One *karāma* story illustrates her power to provide wealth

42 Grandin 1988: 126.

43 Miran 2009: 159.

44 Miran 2009: 146, 156.

for needy people. It is reported that a man went to visit her to ask for a contribution to his marriage. She made a hole in the ground with her cane and Lire (the Italian currency) tumbled out, but when the man returned on another occasion to dig in the same place, snakes crawled out of the ground.[45]

Her residence was a space where people from a multitude of social and cultural backgrounds converged to seek her blessing, believing that she had *baraka*.[46] Tigrè women, for example, "respected Šarīfa 'Alawiyya, gathered around her and loved her very much". Women in particular would visit her at each *ḥawliyya*. They worked in her home and asked for her help for weddings.[47]

She also engaged in charitable works in support of Eritrean communities, and by the late 1930s these activities were fairly well structured. According to Caniglia, she led the Charity Council of the Islamic Community, which she herself had founded in Massawa. Its budget was financed by voluntary offerings as a charity and to propagate the faith, and its main goal was to provide relief for the elderly, for the poor and the sick, and for people who were unfit for any type of work, who received a monthly payment from the Community.[48]

Because she came from a wealthy family, she owned a number of properties in Eritrea. In addition to the cash grants the colonial authorities and travellers offered her, she also received gifts such as livestock, weapons, and products of various kinds that her followers, the Italian Government, and the country's elites offered her in exchange for her assistance. This property was eventually redistributed and offered to the community to realize believers' desires and perform various kinds of charitable work.[49] The Italian authorities were not the only ones to contribute to the operation of this complex social structure she directed: her visitors were also active agents, not only by donating and exchanging gifts during their visits but also by participating in the establishment of important socio-political networks. During the Ethiopian campaign, a delegation of Red Cross nurses and other newly-arrived nursing sisters went to visit her on two occasions (Figures 10–13), the second of which was on

45 Interview with Hāšim Muḥammad 'Alī Blenai on March 2009 in Massawa.

46 The definition of *baraka* is the one provided by Colin 1986. Regarding her *baraka*, in addition to my interviews, see also Böll 2003: 40.

47 Interview with 'Abd al-Raḥīm 'Uṯmān Kekiya on March 2009 in Keren.

48 Caniglia 1940: 36–37. Rivista di diritto coloniale. Bologna: Cappelli, 1940: 254.

49 Interviews with Šarīfa 'Alawiyya's and Aḥmad al-Mīrġanī, on May 2009 in Cairo. See also Commissariato regionale di Massaua, "Per le figlie del defunto Saied Hascem El Morgani", Massawa, 20 maggio 1903; Commissariato di Cheren, "Domanda della Scerifa Alauia per avere in consegna quattro moschetti", Cheren, 23 giugno 1908. Archivio Storico Diplomatico del Ministero degli Affari Esteri (ASDMAE), Archivio Eritrea (AE), 1886–1912 Pacco 43 (Morgani-Adigrat—Varie Eritrea), Fasc. 1 Morgani (1886–1911).

3 January 1936, and as one of the nurses, Elena Pesenti, recalled, the exchange of gifts was common practice: "as always, the visit was interesting, and on this occasion the Sceriffa offered each of us a gift of a beautiful basket of colourful straw. This time, we discovered that you have to give her an offering, and so I gave her an envelope containing 100 Lire through Amecek (Captain Materi's butler) so I would be received by her! We visited her garden, which was full of magnificent tropical greenery, and saw the car the Italian Government had given her, a small red Balilla. We also promised her the basket of sugar flowers the chefs on board had given us for Christmas, and we sent it to her in a nice little box through Amecek the day after".[50] The goods she received were therefore also the result of exchanges that worked by means of a system of gifts and counter-gifts. Her charity was integrated into the colonial wealth system: she introduced sick Muslims to the colonial hospitals in Asmara, where Christian nuns were used, and to other nearby locations, all at the expense of the Muslim Community. The Community also provided for their needs in the event of death.[51] As was the case with Christian missionaries in Africa, curing the sick was not only associated with treating the body, but as well as wider social and religious reforms, it was closely interwoven with saving believers' souls and, of course, religious proselytizing.[52] One area of the charity's activities that Šarīfa ʿAlawiyya promoted was devoted to caring for and assisting the sick, and in the 1930s, this was carried out with the collaboration of the colonial Government. In this way, she inherited not only the *baraka* but also the social role that had belonged to her father, who—as reported in colonial accounts—used to restore sick people troubled by the influence of the *ǧinn* to health. This illustrates both remarkable consistencies in and changes to the Sufis' attitudes to medicine. In the case of the Mīrġanī, to whom the sick and needy would come, we see a gradual movement from endogenous medicine to European methods. In the early 1900s, believers used to visit Muslim shaykhs like Sīdī Hāšim for treatment, whereas in the 1920s and 1930s, the new generation of Sittī ʿAlawiyya showed a growing interest in colonial medicine, with its acknowledged powers. From this moment on, sick people who had previously

50 De Carli 2016.
51 Caniglia 1940: 36–37.
52 Vaughan 1994: 295.

FIGURE 10 *Red Cross nurses visit Sittī ʿAlawiyya (1936).*
PRIVATE COLLECTION OF OTTAVIO DE CARLI, BRESCIA.

FIGURE 11 *A Red Cross nurse, Sittī 'Alawiyya, and a child (1936).*
PRIVATE COLLECTION OF OTTAVIO DE CARLI, BRESCIA.

FIGURE 12 *Red Cross nurses, a colonial officer and Sittī ʿAlawiyya (1936).*
PRIVATE COLLECTION OF OTTAVIO DE CARLI, BRESCIA.

gone to the Mīrġanī were not necessarily treated by them, but were directed towards colonial hospitals.[53]

Baraka, Itinerant Preaching and the Mobility of Pious Women

Pious peregrinations to villages played an important role in propagating both the Islamic and Christian faiths. In the early colonial period, itinerant preachers and missionaries were mainly men, but there were a few women, too. In Eritrea, nuns from the Order of St Anne evangelized in the Cunama area and beyond, not only through education by teaching at schools in Barentu and other places, but also through apostolic tours, especially among indigenous women. St. Anne nuns had been active in Eritrea since at least 1885, when the Italian Government expressly asked for two sisters for the hospital in Assab. The Comboni Missionary Sisters, on the other hand, arrived in 1914 to work at the Regina Elena Hospital in Asmara. They were the most numerous of all the female missionary congregations in Eritrea because they were in charge of health and education: Comboni Missionary Sisters were employed in the Asmara, Massawa, Decamere, and Senafe hospitals, and worked with compatriots and locals alike, both Christian and Muslim. They were also highly mobile, and travelled to villages to visit and take care of those who could not

53 Regio esercito italiano, Comando superiore in Africa al Ministero degli Affari Esteri, 16 gennaio 1887. Archivio Storico Diplomatico del Ministero degli Affari Esteri (ASDMAE), Archivio Eritrea (AE), 1886–1912, Pacco 43 (Morgani-Adigrat—Varie Eritrea), Fasc. 1 Morgani (1886–1911). On this issue, see Bruzzi 2012a. Another case study on the complexity of Islamic and colonial leadership relationships is Northern Nigeria. Here, the Muslim leadership, which ruled during the British administration of the country in the first half of the 20th century, was able to explore modern colonial ideas while still adhering firmly to the matrix of Islam, especially in the field of colonial medicine. In fact, as Shobana Shankar points out, Nigerian emirs modernized and enhanced their authority through cooperation with Christian missions during the anti-leprosy campaign in colonial Hausaland in the 1930s (Shankar 2007). Their representatives were "agents of change", and not merely "compromisers who kept the old apparatus of governance in place and allowed Europeans to impose their idea of civilization". They "believed that religion and religious differences could be subordinated to medical welfare and to political authority". They had submitted to a "Christian" administration "under which they were able to exercise great power. As a consequence, among their people their power grew, not in the mould of pre-colonial aristocracies but as a model of moderation in modernization". See Last 1988: 72; Shankar 2007: 45–68.

travel to hospitals on their own. These trips were one of the tools used by the missionaries for proselytising in more marginal areas.[54]

Not much is known about missionary expeditions by Muslim women in the Horn. Here, the colonial gaze still persisted in portraying a no-woman's-land, a society that for the most part kept Muslim women segregated in domestic spaces. Mobility is one of the recurring differences between the lives of male and female Sufi missionaries in Africa and beyond. The founder of a Sufi order usually left his homeland to begin his journey of initiation, during which he normally studied under the authority of various spiritual masters. This journey was not so common among holy women, however, who were portrayed as being kept separate in voluntary confinement.[55]

At the time of the Islamic renewal, the Sufi master Aḥmad Ibn Idrīs expressly asked his pupils to proselytize in Africa. Although the phenomenon is still relatively unexplored and little known, some studies have shed light on female participation in the re-islamization of the continent through holy peregrinations. One well-known example of this is the *'yan taru*, which was a network of itinerant women teachers from the Tiǧāniyya in Nigeria. Under the supervision and teachings of Nana Asma'u, they travelled to remote rural areas to teach Islam to women in their homes. There is further evidence of the long-term nature in West Africa of this phenomenon of itinerant women preachers travelling from the Maghreb along the pilgrimage route to Mecca.[56]

The case of Sittī 'Alawiya conflicts with the mainstream idea of the segregation of holy women: she was, in fact, a highly mobile socio-religious agent. Her freedom of movement and circulation was eventually hindered by colonial orders that sought to limit any proselytizing that might undermine the *pax coloniale*. In 1914, Commissioner Fioccardi, the Regional Officer in Keren, attempted to prevent her from travelling to the Gash Barka region in the southwest of Eritrea. In many instances, these journeys by influential religious mentors like the *šarīfa* were comparable to the Christian missionaries' strategy of itinerant proselytizing that had led to occasional tensions among local populations, but the excessive numbers of proselytizing Christian missionaries stood in stark contrast to the colonial administrative and political priority of maintaining peace and order.[57]

---

54 Da Nembro 1953. For a history of the Comboni Missionary Sisters in Eritrea, see Fusari 2015.

55 Boissevain 2006: 37.

56 On Nana Asma'u, see Boyd and Mack 2000, 1997.

57 Chelati Dirar 2003: 402. See also Chelati Dirar 2006.

For Sittī ʿAlawiyya , these trips were a key tool for propagating the (Islamic) faith, establishing socio-political networks, and collecting offerings. From the colonial point of view, however, they had the potential to undermine political stability, and so administrators prevented and limited movements by shaykhs within the colonial borders as far as possible.

In 1914, after the famine that caused great damage in the country, Sittī ʿAlawiyya wanted to travel to the Sahel, but both the local authorities and colonial officials opposed the idea, especially because the Commissioner of Barka was collecting tributes and did not wanted her to cross the region until the collection process had been accomplished.[58] This episode is an illustration of the conflicts with the Government relating to the freedom of movement of local religious mentors and colonial control of their economic, religious, and political powers. In a way, the manner in which this political control was exercised and preserved by the colonial authorities echoed biopolitics: Fioccardi, who was the regional administrator in the Keren district at that time, tried to prevent the *šarīfa*'s trip to the Gash Barka region by explaining to her that it was dangerous for her health. He stressed that the region was particularly unhealthy and dangerous. Reporting on their meeting, he wrote:

> Today, the Sceriffa tormented me for two hours on the issue of her trip to Barca [in the South-West of Eritrea]. She very cunningly told me that the Diglal [the Beni ʿAmer authority] had written to her with advice on hygiene, the importance of and reason for which she understands. As I insisted on the issue of Barca's weather conditions and insalubrities, she answered that it would be better to catch a fever than die in poverty. She added that she knew perfectly well that fevers could be fought with quinine.[59]

58 Telegramma—espresso di servizio, Commissario Regionale di Cheren, 23 settembre 1914, Archivio Storico Diplomatico del Ministero degli Affari Esteri (ASDMAE), Archivio Eritrea (AE), 1880–1917, Pacco 1022 (Missioni Politiche—Varie—El Morgani), Fasc. 10 Famiglia El Morgani, 1895–1917.

59 Telegramma—espresso di servizio, Commissario Regionale di Cheren, 29 ottobre 1914, Archivio Storico Diplomatico del Ministero degli Affari Esteri (ASDMAE), Archivio Eritrea (AE), 1880–1917, Pacco 1022 (Missioni Politiche—Varie—El Morgani), Fasc. 10 Famiglia El Morgani, 1895–1917. Prevention by using hygienic and sanitary precautions, such as following special rules of personal conduct, was an extremely important tool for preventing diseases. Here, we can clearly understand the impact of the local authorities' advice given to her by the Diglal. See Bruzzi 2011.

Her emphasis on quinine, which was an important tool for colonial domination in Africa, is remarkable. From the early 1830s in particular, quinine was produced by European companies, and became increasingly significant for colonial conquests. The African continent, which was known as the "white man's grave", was an especially difficult environment for Europeans to penetrate. Malaria had been the main cause of death, especially for newcomers, who had had no opportunity to build up resistance. The introduction and spread of adequate quantities of quinine in the continent had represented a major medical innovation, a technological advance that had enabled and favoured the previous "scramble for Africa" of the late 19th century.[60] This new European technology represented a further "tool of Empire", and did not go unnoticed by local dignitaries, and it is in this context that Sittī ʿAlawiyya's reference to quinine should be understood. During her negotiations with Fioccardi on her trip, she stressed her knowledge of the powers of quinine. In other words, faced with a colonial attempt to use health and safety reasons as a "political techinque" for limiting her freedom of movement, she responded by pointing out her understanding of the effectiveness of both endogenous and exogenous medicines. In the end, on that occasion, as a reaction to the colonial prohibition against her trip, she declared that she was in detention.[61] A number of reports by the Regional Commissioner of Keren in 1915 attest to the fact that she engaged in continuous negotiations with the colonial authorities in order to obtain permission for her trip across the country, especially in the Barka and Sahel regions. Her relationship with the colonial authorities was complex, and involved difficult discussions: it was not merely a simple collaboration. Fioccardi expressed his worry and frustration over the impossibility of completely controlling this "neurotic" and "irritable" woman. He had good

60 According to Headrick, "scientific cinchona production was an imperial technology *par excellence*. Without it European colonialism would have been almost impossible in Africa". Headrick 1981: 72. Curtin 1961: 94–110; Curtin 1998; Headrick 1981. From the early 1900s, the drug became increasingly important for the suppression of malaria, but at first its use was only experimental; the cause of death was associated not only with the disease but also with the incorrect treatment received by patients. Even quinine prophylaxis was not immediately adopted, and it was only when its use spread that death rates among Europeans fell significantly. I have discussed this issue in a published article in Bruzzi 2012a.

61 Telegramma—espresso di servizio, Commissario Regionale di Cheren, 29 ottobre 1914, Archivio Storico Diplomatico del Ministero degli Affari Esteri (ASDMAE), Archivio Eritrea (AE), 1880–1917, Pacco 1022 (Missioni Politiche—Varie—El Morgani), Fasc. 10 Famiglia El Morgani, 1895–1917.

grounds for fearing conflict with her over these travel restrictions, and although freedom of movement across the country depended on the permits and limitations put in place by the colonial authorities, they did attempt to adapt to her demands in the end.[62] Fioccardi observed: "I now believe that to change this irritable and neurotic woman's itinerary is not appropriate, especially in these times. She may act on a foolish whim and not move, declaring herself to be a prisoner, as she did the last time the government forbade her to move due to the famine our populations were suffering".[63]

In certain areas, such as the Cunama region, there was competition between Christian missionaries and Muslim leaders like the Mīrġanī. In the late 1910s, the Capuchin missionaries' proselytizing campaign was enjoying a certain success, and Muslims who worried that some villages whose elites had previously been Islamized were sympathetic to Christian missions confronted the threat and launched a campaign, led by the *Sceriffa*. The Capuchins were worried about her effectiveness as a proselytizer, and very well knew that "wherever she went, villages were *ipso facto* declared to be Muslim". This was why they attempted to block her journey by asking the colonial authorities to intervene. In 1918, a missionary involved in the affair reported: "I went to the Commissioner to protest because the Sceriffa (a sort of Muslim priestess) had received Commissioner Pollera's permission to 'Islamically' exploit certain Cunama villages that adhere to the Mission. My protests, which I admit were too heated, had the honour to reach the Governor in Asmara. I had to apologize to Commissioner Pollera, but I had the satisfaction of seeing the Sceriffa being recalled, and so this sorceress was not able to set foot in villages we consider to be already under our influence".[64] As this passage clearly states, the Capuchins acknowledged her impressive ability to convert indigenous people, and considered her as a rival whose power could be compared to that of a sorceress. The colonial authorities, on the other hand, tended to overlook the religious significance of her journeys and focus on the venal reasons that drove

62 Commissariato di Cheren, Escursione della Sceriffa Alauia Morgani, 9 luglio 1915. Archivio Storico Diplomatico del Ministero degli Affari Esteri (ASDMAE), Archivio Eritrea (AE), 1880–1917, Pacco 1022 (Missioni Politiche—Varie—El Morgani), Fasc. 10 Famiglia El Morgani, 1895–1917.

63 Commissariato Regionale di Cheren, Telegramma Espresso, 25 luglio 1915. Archivio Storico Diplomatico del Ministero degli Affari Esteri (ASDMAE), Archivio Eritrea (AE), 1880–1917, Pacco 1022 (Missioni Politiche—Varie—El Morgani), Fasc. 10 Famiglia El Morgani, 1895–1917.

64 CBMC, p. 22, cit. in Da Nembro 1953: 230.

her to her peregrinations. Her ability to convert the villages she visited to collect offerings, to influence people's behaviour and attitudes, and to impress those who met her cannot be fully understood unless one takes account of the body that is the source of her spiritual and charismatic power; in any event, it was on the surface of this body that her own voice, which was mainly silenced in the archives, could be reheard.

CHAPTER 5

Sufi Women's "Fantasy", Performances and Fashion

Imagination and Desire in Women's Bodies

As the anthropologist and colonial officer Alberto Pollera (1873–1939) observed in his time, Italians expressed "imaginary dreams … of a wonderful ambiance" when reflecting on Africans, especially when they were living in their homeland.[1] These fantasies were reproduced and spread by means of private photographs and postcards that allowed African bodies and landscapes to circulate across borders. Imagination and desire, as well as invention and construction, play a pivotal role when we look at how feminine bodies are represented in colonial narratives and images. The advent of photography—which coincided with the arrival of colonialism and Italian participation in the scramble for Africa—became "a powerful medium that gave a visual form to colonial culture and helped forge a link between the empire and domestic imagination".[2] This new mass medium developed into a true imperial tool that permitted colonial enterprise to be fashioned for a homeland audience. The commercial photography market developed rapidly, and postcards became both a significant mass medium and collector's items between the end of the 19th century and the First World War, and a wave of commodification, objectification, and consumption of indigenous feminine bodies in the illustrated press accompanied colonial military campaigns. Colonial images such as those circulating through the medium of postcards helped "create and sustain tourist desires and fantasy".[3] Photography also participated in the cataloguing and classification of "colonized" peoples. Commercial images created and invented human typologies for audiences in the motherland: in postcards, African faces and bodies are classified by "scene and type". These photographs show anonymous bodies that are only rooted in colonial spaces by the caption beneath them: "Young *madama* in Italian East Africa", or "Young woman in Italian Libya", etc. Influenced by the anthropometry photography employed in

1 In Italian "sogni immaginosi … di un ambiente fantastico" (Pollera 1913: 12), cit. in Sòrgoni 2002: 75.

2 Ponzanesi 2012: 163.

3 Edwards 1996: 197.

 | DOI 10.1163/9789004356160_007

physical anthropology, women are also catalogued according to their supposed "ethnic" identity and sex, age or status ("woman", "young girl", "*madama*", "wife of", etc.).[4] If we study these postcards more closely, in addition to a process of fabrication of supposed ethnic types, we see an example of the manipulation, circulation, and reproduction of images: in fact, the same model might be employed with different captions and descriptions for a different audience, and thus one single body may appear to be rooted in different colonial landscapes.[5] Travel postcards gave remarkable visibility to the "exotic" and "sensual" bodies of African and Asian women. These pictures were often staged in studios or open spaces, according to the photographer's directions, and provided a sense of a-temporality. The hypersexualization of female bodies in Italian colonial images is analogous to cases that have been analysed in other territories under colonial rule, where we find similar portraits of anonymous models whose identities and histories are completely unknown.[6] While their voices may have been silenced in the colonial archives, their bodies are constantly exhibited in stereotypical representations of the black female as close to nature and out of time. These images of a sensual and sexually available "Black Venus" circulated especially, but not exclusively, among soldiers in East Africa.[7] The phenomenon became even more highly organized during Fascism, when the regime distributed photography portraying winking African women in sensual poses to soldiers leaving for the war of conquest in Ethiopia.[8]

One example of this type of image is a series of commercial shots portraying "Bilen" women in "East Africa".[9] Another postcard shows beautiful, bare-breasted models performing a dance that the caption identifies as a "Bilen fantasy" (Figure 13). Although their poor clothing may suggest a servile social class, the form of dance demonstrates an ambiguous role in the empowerment

4 See Palma 1999.

5 Goglia 2005. Studio portraits of women in Tunisia by the famous orientalist photographers Lanhart and Landrock were used for postcards and other visual images that circulated across all North African countries even though they had all been taken in Tunisia. See Castelli, Enrico (ed.), Immagini & Colonie, Montone: Centro di documentazione del Museo Etnografico Tamburo Parlante, 1998: 139. With particular regard to these manipulations and the false nature of postcards portraying African women in the Italian colonies, see Bruzzi 2013, unpublished paper. In my analysis, I used postcards belonging to two private collectors: Beniamino Cadioli and Celsio Bragli. Their collections are duplicated in the newly-established photographic archive at the Casa delle Culture in Modena.

6 Taraud 2012: 11.

7 Ponzanesi 2005; Bini 2003.

8 Bini 2003: 8. Campassi and Sega 1983: 61–62.

9 Mignemi 1984: 102–109.

FIGURE 13 *East Africa—Bilen Fantasy.*
POSTCARD, PHOTOGRAPHER UNKNOWN, PERSONAL COLLECTION.

of these women: it allows them to gain visibility, but at the same time undermines this apparent empowerment by relegating them to stereotypical female roles through the hypersexualization of their bodies.[10]

Unconscious processes such as fantasy and desire were integral parts of the construction of the colonial subject and the relationship established both during colonial encounters and in the empire-building context.[11] Erotic images represent only one of the ways in which women's bodies are fashioned, however: in addition to the erotic styling of these particular images, we find other typologies in colonial postcards, such as portraits of scenes and types, anonymous women and children, women at the market or groups of veiled women in a public space, and yet once again, a common feature is that they are anonymous icons, and seem to be mere objects reduced to commercial commodities.[12] They are images of women whose histories and identities we

10 Yarber 2011.

11 Yeğenoğlu 1998: 2; Pickering-Iazzi 2000: 400–417.

12 See also Pinkus 1995.

do not know: "we know nothing of them, except their bodies".[13] Despite this, the body lies at the very core of the colonial encounter, and deserves special attention in our analysis, as it was on the female body that a blend of fiction, desire, and imagination was staged. In fact, as Alain Corbin has pointed out, the body itself is "a fiction, an ensemble of mental representations, an unconscious framing of images, fading away and reforming along the thread of the history of the subject, with the mediation of social discourses and symbolic systems".[14] A collection of postcards, pictures, travel literature and ethnographies provides a cross-section of society through a representation of women's bodies that goes beyond eroticism. Women's fantasies played a pivotal role in fashioning not only the colonial enterprise, but also holy sites, as we will see, and fed the imaginations of travellers and settlers alike.

Women's *Fantasia* in Sufi Regional Centres

There is a common leitmotif to be found in the colonial jargon in postcards and travel literature: that of *fantasia* (fantasy). In the Italian context, the term *fantasia* became a macro-category that referred not only to erotic images of African women, but also to indigenous dances and musical performances that stirred the colonial imagination. Fantasy—which from a Lacanian standpoint is the support of desire—recalls the idea of imagination, of a strange desire that lies far from reality. As Gianni Dore observed, the word was widely used in both visual and written records from the early colonial period. Originating from the Mediterranean Lingua Franca, it was integrated into Arabic in North Africa and later absorbed into colonial jargon in East Africa. It was employed in the context of a variety of dance and musical performances that took place during ceremonies and events of any kind, and not exclusively during military events, as was often the case in the Maghreb. *Fantasia* became a part of the colonial set, the expression of a reimagination of pre-colonial performances. This macro-category included performances from Libya, Somalia, Ethiopia, and Eritrea that were all very different from one other.[15] It was often employed to describe both military and women's dance and music forms of any kind. One photograph portrays a so-called "Arabic fantasy" in Libya: a group of woman appears leading a musical performance while sitting in a circle on a terrace in the oasis of Ghadames (Figure 14). Here, the ethnographic image of female

13 See Taraud 2012: 11.

14 Corbin, Courtine and Vigarello 2005: 9.

15 Dore 2004: 50.

TRIPOLITANIA - Gadames - Fantasia araba

FIGURE 14 *Tripolitania, Gadames-Arabic fantasy'*
POSTCARD, PRIVATE COLLECTION OF CELSIO BRAGLI, MODENA.

performance is converted into a tourist item to fashion the colonial landscape. The handwritten text on the back of the postcard tells us that it was addressed to a woman and her family, which proves that the consumers and collectors of "women's fantasy" were not necessarily men.[16]

Other postcards (Figures 15 and 16) portray a women's *fantasia* in Keren on the occasion of the death of "the holy man *Shaykh Morgani*", Sayyid Hāšim al-Mīrġanī. The pictures show another kind of performance, one that is seemingly spontaneous and not deliberately staged by the photographer. It is a group of women's gatherings in open air spaces.

When Sīdī Hāšim died, female forms of devotion and piety for the death of Sittī ʿAlawiyya's father became a part of a tourist repertoire for colonial postcards produced in Massawa. A process of commodification invests women's religious performances, fashioning colonial landscapes and cities such as Keren. In 1888, the Italians occupied the city, which was an old caravan station on the way from the coast to Sudan. This region, which was inhabited by Bilen people

16 DeRoo and Johnston made the point that the consumption of erotic images sheds light on issues of sexual freedom and gender identity with regard to female Western collectors and consumers. Hight and Sampson 2002: 14.

FIGURE 15 *Keren—Women's fantasy for the death of Šayẖ Morgani (a holy man), (a).*
POSTCARD 1, GIORGIO ZAFIRACHI, MASSAWA. PERSONAL COLLECTION.

FIGURE 16 *Keren—Women's fantasy for the death of Šayẖ Morgani (a holy man), (b).*
POSTCARD 2, GIORGIO ZAFIRACHI, MASSAWA. PERSONAL COLLECTION.

who had formerly been Christians, went through a process of Islamization during which the Bilen people were encouraged to convert to Islam en masse, partly as a consequence of Egyptian and Beni ʿAmer raids against them in the 1850s and 1860s, and especially after the Egyptian raid of 1854, when a large number of Bilen were killed and nearly 400 women and children carried off into slavery. Conversions increased as a result of these raids and during the subsequent occupation of Keren by the Egyptian Government, led by Münzinger, who was married to a Bilen woman. After the Mahdist revolt, the Egyptians left, and the Italians occupied the region and began to preach Christianity through the establishment of a Catholic mission in the city. Under pressure from external proselytizing powers, the Bilen saw their religious identity as secondary and shifting boundaries were frequent, as the inter-religious marriages and regular conversions clearly testify: common beliefs and religious traditions were adhered to by Bilen groups, Christian and Muslim alike.[17] According to Cerulli, the gods of the peoples conquered by Abyssinian Christianity were worshipped by both the conquered and the conquerors but were converted into minor spirits or deities. According to his interpretation, the Sky-God of Agao, who was called *jār* in the Bilen language, became the possessive spirit of the *zār* cult, which was especially popular among women crossing confessional and geographical borders.[18]

The *zār* overlapped into another practice that was widespread in the region, the cult of saints expressed through a pious visit (*ziyāra*) to living or dead saints. As we have seen in the previous chapter, people used to visit pious figures and holy shrines because they were believed to hold *baraka*. Through *ziyāra*, believers hoped to obtain blessings, as well as relief and teachings or answers to their questions. The saints' residences—or their shrines, if they were dead—sometimes became the centre of a regional cult where gatherings and cross-religious practices were carried out, especially on the occasion of the anniversary of their death (*ḥawliyya*). Attendance at these gatherings was thought of as being therapeutic for the resolution of personal problems. Pious men and women such as Sīdī Hāšim and his daughter Sittī ʿAlawiyya attracted believers, as well as troubled or sick people in *ziyāra*. Pilgrims held religious gatherings, including practices such as *ḥaḍra* sessions, dances, and chanting *ḏikr* or seeking the saint's *barākāt* (blessings), at these blessed places. As was the case with spirit possession cults, it was frequently noted that pious visits were especially attractive to women. Some of the socio-religious practices that were performed at holy shrines involved mainly female communities, who

17 Smidt 2003: 586–588; Trimingham 1952: 165; Pollera 1935: 158–159.

18 Trimingham 1952: 27, 257.

were combining their religious affiliations. Many of the religious practices that are still performed at shrines in Ethiopia today are gender-based and include spirit possession cults.[19] These devotional—but also, as we will see, leisure-time—practices were imagined and represented in colonial postcards and converted into tourist attractions, as can be seen from the "women's fantasy for the death of Šayḫ Morgani" postcards (Figures 15 and 16).

No personality travelling to Keren ever failed to visit Sittī ʿAlawiyya, whose residence was extremely popular, especially among African soldiers. Her home was also described as the setting for *fantasia* performances. According to the Commissioner of Keren, Vittorio Fioccardi, her residence was popular and well-frequented because of her "bizarre" personality, but more particularly due to the "unpunished Bilen fantasy" she habitually lavished on her visitors.[20] As we have seen, during the Italian occupation, which by 1888 included the Keren district, the Bilen people became popular for the beauty of their women, whose erotic portraits were recurring commodities in colonial postcards, which enjoyed especially high circulation in the army. These stereotypical "clichés" portrayed a hypersexualization of women' bodies.

Just as the production, consumption, and circulation of photography stimulated colonial fantasies of the sexuality and willingness of African women, social phenomena such as prostitution were also widespread in the colony. Recruitment into the colonial army had led to a virtual collapse of the subsistence economy and had a huge impact on women's lives. Some women, mainly Christians from Asmara and Keren, were forced to find alternative means of support, and reluctantly found themselves in a position in which they had to meet the Italian demand for prostitutes, domestic servants, and *madamas*.[21] In Asmara, the development of the commercial, military, and industrial sectors led to an increase in services such as bars and restaurants. In the indigenous quarters, "drinking houses" (*sewa* houses), which were mainly run by women, who sometimes prostituted themselves to increase their income, became a major feature of urban social life. *Sewa* houses were places of recreation, and were among the few leisure activities available to the local population. In East Africa, similar drinking places were a "thriving alternative economy, in which

19 Zeleke 2013: 115.

20 Colonia Eritrea, Commissariato di Cheren, Riservato-Urgente, Al Signor Reggente il Governo della Colonia. Oggetto: Grave dissidio seguito da ingiurie tra Morgani e Scerifa, Cheren, 6 settembre 1917. Archivio Storico Diplomatico del Ministero degli Affari Esteri (ASDMAE), Archivio Eritrea (AE), 1880–1917, Pacco 1022 (Missioni Politiche—Varie—El Morgani), Fasc. 10 Famiglia El Morgani, 1895–1917.

21 Ponzanesi 2012: 164. See also Negash 1987; Barrera 1996.

women could seek refuge from the authority of fathers and husbands, selling sex, food, and alcohol".[22]

Women's social lives also included a number of forms of gatherings and more "respectable" leisure activities that were nevertheless subjected to social pressures and controls. When describing the theatrical dimension of regional possession cults in Ethiopia, the anthropologist Michel Leiris observed that the home of the woman who led the *zār* cults was looked on not only as a kind of hotel where even medical and religious functions were performed, but also as a *café chantant* or dance house where ritual performances and profane leisure activities provided travellers with a welcoming atmosphere.[23]

Imagined with erotic tones in colonial postcards and photography, groups of Bilen women used to gather at Sittī ʿAlawiyya's residence in Keren, where they performed dances within a "private" space for a mainly female audience. This might be seen as a strategy for preserving "women's morality", especially as regards a section of the Muslim elites who sought to criticize women's leaders asked women to be ashamed of displaying their bodies and beauty to strangers.[24] But what exactly was this impressive "Bilen fantasy", this particular form of dance through which Bilen women staged their embodied knowledge? Although it was performed within the private space of Sittī ʿAlawiyya's residence, it was condemned by colonial officers like Fioccardi, as well as by a section of the male Muslim elite. Our understanding is that the performance she offered her visitors in Keren may have been an ecstatic dance. As Miran has pointed out, women's *fantasie* were also popular in Massawa from the early days of the colonial occupation, and as colonial accounts suggest, some of these rituals and festive dancing were probably *zār* ceremonies. Miran also raised the issue of the relationship between *zār* and *ḏikr* at Sufi centres, especially at Sittī ʿAlawiyya's residence.[25] In effect, although no information is

22 Justin Willis 2002: 102. Cit. in Locatelli 2009: 233. See also Pankhurst 1974: 159–179.

23 Leiris 1988: 45, 81.

24 Handwritten letter in Arabic with an attached Italian translation, 5 Settembre 1917. Archivio Storico Diplomatico del Ministero degli Affari Esteri (ASDMAE), Archivio Eritrea (AE), 1880–1917, Pacco 1022 (Missioni Politiche—Varie—El Morgani), Fasc. 10 Famiglia El Morgani, 1895–1917. Women's performances and theatre representations assumed a similar "private dimension" in the 1940s. "We were playing in our homes", a female performer emphasized in order to defend her good name in the light of her performances at *suwa* houses. See Matzke 2003: 78.

25 Miran also published Figures 18 and 19 in his monograph on Massawa (Miran 2009: 210–211). He provides very interesting accounts of similar performances—which were very likely to have been *zār* sessions –in Massawa which Italian travellers observed during the early colonial occupation. It is important to make it clear, however, that these pictures

available that clarifies precisely what this dance was, we do know that possession cults—such as the *zār*—were very popular at shrines at the time, especially among slave women, who were involved in the cult's leadership and who, according to a number of authors, were responsible for introducing it into the Middle East. Between the 19th and early twentieth centuries, the *zār* became widespread in Cairo thanks to black female slaves or descendants of slaves, who would perform it at shrines.[26] In early twentieth century Sudan, *zār* and *ḏikr* religious practices were usually performed side by side as complementary expressions of religious devotion on the occasion of Islamic holidays.[27] According to Pamela Constantinides, *zār* spread in Sudan during the Ottoman Conquest (1820–21), developed during the Ottoman-Egyptian period, was repressed during the Mahdiyya, but re-emerged after the establishment of the Anglo-Egyptian Condominium.[28] In Sudan and Egypt, the greatest development of *zār* coincided with the rise and spread of Islamic brotherhoods as the main expression of popular Islam. The term *ḥaḍra*, which denotes Sufi rituals, is often employed to "describe a *zār* session and the holding of *zār* ceremonies at, or in association with, visits to the tombs of Sufi saints—powerful sources of mystical blessings".[29] This is also the case with the so-called *zār ḥaḍra* rituals that are still performed in Ethiopia today. In this context, *zār ḥaḍra* refers to a weekly gathering ritual attended by possessed women that takes place regularly at the shrine. It is a session of prayers, chanting, singing, and dancing, the aim of which is to appease a possessing spirit.[30]

European travellers to Egypt were already reporting on the popularity of ecstatic practices during religious dances or *ḏikr* in the 1860s and 1870s. Klunzinger wrote that "women have adopted a practice (the *zār* cult) which is said to have been introduced by Abyssinian female slaves, and which gradually spread to such an extent that the government felt itself called upon to forbid it". Nevertheless, it is still common among the high and low, especially in Upper Egypt.[31] In effect, by the turn of the century the government and the

---

(Figures 17–19) were taken at Sittī ʿAlawiyya's residence on the occasion of a "women's fantasy" performed in Keren (as observed by Fioccardi), and not in Massawa.

26 Natvig reports in particular the case of a shrine called Šayḫ Bidak. Natvig 1987: 672.

27 While "today the two are firmly distinguished and those who consider themselves pious condemn *zār* as unislamic," *zār*'s diminished status as a practice of popular Islam may owe much to British conservatism (Boddy 2007: 48).

28 Constantinides 1991: 85, 98, 99.

29 Lewis 1991: 13.

30 I am referring here to Zeleke's ethnographic study of a Sufi shrine, the custodian of which was the daughter of the shaykh who founded the centre at Tiru Sina. Zeleke 2010: 63–84.

31 Natvig 1991: 12.

ʿulamāʾ of the Al-Azhar University Mosque were worried about its popularity. A variety of pamphlet and newspaper articles condemning these "common practices" were published in Cairo.[32] By the time of Anglo-Egyptian rule, the *zār* had become so popular that it was seen as a threat to orthodox and legalist Islam. It was banned during the Mahdiyya, and it was also denounced under the Condominium by the conservative Egyptian *ʿulamāʾ* whom the British appointed to official posts in an attempt to marginalize charismatic faiths. Together with a section of the Muslim elite, the British considered *zār* to be one of the "superstitious" practices that marked Sudanese women as more backward than Sudanese men.[33] The Italian official Fioccardi's assertion that this highly popular performance at Sittī ʿAlawiyya's residence in Keren was not punishable, as should have been the case, is especially meaningful if one considers that these ecstatic performances were seen as dangerous and destabilizing for political establishments, and that rulers periodically attempted to ban them in the region.[34] As we have previously mentioned, this was also the case in Sudan during the Mahdiyya, where *zār* was banned and accused of being unislamic. Similarly, the Mahdī was opposed to women's participating in Sufi sessions.[35] In Egypt some years later, the Government attempted to forbid women from performing it at shrines where it was popular.[36] In Cairo, a *fatwā* was even proclaimed against *zār*.[37] In 1878, Emperor Yohannes IV outlawed *zār* dance sessions in Ethiopia.[38] Also Marcel Griaule reported that the Government had issued a proclamation to restrict it. In the 1920s and 1930s, the British administration—granting petitions from a mainly male middle-class section of the Muslim elite—banned "*zār* theatre" and "*zār* parties" performed by lower-class urban women who were living in Aden, but came mainly from Ethiopia and East Africa.[39] Spirit possession in Ethiopia has been interpreted by Michel Leiris (1958) as a cathartic externalization of alterity, and as a theatre of alterity. The colonial view that portrayed the "Bilen fantasy" sheds light on women's performances as a popular attraction for Africans and foreigners alike. One of the female dances that used to be staged at Sittī ʿAlawiyya's home is immortalized in a series of photographs (Figures 17, 18 and 19) that show an

---

32 Constantinides 1991: 87.

33 Body, Wombs and Alien Spirits, p. 132. Constantinides 1991: 87, 91, 93, 96, 97.

34 See, for example, Kapteijns and Spaulding 1996.

35 Voll 1979: 156.

36 Natvig 1991: 178.

37 Muḥammad Rašīd Riḍā's *fatwā* on *zār* is printed in Salah al-Din al-Munajjid and Yusuf Q. Khuri 1970: 48–9, see Natvig 1998: 173.

38 Abbink 2010: 185.

39 Kapteijns and Spaulding 1996.

FIGURE 17 *Arabic Fantasy at* Sceriffa Alauia's *residence, (a).*
E. LO GIUDICE COLLECTION, 47. ISIAO ARCHIVE, ROME.

FIGURE 18 *Arabic Fantasy at* Sceriffa Alauia's *residence, (b).*
PAVONI SOCIAL CENTRE COLLECTION, ASMARA.

FIGURE 19 *Waiting for the Arabic Fantasy at* Sceriffa Alauia's *residence.*
PAVONI SOCIAL CENTRE COLLECTION, ASMARA.

audience of mainly veiled women watching other unveiled women dancing on the patio of Sittī 'Alawiyya's residence. In a region such as Keren, where most residents had recently converted to Islam, the simple dresses of the unveiled dancers might offer "proof" of their servility and different religious belonging. The veiled women in public are clapping to follow a rhythmic dance. It is interesting to note that the men and children are at the bottom of the picture, showing that the performance space was dominantly feminine, but also mixed, and yet if we look at the clothing, social class distinctions may be observed between the lower social strata and a number of aristocratic women. The Bilen socio-political order was hierarchical, and distinguished the warrior aristocracy from the serfs, who were mainly farmers.[40] A feminine "stigma" of the servitude was related to custom. While it was considered possible for a serf woman to turn to prostitution, this was unheard of for aristocratic women, who were asked to guard their chastity and were never seen outside unveiled, while serf girls used to leave their faces uncovered.[41] The mixed-gender public watching the show includes foreign and indigenous travellers and settlers,

40 Smidt 2003: 586.

41 This "stigma" was observed in Beni 'Amer country. See Nadel 1945: 82.

but with a noteworthy separation between the female and male spaces for the audience, with veiled women sitting in front of the unveiled female dancers, while the boys and men are mostly standing at the back.

As we have seen in the previous chapter, the imposition of women's spaces of empowerment around Sittī ʿAlawiyya lay at the heart of the harsh criticism that a section of the Muslim and male elites levelled at her at the Keren mosque. Her residence had also become a "public" space where strangers mingled, and promiscuous conduct there was the justification used by the *imām* of the Keren mosque to challenge her religious leadership.[42]

The captions accompanying this series of photographs describe the scene as an "Arabic fantasy at Sittī ʿAlawiyya's residence". Beyond the "ethnic" ambiguity and the ambivalence of colonial narratives in which the "Bilen" fantasy is now identified as "Arabic", they portray the performances that used to take place at her residence, attracting a substantial public of mainly Africans. In the background, we can also discern the stealthy gazes of curious men watching the show from beyond the walls of the residence. This curiosity and "exoticism" would have made her popular with an audience that included both the local population and foreigners. In the disdainful words of the Commissioner of Keren: "Many visitors go to see her because they have heard about her, just as they go to see a rare animal, because among the things that should be visited in Keren, in addition to the gardens, the School of Arts and Crafts and their pleasant environs, there is the Sceriffa, and over and over again the unpunished Bilen fantasy that she habitually lavishes on her visitors".[43] His crushing remarks draw attention to a taste for exoticism and tourist fashions with regard to both her character and the women's performances and dances that took place on the patio of her residence. The colonial gaze compares the shows at *Sceriffa*'s home to a "freak show" like those that were widespread in Europe from the early 1900s. In reality, considering that the captions are in Italian, it is highly likely that these photos were shown in museums or colonial exhibitions for Italian audiences; at that time, shows and exhibitions of "Zoos Humains"

---

42 Handwritten letter in Arabic with an attached Italian translation, 5 Settembre 1917. Archivio Storico Diplomatico del Ministero degli Affari Esteri (ASDMAE), Archivio Eritrea (AE), 1880–1917 Pacco 1022 (Missioni Politiche—Varie—El Morgani), Fasc. 10 Famiglia El Morgani, 1895–1917.

43 Colonia Eritrea, Commissariato di Cheren, Riservato-Urgente, Al Signor Reggente il Governo della Colonia. Oggetto: Grave dissidio seguito da ingiurie tra Morgani e Sceriffa, Cheren, 6 settembre 1917, Archivio Storico Diplomatico del Ministero degli Affari Esteri (ASDMAE), Archivio Eritrea (AE), 1880–1917, Pacco 1022 (Missioni Politiche—Varie—El Morgani), Fasc. 10 Famiglia El Morgani, 1895–1917.

were fashionable with European audiences and had become a part of popular culture through mass media such as the press, literature, paintings, postcards, and photography.[44] Beyond the folklore and tourist-oriented fashion for these practices at Sufi centres, on which colonial photography has shed light, the audiences attending the performances draw our attention once again to the curiosity, leisure, and entertainment dimension that also captivated Africans, and not only European settlers. Last but not least, the devotional dimension evidently played a pivotal role, despite the fact that the colonial gaze, which was marked by a high degree of scepticism towards African beliefs, tends to overshadow it.

Visiting a Fashionable, Cosmopolitan Woman

The residence of the *šarīfa* in Massawa was built and expanded by the Italians together with the *qubba* of Sīdī Hāšim, which was constructed with funds from both the Muslim community of Massawa and the first Governor of Eritrea, Ferdinando Martini. The residence was a holy space around which social events were held, as well as a gathering place in general and a sort of informal institution. People visited her for various reasons: personal, religious, and social, or to pray, or to ask for financial support or intervention and to resolve problems with the Italian authorities. The *šarīfa* welcomed people from different socio-cultural backgrounds at her residence, whether they were local or foreign, Christian and Muslim leaders and notables, colonial authorities, travellers, soldiers, merchants, or the poor and needy.[45]

One Italian traveller reported that "until recently in our Colony there was no visitor, even a hasty one, that did not go to Keren to visit the woman who represented a living curiosity, because Italian travellers certainly do not cross the threshold of Sceriffa Alauia el Morgani's home to be given a holy title or to make an offering to the holy descendent of the Prophet".[46] Along the prism of the colonial gaze, the "curiosity" and tourist dimension of her image is

44 Bancel, Blanchard, Boëtsch et al. 2004. On colonial museums and exhibitions in Italy, see Labanca 1992.

45 See Caniglia 1940 and my interviews with Šarīfa ʿAlawiyya al-Mīrġanī, daughter of Sīdī Ǧaʿfar al-Mīrġanī, a namesake of Šarīfa ʿAlawiyya bint Hāšim al-Mīrġanī (Cairo, May 2009); Hāšim Muḥammad ʿAlī Blenai, 102 years of age, a follower of the Ḫatmiyya (Massawa, March 2009). ʿAbd al-Raḥīm ʿUṯmān Kekiya (Keren, March 2009).

46 Massara 1921: 306–307. In around 1919, according to Massara, she left the colony to live at her sister's home in Suakin.

stressed, to the detriment of her socio-religious authority, but in actual fact her domestic space was an attractive place not only for believers, but also for non-believers such as Italian journalists, colonial officials, and travellers. These visits provoked rumours among the local indigenous people, who were particularly impressed by her success and the gifts she received from the Government in Asmara. Until the 1920s, her home in Keren was a hub for travellers wishing to visit "a living curiosity",[47] but later on, visits to her residence near Massawa became more frequent. In the late 1930s, Renzo Martinelli, an Italian journalist, led a trip to Eritrea and wrote a book about it, dedicating a section to his visit to her home in Hetumlo—a suburb of Massawa—where her main residence lay close to her father's shrine and the mosque. An entire chapter of his book is dedicated to "La Sceriffa Alauia". He writes: "they told me it would be a good idea to visit *Sceriffa Alauia*. She seems to be a very interesting woman … there is no Muslim coming to Eritrea from the Arabic coast, or from every African and Asian country, that does not believe it to be his duty to go to Hetumlo to prostrate himself in front of ʿAlawiyya or leave a donation in cash or in kind".[48] The visits usually originated from advice from indigenous people, but also from Italian authority figures such as the Governor of Eritrea, Giuseppe Daodiace, who suggested to Caniglia that he should visit her. Italian men who went were highly impressed by her personality and lively intelligence.[49] During the same period, Caniglia wrote a book on the Ḫatmiyya entitled "la Sceriffa di Massawa. La tariqa catmia", in which he wrote at length on the everyday religious activities of this "exceptional" woman, which were marked by an intense timetable of prayers and visits. He reported that in the mornings, she devoted herself to reciting ritual prayers and reading the Qur'an and her grandfather's writings so that she would be able to teach them to believers, after which political authorities and heads of tribes visited and were invited to discuss issues with her and to ask for her help with solving problems and disputes among and within various communities. She played an important role, recalls Kekiya, "a sweet, beautiful role". She solved matters relating to land, territories and agriculture and problems between tribes and families, acting as an intermediary. According to Kekiya's oral testimony: "if there was a serious problem to be solved, people turned to her and she sometimes acted alone or sometimes

47 Colonia Eritrea, Commissariato Regionale di Cheren, 9 agosto 1910. Archivio Storico Diplomatico del Ministero degli Affari Esteri (ASDMAE), Archivio Eritrea (AE), 1886–1912, Pacco 43 (Morgani-Adigrat—Varie Eritrea), Fasc. 1 Morgani (1886–1911). See also Massara 1921.

48 Martinelli 1930: 49.

49 Caniglia 1940: 13; Martinelli 1930: 53.

spoke to the Italians to resolve it. When people wanted something from the Italian government, they would go to her and ask her to intervene or to provide help. She played an important role with Italy. When there was a problem with the Italians, people went to talk to her. When people had any kind of problem they addressed it to her. Even the political authorities, such as the *shumagalle*, sometimes turned to her. She spoke to the Italian authorities and the problem was usually fixed".[50] In the afternoons, recalls Caniglia, she used to receive the *ḫulafāʾ* of the Ḫatmiyya to discuss not only religious matters, but also civil and political topics. She welcomed her visitors in an open-air courtyard that was generally used for communal prayers. She listened to their demands, providing advice and "words of hope and solace", drawing inspiration from the teachings of her father, whose shrines and memory she guarded jealously.[51]

Following a religious ceremonial that can still be found in Ethiopian Sufi centres today, she welcomed visitors with prayers of preaching and blessings. Believers imitated her, raising their hands and preaching God to realize their desires.[52] The afternoon was often the time she reserved for visits that might also include European personalities such as Italian journalists, who were usually received in her garden of lemon and orange trees. In the 1930s, European travellers recounted that they were impressed by her fashion, and their accounts go into great detail, from the furniture in her house to her eccentric clothes. Martinelli, for example, reports that he sat with her on two chairs on two rich and very colourful carpets embellished with red and turquoise gems. Caniglia recalls that he conducted his interviews with her on comfortable Italian-style leather armchairs in her paved garden, which was covered with soft, wide Persian carpets. She offered him a perfumed coffee served in an elegant silver set that she proudly told him was a gift from Mussolini himself. Travellers and oral accounts focus on her precious, vividly colourful and rich clothing, and also report on her impressive personality.[53]

She was, as recalled on 28 October 1935 by an Italian Red Cross nurse, Elena Pesenti Agliardi, who visited her twice with other Sisters of the Red Cross, "the

50 Interview ʿAbd al-Raḥīm ʿUṯmān Kekiya on March 2009 in Keren.

51 Caniglia 1940: 33–34. During the conflict to gain religious leadership of the order, she claimed that she was ready to have her head cut off rather than see anybody other than herself in command at her father's mosque. Colonia Eritrea, Commissariato Regionale di Keren, 20 October 1910. Archivio Storico Diplomatico del Ministero degli Affari Esteri (ASDMAE), Archivio Eritrea (AE), 1886–1912, Pacco 43 (Morgani-Adigrat—Varie Eritrea), Fasc. 1 Morgani (1886–1911).

52 Caniglia 1940: 49. The ethnographic study of the Tiru Sina shrine in Ethiopia led by Meron Zeleke explores the role that women played in conflict resolution in their capacity as guardians of shrines in detail. Zeleke 2010: 63–84.

53 Martinelli 1930: 51; Caniglia 1940: 39.

simulacrum of Muslims' political and religious sovereignty (…) Very clever, cultured, authoritative and resolute, she has an energy that is well-suited to a man, and she also has the value and presence of mind of a man". They visited the shrines and mosque of her father in Hetumlo with Sittī ʿAlawiyya in their bare feet. They were then introduced to a simple living room in which there was a jumble of objects and European furniture "in bad taste", including a sewing machine. "La Sceriffa"—she recalled—"is a woman of an uncertain age. She wears a white skirt of starched cotton, over which she has a tunic of yellow and mauve cloth around her face, with a blue veil, and a shawl of red and yellow manilla on her head covers her hair and falls on to her shoulders. She wears a beautiful chiseled golden girdle. We are warmly received and she responds to our bows and kisses with a Muslim hug."[54] The headscarf merits separate discussion, because veiling and purdah were specific patterns of behaviour that identified an aristocratic Arab status in Northeast African societies. As I have pointed out, the issue of veils was one element of the debate around her challenged religious authority. Her rivals contested this authority, making the point that women's bodies should be kept from the gaze of strangers, while her supporters stressed the fact that she remained carefully veiled. A seasoned traveller like Martinelli noted that her veil was merely symbolic, and that her black Sudanese face was mainly uncovered, unlikely other Muslim women from the region, who would hide their faces completely except for their eyes. Her chest, on the other hand, was covered with incredibly rich silks and satins in a dozen colours. Her dresses were a combination of precious clothes. From under her skirt, "vaguely Japanese black and gold shoes peeped out of very tight silk pants trimmed with satin".[55]

Caniglia, on the other hand, underlines her austerity and her simple, rather small figure, wound up in a gold and red chlamys. She shows "only part of her face, from which her large, intelligent eyes stand out, full of sweetness and expressiveness".[56] Massara noticed that she had a "small but well-proportioned body, with two large eyes and an expressive look, a nice smile … she leaves a pleasant impression that a visitor has met not only a venerated woman of high lineage, but also one of noteworthy and extraordinary excellence …".[57] In the 1930s, the Italian press reported official ceremonies in Massawa that she attended in her capacity as one of the leading African figures of authority. Descriptions of her look depict an eclectic—and somewhat surrealistic and

54 De Carli 2016.

55 Martinelli 1930: 52. To me, these "tight silk pants trimmed with satin" recall the Indian style pants worn by women in Harar.

56 Caniglia 1940: 38.

57 Massara 1921: 306-307.

FIGURE 20 *Portrait of Sittī ʿAlawiyya.*
PHOTOGRAPHER UNKNOWN. MĪRĠANĪ FAMILY PRIVATE COLLECTION, CAIRO.

fantastic—fashion style. One reporter writes that on one occasion "she wore a full dress with black vest, yellow silk shorts and black embroidered slippers. Her head was adorned with a blue medieval zendado worn over a majestic golden crown ... she was welcomed by the authorities and sat on an armchair, with a silk umbrella above her".[58] Another journalist described how on the same occasion she sat like "a queen upon a throne, in muslin veils that covered her body with a confusion of light colours, pinks and blues. She wore precious filigree jewels and (...) held a strange sunshade of refined carved ivory in her hand. Her wide embroidered trousers were tucked into fine open-work socks and she wore Turkish slippers embroidered with metal thread".[59]

Dress has always been one of the most important indicators of class, status, and ethnicity differences in East African coastal society, and the importance of dressing up to one's status, be it actual or desired, was widely recognized in daily practice; indeed, changes in clothing habits was also associated with changing social, cultural, and religious identity.[60] Sittī ʿAlawiyya made great use of dressing up and of adopting and mixing a huge variety of items from different socio-cultural and geographical backgrounds and areas. Her colourful and somewhat jumbled style consisted in an original blend of military, Italian, Christian nuns', Arabic, Turkish, Japanese, Persian, and Indian clothes and accessories, and resulted in a particularly eclectic approach that well expressed her deep cosmopolitan aptitudes and actively participated in fashioning her charismatic image. Besides, her particular fashion and furnishings were an expression of her transnational networks and her openness to the material culture of her overseas visitors.

The Marchioness Targiani, the National Representative of Volunteer Nurses of the Italian Red Cross, also had the occasion to meet the *Sceriffa*, and described her as "a woman who has a great influence upon Muslims. She is considered to be a descendent of the Prophet, but even if she is not, she has the high dignity of her race and character and rich custom, and is accompanied by an interpreter, even though we have the feeling that she understand Italian very well". The Marchioness was accompanying the Princess of Piemonte on her mission to Africa in 1936, and it was during their travels that she went to visit Sittī ʿAlawiyya with the Princess and some volunteer nurses (Figure 21). She recalled the local people's welcome ceremony—a "fantasy"—for the Princess while stressing their feminine whiteness in contrast with the indigenous

58 Perbellini 1936.

59 Barzini 1936.

60 Fair 1998: 46.

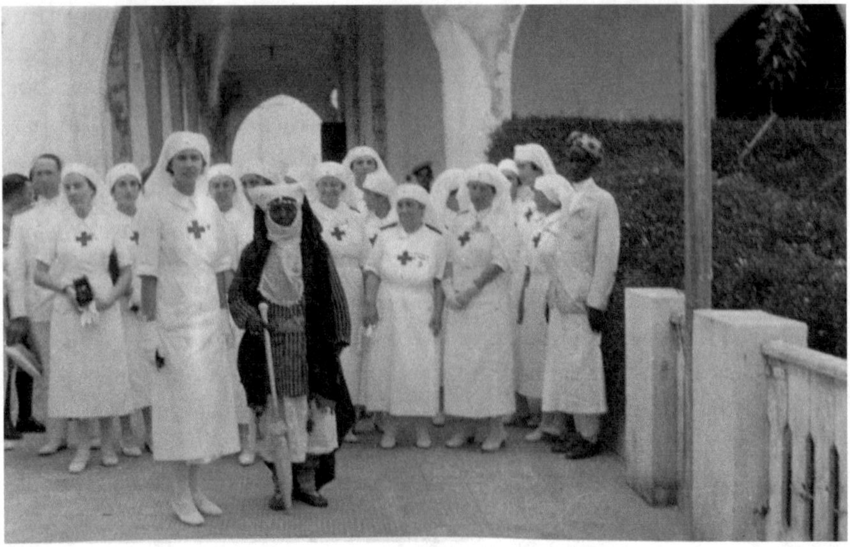

FIGURE 21 *Sittī ʿAlawiyya and the Princess of Piemonte dressed in Red Cross uniform, with other Red Cross nurses (1936).*
PRIVATE COLLECTION OF OTTAVIO DE CARLI, BRESCIA.

blackness: "[…] we pass through Otmlo (*sic*), an indigenous suburb, where all the inhabitants are gathered together and lined up in their multi-coloured costumes. They are of different religions and races, and they wail, clap and play very diverse instruments. It is a spontaneous show of joy for the white Princess, who passes among her black subjects, and in the expression on their colourless faces we see all the expression of their souls. Down the street we pass, and we arrive all of a sudden at the *Sceriffa*'s small dominion. Despite the morning hour, she has organized a party, a celebration, usually called a *fantasia*. It is a true fantasy, a circle of indigenous playing, shouting, and warbling, and in the middle the outstanding dance group is clearly visible. There are three or four women, among the most beautiful, with their festive costumes, almost naked in the draperies of their graceful tunics. Their dance is a rite that is performed at events of sorrow as well as joy, but their movements and attitudes always have a refined and deep character. We watch it perplexed, but do not laugh. The *Sceriffa* is proud to show the Princess the small community of Muslims she rules, and with a broad but resolute gesture she invites her to honour her home. It is a strange residence, a little disjointed, but our government has provided for its restoration. She introduces us into a living room in which she has collected a variety of furniture of local colour mixed with a great variety of

FIGURE 22 *Sittī ʿAlawiyya and Renzo Martinelli at her residence in Hetumlo (1927).* PHOTO PUBLISHED IN MARTINELLI (1930: 55).

FIGURE 23 *Sittī ʿAlawiyya and Renzo Martinelli at her residence in Hetumlo (1927).* PHOTO PUBLISHED IN MARTINELLI (1930: 52).

modern decorations such as a strongbox and an ice-box, and all of this has some significance for her."[61]

Meetings such as this one between African authorities and European personalities called for diplomatic ceremonies that included exchanges of gifts, and offered interpreters and photographers a remarkable role. Even though she was probably fluent in Italian, the duty to provide a reliable interpreter and personal scribe was a part of the ceremony. The interpreter used by Martinelli immediately expressed his respect for her by kissing the tail of her dress.[62] Interviews with journalists, travellers and Italian officials usually ended with a moment for taking photographs, and in fact, as we will see in the following

61 Brayda Gozzi and Zangrossi 2012: 268. I would like to thank Ottavio de Carli, who provided me with his reference as well as access to his precious private collection, which includes photographs and memories written by his great aunt Elena Pesenti.

62 Martinelli 1930: 51.

chapters, the colonial media and photographers gave her particular visibility by filming and broadcasting the visits that journalists such as Renzo Martinelli and Giuseppe Caniglia, and popular Italian figures such as the Princess of Piemonte, Edda Mussolini and the Duke of the Abruzzi, periodically made to her residence.

Sufi women's "fantasy" and performances were not only a part of the colonial set and a product of the colonial imagination; women actively participated in their own empowerment by playing creatively with their audiences' imaginations. In any event, although they always provoked rumours and social pressures, female performances and agency were staged on different sets in spaces within private residences until they were publicized visually in the mass media.

At first, Sittī ʿAlawiyya grew in popularity in the region thanks to her charismatic power and feminine performances such as dance and later *zār* "theatre" or *zār "party"*, but her "hexcentric" character gradually attained a transnational level, and she gained more and more visibility in the public arena by ascending to the colonial stage. Indeed, the Italian media publicized her impressive character through different outlets from the press to travel literature and photography exhibitions, and the more modern visual technologies such as the cinema and newsreels.

CHAPTER 6

Growing Visibility in the Political Arena

Women's Bodies, Photography, and Colonialism

The introduction of photography into North-Eastern Africa quickly assumed an important political function. It became a powerful means of legitimizing, as well as delegitimizing, political leadership, and its spread across Ethiopia produced a veritable war of images.[1] Photography was a visual revolution for 20th century popular culture, and the visual representation of women's bodies was a part of these changes, specifically in the perception of bodies and sexuality. As we have seen, erotic photography representing African women became an expression of the violence of the occupying powers. Several series of photographs portrayed women's bodies as a metaphor for the occupied territories, the possession of indigenous bodies becoming an expression of overseas possession. Visual texts such as photographs and postcards have been analysed in order to shed light on colonial discourses on women's bodies and their representation in African lands under colonial rule;[2] in particular, parallels have been drawn between cartography and woman's bodies, and between photography and colonialism.[3] Erotic photography and postcards showing sensual naked African women's bodies in front of occupied territory are examples of what Sontag called a *predatory act* of taking a photograph, in which female bodies became a sort of metaphor for African landscapes. Indeed, photography and postcards mirror a process of commodification and objectification of female bodies, and have been interpreted as an example of the sexualization of colonial domination, as the expression of a sort of appropriation and possession of feminized colonial subjects. Here, colonialism is a true expression of the violence of the gaze. As Sontag put it, "like guns and cars, cameras are fantasy-machines whose use is addictive ... Still, there is something predatory in the act of taking a picture. To photograph people is to violate them, by seeing them as they never see themselves, by having knowledge of

* This chapter is an extended and revised version of my article 'Femmes, images et pouvoir en contexte colonial: Le cas de l'Érythrée dans l'entre-deux-guerres' (Bruzzi *forthcoming*).

1 Pankhurst 1992: 234–41 and Sohier 2011, 2012.

2 On the Italian colonies, see in particular Palma 1999; Palma 2005b: 39–69; Goglia 1989; Ponzanesi 2012: 155–172.

3 Romani 2008.

 | DOI 10.1163/9789004356160_008

them they can never have; it turns people into objects that can be symbolically possessed".[4] Colonial violence was metaphorically staged through photographs of African women's bodies: the colonial empire was feminized and represented as a metaphor of domination over virgin territories ready to be conquered by a virile, masculine civilization. In this way, taking photographs became an aggressive sexual act, a sort of appropriation and possession of the Other: the colonial subject.[5] Apart from asymmetrical sexual and interracial relationships between white men and black women in the colonial context, the weight of other differences such as religious affiliation and social status should also be taken into account when deconstructing the highly heterogeneous category of the African woman. Moreover, even though images became a privileged medium for representational colonial encounters, their interpretation also seems ambiguous; indeed, a single image may be susceptible to a multiplicity of interpretations, depending on where the focus is directed for its production, circulation, and audience. The use of visual images taken by both the colonial authorities and Sittī ʿAlawiyya sheds light on the visual representation of African women for their political empowerment. The media were also employed as a way of asserting her authority in the political and religious arenas, both regionally and internationally. Apart from the homogenous category of colonized women, one should pay attention to differences in race, class, and religion as portrayed in photographs. Visual images, which are ambiguous and ambivalent by nature, are of great interest because they are able to express the multitude of representations and images that circulated around a single female figure. On the one hand, they explain the use of her image in the context of the colonial political agenda, while on the other, Sittī ʿAlawiyya was always an active agent who used a political and public image to foster her charismatic power. Her visual representation also complicates the previous mainstream colonial representation of Eritrean and Ethiopian women as anonymous objects of colonial photography, and casts doubt on it; she is shown as an active subject who creatively appropriates colonial and visual technology such as photography and cinematography to gain popularity, and, maybe, to communicate her counter-narrative through the way she represents her body.

4 Sontag 1992.

5 Sontag 1992. See also Bini 2003; Ponzanesi 2005. Mallek Alloula (1981) analysed French colonial photographic postcards of Algerian women from the late 19th and early 20th centuries that staged erotic images of harems and belly dancers. The author focuses mostly on Orientalist imaginary and proposes a new interpretation of these postcards, arguing that they no longer represent Algeria or Algerian women, but rather perpetuate a harem fantasy through which French male colonists viewed North Africa.

FIGURE 24 *Sceriffa Alauia and her followers.*
PAVONI SOCIAL CENTRE COLLECTION, ASMARA.

FIGURE 25 *Said Giafer and his caliphs.*
PAVONI SOCIAL CENTRE COLLECTION, ASMARA.

The first colonial photograph known to portray the *šarīfa* is part of a private library collection (Figure 24). It was owned by an Italian priest in Asmara.[6] Miran has dated it in the 1920s (but does not furnish any particular explanation).[7] The caption in Italian is: "Sceriffa Alauia [*sic*] and her followers" (*La Sceriffa Alauia ed il suo seguito*). The Italian term *sceriffa* ("sheriff") recalls the idea of an officer responsible for keeping the peace, and appears in colonial reports and journals as a customary transposition of the noun *šarīfa*, her common Arabic title. The language of the legend—which leads to a particular reading of the image—shows that the photograph's publisher was seeking to take it to an Italian audience in exhibitions. It appears to be a studio photograph: she is posing in the centre of the image with a group of people: armed guards, servants, and dignitaries, and among them several women on her right. The sword she holds in her right hand in the centre of the image follows a model of other contemporary images of groups portraying indigenous male dignitaries. The current representative of the brotherhood in Keren and the *šarīfa*'s descendants in Cairo have questioned the authenticity of this photograph.[8] They did not recognize her because according to them, it does not conform to her official image in that her veil is not covering her chin, as it usually did. In other words, their questions about this portrait's authenticity relate to an "unorthodox" aspect of her public image, which was also pointed out by our interlocutors. In fact, it is very different from the others we have, in which she appears veiled, with her chin carefully covered. Could this photograph, the author of which is unfortunately unknown, actually be a colonial fiction designed to illustrate an exotic cliché for an Italian audience? The way the image is posed reflects the style of the photograph of another group of indigenous dignitaries showing her rival and nephew, Sīdī Ǧaʿfar al-Mīrġanī (Figure 25). The format of the caption suggests that the two photographs would have belonged to the same series of photographs taken for colonial purposes such as exhibitions. While there may be a similarity in the layout of the two photographs, however, the authenticity of the portrait of Sīdī Ǧaʿfar is unquestioned. He appears in person in the centre of the image, surrounded by his entourage, among whom are probably representatives of the brotherhood (Figure 25).

---

6 Pavoni Social Centre Library (Asmara).

7 Figure 24 has also been reproduced in Miran 2009.

8 Interviews with Aḥmad al-Mīrġanī, a descendent of Šarīfa ʿAlawiyya and grandson of Ǧaʿfar al-Mīrġanī (Cairo, May 2009), with *ḫalīfa* Aḥmad, the current representative of the Ḫatmiyya in Keren (Keren, March 2009), and with Šarīfa ʿAlawiyya's a descendent of Šarīfa ʿAlawiyya and daughter of Ǧaʿfar al-Mīrġanī (Cairo, May 2009).

If these two photographs date from the 1920s, they would have been taken at a time when the two authorities were competing for religious leadership in Keren. As we have seen, the authority of the *šarīfa* had been challenged during this period. The common arguments her rival and his entourage employed to discredit her leadership related to gender roles and the habits that would be appropriate for a respectable Muslim woman in a public space. They called on Islamic orthodoxy in order to delegitimize the public and political authority of women. In particular, they criticized the fact that the *šarīfa* was accustomed to receiving foreign visitors at her residence, arguing that the female body should be shielded from prying eyes, and that religion forbade its being shown to people who were not a part of the family circle.[9]

Notwithstanding the debate regarding the authenticity of this first photograph of her, the representation it portrays is still worthy of note. It introduces to the Italian audience—to which it was apparently addressed—a woman of power with a sword encircled by armed men, women, and other "followers". The sword, which is a recurring symbolic element of colonial portraits of local dignitaries, is the queen of all Islamic weapons: it is a sign of the power of the warrior. In the 7th century, Ḫālid ibn Wālīd, the Arab general who led the first battle against the Meccan Qurayshites, received the epithet "Sword of Islam" from the Prophet. According to al-Ṭabarī, the Prophet had seven types of sword.[10] Oral stories reported by her descendants in Cairo relate that the *šarīfa* owned several weapons, which were mostly gifts she had received, including from the Italian Government.[11] There were also rumours that she always carried a gun made of gold,[12] a precious metal that is not always associated with orthodoxy in Islam. These two references—wearing a veil in a particular way and carrying a gold gun—introduce the question of the relationship between religious orthodoxy and the legitimacy of her authority, a recurring issue throughout her life.

Apart from the controversy regarding the authenticity of the photograph "La sceriffa Alauia [*sic*] ed il suo seguito", we can look at other undoubtedly authentic early portraits of her belonging to the Luce Institute. Established by Luciano

9 On this issue, see also Bruzzi 2006; Bruzzi and Zeleke 2015.

10 Chebel 1995: 55.

11 A letter of greeting (only the Italian translation is available; the original Arabic version is not) from Šarīfa ʿAlawiyya was sent to Mussolini for his gift, a carbine, in 1938. Archivio Storico Diplomatico del Ministero degli Affari Esteri (ASDMAE), Archivio Storico Del Ministero Dell'Africa Italiana (ASMAI), Dir. Gen. Affari Politici, el. III, cart. 103. Borruso 1997: 41.

12 Interview with Aḥmad al-Mīrġanī on May 2009 in Cairo.

De Feo in Rome in 1924, the Istituto Luce (Educational Cinematographic Union) was a public entity funded entirely by the public sector—but with private legal status—devoted to distributing films with an educational and informative purpose. Mussolini himself chose the name *Luce* and immediately saw this media tool as an important ally for the Fascist regime's instruction, education and propaganda[13] The first unit of the LUCE Photographic Service, which was created in 1927, was the news ("*cinegiornali*", newsreel) department, from which a number of early images of the *šarīfa* circulated. These photographs (Figures 26 and 27) were taken during the East African travels of Prince Luigi Amedeo of Savoy-Aosta (1873–1933), Duke of the Abruzzi, an Italian nobleman and popular explorer (who appears on the left of the pictures). The *šarīfa* appears at his side in two photographs, while a third commemorates a similar meeting between the Duke and her relative, Sīdī Ǧaʿfar al-Mīrġanī. Unlike in the previous photograph, the authenticity of which has been challenged, she is not posing for the camera this time: the movement of the subjects in the images testifies to the speed with which the photographs were taken. They date from May 1927, and were taken on the patio of her residence close to Massawa, the main port of Eritrea, when the Duke travelled into the region. Prince Luigi Amedeo of Savoy-Aosta, Duke of the Abruzzi, who was a grandson of King Vittorio Emanuele II of Italy, was a mountaineer, sailor, and explorer from the Royal House of Savoy. In 1918, he left to "discover" Somalia, where he finally married a Somali Princess and spent the last years of his life.[14] These images, which were shot with a colonial camera, were taken in 1927, and show the *šarīfa*'s first official meeting with such a popular Italian figure from the colonial establishment.

The photographs were taken near the large house where she lived, which, according to her descendants, was built by the Italian authorities, together with another building that was reserved for receiving guests and pilgrims. Her house also included a mosque, a patio, and the shrine where her father was buried.[15] These two photographs show the *šarīfa* veiled (we should notice that her chin and neck are carefully covered here), with a decorated scarf across her forehead. She is wearing shoes and socks, a mark of class and status differences in society, because the absence of shoes was an immediately visible sign that identified a member of the servile class. The shape of her body is completely concealed from the public eye thanks to the rich, ornate clothes she wore,

13 Laura 2000: 21.

14 Basile 2010; Dell'Osa 2010.

15 In fact, also according to colonial sources, her father's shrine was built with government funding. Romandini 1984.

FIGURE 26 *The Duke of the Abruzzi's travels in Abyssinia. The sceriffa Alaluja El Morgani* (*sic*) *pays homage to the Duke of the Abruzzi.* Reparto Attualità: 1927. 07.05.1927. La sceriffa Alaluja o Alabuia El Morgani accompagnata dai rappresentanti della missione—campo medio, cod. foto: *A00000394*.
ISTITUTO LUCE CINECITTÀ HISTORICAL ARCHIVE, ROME.

which marked her high social status.[16] One more detail attracts our attention: the parasol a servant or guard is holding next to her. A sign of sovereignty in the

16 On issues of dress as social and status markers, see in particular Fair 1998: 63–94. She points out (on p. 74) that "in 19th-century Zanzibar, clothing served as an important and visually immediate signifier of class and status difference. As is the case with many of the world's cultures, the clothing of wealthy members of society was far more ornate than that of the working or servile classes. Islam, as the religion of the ruling Omani aristocracy as well as the majority of coastal inhabitants, also contributed additional symbolic markers of status. Free believers, both male and female, were obliged to cover their heads, while slaves, even if they had converted to Islam, were forbidden from wearing a cap or veil, suggesting that the class interests of the dominant members of society overrode religious prescriptions. The bodies of the elite were also elaborately adorned and almost entirely covered, while those of the poor or servile were concealed only to the extent that an individual's social and financial position allowed."

FIGURE 27 *The Duke of the Abruzzi's travels in Abyssinia. The sceriffa Alaluja El Morgani (sic) pays homage to the Duke of the Abruzzi.* Reparto Attualità: 1927. 07.05.1927. La sceriffa accompagnata dai membri della missione—campo medio, cod. foto: *A00000435*.
ISTITUTO LUCE CINECITTÀ HISTORICAL ARCHIVE, ROME.

ancient Islamic world—and also in Ethiopia—the parasol accompanies her portrait in a number of the images that are preserved in the Luce archives. It is an accessory that, like her shoes and socks, shows her status (shoes and socks had formerly been the exclusive symbols of political authority and wealth). Similarly, the car behind them is an important and impressive status symbol for the time. Finally, her white veil is also an interesting accessory: it is a remnant of the Ottoman heritage, recaling a fashion that was popular among Ottoman-Egyptian aristocratic women in Cairo in the 1920s.[17]

For propaganda purposes, the caption "The Sceriffa Alaluja El Morgani (*sic*) pays homage to the Duke of the Abruzzi" reverses the meaning of the moment that is immortalized in the photograph. In fact, contrary to what the caption says, it is the Duke who was visiting her residence and paying tribute to her,

17 See, for example, the portraits of Safiyya Zaghlul and other aristocratic women in Baron 2005.

not the other way round. In this fabricated reversal of the interpretation of the image, we see a shift between the reality of the moment as it was lived and observed on the ground and the representation expressed and broadcast by the Luce Institute in the context of its propaganda, the principal aim of which was to celebrate the Duke's prestige in the region.

As we have seen in previous chapters, Sittī ʿAlawiyya became extremely popular in the country from the early 1920s, especially among the Muslim and lowland people who used to visit her and perform *ziyāra* at her residence.[18] This official meeting with a popular Italian explorer echoes other meetings, some informal and others less so, that the Italian authorities and travellers used to have with her at her residence. In 1927, it was the turn of the daughter of the Duce, Edda Mussolini, who went to visit the *Sceriffa* with Governor Zoli and Commissioner Cancilla in the course of her travels along the Red Sea, and later it was the turn of Caniglia and Martinelli, who wrote travelogues that recounted her impressive personality.[19]

What distinguishes this picture with the Duke is the fact that it is the first visual documentation produced by Luce that reveals a desire to make the event noteworthy. If we study the movement of the characters involved, we see that there was no question of preparing a stage or striking a particular pose; rather, it looks like a snapshot taken in the midst of some activity. The meeting between these two key figures became a media-staged event that could be broadcast beyond colonial borders.

Growing Popularity Broadcast through Visual Media

When the *Unione Cinematografica Educativa* (L.U.C.E.) was established in 1924, it was one of the earliest State-owned cinematographic production companies in Europe. It was also the first public production company devoted entirely to educational and didactic cinema. Its name was presented in a theatre in Rome

18 This popularity was well-documented after 1915 in reports from local Commissioners such as that filed by Fioccardi. See, for example, Colonia Eritrea, Commissariato di Cheren, Riservato-Urgente, Al Signor Reggente il Governo della Colonia. Oggetto: Grave dissidio seguito da ingiurie tra Morgani e Sceriffa, Cheren, 6 settembre 1917. Archivio Storico Diplomatico del Ministero degli Affari Esteri (ASDMAE), Archivio Eritrea (AE), 1880–1917, Pacco 1022 (Missioni Politiche—Varie—El Morgani), Fasc. 10 Famiglia El Morgani, 1895–1917.

19 Martinelli 1930: 55.

in November 1924 on the occasion of the projection of its first film: *Aethiopica*, a documentary on Ethiopia, which was the most exotic place for the Italian imagination at the time. From October 1926, following an edict that made the projection of one or more L.U.C.E. documentaries compulsory in all Italian cinemas, its productions were always projected as an addition to the regular programming. The creation of newsreels—the *Giornale Cinematografico Luce*—would follow, but would focus mainly on documentaries rather than on political events.[20] The question of whether Luce newsreels circulated, or were even received, in Africa has not been fully answered, although certain specific contributions have shown its political and social importance beyond Italy's borders, in particular in a context such as that of Tunisia.[21] There, as in other African and Middle East countries, the Institute's propaganda was remarkable in the context of the Mediterranean and Islamic imperial policy that was being actively promoted by the the Fascist regime, especially in the 1930s. As we will see in more detail in the following chapters, the *šarīfa* gained high visibility in the Italian media as a result of this propaganda.

Luce broadcast another meeting between the Duke of the Abruzzi and the *šarīfa* some years after the one photographed at her residence in 1927. A silent documentary lasting little more than eighteen minutes, it was shot during a second visit to Massawa led by the explorer. It was produced on this occasion by the *Istituto Nazionale Luce*, and offers a posthumous retrospective of the life of the Duke of the Abruzzi. It was entitled "Perspectives and memories of the Duke of the Abruzzi during his travels in Abyssinia. A commemoration of Luigi of Savoy, Duke of the Abruzzi",[22] and celebrates the most meaningful moments in the life of the explorer, who died in 1933. Among the recollections of the Duke's travels in Abyssinia at the end of the 1920s, it mentions his meeting with the *šarīfa* in Massawa: the subtitles read: "the Sceriffa Alabuia el Morgani (*sic*), a great saint venerated by thousands, pays tribute to the Duke …".[23] The scene lasts about one minute, and begins with a clip of the *šarīfa*, who is identified as a "saint", arriving with two other uniformed representatives of the Italian authorities at the palace where the official ceremony was to take place,

20 Laura 2000: 21, 44–50.

21 See Corriou 2010: 203–236.

22 Istituto Nazionale [1932–37] « Aspetti e ricordi di S.A.R. il Duca degli Abruzzi nel suo viaggio in Abissinia. Rievocazione di Luigi di Savoia, Duca degli Abruzzi », Istituto Luce Cinecittà Historical Archive.

23 Ibid. min.: 09.60.

apparently the Governor's Palace in Massawa[24] (Figure 28). They climb the steps, followed by local dignitaries and servants. Behind them, at the bottom of the steps, the car that brought them to the ceremony and the watching crowd can be seen. The next scene shows other Muslim dignitaries, among them Sīdī Ǧaʿfar al-Mīrġanī and other representatives of the brotherhood. Even though the sequence is very short, the way it is staged introduces the *šarīfa* as the guest of honour at the ceremony. Despite the fact that the entire documentary is aimed at an Italian audience to celebrate the Duke, one might hypothesize that it was also crucial for a Muslim audience in order to stress the public visibility of the *šarīfa*, and that this might be further evidence of her charismatic power; or was her widespread popularity the main reason behind the respect the Italian authorities customarily expressed for her in public? The former interpretation does not exclude the latter, however: in fact, while the colonial archives restate the prestige she enjoyed among colonial subjects, oral narratives collected on the ground in Eritrea and Ethiopia stress the influence she had on Italians. Ultimately, her widespread visibility during official ceremonies may have enhanced her charismatic authority.

Between 1927 and 1945, the Luce Institute produced the most significant newsreels (*cinegiornali*) of the Fascist era, *Il Giornale Cinematografico Luce*. According to a review of the company, the *Cinegiornale Luce* had a huge domestic audience in 1929.[25] As with its documentaries, Luce newsreels included short films that were shown in all Italian cinemas with the dual aim of educating and amusing. Curious, exotic, or exceptional events taking place overseas were among the range of issues covered. This was the case with a newsreel that broadcast a "Muslim reception committee offered in honour of the Governor, Admiral De Feo" that took place in 1937 (Figures 29–31). The film records the arrival of Governor De Feo in Massawa.[26] The short sequence of approximately one minute is made up of four scenes. It opens with the title "Massawa" at the centre of the image. In the lower right-hand corner of the screen there is the abbreviation "AOI" (Italian East Africa), and at the top an eagle, the logo of the Luce Institute. A female voice-over comments on the brief sequence in Italian, placing the event at the time of the death of the *šarīfa's* mother:

---

24 If one compares the Governor's Palace that appears in the sene from 07.53 to 08:03 with that appearing from 10:08 to 10:21 in « Aspetti e ricordi di S.A.R. il Duca degli Abruzzi nel suo viaggio in Abissinia. Rievocazione di Luigi di Savoia, Duca degli Abruzzi », Istituto Luce Cinecittà Historical Archive.

25 Laura 2000: 52.

26 Appointed Governor of Eritrea in 1937, he would remain in the post only for a short time, from 1 April to 15 December 1937.

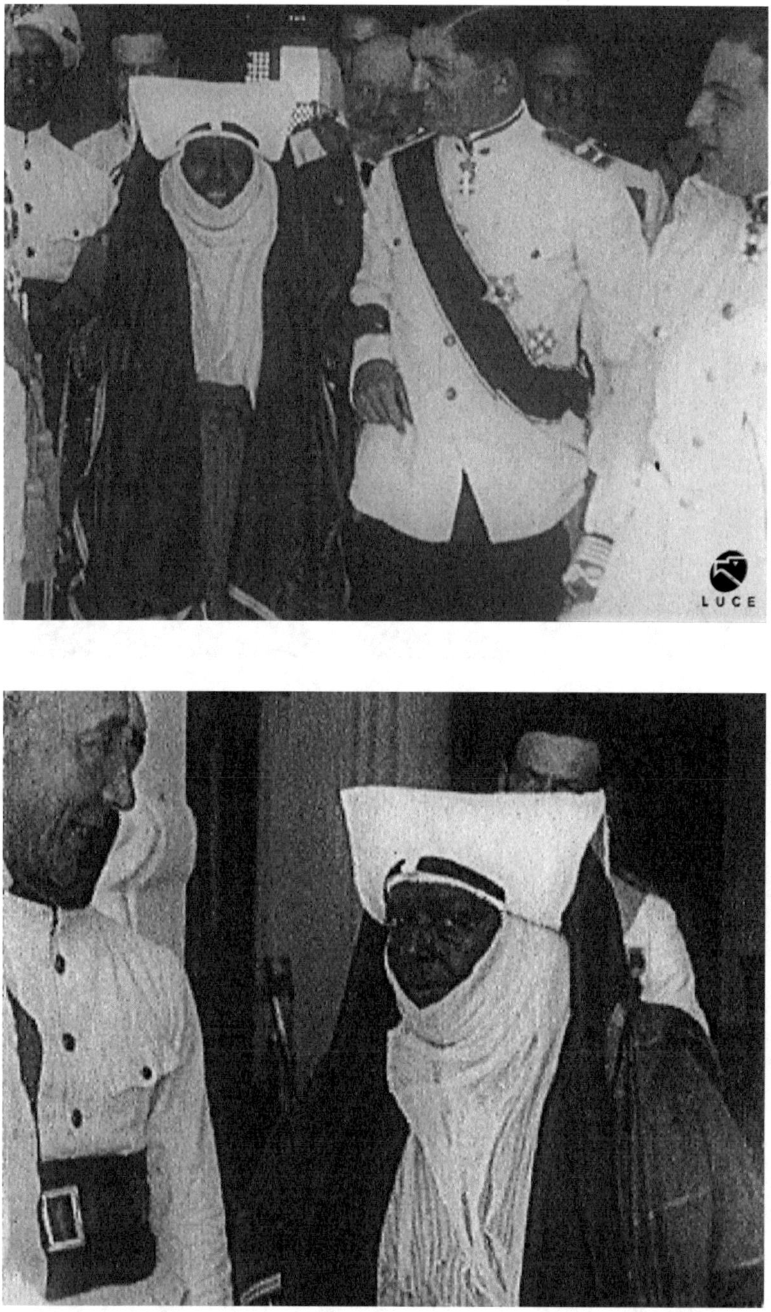

FIGURE 28 *Luce National Institute [1932–37], memories of the Duke of the Abruzzi during his travel in Abyssinia.* Aspetti e ricordi di S.A.R. il Duca degli Abruzzi nel suo viaggio in Abissinia. Rievocazione di Luigi di Savoia, Duca degli Abruzzi. ISTITUTO LUCE CINECITTÀ HISTORICAL ARCHIVE, ROME.

FIGURE 29 *A Muslim community welcome ceremony in honour of the Governor Ammiraglio De Feo in Massawa (08/12/1937), Newsreeel B1215, m. 00-46-50/00-47-17, (a).*
ISTITUTO LUCE CINECITTÀ HISTORICAL ARCHIVE, ROME.

"The Muslim community of Massawa gathered around the magnificent new mosque and offered a welcome to his Excellency Governor Admiral De Feo on the occasion of the death of the mother of Sceriffa Alauia El Morgani (*sic*), who sees herself as the only direct descendent of the Prophet Mohammad, and who has recognized the Duce of Fascist Italy [*Mussolini*] as the great protector of the Muslim world".

Again, we see a shift between the subtitles—which introduce a "welcome offered by the Muslim community in honour of Governor Admiral De Feo"—and the filmed images. Was the Governor's visit really the main reason for the ceremony, or had it been organized to inaugurate the new mosque in honour of the *šarīfa*'s mother, to whom the Italian colonial Governor went to pay homage? If we look carefully at the images taken around the mosque, we might conclude that it is more a case of a celebration organized on the occasion of the inauguration of the mosque (in honour of the *šarīfa's* mother, and not simply for the Governor's visit to Massawa.

Certainly, the Institute's rhetoric suggests a very different discourse: the newsreel shows the ceremony to demonstrate the support and respect Muslim

FIGURE 30 *A Muslim community welcome ceremony in honour of the Governor Ammiraglio De Feo in Massawa (08/12/1937), Newsreeel B1215, m. 00-47-17/00-47-26 (b).*
ISTITUTO LUCE CINECITTÀ HISTORICAL ARCHIVE, ROME.

FIGURE 31 *A Muslim community welcome ceremony in honour of the Governor Ammiraglio De Feo in Massawa (08/12/1937), Newsreeel B1215, m. 00-27-26/00-47-38 (c).*
ISTITUTO LUCE CINECITTÀ HISTORICAL ARCHIVE, ROME.

subjects showed the Governor of the Colony. It also aimed to illustrate the colonial works carried out for the benefit of Muslims so as to improve the international pro-Islamic propaganda that Mussolini had inaugurated in March of the same year during his journey to Tripoli, when he publicly claimed to be the "Sword of Islam".[27]

Suggesting a reassuring image, as well as extraordinary and exotic pictures of overseas territories to the Italian audience, the *šarīfa* is once again placed at centre stage. Accompanied by the words of the commentator, the images of the first thirty-second sequence roll. After showing the exterior of the mosque, the new minaret, from which (apparently Italian) flags are flying, is filmed from top to bottom. Then we are immediately led into the interior of the mosque, where we discover its beauty, from its columns and arches to the fine setting of the dome (Figures 29).

A cut leads to the second sequence, in which Governor De Feo, accompanied by other uniformed colonial authorities, is seen marching and giving the Roman salute to the crowd, which responds in the same way. In the crowd, one detail draws our attention: a woman, apparently an Italian settler, wearing a clear robe and a woman's hat according to the fashion of the time, is giving a Fascist salute to the authorities that accompanies the entire sequence of the march. Another cut takes us to a short scene of less than two seconds that shows a group of carefully-veiled Muslim women attending the ceremony. This juxtaposition of these images of women is interesting to note in the colonial context; we see the contrast between these two representations: compared with an anonymous group of indigenous veiled Arab/black women, the producers have placed a single white woman, who symbolically represents active support for colonial and Fascist policy, in the foreground (Figure 30).

The final scene, which lasts about thirteen seconds and is made up of four shots, focuses on images of the *šarīfa* welcoming Governor De Feo (on her left) and other Italian and indigenous representatives, apparently at the entrance to the mosque (Figure 31). To her right, an Eritrean man wearing ceremonial clothes reads an official declaration. The *šarīfa* seems to be in charge in the scene, and asks for silence from the attending crowd with a gesture. On their left (on the right of the image), a group of colonial settlers in plain clothes stare at the camera, while in the background (behind De Feo and the *šarīfa*), we see other colonial and indigenous authorities. The presence of the camera, which is an integral part of the scene, is clearly noticed by the audience, as well as by the two dignitaries who agreed to memorialize this official meeting on film.

27 On this event, see Wright 2005.

Half the images in the newsreel celebrate the Italian renovation works on the Massawa mosque, which were intended to show how colonial policy aims to protect Islam. They expressed the practical implications of the highly pro-Islamic and pro-Mediterranean policy that Mussolini claimed to be promoting in 1937. As we will see in the next chapter, as a result of this particular propaganda discourse, the *šarīfa* gained high visibility in the media.

In Italy, her image was mainly as an icon of indigenous support for Fascist policy, and as an example of Orientalist and exotic repertoires. While it may be difficult to evaluate the impact of the circulation of her images in Eritrea and internationally, a number of points are worthy of note. Some portraits of her attending colonial official ceremonies were still being conserved by representative members of the brotherhood in Asmara in 2005, which testifies to her prestige in colonial times. It seems likely that these images may have circulated among the Eritrean elites, but probably only in very limited quantities, as it was a Muslim society with iconoclastic leanings. Moreover, owing to the high cost of reproducing images, photography was a sign of prestige and wealth limited to a small, privileged group.[28]

The circulation of short movies and newsreels, on the other hand, may not have been limited to cinemas in Italy, but might also have been broadcast in Italian Northeast Africa and other foreign territories where Luce's propaganda was active. In Ethiopia, for example, where there were forty cinemas in 1939 (and fifty-five in 1940), the regime considered the cinema to be an important tool for imperial propaganda.[29] Here, her image was discursively construed as that of an active supporter of the Italian occupation.

While the *šarīfa* was influential in the Muslim community in Eritrea throughout the colonial period, she only became popular in Ethiopia in the 1930s, after her trips there and during the Italian occupation (1936–1941). In Harar, the main centre for Islamic teaching and learning in the Horn of Africa, where a mosque was built in her honour, her portrait was hung in the residences of the indigenous shaykhs.[30] Another image of her was published later on in Addis Ababa to accompany a front-page article in an Arabic newspaper announcing her death in 1940.[31] This was *Barīd al-Imbirātūriyya*, the Arabic

28 Abebe 2003: 21.

29 Ben-Ghiat 2008: 182–183.

30 Interviews with Ay Rawda Qallu on November 2009 in Harar. For the general historical context see Braukamper 2004.

31 "Al-Šarīfa al-Mīrġanī died. Sadness prevails among all Muslims" (in Arabic), in *Barīd al-Imbirātūriyya*, Year v, No. 156, Addis Ababa, 27 October 1940—XVIII (the Mīrġanī family Private Collection, Cairo). *Barīd al-Imbirātūriyya* was an Arabic-language version of the

version of the Fascist journal *Il Corriere dell'Impero*, which was published in Addis Ababa during the Italian occupation. The same year, a book devoted to her—entitled "The Sceriffa of Massawa"—was published by Giuseppe Canaglia (1940) in Italy (Figure 32).

Her visibility was reaffirmed on the occasion of other public ceremonies that were documented and promoted on film to show and foster international support for the regime. In 1938, a year after the sequence filmed in Massawa for the inauguration of the renovated mosque, she accepted an invitation from the Government to visit Rome on the occasion of the anniversary of the foundation of the Italian Empire in East Africa that had been pronounced by Mussolini on 9 May 1936, following the conquest of Ethiopia. At the celebrations in Rome, she was the only woman among the African dignitaries who went to Palazzo Venezia to meet Mussolini.

The event was broadcast by the propaganda system, once again thanks to the Fascist media; among the Luce archives we found a newsreel of the event lasting little more than a minute highlighting the participation of a woman among the dignitaries.[32] The female voice-over comments on the images as follows:

> The Duce [*Mussolini*] received fifty leaders and notables at Palace Venezia from Libya and East Africa who had gathered in Rome to pay homage to the Emperor and Founder of the Empire. A woman stands out among them, Sceriffa Alauia al-Morgani [*sic*], a descendant of the Prophet, who expressed to the Duce the deep feeling of loyalty that drives all Muslims in the Empire. Her attendants, who are wearing luxurious traditional clothes, are all valiant old warriors on whose chests shine signs of the respect they have earned on the battlefield. Among those paying homage to the Duce were Prince Slaina Qaramanli [*sic*] in the name of the Libyan people, Lecce Ghiéta Claimanós [*sic*], representing the Coptic clergy, Ras Ailùte Claimò [*sic*] for the Amahra people, Dejjià Kailé Salassié Gustà for the Tigray people, Dejjà Beia Ibrahim for the Eritreans, the very valiant Sultan Olò Dimle, leader of the Shabeli [*sic*], and Sultan Abba Giobbi Gumai [*sic*], in the name of the Galla people. The Duce agreed to pose before the lens in a group with these loyal individuals, who will keep a

Fascist newspaper "Il Corriere dell'Impero", and was published in Addis Ababa during the Italian occupation.

32 Giornale Luce, B1307, 18/05/1938 "Roma. 50 capi e notabili della Libia ricevuti da Mussolini", Istituto Luce Cinecittà Historical Archive, Rome.

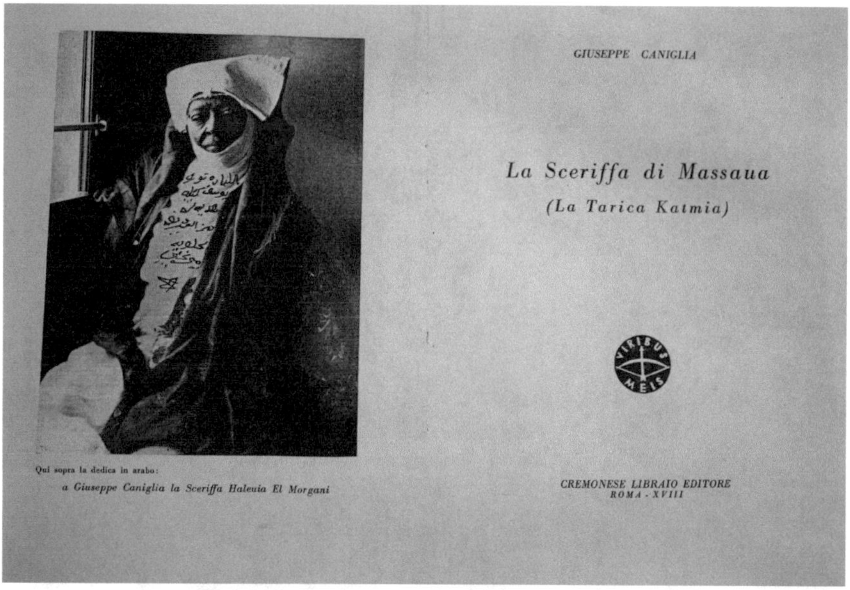

FIGURE 32 *Giuseppe Caniglia's book 'La Sceriffa di Massaua'.*
CREMONESE LIBRARIO ED., ROME, 1940.

> memorable souvenir of the kind welcome they have received and the magnificence of the Imperial *Urbe*.

In fact, there is a photographic portrait of the notables, with Mussolini and the *šarīfa* in the first row (Figure 33).[33] The same communication was also presented in the contemporary written press, such as in *Gli Annali dell'Africa Italiana*, which reports that the *šarīfa*, "a descendant of the Prophet" Muḥammad, attended the ceremony.[34]

As in other photographs from the 1930s, she appears carefully veiled and wearing trousers under her robe. She conformed with this particular dress code in all the images that were circulating in Italy at the time, and her fascinating dress was certainly also an expression of the staging of a charming power to an Italian audience.

---

33 Published by Goglia 1989: 272.

34 *Gli Annali dell'Africa Italiana*, Year 1—No. 2—August 1938—XVI—Rome, Casa Editrice A. Mondadori, p. 712.

FIGURE 33 *Sittī ʿAlawiyya and Mussolini at Palazzo Venezia (Rome) in 1938.*
ISTITUTO LUCE CINECITTÀ HISTORICAL ARCHIVE (BY GRACIOUS PERMISSION OF THE BORRUSO FAMILY), ROME.

The Fascist discursive construction of the image of Sittī ʿAlawiyya in the context of its political propaganda is undeniable; indeed, she was part of a political project promoted by the regime to gain popular support internationally, in the Empire and beyond in the Middle East.

While the colonial discourse may be clear, an interpretation of her own rhetoric may be considerably more complex to decode because we have no written sources from the *šarīfa* herself, and her voice has mostly been screened by the colonial media and reports. Of course, we know that she took on political responsibility on behalf of her people, who were predominantly Muslims under Italian occupation, in the form of an intermediary with the colonial power. With the exception of oral stories gathered in Northeast Africa, however, we mainly have images and her fashion style to counter or complement the colonial narrative. The image she actively portrays through her style of clothing deserves our special attention, particularly if we consider it in the context of the motherland's Fascist, Christian society.

Two particular details attract our attention in the photograph in which she appears with Mussolini: her veil and the trousers she wears under her tunic. Military trousers are a sign of masculinity and power, which according to her descendent from Cairo were the inspiration for her nickname *al-ḥarbiyya*, "the warrior". The veil she wears during her meeting with Italians in all the images from the 1930s is very different from the one we see in the previous photographs (Figures 20, 24, 26, 27); it is a scarf with both Islamic and Christian designs (Figures 28, 31–33). Sufi shaykhs in Ethiopia used to dress in a style that integrated eclectic features and symbols and revealed the intercultural and interreligious dynamics that are generally welcomed by Sufi intellectual understandings and practices. For Sufis, the mystical nature of religion is crucial: its very essence is mystical love. The theme of love often appears in oral narratives describing the *šarīfa*: for example, it has frequently been reported that she loved Italians as much as she did her compatriots. This controversial narrative depicts her as an impartial mediator, but did her authority actually derive from her role as an intermediary and a truly noteworthy capacity to influence the Italian authorities? Oral narratives stress her status as a *walī*, a person close to God, which was proved by a number of reports of *karāmāt* (miracles) that it is claimed she performed.[35] Her mediation between the colonial power and the Muslim population fostered her legacy of religious and political authority, and she gained great visibility through the colonial media, not only in Eritrea, but also internationally.

Visibility, Visuality and Power in Portraits of the *Šarīfa*

Visual data are frequently used in women's and gender studies as a meaningful transdisciplinary tool for historical analysis. The invisibility of women and their marginalization from the great historical narratives have led researchers to study the subjectivities of women from a number of sources, not only written but also oral and visual. Despite this, a close analysis of iconographic sources reveals the need to distinguish between visibility, which is the act of making something visible, and visuality, which has a discursive connotation.[36]

35 Interview with Aḥmad al-Mīrġanī, a descendant of Šarīfa ʿAlawiyya and nephew of Ǧaʿfar al-Mīrġanī (Cairo, May 2009); *ḫalīfa* Aḥmad, the current *ḫalīfa al-ḫulafāʾ* of the Ḫatmiyya in Keren (Keren, March 2009); Šarīfa ʿAlawiyya, a descendant of Šarīfa ʿAlawiyya and daughter of Ǧaʿfar al-Mīrġanī (Cairo, May 2009).

36 Hayes 2006: 521.

In Eritrea, as in other African countries, we see an extensive production of portraits of local women thanks to the colonial camera, whereas their voices are virtually absent in the colonial archives. As I have pointed out, there is a huge number of images of unclothed bodies and naked, sensual Eritrean women representing the so-called *madame* in private photographs and postcards. The visibility of women's bodies in colonial portraits was an expression of colonial violence. A critical analysis of these visual data raises several questions regarding the wide circulation and receipt of images.[37] Colonial photographs of Eritrean women show similarities to those of other colonized women in countries such as in Algeria, which is itself a well-explored case study.[38] Here, as elsewhere, a critical analysis of the visual data shows that the visibility of women's bodies does not necessarily translate into empowerment.[39] Women often appear as merely passive objects in photographs, and not as active subjects. If we compare the case of Sittī ʿAlawiyya with portraits of the so-called Eritrean *madame*, whose sensual body became an exotic metaphor for the virgin territory of the colony, it is clear that one of the peculiarities that distinguishes representations of the *šarīfa's* body is the desire to give visibility to an unchallengable respectability, concealing her sexuality and shielding it from prying eyes. While, as Silvana Palma has pointed out, the body of the *madame* was a colonial icon of sexualized beauty, the expression of an illegitimate and asymmetric relationship, a space for interaction and conflict between colonizers and colonized, the body of the *šarīfa* was presented like that of a saint, untouchable and asexual, or a holy intermediary. She demands respect, and expresses her acknowledgement of a morality she shares with the Christian colonizers; her veil reflects the strictness of Islam while at the same time comparing her to a Christian nun. As has been pointed out, among the visual repertoires of women in the colony, nuns had exceptional visibility in the public sphere. Their veils in particular gave a sense of respectability to the representation of their bodies in colonial pictures.[40] Similarly, in colonial portraits, the bourgeois clothes worn by Italian women imbued them with a sense of respectability and superiority compared with the colonized population.[41]

Although Sittī ʿAlawiyya's image was broadcast through the colonial media to good effect, we also see that she actively promoted a particular public

37 DeRoo 2002: 159–171.

38 Alloula 1981 amd Taraud 2012.

39 Hayes 2006: 3.

40 See Di Barbora 2012.

41 See Spadaro 2013.

image through her clothing: that of a universal, and not necessarily, or exclusively, Islamic, religious authority. Her clothing seems to convey a message to Christians and Italians that she herself is also willing to co-opt, and as a result, her portrait can also be considered to be a mirror of a discourse that she herself actively conceived.

Her body was a potential battlefield for a number of political and social conflicts, however. This complex situation is revealed in another photograph from an Arabic journal dating from that time, although unfortunately, its exact date and origin are unavailable (Figure 34).

The *šarīfa* is represented at the centre of the image holding a sword and wearing special clothing.[42] The Arabic caption states: "The uncrowned Queen of Eritrea, a woman known as *šarīfa*, who rules a large area of Eritrea occupied by Italians and lives in a palace outside Massawa. In the photograph she is wearining men's clothes and holding a sword in her left hand".

The epithet "uncrowned queen" was often employed with reference to her, and was still invoked during my interviews in Eritrea, which confirmed that her political authority was effective but informal.[43]

As used here, the sword is a symbol not only of political power, but also of the masculinity that transpires from her posture: she is sitting with her legs open and wearing trousers under her tunic like a man. In this image she is not wearing her special veil, but a hat typical of the Arabic peninsula. Why is the *šarīfa* dressed like this? Who was the intended audience for this portrait? What were the producer's aims and what was it intended to be used for politically? These are difficult questions to answer because we do not currently have any more information on the origin of the journal from which this article is taken. If we look at her posture, however, sitting with her legs open, the representation seems far more disreputable than it is positive. The Arabic hat and the scarf leave her chin uncovered, unlike other portraits of her from the 1930s, where she covers it carefully. The statement in the caption that she "is wearing men's clothes" recalls a negative connotation in a number of Islamic traditions relating to *ḥadīṯ*s that forbid women from trying to look like men in their dress and movements, as well as masculine women in general. According to her descendants, there were (mainly defamatory) rumours about her habit of

42 Mīrġanī family Private Collection, Cairo.

43 Interwiew with Aḥmad al-Mīrġanī, Šarīfa ʿAlawiyya's and grandson of Ǧaʿfar al-Mīrġanī (Cairo, May 2009); *ḫalīfa* Aḥmad, current *ḫalīfat al-ḫulafāʾ* of the Ḫatmiyya in Keren (Keren, March 2009); Šarīfa ʿAlawiyya, a descendant of Šarīfa ʿAlawiyya and daughter of Ǧaʿfar al-Mīrġanī (Cairo, May 2009).

ملكة مستعمرة اريترة غير المتوجة : سيدة مسلمة تعرف باسم «الشريفة»
تحكم جانبا كبيرا من المستعمرة الايطالية وتسكن فى قصر خارج مدينة
مصوع . وهى فى الصورة بملابس الرجال وفى يسراها سيف

FIGURE 34 *The uncrowned Queen of the Eritrean colony.*
UNKNOWN NEWSPAPER, MĪRĠANĪ PRIVATE COLLECTION, CAIRO.

wearing men's clothes and acting like a man.[44] This curious portrait is more likely to be a forgery prepared by her adversaries than an authentic photograph; at the time, her image enjoyed an international circulation that could be politically exploited, and not only by Italians and her followers. After all, the introduction and circulation of photography was rapidly used for political purposes in Ethiopia in the context of a veritable "war of images".[45] One well-known example of the political use of photography is that of Lijj Iyasu, the ephemeral Christian sovereign of Ethiopia from 1909 to 1916, whose political enemies used photographs of the prince wearing Muslim clothing to accuse him of converting to Islam. This controversial portrait, which was assumed to be proof of his apostasy, led to his downfall, and yet, as recent literature has recalled, Iyasu himself actively used his political image to represent multiple identities of his reign: by posing in front of the camera in Muslim clothing, he was seeking to demonstrate his interest in Ethiopian Muslims and maintaining a political alliance with them.[46] The public and media visibility of Sittī ʿAlawiyya participated in fostering her charisma as much at a local as an international level. The colonial authorities (and possibly also her enemies) used her political image, as she herself did. By posing for colonial cameras, she had decided to actively take on a political visibility. She chose to enter the country's political sphere by acting as a mediator in negotiations between the colonial establishment and indigenous interests. The portraits of her that circulated in the new media (photographs, the press, newsreels, etc.) allowed her to show her political power at an international level, even in her absence.[47]

In these portraits, Sittī ʿAlawiyya expresses a cosmopolitan identity by wearing overseas garments in an original style. Dressed in a pair of military trousers and a special veil, she shows an eclectic attitude, and her image is the mirror of a cultural negotiation between Christian and Muslim moral values. At the same time, recourse to photography as a political medium is employed to good advantage, and she shows her interest in employing it to promote her image. In effect, the use of photography in the political arena is a part of the process

---

44 Interwiew with Aḥmad al-Mīrġanī, a descendant of Šarīfa ʿAlawiyya and grandson of Ǧaʿfar al-Mīrġanī (Cairo, May 2009); *ḫalīfa* Ahmad, current *ḫalīfat al-ḫulafāʾ* of the Ḫatmiyya in Keren (Keren, March 2009); Šarīfa ʿAlawiyya, a descendant of Šarīfa ʿAlawiyya and daughter of Ǧaʿfar al-Mīrġanī (Cairo, May 2009).

45 Pankhurst 1992: 234–41.

46 Sohier 2011.

47 Her case is comparable to that of the elite of the Ethiopian Empire as analysed by Estelle Sohier. On the use of photography in Ethiopia by Menelik and Taytu, see Sohier 2012.

of mediatization of political power that was on the increase in 1920s North-Eastern Africa. She demonstrates a creative appropriation of the visual media, especially through dressing up. While the camera may have been a prerogative of the colonial power, she formulated her own rhetoric through a representation of her body that would circulate in the press, photography and cinematography of the Empire. The circulation of these images beyond the Eritrean border helped increase her popularity both internationally and regionally. She was presented as a symbol of emancipation for Muslim people at large, not only in Italy but also, as we will see in the chapters that follow, in Ethiopia and beyond. In the end, although the camera was principally monopolized by the colonial power, African women from the elites, such as a Muslim shaykha like Sittī ʿAlawiyya or an Ethiopian Queen such as Taytu, formulated their own rhetoric through images of their bodies, one that could circulate in the press, photography and cinematography of the Empire. Finally, differences in class and religious affiliation had a profound effect on the process of appropriation of visual media to display images of the self.

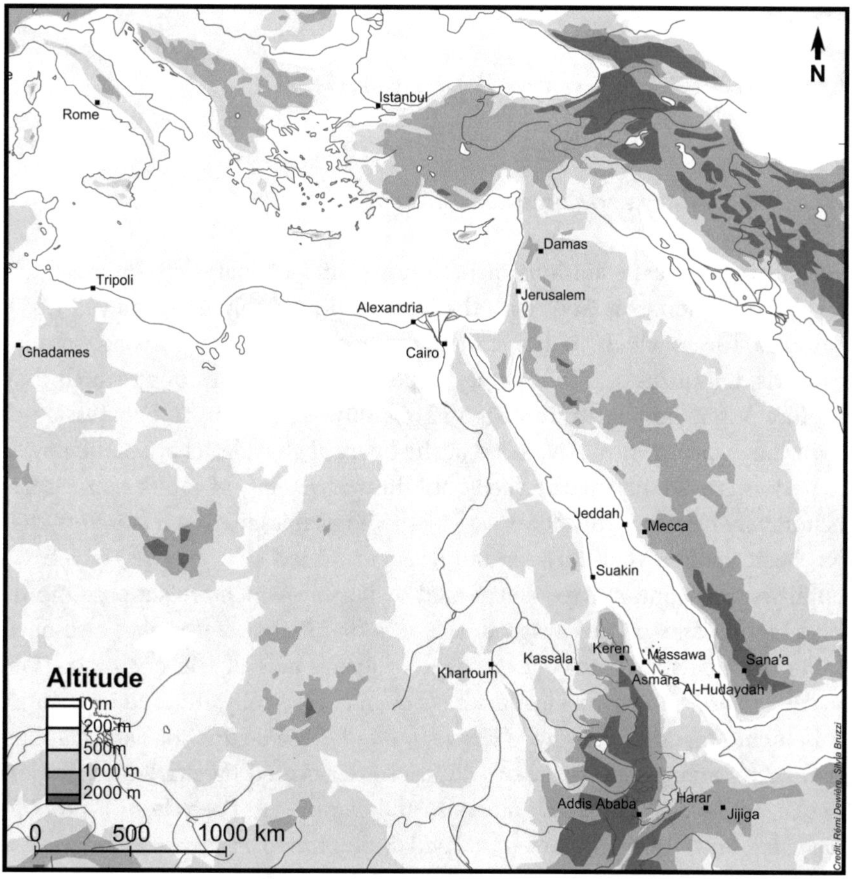

MAP 3 *Mediterranean and Red Sea region.*

CHAPTER 7

Marvels, Charisma and Modernity

Performed and Contested *Karāmāt*

Sufi hagiographical traditions include repertoires of marvels (*karāmāt*) performed by "Friends of God" with the intervention of the divine power. These *karāmāt* stories, which are transmitted orally or written down in hagiographical texts, tell of the shaykhs' ability to perform wonders through which they acquire public popularity, respect and possibly veneration. The possession of knowledge is known to have been at the heart of shaykhs' charismatic power to perform these spectacular deeds, but the authenticity of saints' marvels has historically been a highly controversial theological issue. One distinction that has been made is that between miracles performed by a prophet, which are public actions, and marvels performed by a saint, which are supposed to be kept hidden and are not a sign of a prophetic mission. Both types also need to be distinguished from deceptive and illusory acts of trickery, divination, magic or sorcery. Spiritual leaders have been periodically attacked by their rivals, including other Sufis, who have exploited these distinctions and claimed that their "marvels" were essentially tricks performed by charlatans. In particular, the act of "divulging marvels" and aspiring to the role of a prophet has frequently been criticized.[1] Sayyid Muḥammad al-Idrīsī (1876–1923), a great-grandson of the Moroccan Sufi master Aḥmad ibn Idrīs and the representative of the Idrīsī tradition in Yemen, was accused of having resorted to technical devices such as electricity, phosphorus, aniline and the like to impress his followers, who believed he was able to perform marvels. His rivals accused him of "charlatanry" because of his use of "devious" devices such as a battery to shock his visitors, a light bulb over the entrance to his house that lit up when he passed under it and most notably his use of the phonograph, which was the topic of a series of treatises written by his rivals who denounced it as a devilish illusion. The introduction of Western technology stimulated lively debates in Islamic circles on the Red Sea and across the whole Muslim world. These were related in part to broader political conflicts, but also to cultural changes that had their origins in the debate on reform, Islam and modernity. One typical, complex example is "the phonograph affair", which pitted Idrīsī and Ḫatmī shaykhs in Yemen against each other at the time of the Ottoman ad-

1 Gardet 1997: 615–616.

 | DOI 10.1163/9789004356160_009

ministration (1849–1911).[2] During this period, the cosmopolitan port of al-Hudayda, in the coastal region of Thiama, was the main centre of both Ottoman power and Mīrġanī religious influence in the country. As was the case along the African shore of the Red Sea, the Ḫatmiyya acted as mediators in the city between the locals and the Ottoman administration. By 1909, a number of tribes had recognized their rival al-Idrīsī as their *imām*—that is, as both their political and spiritual leader—in the regions of ʿAsir and Thiama, which were in a state of anarchy at the time. Here, al-Idrīsī remedied the failures of the Ottoman administrators to act as mediators in disputes between tribal fractions. In 1911, after his reputation had soared thanks to his successes as an arbitrator in resolving conflicts between tribal groups, Muḥammad al-Idrīsī led a rebellion against the government, armed by the Italians. His enemies spread rumours to undermine his authority, slandering him with claims that has was a false leader, a charlatan and a pretender. In particular, European accounts accused him of producing fake miracles by employing modern gadgets and chemical tricks, and more specifically the phonograph, to perform them. A Ḫatmī shaykh nicknamed al-Fawānīs, who was based in al-Hudayda, where anti-Ottoman attitudes were less marked, also published a series of writings that denounced the gramophone—"the talking box"—as a devilish illusion created to astonish believers.[3] New inventions in general had the potential to foment popular astonishment and wonder, thereby provoking debates in Islamic circles and among *ʿulamāʾ*, and this particular new device, which was able to reproduce recorded sound and music, and was introduced in the Ottoman capital before 1895 and later in other towns across the Empire, become a controversial topic because it was considered "an infedel's work".[4] Despite this, it gained popularity rapidly and spread across other areas of the Empire, including al-Hudayda, through both Ottoman and European networks. Al-Fawānīs agreed with the opinion of other *ʿulamāʾ* that "the talking box" was illegal. As reported in the text translated by Nicola Melis, the Ḫatmī shaykh argued that it was associated with the "paranormal", and that it was illegal to listen to the sounds of the box and to sit around it because "a voice transmitted from an inanimate object is like a miracle. However, this box uses gimmicks, unlike the miracles of the pious and the saints, which do not. (...) It is forbidden to listen to any sound like this, for it is like magic. Sitting around the box, listening to the sound

2 Hofheinz 1995: 105. See Archivio Storico Diplomatico del Ministero degli Affari Esteri (ASDMAE), Archivio Eritrea (AE), 1886–1912, P. 1043/4. On Sayyid Muḥammad al-Idrīsī and the Idrīsī State in the ʿAsir, see Bang 1996: 68–130.

3 Bang 1996: 84–101. See also Hofheinz 1995; Melis 2012: 107–152.

4 Melis 2012: 125.

and the flow of poems and songs from within it is considered to be an act of worship". He also claimed that even if the gramophone were to transmit the word of God, it would forbidden to listen to it because it was an inanimate body talking like a prodigious device that caused astonishment.[5] As Nicola Melis has suggested, it is also worth noting that this reasoning made the question of the gramophone a part of the widely-debated issue among *ʿulamāʾ* regarding the prohibition of instruments, as well as singing and amusement in general. In this instance, as was the case with other Muslim reformers, the order followed a reformist Naqšbandī tradition of banning instrumental music. The Ḫatmī shaykh argued that amusement, including flutes and drums, was unnecessary, and that sitting and listening to these instruments was prohibited.[6] But not all members of the Ḫatmiyya in the region shared his puritanical approach: as we have seen, performances of music and dance used to take place regularly at the residences of the Šarīfa ʿAlawiyya in Eritrea, and were actively promoted by her, and contributed to creating an aura of fascination around her religious centre. As was also customary at the time, in Aden, on the opposite shore of the Red Sea, the festivals at shrines also had a festive—if not actually "carnival-like"—atmosphere, with entertainment that included dances performed by women.[7]

The Ḫatmiyya, like the Salafism trans-regional ideology, the scripturalist reform movement that spread across the Islamic world from the middle of the 19th century, was shaped by local and historically contingent institutions, power structures and social practices. The spread of Salafism in the Indian Ocean enjoyed a certain amount of success, including the banning of *zār* rituals in the 1920s and of mixed dancing associated with annual festivals at shrines, on the grounds that they needed to face a process of negotiation and accommodation to local contexts. A number of Salafi preachers accused the Sufis and their followers of supporting flawed doctrinal practices such as *ḏikr* and the veneration of saints, which led to moral depravity.[8] However, other prominent members of the Arab Islamic Reform Club, which brought together people who had been involved in the anti-*zār* campaign in Aden and sought reforms in society,

5 Melis 2012: 132–133.

6 Melis 2012: 139.

7 As Irene Di Targiani Giunti wrote in her memories of her visit to Sittī ʿAlawiyya, on that occasion the *Sceriffa* had "organized a party, a jubilation, which is usually called a *fantasia*. It is a real fantasy, a circle of indigenous playing, shouting and warbling, with and the outstanding dance group clearly visible in the middle. There are three or four women, among the most beautiful, with their festive customs, almost naked in the draperies of their graceful tunics. Their dance is a rite that is performed at events of sorrow as well as of joy, but their movements and attitudes have always a refined and deep character". Di Targiani Giunti 2012: 268. In this period, this festive atmosphere was also present at Sufi festivals in Aden: Reese 2012: 75.

8 Reese 2012: 72–73–84.

focused on individual moral conduct rather than ritual practices. They considered themselves to be "lovers of the saints", and acknowledged that *ziyārāt* to shrines were spiritually edifying. One author, for example, agreed that the guardians of the saints' shrines could provide spiritual guidance, thereby becoming a "benefit" to society. He offered the example of another female guardian of a shrine, Šarīfa ʿAliya, the sister of Sayyid Hāšim al-Bahr, whose shrine was at the centre of one of the most popular Sufi festivals in Aden.[9]

The anti-Sufi critics, led by Muslim reformers such as Muḥammad Rašīd Riḍā, promoted the idea that the decline of Muslim civilization and the rise of European colonialism were related to the fact that the adoption of useful Western innovations was being impeded by Muslim scholars and mystic traditions. Contrary to the mainstream Salafi attack on the Sufi orders, however, the Ḫatmiyya was very far from mounting strong opposition to innovation and modern technology: rather, the order challenged the misleading dichotomy between European "modernization" and Islamic "traditionalism". Although they were part of a reformed Sufi order, its representatives adapted themselves to the colonial establishment and promoted a number of ideas, devices and infrastructures associated with the colonial model of "modernity" more or less actively. The al Fawānīs perspective on the banning of the gramophone is not representative of the Ḫatmiyya opposition to the introduction of all innovations and technology in the region: on the contrary, the order and its followers were especially involved in the integration of Western technology. Moreover, the charisma (*karāma*) of the Mīrġanī representatives was also related to the wonders of modernity as well as to the popular astonishment at their use of these new status symbols. Like other religious authorities in Africa and beyond, the Mīrġanī "fashioned their own visions of modernity".[10] In effect, as we will see, the Mīrġanī family's charisma was linked to the networks they had established with the colonial establishment, their involvement in the modernization process and their successful role as arbitrators in the resolution of both local and regional conflicts. Besides, although theologically speaking the debates on the authenticity of the marvels of a saint were highly controversial,

9 Reese 2012: 85. They attacked conspicuous consumption, which was considered to be a cause of "the decline of morality" during festivals in Aden. By contrast, as Reese suggested, "supporters of one of the most important festivals, that of Sayyid Hāšim al-Bahr, quickly sent their own letter to the Residence denouncing the club's actions and arguing that the activities surrounding the *ziyāra* represented a financial boon to the community. They claimed that more than 20,000 people attended the festival of Sayyid Hāšim annually and that each of them spent a minimum of five rupees. Money earned at the festival, they argued, enabled many of the poorest of Aden to make it through the year, and any curtailing of activities would cause untold hardship" (Reese 2012: 78).

10 Comaroff and Comaroff 1992: 5.

a number of *karāmāt* stories continued to circulate among believers that gave a charismatic aura to the principal representatives of the order.

Modern Enchantment: Colonial Technologies and Infrastructures

For many years, the modernization paradigm claimed that modernity led to "disenchantment with the world" through a process of rationalization, secularization and bureaucratization, and that science demystified wonders and marvels, secularism replaced spirituality and reason marginalized the imagination; a more recent historiographical position argues, however, that "there are forms of enchantment compatible with, and even dependent upon, those tenets of modernity usually seen as disenchanting the world".[11] Across the Muslim world, Sufi orders have experienced the strain of modernization and adjusted to the social transformations associated with technological and economic changes in different ways.[12] The Ḫatmiyya is one example of how Sufi orders have negotiated the processes of modernization beyond the simplistic dialectic that for a long time contrasted modernity with tradition, or rationalism with ecstatic religion.[13]

In Eritrea, as in Sudan, the Ḫatmī representatives adopted a reasonably positive approach towards the colonial activity of building both religious and civil modern infrastructures. From the earliest period, colonial policy focused on building mosques in urban areas and favouring Muslim urban elites such as the Mīrġanī, to the detriment of other Muslim shaykhs in more marginal areas.[14] In this way, a specific form of Islamic modernity was supported over other, more peripheral, forms of religiosity that were perceived as being dangerous because they lay beyond colonial control: one famous Muslim holy family in the Sahel was that of ʿAd Šayḫ, while in particular there was a very well-known shaykh named Seidna Mustafa outside Agordat who was reputed to be a learned man and a healer, whom people from all the regions of Eritrea travelled to visit for his marvels.[15] Despite the ʿAd Šayḫ family's religious influence among Muslims, the first Governor of Eritrea, Ferdinando Martini, had

11 Saler 2006: 702.

12 See Van Bruinessen and Day Howell 2007.

13 Saler 2006: 692–716; Van Bruinessen 2009: 125.

14 In Massawa, for example—as Jonathan Miran observed—urban Muslims and their institutions were privileged by Italian authorities. They were considered to be the most "civilized" and "westernized" (Miran 2005: 195).

15 Interview with Faqīh Aḥmad on September 2004 in Keren. The full text has been reported in Bruzzi 2005. On the ʿAd Šayḫ in Eritrea, see Miran 2009: 184–187.

instituted a policy that sought to undermine their authority by adopting a series of provisions. In 1903, he cut the group and its authorities out by placing their areas of influence, namely the Barka and Sahel-Samhar regions, in different districts (*Commissariati*), and one year later he cancelled the tax exemptions that had been previously granted them by the Egyptians. To counterbalance and weaken ʿAd Šayḫ's influence, the Governor also supported the religious authority of the Ḫatmiyya among the Tigré people.[16] In this way, as can also clearly be seen from colonial photography, the Italian religious policy was to pit a more "civilized", modern Islam against the less civilized version. In contrast to the nomadic structure of the ʿAd Šayḫ mosque in the Sahel, the Government heavily promoted a particular form of Islam, which was celebrated by extensive building projects or by renovating mosques in the main Eritrean urban centres such as Tesseney, Barentu, Agordat and Keren (Figures 35–40).[17]

Karāmāt stories that are transmitted orally today in Eritrea and Ethiopia celebrate the *karāma* and charismatic power of Sittī ʿAlawiyya, recounting that not only did Italian officers follow her wherever she went, but that she also built several mosques in Ethiopia.[18] This promotion of the construction of new mosques across the region was also attributed to her sister Sittī Maryam, who supported the building of small village mosques in Sudan that followed a model similar to the one promoted in Ethiopia during the Italian occupation, and were viewed as being in line with Sittī ʿAlawiyya's wishes. The Sceriffa showed deference to Vittorio Piola Caselli, the Commissioner of Agordat, because he was responsible for the construction of mosques as a part of his development plan for the lowlands. [19]

The order was also a supporter of the establishment of a "modern education system" among Muslim communities in the colony. In 1911, the Italian Government opened the Salvago Raggi School, the first school of arts and crafts for the sons of Muslim chiefs and local notables, in Keren (Figure 41). It was based on the model of British colonial schools in Sudan and Egypt, and established to train future interpreters, clerks and skilled workers in

16 Miran 2010: 45.

17 On this issue, see also Chapter 9.

18 Interviews with Ay Rawda Qallu on November 2009 in Harar (Ethiopia), with Aḥmad al-Mīrġanī and Šarīfa ʿAlawīyya on May 2009 in Cairo.

19 Vittorio Piola Caselli, *Schedario dei capi tribù*, Piola Caselli Archive in Rome. For a study on these files see Gianni Dore, forthcoming. On this issue see chapter 9. On Sittī Maryam's activity in Sudan see Voll 1969: 573. On Italian building mosques activity in Ethiopia, see Hussein Ahmed 2007b, 104; Sbacchi 1985: 162–163.

FIGURE 35 *'Ad Šayḫ's Mosque in Camcena [Camceua]. Lidio Cipriani Collection, 20/A-15.*
ISIAO ARCHIVE, ROME.

FIGURE 36 *The new mosque in Tesseney (1930s). Section 1 (Ex Armadi), Eritrea, E6B Culto Musulmano VII 1–2.*
ISIAO ARCHIVE, ROME.

FIGURE 37 *The renovated mosque in Barentu (1930s). Section 1 (Ex Armadi), Eritrea, E6B Culto Musulmano* VI *1–2.*
ISIAO ARCHIVE, ROME.

FIGURE 38 *The school and the mosque, Agordat. Section 2 (ex schedario), Eritrea, E 17 Istruzione. Altre 3.*
ISIAO ARCHIVE, ROME.

FIGURE 39 *The mosque, Agordat (1930s). Section 1 (Ex Armadi), Eritrea, E6B Culto Musulmano V 1–3.*
ISIAO ARCHIVE, ROME.

FIGURE 40 *The New Mosque, Keren (1930s). Section 1 (Ex Armadi), Eritrea, E6B Culto Musulmano III 12.*
ISIAO ARCHIVE, ROME.

crafts and modern agricultural practices.[20] Here, Eritreans could attend printing, carpentry and blacksmithing classes up to the fourth level. At first, Muslim families proved to be reticent, and were reluctant to send their sons to the school, fearing an attempt by the colonial authorities to sponsor the proselytism of Catholicism. It was rumoured that Christian prayers were said at the school, and that the kind of education that was provided there might lead to conversion to Catholicism. Sayyid Ǧaʿfar al-Mīrġanī worked to revive the school by enrolling one of his own sons, Sayyid Bakrī (b. 1911), and after attending Qur'anic studies under Šayḫ *ḫalīfa* Ǧaʿfar in a Sudanese religious school (*ḫalwa*), Sayyid Bakrī studied at the Italian school, where he learned Italian and afterwards pursued his study of Arabic and Islamic sciences with two

FIGURE 41 *Salvago Raggi School, Keren. Section 2 (ex schedario), Eritrea, E17 Istruzione. Altre 2.* ISIAO ARCHIVE, ROME.

20 Negash 1987, 79–80; Negash 2005: 110; Colonia Eritrea, Istruzione Pubblica (Asmara: n.p., 1914), 9. Commisariato di Cheren, 12 Luglio 1918, Scuola di arti e mestieri in Cheren. Pregi, difetti e proposte. Archivio Storico Diplomatico del Ministero degli Affari Esteri (ASDMAE), Archivio Storico Del Ministero Dell'Africa Italiana (ASMAI), Vol. 3, Pacco 37, Busta 4.

teachers, Šayḫ Muḥammad Ḥamīd and Šayḫ al-Maḥǧūb.[21] Although at first a number of locals resisted enrolling their sons at the school, they were later persuaded to follow Sayyid Ǧaʿfar al-Mīrġanī's example.

Sayyid Ǧaʿfar al-Mīrġanī's activities had a remarkable effect on the promotion, study and spread of Islam in the region. He brought many Muslim scholars—mainly from Massawa, but also from Agordat and Asmara—to his religious centre in Keren, which is how a system of representatives—or *ḫulafāʾ*—of the order, whose task was to spread Islam, was established. This goal was also pursued through colonial institutions and infrastructures. One of these representatives, *ḫalīfa* Ǧaʿfar, worked as a teacher at the Salvago Raggi School in Keren, where he taught Arabic writing and the teachings of the Qur'an.

Through the hierarchical *ḫulafāʾ* system, which formally acted under the authority of Sayyid Ǧaʿfar, the socio-religious organization of the order became highly centralized.[22] In Sudan, there were three degrees of shaykh of the order: the shaykh *al-taḥqīq*, the *muršid* (spiritual guide) or *murab* (educator); the shaykh *al-tabarruk*, also called the *ḫalīfa*, *nāʾib* or *naqīb*, whose position and *baraka* was dependent on the Mīrġanī family; and the shaykh *al-qirāʾa*, who was a teacher of the Qur'an and Islamic sciences, but not of Sufism.[23] In addition, as the colonial authorities noted, three levels of *ḫalīfa* were recognized in Eritrea. The highest was *ḫalīfat al-ḫulafāʾ*, the main Mīrġanī representative of all secular and religious affairs for the order in his area. Then there was the *ḫalīfa muqaddam al-ḥaḍra*, who could also replace the *ḫalīfat al-ḫulafāʾ* when he was not available during religious ceremonies, and was also the person who began to chant the collective *al-ḥaḍra* prayer. Finally, there was the simple *ḫalīfa*, another representative of the order who followed the previous two during ceremonies.[24]

The *ḫulafāʾ* presided at weddings and funerals, rituals that until then had been performed according to the inclinations of each individual group. For Muslim funerals in the area, a *ḫalīfa* was sent from Keren. After the burial, the

---

21 *Al-Zamān*, Asmara, 10 July 1954. Mīrġanī private archive, Cairo.

22 Interview with Faqīh Aḥmad on September 2004 In Keren. The full text has been reported in Bruzzi 2005.

23 Karrar 1992: 126.

24 Colonia Eritrea, Commissariato Regionale di Massaua, Oggetto: Reclami della Sceriffa Halauia El Morgani, Massaua, 24 August 1910. Archivio Storico Diplomatico del Ministero degli Affari Esteri (ASDMAE), Archivio Eritrea (AE), 1886–1912, Pacco 43 (Morgani-Adigrat—Varie Eritrea), Fasc. 1 Morgani (1886–1911).

prayers lasted for three days, and on the fourth day, the Qur'an was read.[25] Their involvement at funeral ceremonies is characteristic of the Ḫatmiyya, which was—and still is—the only order in Sudan that chants portions of the founder's poem of praise for the Prophet, *al-Nūr al-Barrāq*, at the funerals of his followers.[26] In the case of weddings, the spouses went to Sayyid Ǧaʿfar to receive his blessing seven days after celebration of the marriage, and on this occasion he would give a *kufiyya* to the bridegroom as a gift. In the evening, the *ḫulafāʾ* and other Muslims followers gathered at Sīdī Ǧaʿfar's residence to perform the *mawlid*, the collective prayer celebrating the birth of Prophet in which all the saints were mentioned. This usually took place twice a week. During the month of Ramadan, *ḫulafāʾ* and Muslim followers would perform *Salāt at-Tarāwīḥ* at the home of Sīdī Ǧaʿfar, where the courtyard would be filled with believers.[27] It was the aim of colonial policy that his religious authority and his collaboration with the Italians should prove decisive for the maintenance of law and implementation of the government's individual directives, and so Sīdī Ǧaʿfar, in his capacity as leader of the Ḫatmiyya in the colony, was introduced as the official head of Islam in Eritrea. This influential and collaborative religious authority was presented in colonial propaganda, for example in contemporary photographs in which he was pictured surrounded by his *ḫulafāʾ* while visiting the lowland regions of Eritrea to collect taxes or presiding over the inauguration of colonial infrastructures (Figures 42–44, 50). In general, the order supported the introduction of the new ideas and modern infrastructure projects promoted by British and Italian authorities on the one hand, while on the other they worked to mediate with those who were resisting them and to alleviate the negative impacts of the social, political and economic changes under way. In Sudan, Šarīfa Maryam agreed with the British government to support actions in women's education and the development of modernization projects in Eastern Sudan, and intervened as a mediator between the local people and the administration. On the one hand, she showed that she was open to the introduction of economic modernization works, while on the other, she intervened if the ongoing process was causing conflict in the country, for example by contributing financially to the support of Suakin traders who had been affected by the government's decision in 1906 to gradually transfer port traffic from Suakin

25 Interview with Faqīh Aḥmad on September 2004 in Keren.

26 Yūsuf al-Ḫalīfa ʿAbd al-Raḥmān, *al-Jawāb al-kāfī fī'l-iǧāba ʿan as'ila fuhūm al-muslimīn ʿāmmatan wa-ahl al-ṭuruq al-ṣūfiyya ḫaṣṣatan*, Cairo (n.d.), 24. Cit. in Karrar 1992: 164.

27 Interview with Faqīh Aḥmad, *ḫalīfat al-ḫulafāʾ* on September 2004 in Keren.

to Port Sudan.[28] The Ḫatmiyya also favoured the completion of two areas of the Gash irrigation project in Sudanese territory, and received a message of appreciation from the British Governor-General. In 1923, Sayyid ʿAlī al-Mīrġanī and other notables visited the Al Jazirah region to promote the project to combat the resistance that was spreading at the time.[29] Two years later, in 1925, the British completed the building of the Sennar dam, close to Sennar town, which was to provide water for crop irrigation in the Al Jazirah region, and the Italo-British Agreement was signed in Khartoum for the use of water from the River Gash. The agreement was made with Gasparini, the Governor of the Eritrean Colony, who had promoted the water works for irrigating fields in Tesseney.[30] The Italian project to use water from the Gash dated back to 1905, with the first feasibility studies carried out by the Italian engineer Nicola Coletta (followed by those of engineers G.B. Nobile and L. Avetrani in 1905–06), but the works only began in 1924. They included the construction of the dam and an artificial lake to store water in Tesseney, the Eritrean city located closest to the River Gash that thanks to the dam became the main centre for the production of cotton in Eritrea and "one of the major examples of industrial colonization undertaken by Italy", for the cotton industry.[31] Sīdī Ǧaʿfar's attitude towards projects such as this echoed that of his relatives in Sudan, who were favourable to this type of development work and the construction of an infrastructure that has been begun by the colonial authorities in the region.

The solemn celebration of the inauguration of the Tesseney dam was recorded on film and in photographs. The inauguration of the commemorative plaque for the dam in Tesseney was filmed by the Luce Institute in 1928 during the visit of Prince Umberto of Piemonte to Eritrea with both political and religious authorities, Eritreans and Italians alike, in attendance.[32] Muslims were represented by Sīdī Ǧaʿfar and his son Sīdī Bakrī, who participated in the celebration with their followers (Figures 42–44). Sīdī Bakrī had begun to attend official colonial celebrations with his father in 1924, and despite his tender years, he soon began to take on a significant political role in the colony as a mediator in conflict resolution. According to *Al-Zamān*, in 1925, at the request

28 Grandin 1988: 125. Grandin also observed that in 1947 Sittī Maryam acted as mediator in order to in alleviate the consequences of port worker strikes that risked paralysing commercial traffic.

29 Voll 1969: 573.

30 *Bollettino Ufficiale della Colonia Eritrea*—anno XXXVI, Asmara, 15 ottobre 1927, p. 253.

31 *Consociazione Turistica Italiana* 1938: 225–226; Coletta 1907.

32 See Istituto Nazionale Luce 1928 Il viaggio del Principe Umberto in Eritrea—Da Tessenei ad Agordat, see minute: 5:15. Available on-line: http://www.archivioluce.com/archivio/.

FIGURE 42 *Visit and inauguration of hydraulic works in Tesseney. Meeting with Morgani, 1928. Section 1 (Ex Armadi), Eritrea, E4BII III. Visita del Principe ereditario S.A.R duca di Piemonte 33–38(a).*
ISIAO ARCHIVE, ROME.

of the Italian authorities, he successfully intervened in local resistance to a settlement in the recently-founded town of Tesseney.[33]

Both Christian and Muslim authorities attended the ceremony at the Tesseney dam, giving their blessing to a project that was a true example of the marvels of modernity. Attendance by the Mīrġanī at spectacular inaugurations of modern building projects was not limited just to civil infrastructures but also included religious buildings, both mosques and churches. In February 1936, Red Cross nurse Elena Pesenti saw Šarīfa ʿAlawiyya attending the blessing of an Orthodox Church built on stilts close to the Taulud dam in Massawa (Figure 45), and recalled the event with these words:

> We attend the procession, which is made up of priests in rich vestments some bearing large silver crosses in their hands, and other smaller, very fine jewellery. Others hold tiny instruments, also in silver, that clang

33 *Az-Zamān*, Asmara, 10 July 1954, Mīrġanī private archive, Cairo (a).

FIGURE 43 *Visit and inauguration of hydraulic works in Tesseney. Meeting with Morgani, 1928. Section 1 (Ex Armadi), Eritrea, E4BII* III. *Visita del Principe ereditario* S.A.R *duca di Piemonte 33–38 (b).*
ISIAO ARCHIVE, ROME.

FIGURE 44 *Visit and inauguration of hydraulic works in Tesseney. Meeting with Morgani 1928. Section 1 (Ex Armadi), Eritrea, E4BII* III. *Visita del Principe ereditario* S.A.R *duca di Piemonte 33–38 (c).*
ISIAO ARCHIVE, ROME.

FIGURE 45 *Orthodox Church inauguration with the participation of all religious, civil and military authorities (Massawa, 2 Febrauary 1936).*
PRIVATE COLLECTION OF OTTAVIO DE CARLI, BRESCIA.

> when moved. Some have gorgeous heavy gilt silver crowns on their heads. There is a Coptic bishop with a large black cope embroidered in gold, a long robe of purple silk and a black hat. He has a magnificent gold chain with a cross with precious stones. There are the civil and military Italian authorities, and the *Sceriffa* also arrives by car dressed in lace trimming, with her face covered by a veil. She is welcomed with signs of great respect.
>
> A concert of strange instruments accompanies the ceremony: there are long metal and leather trumpets, large drums and small drums, with the addition of violins and metal discs that emit strange sounds when agitated. The procession crosses the bridge that joins the Church to the ground and winds along slowly. As it passes, the women emit cries of joy and greeting, a singular cry that we are not able to imitate. Then, the procession ends and there is a long sermon by the Primate, to whom the *Sceriffa* responds with a greeting […].[34]

Religious rituals and the charisma of the authorities were accompanied by the enchantment of European technology. For example, Sittī ʿAlawiyya arrived at the ceremony in her small red car, a Fiat Balilla, a gift from the government that, as shown in several photographs of the time, she enjoyed showing off.[35] The car—like the technological sector of which it was a part—was a symbol of Western technology in Africa imported from Europe, and was rapidly absorbed, transformed and adapted to the conditions and needs of Eritreans.[36] In general, the Mīrġanī publicly used and promoted symbols of modernity, including a number of European conveniences, that proved their wealth and charisma. It is significant to note here that according to the current *ḫalīfat al-ḫulafāʾ* in Keren, Sīdī Ǧaʿfar, was the first Eritrean to possess a car in Keren. As he recalls it:

> Every Friday, Sīdī Ǧaʿfar prayed at the main mosque, which had been built by the Italians, where he was the *imām* and led prayers. He covered the route from his home to the mosque in a carriage with a rider until the Italians gave him a car, first a Fiat 14, then a Ford 4 cylinder. They taught Muktar Awshik, who became his personal driver, to drive.[37]

---

34 De Carli, 2016: 155–156.

35 De Carli 2016: 126.

36 Bellucci and Zaccaria 2012.

37 Interview with Faqīh Aḥmad on September 2004 in Keren. The full text has been reported in Bruzzi 2005.

This was certainly impressive at that time if one considers that the first automobile made its appearance in Eritrea in 1900, and that in the early 1920s only four or five Eritreans had a driving licence.[38] The public display of these European status symbols fostered the Mīrġanīs' charismatic authority. In addition to owning cars, which were highly prestigious objects at that time, the colonial authorities gifted them with modern weapons for their personal use and for use by the militias they had at their disposal. These donations of modern weapons, together with decorations of merit and medals, were made publicly on the occasion of official ceremonies (Figures 46–47).

A colonial photograph (Figure 47), for example, portrays a ceremony in which Governor Gasparini donated a Flobert carbine to Sīdī Bakrī, who was about thirteen at the time. Some years later, in 1938, Mussolini in person offered Šarīfa ʿAlawiyya a carbine.[39] According to the current *ḫalīfat al-ḫulafāʾ* of Keren, Sīdī Ǧaʿfar had a group of armed men with ammunition given him by the Italians. They were his bodyguards, and were called the *walīd al-bayt* (homeboys).[40] The provision of arms and the impact of the supply of modern weapons by the colonial authorities to the local elite is highly significant, as it is in some way precisely in the superiority their possession provided that not only colonial power and its very legitimacy but also the power of local elites resided. The "tools of Empire", the new European technologies and devices that assisted the scramble for Africa, were regarded with great interest by African people and dignitaries.

The Mīrġanī were not only political intermediaries, but also in some sense *passeurs de culture*, playing a role in the process of transferring the socio-cultural and economic innovations that were imported from Europe. As we have seen, another example of this mediatory role is their approach to colonial medicine and the colonial medical system. When the sick and needy went to them to be restored to health, we see a gradual change from the use of endogenous medicine to European treatments. In the early 1900s, believers used to visit Muslim shaykhs such as Sīdī Hāšim to be treated with Islamic remedies, whereas in the 1920s and 1930s, the new generation, that of Sittī ʿAlawiyya, showed a growing interest in colonial medicine (such as quinine) and their efficacy. From this moment on, sick people who had previously gone to

38 Bellucci and Zaccaria 2012: 241–242.

39 Archivio Storico Diplomatico del Ministero degli Affari Esteri (ASDMAE), Archivio Storico Del Ministero Dell'Africa Italiana (ASMAI), Dir. Gen. Affari Politici, el. III, cart. 103. Cit. in Borruso 1997: 41.

40 Interview with Faqīh Aḥmad on September 2004 in Keren.

FIGURE 46 *Sayyid Ǧaʿfar pays homage to Governor Gasparini, Asmara (1924?). Section 2 (ex schedario), Eritrea, E 4 B/II 1. Asmara. Il Giafar Morgani rende omaggio al Governatore dell'Eritrea Gasparini.*
ISIAO ARCHIVE, ROME.

FIGURE 47 *The Governor donates a Flobert carbine to the son of the Commissioner Sayyid Ǧaʿfar al-Mīrġanī, Asmara. Section 1 (Ex Armadi), Eritrea, E4BII 1. Cerimonie alla presenza del Governatore Gasparini 3–14. Asmara, Il Governatore distribuisce decorazioni al merito, medaglie ed armi, ai capi e ai notabili (1924?).*
ISIAO ARCHIVE, ROME.

the Mīrġanī were not necessarily treated by them, but rather sent by them to colonial hospitals.[41]

The process of transferring Western technological advances to the local elites—whether in the form of "tools of Empire" or "marvels of modernity"—was characterized by complex dynamics of negotiations in which intermediaries and *passeurs* such as these played a pivotal role.

Mediating Conflicts

One common role that is played by Muslim shaykhs and saints is that of mediators in conflict resolution. Their successes as arbitrators are popularly reported in *karāmāt* stories as proof of their charismatic power. The socio-economic role played by Sufi brotherhoods in Africa in opening up new arable land along the banks of rivers donated by local clans is frequently emphasized, often mirroring the role played by these shaykhs in resolving land disputes between local populations.[42] It was not only believers who turned to Muslim shaykhs as intermediaries in cases of regional disputes: the colonial authorities did so too. From the time of the Mahdiyya conflict to the end of the Second World War, the Ḫatmiyya secured a leading role in both trans-regional and international conflicts and regional disputes. It is reported, for example, that Sīdī Bakrī intervened to solve conflicts that arose among residents in the context of the environment planning for the Tesseney area with vast agricultural development project to exploit the waters of the River Gash. When the city of Tesseney was founded in 1925, people refused to live there because of the epidemics that were common at the time, so the Italian authorities invited Sīdī Bakrī to encourage people to live in the city, as a result of which people arrived. When he went there, people began to build homes, and from that moment life began in the city, where he stayed for some years before returning to Keren in 1927. Like other members of the order, he visited the various people of the country by invitation to seek reconciliations and to guide them according to Islamic teachings and values. At his death, he was celebrated not only for his qualities as a pious man, and as generous, humble and devoted to God, but also

41 Caniglia 1940: 36–37. See chapter 4.

42 For an interesting ethnographical case study observed among the Oromo in Ethiopia, see Zeleke 2010: 63–84; Zeleke 2015. The mediation role of the Sufis is acknowledged in all Muslim societies: see, for example: Tanvir 2014.

for his role in solving family disputes, disagreements and conflicts through his "appropriate" directions.[43]

The mediatory role played by Sittī ʿAlawiyya is reported in oral accounts that are widespread across Eritrea, while her problem-solving skills were acknowledged in colonial reports:[44] in particular, *karāmāt* stories report her as an arbiter in conflict resolution affecting Eritreans and Italians alike.

Sittī ʿAlawiyya's conciliation and conflict mediation activities are related as examples of her *karāma*. One of them is still told today, and relates to her mediation in a dispute that had arisen between Italy and Sultan Hanfare of Awsa: her relatives report a family tradition that she negotiated to resolve a conflict between the Italian government and the Sultan in the 1930s.[45]

Relations between Italy and Sultan Yayyo of Awsa and later his son Sultan Muḥammad Yayyo experienced ups and downs. At first, the Sultan opposed Italian expansion into the Danakil region, at least before negotiations in 1928, and it was only in June 1936 that the Awsa become part of the Italian colony of Eritrea as an extension of the Danakil province and the Sultan began to be regularly remunerated by the Italian government. He also received diplomatic gifts from the Italian government in the form of a car and a residence in Assab.[46]

The Italian mission in the territory began in March 1936 in the context of the Second Italo-Ethiopian war, when the Awsa country seat of Sardò was occupied by an Italian contingent led by Colonel Ruggero.[47] The bloodless occupation of Sardò was considered to be a political success because it took the area from the Ethiopian Empire almost without resorting to arms, and with the use of just a few hundred irregulars. The success of the mission was recalled by Colonel Ruggeri, its leader, in these terms: "In 1936 a difficult expedition was carried out from Beilul to Sardò, 350 kilometres across the most terrible desert, which had previously been done just twice by whites. It was necessary to involve chief Haban Amoda (sic) and his brother as guides. This

---

43 *Al-Zamān*, Asmara, 10 July 1954, Mīrġanī private archive, Cairo. The article was published on his death.

44 Interview with ʿAbd al-Raḥīm ʿUṯmān Kekiya on March 2009 In Keren; Cheren, 6 September 1917, Colonia Eritrea, Commissariato di Cheren, Riservato-Urgente, Al Signor Reggente il Governo della Colonia. Oggetto: Grave dissidio seguito da ingiurie tra Morgani e Scerifa. Archivio Storico Diplomatico del Ministero degli Affari Esteri (ASDMAE), Archivio Eritrea (AE), 1886–1912, P. 1022.

45 Interview with Aḥmad al-Mīrġanī on May 2009 in Cairo.

46 Soulé and Piguet 2009: 259.

47 Soulé and Piguet 2009: 253–254.

was achieved by means of a clever policy that consisted in providing Haban Amoda with a letter from Šarīfa Celanja (*sic*) which, when tied to the ankle, became a talisman against snake bites, and in procuring a medicine for his brother that was intended to enable him to satisfy his four women despite his age." The Italian colonel's report testifies that the Italian authorities also trusted her and welcomed her actions, including resorting to the marvel of her talisman, in military and political expeditions. One open question might be what this letter from the *šarīfa* said. Was it a diplomatic letter like those she sent to other Ethiopian shaykhs during the Italian occupation? It is worth noting that, just as Italian officers integrated the astonishing marvel of a "talisman" into their military strategy, they also believed in the enchantment of modern technology, in some cases to the point where they considered it to be the gift of a divine power. During his mission in the region, Colonel Ruggero's deputy, Simon Pietro Mattei, recalled that "because I had flown very low, I returned to the field with holes in my wings, but I never fired a shot: I wanted everybody to realize that our strength came from God, that we were invulnerable and invincible".[48]

The *karāma* story of Sittī ʿAlawiyya tells that Sultan Hanfare was able to control bees. When the Italians attacked him he fought back using bees as weapons: bees against modern Italian arms. Sittī ʿAlawiyya warned the Italians of this, but they did not believe what she was saying. Finally, she told the Italians not to become involved in a war against Sultan Hanfare, and that she would talk to him to make a deal so that Italians could travel in the Danakil region. She managed to arrive at an agreement and as a reward the Sultan gave her a building that was built at the side of her residence in Hetumlo as a gift, but it is said that something happened to her there, although no one knew what exactly, but something did afflict her and some time after her return to Eritrea, she died.[49]

Other sources also report that Šarīfa ʿAlawiyya led a successful mission in 1937 to reach an agreement between the Italian Government and Sultan Muhammad Yayyo Hanfare of Awsa that included a delegation of three Eritrean traders, including Ḥasan Idrīs Kurdī. Eritrean traders from Massawa were interested in maintaining a state of peace and safety along the caravan routes, but this was dependent on political agreements to resolve the conflicts

48 Del Boca 1992 ("Verso la mitica Sardò").

49 Interview with Aḥmad al-Mīrġanī, son of Šarīfa ʿAlawiyya's bint Sīdī Ǧaʿfar on May 2009 in Cairo. The same story was reported to me during an interview with Hāšim Muḥammad ʿAlī Blenai, 102 years of age, Ḫatmiyya fellow on March 2009 in Massawa.

between the Italian government and the Sultan. In any case, after the formal annexation to Eritrea, the Italian garrisons in the Awsa were very limited, but the Italians provided the Sultan's army, which numbered 6,000 men and was associated with the so-called "Banda Dancala", a different military unit from the Eritrean and Somali askaris, with modern equipment.[50] Later on, in 1939 Sultan Muḥammad Yayyo of Awsa lead a delegation to Mussolini in Rome that included the *wazīr* Yayyo Hammadou, Muḥammad ʿAbdu Salām, *qāḍī* of the Awsa and his secretary, Ibrāhīm Dit Haysama Omar (sic).[51] The alliance between the Sultan and the Italian government proved to be a strategic one during the Second Italo-Ethiopian war. The Italian authorities promoted a policy that had the purpose of strengthening relations with local authorities, including through the Eritrean religious authorities, especially with Muslims representatives such as Sultan Muḥammad Yayyo of Awsa and the family of Abba Jaffar, the former Sultan of Jimma, in south-western Ethiopia.[52]

Sittī ʿAlawiyya's role in strengthening her religious networks with Muslim shaykhs of the occupied country in order to make agreements with Italy was remarkable in this context. They included Šayḫ ʿAbdulwahāb ibn Šayḫ Yūnus (1839–1942), one of the greatest *ʿulamāʾ* of the 19th century Bale, a public figure and a mediator between society and the government, first with Haile Selassie and then with Italy during the occupation. During the Second Italo-Ethiopian war, he worked with the Italians in the context of the diplomatic strategy Italy was pursuing in the country by using Muslim figures as intermediaries to communicate with the people. In particular, Sittīnā ʿAlawiyya sent a diplomatic letter from Eritrea to Šayḫ ʿAbdulwahāb that played an important role in helping the Italian government to be accepted by the people of Bale. According to Saru's informant, Šayḫ Kamāl, "around the time of the Italian occupation of Ethiopia in 1935, she sent a diplomatic letter with the Italians to Bale, in which, drawing upon her Muslim background as *šarīfa*, she urged the Muslims of Bale to accept Italian rule. Unfortunately the letter itself

---

50 Soulé and Piguet 2009: 254.

51 The meeting gained visibility in the Italian media and Luce Institute newsreel, see: Giornale Luce B1547, 12/07/1939, Italia Roma, available on-line: http://www.archivioluce.com/archivio/. Istituto Luce Cinecittà Historical Archive, Rome. Regarding the subsequent meeting between Mussolini and the Sultan of Awsa, Soulé and Piguet (2009: 259) pointed out that: "À cette occasion, Mohamed Yayyo est reconnu comme le chef de toute la Dancalia et il obtient de nouvelles armes pour les milices afar. Le 8 juillet 1939, Mussolini recevait en audience le sultan Mohamed Yayyo dans la salle de la Victoire du Palazzo Venezia qui lui offrit le tapis précieux que Lidj Iyassou avait donné à son père".

52 Soulé and Piguet 2009: 260; Sbacchi 1997: 165.

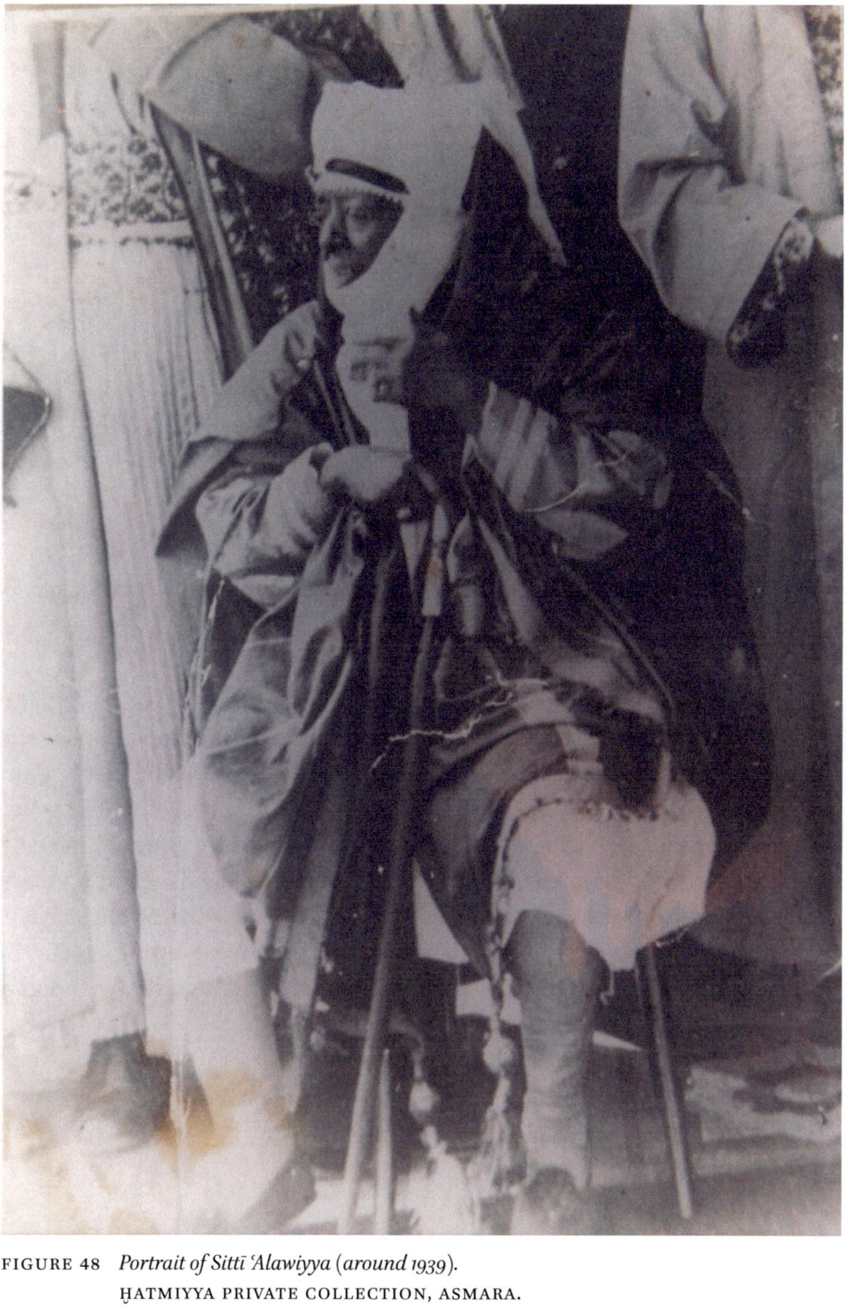

FIGURE 48 *Portrait of Sittī ʿAlawiyya (around 1939).*
ḪATMIYYA PRIVATE COLLECTION, ASMARA.

FIGURE 49 *Visit of East African notables in Rome, late 1930s.*
PHOTOGRAPHER UNKNOWN, MĪRĠANĪ FAMILY PRIVATE COLLECTION, CAIRO.

is now lost. ʿAlawiyya influenced the people of Bale through her diplomatic letter and less formal communications with the shaykhs. Among the *ʿulamāʾ* she sent a fraternal letter to Šayḫ ʿAbdulwahāb Šayḫ Yūnus saying that both of their dynasties were descended from a holy man who came from Hejaz. Her main role was peacekeeping at the time of the change of regime (from Haile Selassie to Italy). Additionally, being a Muslim woman helped her put pressure on society".[53] She also strengthened important contacts with Muslim shaykhs through other Ethiopian regions, as was particularly the case during her stay in Harar and Jimma, where she was recognized as a religious authority and as a person with extensive *karāma*.

53 Sartu 2013: 93. On Šayḫ ʿAbdulwahāb ibn Šayḫ Yūnus. See also Østebø 2008: 84.

CHAPTER 8

Military Bodies: Askaris, Officials and "the Female Warrior"

Religious Intermediaries and Regional Networks

The Italian authorities declared their intention to grant religious freedom to all colonial subjects in the earliest days of the colonial occupation, but it was clear that religious freedom was secondary to the maintenance of "public order";[1] the principal purpose was to preserve the *pax coloniale* by dedicating special attention to religious policies. Islam was the majority faith in the Northeast African colonies, and the Italian authorities, with their Christian identity, strove to prevent any situation that might incite religious clashes. In Somalia, British and Italian colonial penetration and the expansion of the Ethiopian Empire were perceived as an expression of "Christian" penetration in the *Dār al-Islām* and led to a gradual, widespread use of religious language on the part of Somalis. As in other colonial contexts, both opposition to and cooperation with the colonial authorities were led by Islamic brotherhoods that had established themselves in the territory during the period immediately preceding colonial penetration. Personalities such as Sayyid Muḥammad ʿAbdille Ḥasan (1899–1920), a representative of the Ṣāliḥiyya order in Somalia, played a preeminent militant role against colonial rule, while certain representatives of the Qādiriyya order, such as Šayḫ Uways from Brava, favoured negotiations and a more moderate stance.[2]

In Eritrea, the colonial political guidelines adhered to a notion that was lucidly expressed by the Regional Commissar of the Gash-Barka region when he identified the Mīrġanī as privileged religious intermediaries for guaranteeing socio-political stability among Muslims: "it is very unlikely that people who are led by a wise religious orientation will become victims of fanatical zeal, and that they will complain that because our Government is Christian it might always seem as though it is not paying sufficient attention to the religious affairs of Muslims".[3] The Mīrġanī were supported in their capacity as *šarīf* as, "authentic"

1 Marongiu Buonaiuti 1982: 18–19.

2 Battera 1998: 155–185. Samatar 1992.

3 Governo dell'Eritrea, Commissariato Regionale del Barca, 6 dicembre 1910. Archivio Storico Diplomatico del Ministero degli Affari Esteri (ASDMAE), Archivio Eritrea (AE), 1886–1912, Pacco 43 (Morgani-Adigrat—Varie Eritrea), Fasc. 1 Morgani (1886–1911).

 | DOI 10.1163/9789004356160_010

descendants of the Prophet and lawful authorities, who were in a position to resist other Muslim authorities and "holy men" who wished to "threaten order and breach the peace" in the country, especially in the Gash-Barka region.[4] This assumption paved the way on the one hand for progressive involvement in political affairs and regional conflicts on the part of the Ḫatmiyya, and on the other in its members' growing involvement in the security apparatus, represented by the military sector. The threefold focus of this chapter will be a review of the way religious affiliations overlapped with public order, the enrolment of African soldiers (askaris) in the colonial army, and the awarding of colonial military decorations, my aim here being to shed light on the role of the Ḫatmiyya as a social body—one among several, of course—that exerted influence within the army and the security apparatus.

When Italian troops seized Massawa, Sayyid Hāšim was already a popular figure among the irregular soldiers who had previously enlisted in the Egyptian garrison, such as the *bashi-bazouk* (literally "damaged head"), irregular enlisted units in the Ottoman Empire including Sudan, which mainly led police operations and acted as escorts and tax collectors (in return for which they were exempted from taxation). They had been released from their service to the Egyptians as a consequence of the Italian occupation of the Eritrean port, but—as was also the case with the British in Sudan—the Italian authorities decided not to discharge them but rather to integrate them into the colonial army, and so, when the Egyptians left, they passed into the Italian ranks. Photographic records portray some of the salient moments in the creation of the corps of African soldiers from the time the colonial army landed in Massawa before the dismantling of the condominium regime with Egypt to its transfer to the Italian armed services.[5] As a sign of respect and gratitude for securing continuity in their military career through their appointment to the Italian army, a number of them sent charitable gifts, such as coffee, to Sayyid Hāšim in Massawa.[6] A similar tribute was paid by the askaris—and their Christian wives—through pious visits to the ruins of the Ḫatmiyya

4 Pollera 1935: 286–287.

5 Warburg 2013: 211; Palma 2005b: 60, see in particular notes 69 and 70. See also Scardigli 1996: 13.

6 Severals *bashi-bazouk*, for example, when they were released from their service to the Egyptians and later enlisted in the Italian army, were happy to see their position assured and offered the Mīrġanī a handful of coffee or some other item. Regio esercito italiano, 16 gennaio 1887. Archivio Storico Diplomatico del Ministero degli Affari Esteri (ASDMAE), Archivio Eritrea (AE), 1886–1912, Pacco 43 (Morgani-Adigrat—Varie Eritrea), Fasc. 1 Morgani (1886–1911).

shrine and mosque in Kassala when the city was "liberated" by the Mahdiyya thanks to their vital contribution to the battle.[7] The negotiations conducted by the Mīrġanī with colonial officers and their political negotiations and collaborative economic attitude towards the Government reflected not only their personal interests, but also—more notably—those of their members. The Hadendowa, Beni ʿAmer and ʿAfar people—among whom the Ḫatmiyya was particularly influential—were progressively integrated into the colonial economy through mediation conducted by the local and traditional elites.[8] After all, the Ḫatmiyya was well established in the colonial system both economically and politically: as a religious organization, the order had incorporated a preexisting religious formation "into a new supra-community *ṭarīqa* network" by means of which its representatives, such as *ḫulafāʾ* and *ḫalīfat al-ḫulafāʾ*, were appointed and linked together in a trans-ethnic, cross-regional organization across a broader area.[9] This method of expansion was driven by integrating "traditional" religious figures such as *faqīh* and *qāḍī* into the organization and appointing them as *ḫulafāʾ* of the order. For example, the *qāḍī* of Massawa, Šayḫ Muḥammad Nūr ʿAbd Allāh Sirāǧ, was appointed as *ḫalīfat al-ḫulafāʾ* of the port by ʿUṯmān Tāǧ al-Sirr. It was general practice in the order to grant offices such as this to an individual who already had a government function, as was clearly the case with the afore-mentioned *qāḍī* of Massawa.[10] Other *ḫulafāʾ* occupied educational offices in Muslim communities: one noteworthy example of this trend is Sayyid Ǧaʿfar's namesake *ḫalīfa* in Keren, who taught Arabic in the colonial Salvago Raggi School and was also the *imām* of the city's main Mosque.[11] It was not only religious personalities who became a part of the system, however: the order also co-opted key figures from the political and economic establishment as both *ḫulafāʾ* and mere followers. Several followers of Šarīfa ʿAlawiyya were askaris who worked for the Government, but, at the

7 Fiaschi 1896: 28. For the general context see Cesari 1913; Scardigli 1996: 13. For a study on the history of Sudanese slave soldiers in the context of the Anglo-Egyptian re-conquest of Sudan, see Lamothe 2010.

8 Negash 1986: 47–48.

9 O'Fahey and Radtke 1993: 79. Cit. in Miran 2005: 187–188. See also Vikør 2000: 441–476.

10 Colonia Eritrea, Commissariato Regionale di Massaua, 24 agosto 1910. Archivio Storico Diplomatico del Ministero degli Affari Esteri (ASDMAE), Archivio Eritrea (AE), 1886–1912 Pacco 43 (Morgani-Adigrat—Varie Eritrea), Fasc. 1 Morgani (1886–1911).

11 Commissariato Regionale di Cheren, Verbale di sommarie informazioni, 5 settembre 1917. Archivio Storico Diplomatico del Ministero degli Affari Esteri (ASDMAE), Archivio Eritrea (AE), 1880–1917, Pacco 1022 (Missioni Politiche—Varie—El Morgani), Fasc. 10 Famiglia El Morgani, 1895–1917.

same time they supported her and looked on her as their leader.[12] This was the case with the *ḫalīfa* ʿAlī Muḥammad (b. 1898 in Khartoum) who worked as the *šarīfa*'s counsellor for a number of years. He assisted the Mission of Governor Gasparini in Yemen (1927), of which Sīdī Ǧaʿfar al-Mīrġanī was also a member. He was awarded the Colonial Order of the Star of Italy, and accompanied the *šarīfa* on her visit to Mussolini in Rome in 1938.[13] The *šarīfa*, whose epithet was "the warrior" (*al-ḥarbiyya*), "the one who dresses like a warrior" (*al-lābisa ḥarbiyya*), was particularly influential within one section of the colony's military class, and here we can observe a sort of continuity with the popularity her father Sayyid Hāšim had enjoyed among the irregular soldiers. According to Commissioner Fioccardi, no one who travelled to Keren failed to pay her a visit, and her residence was especially frequented by soldiers, with whom she was extremely popular.[14]

The main function of Eritrea—the so-called "first-born colony" ("colonia primogenita")—was to produce the soldiers who were required to consolidate the Italian colonies in Libya and Somalia. By 1914, recruitment had reached a number slightly over 10000. The military sector was vast, and the army was a prestigious centre for recruitment into the money economy.[15]

In a way, a part of the country's military and trade sector was co-opted into the Ḫatmiyya organization: the *šarīfa's* principal "domains" were the *Azienda Trasporti*, the transport company of Asmara and the Keren Battalion, and they were her most important donors. When she visited Asmara, she and her large entourage would be hosted by the *Azienda Trasporti*, where she would hold private talks with the *scium-basci* Muḥammad Aberra Hagos.[16] The higher ranks of the army—who had been decorated by the government—were appointed as representatives of the order: influential figures in the colonial economy and policy such as Maḥmūd Ibrāhīm Muḥammad and the above-

12 Interview with Šarīfa ʿAlawiyya, namesake and descendent of Šarīfa ʿAlawiyya and daughter of Ǧaʿfar al-Mīrġanī on May 2009 in Cairo.

13 Puglisi 1952: 12.

14 Colonia Eritrea, Commissariato di Cheren, Riservato-Urgente, Al Signor Reggente il Governo della Colonia. Oggetto: Grave dissidio seguito da ingiurie tra Morgani e Sceriffa, Cheren, 6 settembre 1917. Archivio Storico Diplomatico del Ministero degli Affari Esteri (ASDMAE), Archivio Eritrea (AE), 1880–1917, Pacco 1022 (Missioni Politiche—Varie—El Morgani), Fasc. 10 Famiglia El Morgani, 1895–1917.

15 Negash 1986: 48-. See also Tekeste Negash 1987.

16 Telegramma espresso di servizio, Commissariato Regionale di Cheren, 4 settembre 1917. Archivio Storico Diplomatico del Ministero degli Affari Esteri (ASDMAE), Archivio Eritrea (AE), 1880 -1917, Pacco 1022 (Missioni Politiche—Varie—El Morgani), Fasc. 10 Famiglia El Morgani, 1895–1917.

mentioned Muḥammad Aberra Hagos, both of whom were appointed simultaneously as *ḫulafā'* of the Ḫatmiyya and *scium-basci* (sergeant) in the colonial army (the highest military rank available to African soldiers in the Italian armed forces), may be found among their number. As in other contexts, a military career offered social mobility, and was one way of achieving higher social status.[17] After Maḥmūd Ibrāhīm enlisted in the *Regio Corpo Truppe Coloniali d'Eritrea* and took part in the Campaign in Libya in 1913–14, he was first promoted as a *muntaz*, then as a *buluc-basci*, and finally as a *scium-basci* in 1923. He was made head of the Eritrean Municipal Guard of Asmara (1932–33) and then performed the same function in Keren until 1937. Another appointed *ḫalīfa* of the Ḫatmiyya, Muḥammad Aberra Hagos, was a *scium-basci* and head of the Eritrean Transport Company of Asmara. After studying at the Salvago Raggi School in Keren, he devoted himself to trade, and in 1928 established the first Public Transport Company for Eritreans. He also worked for the Government in the Economy Department.[18] When Sīdī Ǧa'far appointed Muḥammad Aberra Hagos as his *ḫalīfa*, Sittī 'Alawiyya offered him a higher position, and he was nominated as her *ḫalīfat al-ḫulafā'* in 1917. This episode was the cause of yet another dispute between the two Mīrġanī over leadership of the order. On this occasion, Sittī 'Alawiyya also appointed three *ḫulafā'*: two *scium-basci* and a Jabarti. Sīdī Ǧa'far denounced these appointments to the Government as unlawful, and asked the Italian authorities to intervene to oblige the three "unlawfully" elected men to turn their appointments down. Apart from providing insight into internal conflicts within the Sufi order, the dispute also demonstrates how the order infiltrated the higher ranks of the military and the security services. In effect, as Commissioner Fioccardi observed, it was not a good thing for the government for non-commissioned officers to be hierarchically dependent on other authorities outside the colonial army: "They are people of special significance, they exercise influence and authority over their subjects that deviate from the aims for which the regulations established their rank; they become collectors from their subjects for the benefit of holy men".[19] In truth, the fact that key indigenous figures working for the colonial army were co-opted into the order gave rise to controversial conflicts of interests: some regular and irregular militias were acknowledged to be at the disposal

17 For the Sudanese case, see Lamothe 2010.

18 Puglisi 1952: 189 and 207.

19 Colonia Eritrea, Commissariato Regionale di Cheren, Cheren—28 agosto 1917. Archivio Storico Diplomatico del Ministero degli Affari Esteri (ASDMAE), Archivio Eritrea (AE), 1880 -1917, Pacco 1022 (Missioni Politiche—Varie—El Morgani), Fasc. 10 Famiglia El Morgani, 1895–1917.

FIGURE 50 *Italian East Africa. Morgani crosses subject regions to collect tributes.* E. LO GIUDICE COLLECTION, 49. ISIAO ARCHIVE, ROME.

of the Mīrġanī, and the government provided Sayyid Ǧaʿfar with an armed militia that made up his bodyguards.[20] One colonial photograph portrays Sayyid Ǧaʿfar riding a camel surrounded by a group of people including members of the camel corps, some of whom are wearing askaris uniforms (Figures 50–51).

The caption to the photograph states that he was crossing the regions that were subject to colonial rule to collect tributes.[21] This is misleading and ambiguous, however, because in fact, the Mīrġanī used to cross the region to preach and collect offerings for their own order, but only after the government had completed its collection operations.[22]

20 Interview with Faqīh Aḥmad on September 2004 in Keren.

21 Another photograph (Figure 51) of the moment that is immortalized in this one is in the Pavoni Social Centre Archive (Asmara), but it has a different (and simpler) caption: "Sayyid Ǧaʿfar rides a camel".

22 Colonia Eritrea, 1914, Commissariato Regionale di Cheren, telegramma espresso 23 settembre 1914; Viaggio del Morgani nel Barca e nel Gasc-Setit, Viaggio Morgani 16 febbraio 1915 Commissariato Regionale del Barca. Archivio Storico Diplomatico del Ministero degli

FIGURE 51 *Sayyid Ǧaʿfar rides a camel.*
PAVONI SOCIAL CENTRE COLLECTION, ASMARA.

According to the Regional Commissioner of Barka, the conflict between Sayyid Ǧaʿfar and Šarīfa ʿAlawiyya was connected with economic interests that their entourage in particular promoted in their capacity as collection agents in order to secure offerings from new followers and adherents. In this sense, the *šarīfa's* decision to establish her residence in Keren was related to the need to demand oblations from Muslims from the North-West region of the country. This was a reaction to Sayyid Ǧaʿfar's frequent new appointments of *ḫulafāʾ* who had channelled funds to Keren—reaching not only Kassala, but also Massawa, which was the *šarīfa's* main centre of influence.[23]

On the other hand, the conflicts of interest involved in being affiliated with the order and simultaneously holding government office demonstrate the underground agency of the Mīrġanī and their entourage, which found it easy to evade colonial control, but while the representatives of the order who were working for the government were undoubtedly mired in a controversial

Affari Esteri (ASDMAE), Archivio Eritrea (AE), 1880–1917, Pacco 1022 (Missioni Politiche—Varie—El Morgani), Fasc. 10 Famiglia El Morgani, 1895–1917.

23 Governo dell'Eritrea, Commissariato Regionale del Barca, 6 dicembre 1910. Archivio Storico Diplomatico del Ministero degli Affari Esteri (ASDMAE), Archivio Eritrea (AE), 1886–1912 Pacco 43 (Morgani-Adigrat—Varie Eritrea) Fasc. 1 Morgani (1886–1911).

conflict of interest, this conflict was even more evident in the case of the order's leader: Sayyid Ǧaʿfar resorted to his dual qualification as the officially recognized leader of the order in Eritrea and as a decorated *Grande Ufficiale* of the colony, and later on as *Grand Cordon* (Knight Grand Cross) in his exchanges with the native population, notably in his correspondence in the colonial territory (Figures 52–53).

These titles provided him with an acknowledged authority that was both religious and political.[24]

Despite this official recognition, Sayyid Ǧaʿfar lacked the charismatic authority the colonial officials would have wanted to see when they invited him to establish his residence in the Colony. Two Regional Commissioners, Fioccardi and Pollera, were in agreement that his activities were actually being manipulated by his mainly Sudanese *ḫulafāʾ*, who advised him but who effectively continued to be appointed by the Mīrġanī from Kassala. Indeed, there was a gap between the official colonial discourse, which sought to present him as a faithful and cooperative authority, and his behaviour and the activities he and his representatives carried out underground. The authorities were aware of this to some extent, and were suspicious of the reliability of the political activities that he—and especially his representatives—were carrying out in the country independent of government guidelines. In some instances, they also took measures against some of Sayyid Ǧaʿfar's *ḫulafāʾ*, as in the case of the expulsion of *ḫalīfa* Faqīh Macchi (sic), which had been requested by the Diglal. In the summer of 1913, the Regional Commissioner of the Barka and Gash-Setit, Alberto Pollera, informed the government of the underground activities being directed by Sayyid Ǧaʿfar's Sudanese *ḫalīfa* Mussa Muḥammad, who was his *factotum*. Mussa Muḥammad was regarded as being responsible for the order's involvement in clandestine affairs relating to two personalities who had long been fugitives after being accused of murder, and who were eventually arrested in Barentu. They were found to be in possession of letters from Sayyid Ǧaʿfar to a local chief asking him to offer protection to them and another three fugitives. As a result of this murky matter, colonial officials sought to interfere in the selection and appointment of the *ḫulafāʾ*, and attempted to convince Sīdī Ǧaʿfar to appoint Eritreans, who were well accepted by the government, and to stop appointing Sudanese. Their attempts were unsuccessful, however, in part because his authority within the order was too weak, to the extent that the Mīrġanī from Kassala even continued to exercise

24 After a Royal Decree of 22 September 1932 revoked Muḥammad Idrīs al-Sanūsīʾ award of the highest colonial distinction, the *Grand Cordon*, it was awarded to the leader of the Ḫatmiyya in Eritrea, Sīdī Ǧaʿfar. *Gazzetta Ufficiale del Regno d'Italia*, anno 74°, Roma, mercoledì 22 marzo 1933. no. 68, pp. 1186–1187.

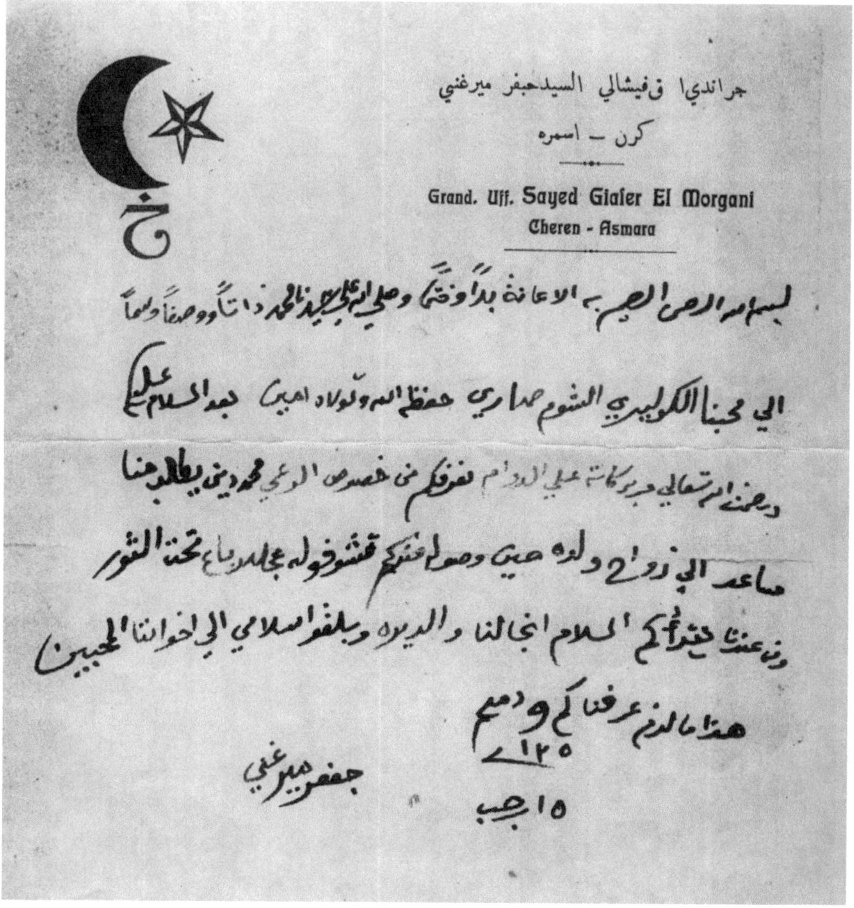
جراندي اوفيشالي السيدجعفر ميرغني
كرن – اسمره
Grand. Uff. Sayed Giafer El Morgani
Cheren - Asmara

جعفر ميرغني
١٥ رجب

FIGURE 52 *Letter from Sayyid Ǧaʿfar (Keren and Asmara).*
MĪRĠANĪ FAMILY PRIVATE COLLECTION, CAIRO.

their influence in Eritrea, especially in the Western areas. In a way, this situation proved that the Italian government's attempt to create an autonomous Eritrean branch of the order under the leadership of Sayyid Ǧaʿfar was not especially effective, because the centre of Kassala in Sudan also continued to be influential in the Eritrean lowlands.[25]

25 Governo dell'Eritrea, Commissario regionale del Gasc e sestit, Oggetto: Azioni del Morgani. Cheren, 6 giugno 1913. Archivio Storico Diplomatico del Ministero degli Affari Esteri (ASDMAE), Archivio Eritrea (AE), 1880 -1917, Pacco 1022 (Missioni Politiche—Varie—El Morgani), Fasc. 10 Famiglia El Morgani, 1895–1917.

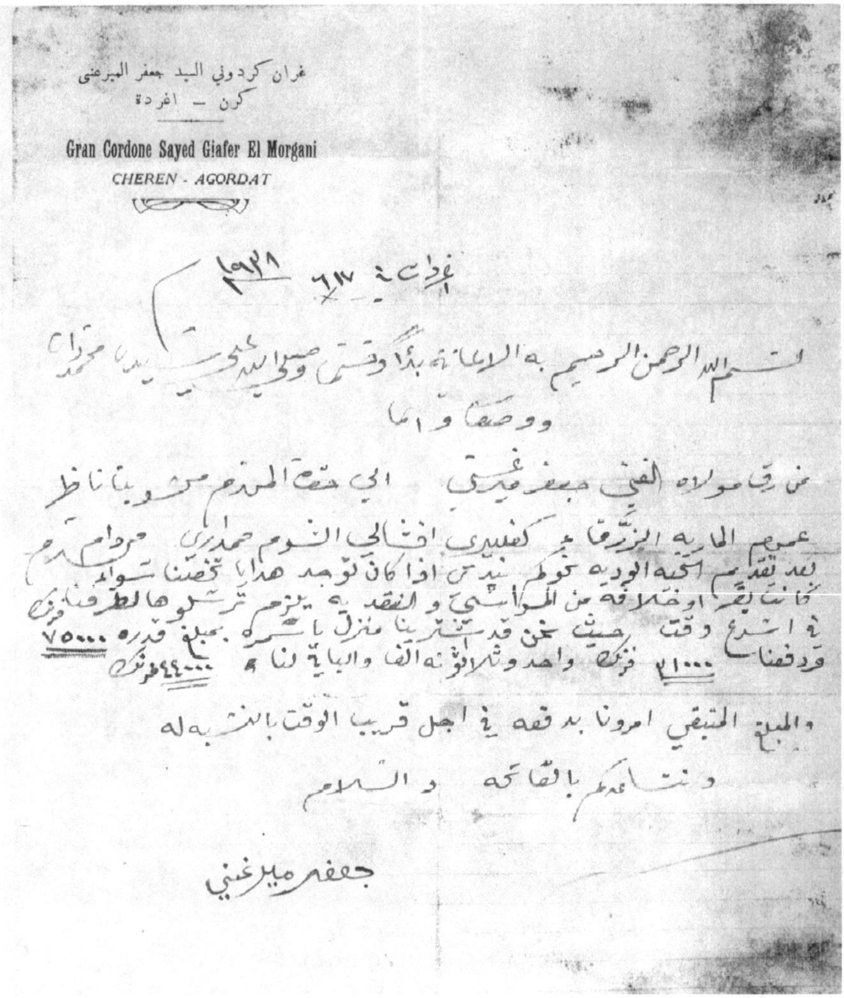
غران كردوني السيد جعفر الميرغني
كرن – اغردة

Gran Cordone Sayed Giafer El Morgani
CHEREN - AGORDAT

بسم الله الرحمن الرحيم وبه الإعانة بدءاً وختماً وصلى الله على سيدنا محمد [illegible] وصحبه وسلما

[illegible]

والمبلغ المتبقي امرونا بدفعه في اجل قريب الوقت بالنسبة له

ونسامحكم بالفاتحة والسلام

جعفر ميرغني

FIGURE 53 *Letter from Sayyid Ǧaʿfar (Keren and Agordat).*
MĪRĠANĪ FAMILY PRIVATE COLLECTION, CAIRO.

Until the First World War, as representatives of a centralized organization with extensive influence, the Mīrġanī were the favoured intermediaries between British officials and the Sudanese in Sudan. In 1916, Wingate publicly acknowledged the loyalty displayed by the Mīrġanī to the Government and their important role in the introduction of some of the reforms that were considered necessary for the country's administration. In the post-war period, however, with the introduction of the Native Administration in Sudan, the situation began to change, and other groups began to play important political roles.[26] The Italian authorities in Eritrea adopted similar religious policies towards them, consulting them as intermediaries, especially when they needed to deal with the Muslim population of the lowlands. A prominent public role was reserved for Sayyid Ǧaʿfar and Sittī ʿAlawiyya by the colonial authorities during official ceremonies, similar to the situation in Sudan with Sayyid ʿAlī, who was treated as the unofficial leader of the country until the 1920s. In 1921, according to British intelligence, the Ḫatmiyya was the most popular and most followed *ṭarīqa* in Sudan.[27] As we have said, the Eritrean branch of the order, which was officially represented by Sayyid Ǧaʿfar, was, in fact, directed by his *ḫulafāʾ*, who were mainly of Sudanese origin. The Mīrġanī from Kassala continued to appoint their representatives in Eritrea, and it was they who effectively manipulated the activities of the Italian-appointed leader of the order in the colony.[28] On the other hand, although she was not officially recognized by the Government, Sittī ʿAlawiyya had real socio-religious authority and great political influence, especially in the region of Massawa, but also through her regional networks, which extended well beyond the colonial borders.

Enlisting Askaris and Colonial Propaganda

Especially from the time of the Italo-Turkish war in Libya (1911–12), colonial policy began to look on Eritrea as a military colony, mainly as a source for enlisting askaris. As Uoldelul Chelati Dirar has noted, colonial legislators report the "myth" of enthusiastic voluntary enlistment by Eritreans into the colonial army, but despite this, the colonial gaze passes over the coercion and power dynamics that influenced "voluntary" recruitment, and oral sources insist on the motives of prestige that drove Eritrean men to enlist in the army, such as enjoying the image of the successful soldier, acquiring a wife, or having a taste for adventure. Enlistment was not necessarily or always due to economic reasons.[29] The experience of the Italian campaign in Libya in 1911–1912 had a

26 Voll 1969: 565, 573.

27 Voll 1969: 574–583.

28 Governo dell'Eritrea, Commissario regionale del Gasc e Sestit, Oggetto: Azioni del Morgani. Cheren, 5 giugno 1913. Archivio Storico Diplomatico del Ministero degli Affari Esteri (ASDMAE), Archivio Eritrea (AE), 1880 -1917, Pacco 1022 (Missioni Politiche—Varie—El Morgani), Fasc. 10 Famiglia El Morgani, 1895–1917.

29 Chelati Dirar 2007: 50–51; Volterra 2005: 76–79. See also Chelati Dirar 2004.

huge impact in Eritrea, and on that occasion, the impressive participation by Eritrean askaris in the war was given considerable visibility in both Italy and Eritrea. The colonial media and propaganda machine become particularly active in promoting their mobilization and celebrating the quality of their fighting skills, exalting the Eritrean askaris as examples of "martial races".[30]

On the other hand, at an international level, Italian propaganda took action to limit voices against the war in Libya that were being raised through Turkish emissaries among Muslim countries at the time, such as on the opposite shore of the Red Sea, along the Arabic peninsula.[31] In Egypt, which lay at heart of the Italian policy to seek a consensus in the region, the Mīrġanī became especially involved in anti-Turkish propaganda. The *šarīfa* sent a letter to the Mīrġanī in Alexandria asking them to intervene to restrain and counterbalance the anti-Italian propaganda that was widespread in Arabic countries after the occupation of Tripoli.[32] Her letter, which was initially addressed to her relatives in Alexandria, was later considered by the Italian Ministry of Foreign Affairs to be worthy of being published so as to give prominence to her claims regarding the special treatment reserved for Muslims in the Italian colonies. The *šarīfa* had sent the letter to Alexandria just a couple of months after the beginning of the war, at the end of December 1911. She was well informed about the rumours circulating in Egypt against the Italian government in a general context of popular opposition to the colonial occupation of Libya. In particular, the Italians were alleged to be interfering in Muslims' religious affairs and offering bribes to make Muslim women turn to prostitution. In response to these rumours, the *šarīfa* stated that the Italians practiced their own religion in Eritrea, and left Muslims to follow theirs, and that they did not interfere in religious affairs except to help Muslims profess Islam, building mosques and shrines and paying Muslims salaries as teachers, *qāḍī* and so on. Through these arguments, she asked her relative in Egypt to tone down the rumours against Italy.[33] Opposition to the Italian conquest was led by the Sanūsiyya Sufi order, which

30 See Zaccaria 2012. On the notion of "martial races" in the British Empire, see: Streets 2004: 241.

31 Zaccaria 2013: 218.

32 Ministero degli Affari Esteri, Oggetto: Musulmani in Tripolitania, Roma, 20 gennaio 1912. Archivio Storico Diplomatico del Ministero degli Affari Esteri (ASDMAE), Archivio Storico Del Ministero Dell'Africa Italiana (ASMAI), Vol. 2, Posiz. 104/1 1911–1912, Fasc. 12. See also Erlich 1994.

33 Commissariato di Cheren, 21 dicembre 1911, Lettere della sceriffa Alania al Morgani. Archivio Storico Diplomatico del Ministero degli Affari Esteri (ASDMAE), Archivio Storico Del Ministero Dell'Africa Italiana (ASMAI), Vol. 2 Libia, Guerra italo-turca 1911–1912, Posiz. 104/1 1911–1912, Fasc. 12 Guerra italo turca.

owed its loyalty to pan-Islamic positions associated with the Ottoman Empire. Internationally, several Muslim countries contributed to the anti-colonial movement, with growing numbers of arrivals of aid and volunteers in Libya from Egypt, Algeria, Tunisia, Chad, and India to fight the Italian colonial army.[34]

In Eritrea, on the other hand, the Ḫatmiyya expressly sided with the anti-Ottoman party and promoted the enlistment of askaris. Both Sittī ʿAlawiyya and Sīdī Ǧaʿfar organized fundraising campaigns among the native population in support of the families of askaris who had died or been injured in Tripolitania.[35] Beginning at the end of 1911, the campaign "for the fallen and injured in Tripolitania and Cyrenaica" saw popular participation in all the colony's territories, with the significant participation of Muslim notables in Massawa and Keren, which was emulated by the Christian and Greek communities.[36] At official events, Sīdī Ǧaʿfar also incited the Eritrean askari battalions to fight the Turks. On 31 January 1912, the Italian government organized a solemn ceremony in Massawa with the participation of military and civil dignitaries to bid farewell to the Eritrean battalions who were leaving for Libya by steamship. The day after, another demonstration took place with the participation of the *abuna* of the Orthodox Church and Sīdī Ǧaʿfar, as representative of the Ḫatmiyya. Both the *qāḍī* of Massawa—who was also the *ḫalīfat al-ḫulafāʾ* of the *ṭarīqa*—and the Prior of the Bizen Monastery blessed Muslim and Christian askaris and encouraged them to uphold the honour of the colonial army.[37] An evocative article in *Rivista Coloniale* celebrated this event, reporting on the widespread stereotypical arguments circulating in the Italian media and propaganda of the time, such as the bravery and exceptional qualities of the Eritrean askaris employed in the colonial war:

> ... We must be grateful to the Italian-Turkish war, which in addition to awakening the national consciousness, drew the motherland's attention to that abandoned land, which other more practical nations envy us for, and which a few years ago the majority of our politicians had classified

---

34 Ahmida 1994: 118.

35 Telegramma Cheren, 26 dicembre 2011; Bollettino Ufficiale della Colonia Eritrea, 21, 9, 29 feb. 1912, pp. 30–32. Archivio Storico Diplomatico del Ministero degli Affari Esteri (ASDMAE), Archivio Eritrea (AE), 1880–1917, Busta 608, Fasc. 2. Cit. in Zaccaria 2012: 36.

36 Zaccaria 2012: 36–39.

37 Zaccaria 2012: 35. See also: 30 gennaio 1912, Telegramma in arrivo da Asmara a Roma; 1 febbraio 1912, Telegramma in arrivo da Massaua a Roma. Archivio Storico Diplomatico del Ministero degli Affari Esteri (ASDMAE), Archivio Storico Del Ministero Dell'Africa Italiana (ASMAI), Vol. 2 Posiz.115/1 Fasc. 2.

> as an acquired damage that needed to be suffered for motives of national self-respect. Today, Eritrea is recognized as a good place for providing soldiers, if for no other reason, and we are adding soldiers whom no other colony, we can say without fear of contradiction, is able to recruit. In fact, the Eritrean native soldier possesses all the best qualities for a colonial war. He is tireless when on the march and very quick when running, he is frugal and brings together the many advantages of disdain for death, which is typical of all oriental populations, impetus and ferocity in battle and iron discipline in executing orders. Eritrea therefore wanted to greet its soldiers in a dignified manner, and without mentioning the official ceremonies, we can say that on the occasion in Massawa, all the native notables of the colony, Christians and Muslims, and the Morgani, authentic descendants of the Prophet, gathered together with the authorities, who, having brought together the Muslim askaris, made a speech encouraging them to fight the usurpers of the caliphate.[38]

This discourse lays emphasis on the distinction between the prophetic ancestry and legitimate religious authority of Sīdī Ǧaʿfar in Eritrea, and the wholly unlawful power of the Ottomans in Libya. The propaganda also appealed to the authenticity of the Islamic faith. In this instance, Sayyid Ǧaʿfar, in his capacity as lawful descendant of the Prophet, played an important role by supporting the war against the "Turks", who were accused of being illegitimate heirs of the caliphate and "false Muslims".[39]

This argument was reported in detail in Italian propaganda, the aim of which was to give visibility to the antagonism of the Muslim communities towards the fracturing Ottoman Empire in its former territories and provinces and to affirm the friendship between Italy and Islam. After all, this period of the Libyan war was merely the prelude to the First World War, and saw growing appeals from the European powers to pro-Islamic attitudes to seek the support of their African colonies on the one hand, and to promote the appointment of Muslim soldiers in colonial armies on the other.[40]

According to the Italian propaganda discourse, the reporter could also claim that:

---

38 *Rivista coloniale: organo dell'Istituto coloniale italiano* (1906–1927). Rome: Unione coop. Editrice. 1912: 206.

39 Bruzzi 2006: 435–453.

40 With regard to British propaganda that claimed to be a Muslim power during World War One, see Reynolds 2001: 605. For the French case, see, for example, Renard 2013.

... the awakening of anti-Turkish attitudes on the part of natives is natural. Above all else, it is an ancient hatred against the ancient tyrants that is awakening. And certainly today in Eritrea, the old men frequently evoke ancient traditions to incite hatred of the Turks, because in Eritrea, as in Yemen, the Turk is considered to be a false Muslim, a usurper of the rights due to the real descendants of the Prophet. It is enough to ask Morgani, a Muslim holy man revered throughout East Africa who claims to be a direct descendant of Mohammed, to hear what he says about Muslim Turks and the Caliph of Constantinople, whom he regards as a usurper of rights. But the best evidence of all will be provided by the Eritrean battalion as soon as they arrive in battle. We are absolutely sure of this. Our askaris have already fought against the Mahdi; many of them were Muslims, but they have done their duty just like the rest....[41]

It is worth noting that the contribution of the Eritrean and Muslim askaris to the Italian war in Libya brought back memories of their participation in the conflict against the Mahdī in Sudan, which was also not only an anti-colonial movement but also a religious war in which opposing sectarian parties employed Islamic rhetoric to legitimize their political agendas.[42] In Libya, too, and later on during the First World War, conflicts within the Muslim community played an important role and channelled rival parties towards their claim of "Islamic authenticity"; while the Sanūsiyya order swore allegiance to the Ottomans, and led a *ǧihād* against the "unbelievers", the Ḫatmiyya, its traditional rival, sided with the Allies and accused the Turks of being "usurpers of the caliphate".[43]

During the First World War, the Mīrġanī openly asserted their anti-Ottoman position at a supra-regional level. In 1917, Sayyid ʿAlī al-Mīrġanī who was in touch with the leaders of the Arabic revolts against the Ottomans, wrote to Šarīf Ḥusayn of Mecca from Sudan congratulating him on his victories in the Arab revolt.[44] From Egypt and Eritrea, too, the Mīrġanī family sided with the

---

41 *Rivista coloniale: organo dell'Istituto coloniale italiano* (1906–1927). Rome: Unione coop. Editrice. 1912: 206.

42 A comparison with the war against the Mahdī is also offered in Sittī ʿAlawiyya's letter. Commissariato di Cheren, 21 dicembre 1911, Lettere della sceriffa Alania al Morgani. Archivio Storico Diplomatico del Ministero degli Affari Esteri (ASDMAE), Archivio Storico Del Ministero Dell'Africa Italiana (ASMAI), Vol. 2 Libia, Guerra italo-turca 1911–1912, Posiz. 104/1 1911–1912, Fasc. 12 Guerra italo turca.

43 On the Sanūsiyya role in promoting enrolment, see Koloğlu 2007: 126.

44 Voll 1969: 458.

Allies against both the "Turks" and the Sanūsiyya in Libya during World War One,[45] and their support for England and the Allies was reported on several occasions. In a 1914 propaganda article entitled "A descendent of the Prophet against the holy war" Reuters reported that:

> Sceik Said el Morghani, a direct descendent of the Prophet, who enjoys great influence in Egypt, Arabia and Sudan, has sent a telegraph strongly deploring the Turkish Government's activity and the war against Great Britain and the Allies. Morghani declares that "Turkey is sacrificed to German ambition. By placing themselves under Germany influence, those who hold authority in Constantinople have alienated the good feelings of Muslims across the entire world, and they will drag the Turkish people to certain ruin. Morghani declared his and his followers' most sincere and loyal devotion to England, to which Muslims are highly indebted. Sceik Yusee Elhindi (sic), a religious personality of great authority, has made a similar claim, and protestations of loyalty have been sent from all the leading shaykhs and ulema in Sudan".[46]

In the post-war period, Sayyid Ǧaʿfar was decorated with the highest colonial honours as a reward for his commitment to supporting the *pax colonial* not only in Eritrea but also on the Libyan front. A Royal Decree of 29 January 1929 decorated him with the 2nd Class Degree of the Colonial Order of the Star of Italy, that of Grand Officer (*Grande Ufficiale*). The Colonial Order of the Star of Italy (*Ordine coloniale della Stella d'Italia*) had been created by King Victor Emmanuel III on 18 June 1914 as a colonial order of knighthood to reward soldiers deployed to the colony of Libya. Some years later, at the end of October 1932, another decree awarded him the highest colonial decoration, the Knight Grand Cross, in his capacity as "leader of the tariqa in the Eritrean Colony". His decoration coincided with the revocation of both decorations from Sīdī Muḥammad Idrīs al-Sanūsī, who was in exile in Egypt at that time following a brief parenthesis of negotiations with the occupying powers between 1916 and 1923, when the Italian authorities had lent support to his authority, providing him with armed forces and allowing him to adopt the symbols of government in

45 For the text of the Ottoman proclamation of *ǧihād* in 1914, see Lewis 1975: 157 and Erik-Jan Zürcher 2016.

46 This is my own translation from Italian to English. See "Un discendente del Profeta contro la guerra santa", *L'Idea Nazionale*, 17 novembre 1914. Archivio Storico Diplomatico del Ministero degli Affari Esteri (ASDMAE), Archivio Eritrea (AE), 1886–1912 Pacco 43 (Morgani-Adigrat—Varie Eritrea) Fasc. 1 Morgani (1886–1911).

a semi-independent Emirate in Cyrenaica.[47] In June 1930, a government decree ordered the closing of the zawiyyas of the Sanūsiyya and the confiscation of all their assets in Libyan territory.[48] The pacification of "Libya" was only declared after the execution of the Libyan rebel leader ʿUmar al-Muḫtār on September 1931. One year later, in addition to Sayyid Ǧaʿar, the Italian Government awarded the Knight Grand Cross decoration to another indigenous figure, Šarīf al-Gharyānī (1877–1945), a Libyan religious shaykh and statesman.[49] He acted as an intermediary between the resistance leaders and the Italian government in Libya, and had been accused of being a traitor who had been partly responsible for the capture of ʿUmar al-Muḫtār.

From the mid-1930s, the deterioration of the British-Italian conflict created tensions within the Ḫatmiyya, whose main centre was located at the heart of the disputes between the two colonial powers in Northeast Africa. During World War Two, which spread to the region in June 1940, the British authorities considered Sayyid ʿAlī al-Mīrġanī to be a very influential figure, and he was given a seat on the Advisory Council for the Northern Sudan, which had been formed during the war.[50] The situation was different in Eritrea, the other front, however, where the Mīrġanī representatives, who had been regarded as advisors and intermediaries throughout the Italian occupation, occupied a controversial role, mostly because of their close ties with the Sudanese branch of the Ḫatmiyya, which was under British influence.

Italian colonial policy between 1935 and 1941 was marked by racism. During this period, a series of provisions were issued that aimed at separating the colonial settlers from their subjects.[51] According to an article from the Mīrġanī private archive in Cairo, Sīdī Ǧaʿfar condemned the Fascists' racial policy, and his political position would emerge in a speech reported in an Arabic article published during that time entitled *Islam and Freedom*,[52] which stressed the change in the collaboration with the Italians that had been attributed to Sīdī

47 See Ryan 2012.

48 Marongiu Buonaiuti 1982: 254.

49 Gazzetta Ufficiale del Regno d'Italia, anno 70° Roma—Mercoledì, 30 gennaio 1929, anno VII, n. 25, p. 489; Gazzetta Ufficiale del Regno d'Italia, anno 74° Rome—Mercoledì, 22 marzo 1933, anno XI, n. 68, pp. 1186–1187.

50 Voll 1969: 417.

51 For a study on inter-racial legislation and relationships in Eritrea, see Sorgoni 1998; On racism in Fascist colonialism, see: Goglia 1988; Goglia 1992; Pankhurst 1987: 32–51. For a study on local perceptions of racist laws in oral memories, see: Volterra 2005: 140–154.

52 The origin of the newspaper from which this article is taken is unknown. The original document belongs to the Mīrġanī family's private collection, Cairo. I assume the article would have been published in Sudan or Egypt as part of anti-Italian propaganda. The date handwritten on the article is 1938, but this is probably approximate, and it should be post-

Ǧaʿfar during the colonial period, arguing that he now claimed to be aligned with the democratic forces and had lent his political support to the British front opposing the Italian rule. It is of interest to note that this discourse made reference not only to pan-Islamism but also to pan-Arabism; in fact, he claimed that "according to the teachings of our religion, every Islamic believer and every person of Arabic blood disdains every violation and cupidity. As Arabs who are proud of our dignity, we fight strongly against every injustice or cupidity. It has made me suffer to see advocates of discrimination on the basis of colour in recent days. This is a new position that disagrees with the teachings of our religion and our Arab traditions, and which asserts claims for laws that are not established in our orthodox religion, in which no human being is superior to another except as regards his piety".[53]

There are two verses in the Qur'an that contain a reference to the issue of colour and race. The first states: "Among the signs of Allah are the creation of the Heaven and of the Earth, and the diversity of your languages and colours. Lo! Herein indeed are portents (signs) for men of knowledge".[54] The second states: "O mankind! Lo! We have created you from a male and female, and We have made you into nations and tribes, so that ye may know one another. Lo! The noblest of you in the eyes of God is the most pious, for Allah is Knower and Aware".[55] There are also several *ḥadīṯs* that claim that all humans are equal, one of which is often reported as having been taken from the Prophet's last sermon. It reads: "All mankind is from Adam and Eve, an Arab has no superiority over a non-Arab nor does a non-Arab have any superiority over an Arab; also a white has no superiority over a black and a black has no superiority over a white, except by piety and good actions". Sīdī Ǧaʿfar seems to be making a reference to this *ḥadīṯ* in his speech.

In his discourse entitled "Islam and Freedom", Sīdī Ǧaʿfar appealed to pan-Islamism and pan-Arabism to confront a new Fascist colonial policy that was being pursued through racially discriminatory laws during this period, justifying his alignment with the British by pointing out the conformity of democratic values with Islamic orthodoxy.[56]

---

dated to 1940, when the East African campaign took place. According to Aḥmad b. Sittī ʿAlawiyya bt. Sīdī Ǧaʿfar al-Mīrġanī, this speech was delivered in the Agordat area.

53 A complete version of this speech has been published in Bruzzi 2012b.

54 Qur'an, XXX: 22—Pickthall's translation, Muslim World League, Rābita Mecca al-Mukarramah, 1977.

55 Qur'an, XLIX: 13. See Fadel Abdallah 1987: 42.

56 This discourse appealing to "democratic values" would be presented in Sudan with the support given by the Ḫatmiyya to the Democratic Unionist Party (DUP). On the position taken by the Ḫatmiyya in post-World War Two Sudan, see: Omer Beshir 1977; Daly 1991; Warburg 2003.

Finally, he anticipated the devastating effect of the war, which would reach its climax in 1941 at the Battle of Keren, the headquarters of the Eritrean branch of Ḫatmiyya, the theatre of one of the bloodiest battles of the Second World War's East African Campaign. Sīdī Ǧaʿfar's speech might be placed in the context of local disagreements with racist Fascist policies, which would have fostered local disaffection towards the Italian government and divisions between supporters of the Italian and British military forces. At the time of this speech, which urged Muslims to espouse the democratic cause and support the British, he was on the point of withdrawing from Keren to Agordat towards the Sudanese border, or perhaps had even already done so.[57] According to a widely-reported oral account in Keren, Sīdī Ǧaʿfar dreamed of being buried in Kassala; after his retreat to Agordat, leaving his first son, Sīdī Bakrī, in Keren, he moved to Tesseney, where he died in 1943, and he was finally buried in Kassala, beyond the Eritrean border.[58]

Throughout the war, the two Eritrean representatives of Ḫatmiyya, Sīdī Ǧaʿfar and Sittī ʿAlawiyya would yet again demonstrate the differences in their approaches to the Italian government, and Sīdī Ǧaʿfar in particular would confirm his preference for his Sudanese links.

The Defeat of Italy

Sittī ʿAlawiyya remained in Massawa until the outbreak of the Second World War, when she finally moved to Keren.[59] Her activities remained rooted in Eritrean interests, and while Sīdī Ǧaʿfar assumed a pro-British position, in line with that of the Sudanese branch of the Ḫatmiyya, Sittī ʿAlawiyya seemed to be more involved with the Eritrean branch. Significantly, they were buried in Eritrea and Sudan respectively, thus confirming the principal ties they had maintained throughout their lives.

A number of oral traditions on Sittī ʿAlawiyya's role during this period are available. One of these stories was related to me by a relative of Sittī ʿAlawiyya al-Mīrġanī. As she told it, during World War Two, Sittī ʿAlawiyya al-Mīrġanī went to Kassala, and the Italians followed her there. The British authorities

57 According to Aḥmad al-Mīrġanī, son of Sittī ʿAlawiyya's bint Sīdī Ǧaʿfar al-Mīrġanī, the speech was delivered in the Agordat area. Interview with Aḥmad al-Mīrġanī on May 2009 in Cairo.

58 Interview with Faqīh Aḥmad, *ḫalīfat al-ḫulafāʾ* of Keren on September 2004. The full text has been reported in Bruzzi 2005.

59 Interview with Sittī ʿAlawiyya's bint Sīdī Ǧaʿfar al-Mīrġanī on May 2009 in Cairo.

asked Sīdī ʿAlī al-Mīrġanī to meet her in Kassala and to ask her not to go there or to Sudan any more, as the Italians would follow her if she did.[60]

Another version of this story was related to me as an example of *karāma* performed by the *šarīfa* in that period: Sīdī ʿAlī al-Mīrġanī told her not to go to Sudan to prevent the Italian army from following her, and because she decided not to make any further trips to Sudan, she prevented the Italian army from invading the country.[61] This tradition stresses her involvement with and influence over the Italian occupation of Sudan, which took place in June 1940.

As Warburg has noted, the Italian conquest of the Kassala region seems to have been detrimental to Sayyid ʿAlī al-Mīrġanī's fortunes. Because of the close relations his Eritrean relatives had with the Italian authorities, he believed that the government was suspicious of him.[62]

According to a popular tradition in Sudan that has been reported by Voll, "when the Italians occupied Kassala, Sayyid Muḥammad ʿUṯmān and Ḥasan (sons of Sayyid Aḥmad and nephews of Sayyid ʿAlī) assumed real leadership in the occupied area and dealt with the Italians. At the same time the Sayyids and others, including Sayyid ʿAlī's representative in Kassala, ʿAbdallah Faqiri, helped refugees escape and sent out information of the greatest value to the British forces. The major contribution of the Sayyids was that their prestige and leadership made it possible for Kassala to survive two evacuations and occupations with a minimum of public disorder".[63]

These stories emphasize the intermediation role of Mīrġanī representatives in this period. According to Voll, too, the Mīrġanī had an important part to play in the course of the conflict, especially in Eastern Sudan, during a crucial period when the threat of an Italian invasion from Ethiopia and Eritrea appeared to be imminent.[64] Kassala and Keren were the principal centres of the brotherhood in Sudan and Eritrea respectively, and they were the main targets of the Italian-British conflict in the region. Their strategic position explains why Italy and Britain reserved special attention for the Ḫatmiyya during the war.

After the Italian occupation of Kassala on July 1940, the British stated that Ḫatmiyya, which was the centre of the order near Kassala and the location of Sayyid al-Ḥasan al-Mīrġanī's tomb "should remain as a sanctuary whatever happened".[65]

---

60 Interview with Sittī ʿAlawiyya's bint Sīdī Ǧaʿfar al-Mīrġanī on May 2009 in Cairo.

61 Interview with Hāšim Muḥammad ʿAlī Blenai, 102 years of age and a follower of Ḫatmiyya, on Mars 2009 in Massawa.

62 Warburg 2003: 108.

63 Voll 1969: 586.

64 Voll 1969: 585–586.

65 Voll 1969: 587.

At the same time, following the Italian bombardment of Omdurman, it was stated that the Italians would never attack Sayyid ʿAlī's quarters.[66] According to another *karāma* narrative, Sayyid ʿAlī al-Mīrġanī foresaw the bombardment of Kassala: "It is told that the Italians sent a message to the Mīrġanī family in Kassala that they would bomb the town at 4:00 a.m. on a certain day and suggested that they leave. Sayyid ʿAlī, who was in Khartoum, was informed, and told the family to stay. That night, in an impossibly short time, he made the round trip from Khartoum to Kassala by car. While he was in Kassala he went to the mountain at 4:00 a.m. and wrote something in the air with his finger, and the bombing was prevented by this action".[67]

This is certainly a *karāma* narrative that celebrates the *baraka* held by Sayyid ʿAlī during the conflict between the Italian and British governments, but it also tells us of the care taken by the Italians with regard to the Mīrġanī.

To sum up, on the one hand there was the British link with Sayyid ʿAlī and Šarīfa Maryam al-Mīrġanī, while on the Eritrean side there was the well-established relationship between Italian authorities and Sittī ʿAlawiyya.

The final stage of Italian rule has been symbolically associated with Sittī ʿAlawiyya al-Mīrġanī's death. In particular, the current *ḫalīfat al-ḫulafāʾ* in Keren associated her death with the pain she was suffering due to the impending Italian defeat.[68] This subsequent interpretation underlines how deeply entwined Sittī ʿAlawiyya al-Mīrġanī's and the Italian authorities were.

In *Barīd al-Imbirātūriyya*, an Arabic newspaper published by the government in Addis Ababa during the Italian occupation, her death was announced with references to Muslim grief and mourning in the Italian Empire, and the fact that she had always been very close to the government was cited: "Al-Šarīfa al-Mīrġanī has died. Sadness prevails among all the Muslims of the Empire.... She was always close to the Italian government".[69]

For her entire entourage, the *šarīfa's* passing especially represented the loss of an eminent mentor in a crucial period, and the *qaṣīda* composed by her *ḫalīfa* on this occasion lamented the coming of much harder times because of

66 SMIS (Sudan Monthly Intelligence Summary), no. 73, Aug.–Sept. 1940, FO 371/24633, "following an Italian bombardment of Omdurman, the Khatmiyya leaders spread a rumour that the attack was directed against Sayed Abdel Rahman personally, since all the bombs fell in the Abbasia district. The Italians, it was pointed out, would never attack Sayed Ali's quarters", cit. from Warburg 2003: 108.

67 Voll 1969: 563.

68 Interview with Faqīh Aḥmad on September 2004 in Keren, see Bruzzi 2005.

69 "Al-Šarīfa al-Mīrġanī has died. Sadness prevails among all the Muslims of the Empire" (in Arabic), in *Barīd al-Imbirāṭūrīa*, Year V, no. 156, Addis Ababa, 27 October 1940—XVIII (The Mīrġanī family Private Collection, Cairo).

the loss of her protection (Figure 55). It is also reported that after the defeat of the Italians, the British took possession of her considerable wealth.[70]

The ongoing conflict caused internal divisions among Muslims. During the later years of World War Two, the British authorities appealed to Maryam al-Mīrġanī to intervene to solve a conflict that had arisen between the Beni ʿAmer and Hadendowa in the Eritrean-Sudanese region.[71] These two populations were those from which Sittī ʿAlawiyya al-Mīrġanī and Sittī Maryam al-Mīrġanī respectively descended on their mothers' side.

After 1940, during the East African campaign, the support lent by the Mīrġanī representatives in Eritrea to Italian policy suffered a significant breakdown. The death of Sittī ʿAlawiyya al-Mīrġanī on the one hand, and the alignment of Sīdī Ǧaʿfar al-Mīrġanī with the political position taken by the Sudanese branch of the Ḫatmiyya on the other, marked the end of Mīrġanī support for the Italian government. It is hard to conceive of this break as a true anti-colonial movement, since it was still at an early stage in Eritrea in this period;[72] however, as Volterra has pointed out, the racial laws and the idea of a separate society contributed to the political reprocessing of a minority within Eritrean society that began to look on the end of the Italian occupation as their only option.[73]

As al-Shahi has written, the continuity of the Ḫatmiyya in Sudan as both a religious and political organization was marked by a particularly flexible and moderate attitude to both religion and politics.[74] This ability to accommodate several contexts also showed itself in Eritrea, where the *ṭarīqa* representatives played a significant mediation role between the colonial authorities and the local population. The Mīrġanīs' political support for the Italian government reached a turning point when the change in international stability placed the Ḫatmiyya in a particular position, divided as it was between the British front in Sudan and the Italian front in Eritrea. During the crucial years of World War Two, the political collaboration that had been provided to the Italian government by Sīdī Ǧaʿfar and Sittī ʿAlawiyya throughout the colonial occupation was finally no longer on offer.

---

70 Carlo Piola Caselli, the nephew of the former Commissioner of Agordat, recalled the story about the *Sceriffa's* treasure he had heard from his uncle.

71 Voll 1969: 593.

72 Volterra 2005: 147. As Volterra points out, in his work on anti-colonial resistance in Eritrea, Tekeste Negash only considers Ethiopian resistance within the period between 1935 and 1940, Negash 1986.

73 Volterra 2005: 147.

74 Al-Shahi 1981: 13. On the Ḫatmiyya's role during during the British Occupation (1941–1949), see Venosa 2013.

CHAPTER 9

A Female Icon of Muslim "Emancipation" for the Conquest of Ethiopia (1936–1941)

Building Mosques: Muslim Policies from Libya to Ethiopia

During a visit to Tripoli in 1937, Mussolini presented himself to the Libyan people as the "Founder of the Empire" and "Defender of the Prestige of Rome, the Common Mother of all Mediterranean Peoples".[1] As Wright has pointed out, his visit reached its pinnacle of euphoria when the Duce declared himself the "Sword of Islam" at a ceremony during which, as a symbolic gesture, two Libyan soldiers who had participated in the Ethiopian campaign offered him the Islamic sword.[2] The purpose of this flagrant act of propaganda was to allow Fascist Italy to display its support for Muslim peoples internationally, in particular in the context of its Mediterranean policy.[3] Italian Muslim policy had a long history in Eritrea: it had already been in effect during the governorship of Ferdinando Martini (1897–1907) as a means of achieving local consensus and preserving the pax colonial. This policy of sponsoring Islam was perpetuated during the Fascist period—as is well-documented in the IsIAO photographic archives—when a number of mosques were built around the country in the 1930s.[4] Great "works of assistance and protection" for Muslims in Eritrea included the Mosque of Massawa (which was destroyed in the 1923 earthquake), the Islamic Court in Asmara, the Salvago Raggi School of Arts and Crafts in Keren and the Italo-Arabic school in Massawa. In Ethiopia, a number of inauguration ceremonies were celebrated during the occupation at the mosque and Qur'anic school in Harar and the Islamic schools in Jimma and Addis Ababa, but mosques and Qur'anic schools were also built and renovated in Libya.[5] It

1 Wright 2005: 121. See Governor-General Italo Balbo's Proclamation to the Libyan people, March 10, 1937. Cit. by J.L. Wright.

2 Wright 2005: 124.

3 On Fascist policy in the Middle East, see De Felice 1988; Arielli 2011: 385–407; Baldinetti 2011: 408–436; MacDonald 1977: 195–207.

4 A histographical overview of Italian Muslim policies in Eritrea is provided by Miran 2005: 195–203. See in particular Romandini 1984, Romandini 1985; Marongiu Buonaiuti 1982: 249–291.

5 See R. d. C, *L'Italia per i suoi sudditi musulmani*, in "Rivista delle Colonie", September 1938—XVI; Photographic evidence of the Italian enterprise of building or renovating mosques in

was mostly during the term of office of Italo Balbo, who was Governor-General from 1934 to 1940, that an explicit Muslim policy was implemented in Libya, but it was merely nominal, and it was not sufficient to counteract the deprivation suffered by the Libyan population during and after the brutal "pacification campaign".[6] It was also clear that the policy was not aimed at assimilating Muslim communities, but rather at creating a parallel status for them within the Fascist system.[7] The political strategy of "fascistizing" Arabs was promoted through education, "special citizenship", and the Muslim Association of the Lictor, but ultimately the "Fascist political indoctrination project" proved to be a failure.[8] Conversely, religion and religious elites played a crucial role not only in the context of the resistance movement, but also as an element of colonial policy itself. In Libya, as in other African countries in the colonial context, the boundaries between collaboration and resistance were ambiguous. Beyond the well-known resistance movement, which was led mainly by the Sanūsiyya Islamic brotherhood, lays a complex web of negotiations with the colonial powers, so it is far more accurate to describe the relationship between most Muslim notables and the Italian colonial authorities as ambivalent.[9]

Pan-Islamism was an argument that was used extensively in Fascist propaganda during the Ethiopian war. Military cooperation between the Italians and Muslims, mainly the Oromo, Danakil, Eritreans and Somalis, was a question of strategy: Muslim soldiers were seen as being more loyal, and their recruitment into the colonial army was portrayed as a sign of trust. Entirely Muslim battalions were employed against Amhara resistance because they were considered to be a political and military deterrent, and besides, the war offered Muslims a chance to declare a holy war against the Amhara regime, which had persecuted them, and they were rewarded with concessions after the war, some attaining positions of honour at official ceremonies. After the war ended, they were granted religious freedom, *qāḍīs* replaced Amhara judges, Arabic was taught in Muslim schools, and a number of newspapers began to publish an Arabic section. Mosque building was pursued throughout the occupation (1936–1941),[10] and the construction of a new mosque in Addis Ababa by the Italians, ordered by Mussolini himself, stands as a symbol of a policy of

Eritrea in the 1930s is available on Asmara, Massawa, Keren, Assab, Agordat and Barentu. See: Sezione 1 (Ex Armadi)—Eritrea—E 6 B Culto musulmano, IsIAO Archive (Rome).

6 See Cresti 2011. Regarding the early Italian Islamic policy in Egypt see Baldinetti 1997.

7 Goglia 1988: 35–53; Di Pasquale 2012.

8 Di Pasquale 2012: 5.

9 Baldinetti 2009.

10 Sbacchi 1985: 162–163.

declaring support for Muslim communities, to the detriment of a supposedly predominantly Christian Amhara resistance.[11]

This colonial policy of influencing and supporting the building of mosques in occupied territories in Africa was not unique to Italy; France, for example, pursued a similar policy in West Africa. It was a way of expressing the superiority of colonial civilizations, as the style and design of these mosques acquired a political dimension, and mosque construction was seen as being instrumental to controlling Islam and selecting which religious authorities should be supported and which should be marginalized.[12] Recent studies have criticized previous approaches and paradigms that emphasized Arab and Muslim leaders' sympathies for—and collaboration with—Nazism and Fascism in the Middle East and North Africa,[13] and this historiographical approach has recently been questioned in Ethiopia, too.[14] In reality, the so-called Islamic policy practiced in Ethiopia under Fascism during the second Italo-Ethiopian war was an element of the propaganda spread by the Italian press, and it must be juxtaposed with the endogenous data from Ethiopia if its effectiveness and impact are to be fully explored. In order to achieve this, we will refer to both the colonial descriptions and representations expressed through Fascist propaganda and the individual memories on Sittī ʿAlawiyya, who enjoyed considerable visibility in both Italy and Ethiopia at that time through her role as a female religious leader.[15]

A Female Icon of Muslim "Emancipation"

In 1938, two years after the declaration of the pacification of Ethiopia and the foundation of the Empire in May 1936, celebrations were held in Rome to commemorate the anniversary of the foundation of the Italian Empire. Selected notables and dignitaries from East Africa and Libya were invited to Rome to celebrate this anniversary and were greeted by Mussolini at a ceremony at Palazzo Venezia.

11 Alvisini 2000: 511. As the author points out, and as I note later in this chapter, the new mosque in Addis Ababa was intended to be a reward for Muslim Oromo cooperation during the war.

12 Cantone 2012.

13 Freitag and Gershoni 2011.

14 Hussein Ahmed 2007b; Ahmad Hassen 2000.

15 This chapter is a revised version of my forthcoming article in *Aethiopica*.

The national press was particularly active in reporting this event, which offered a fitting opportunity to demonstrate that there was a consensus on Italian imperial policies in East Africa and in the Mediterranean region. The official line stressed the "emancipation" policy put in place by the Fascist government during the war in favour of "oppressed" Ethiopian Muslims (1935–1936); this discourse was the foundation of Italian propaganda during the occupation of Ethiopia[16] and was also widely mobilized internationally in order to gain Muslim support in the Mediterranean region and the Middle East.[17] On this occasion, the Fascist press and newsreels underlined the presence of a woman, the *Sceriffa Alauia el Morgani*, as the representative of Eritrean Muslims among the African colonial notables received by Mussolini at Palazzo Venezia. As a religious authority whose prestige was reportedly widely recognized among Muslims, she ardently declared Islamic support for the Fascist regime. The meeting between the African dignitaries and Mussolini was immortalized in a photograph taken by the Luce Institute which showed her in the foreground, side by side with the Duce, surrounded by the other notables.[18] Her presence there was intended to attest to Mussolini's high regard for Muslims in the process of constructing the Empire.[19]

The presence of the *šarīfa* lent a particular flavour to this news item that was at once exotic and reassuring. According to the Italian press, the *Sceriffa's* "undisputed" legacy and authority were ensured by her line of descent from the Prophet. Some years later, a book entitled *La Sceriffa di Massaua* was published about her. It was a work of propaganda the purpose of which was to celebrate the Empire's wonders and exotic territories, and included a report of an interview with the *Sceriffa* that the author, Giuseppe Caniglia, claimed he had recorded during his visit to her residence in Eritrea. He recounts that when discussing her trip to Rome and her relationship with the Italian government, she exclaimed: "Since God wanted the *Duce* to take charge of the protection and defence of Islam, my tariqa [Sufi brotherhood] also acquired importance

16 Sbacchi 1985: 163; Alvisini 2000: 4; Borruso 2001a: 1–45; Borruso 2001b: 57.

17 De Felice 1988; Wright 2005; Arielli 2010.

18 Giornale Luce B1307 18/05/1938 Roma, '50 capi e notabili della Libia ricevuti da Mussolini'. Istituto Luce Cinecittà Historical Archive; 'Il Duce riceve 50 notabili della Libia e dell'Africa Orientale', *Corriere Della Sera*, Milano—Giovedì 12 Maggio 1938; *Gli Annali dell'Africa Italiana*, 1/2, agosto 1938: 712. The photograph is published in Goglia 1989: 272 and in Borruso 1997: image no. 57. See also the interview with *Sceriffa Alauia El Morgani*, in 'Il Sovrano riceve alla Reggia i notabili dell'Africa italiana. I capi indigeni rinnovano il giuramento di fedeltà alla Dinastia e all'Italia fascista', Roma 13 maggio, *Il Corriere della Sera*, Milano—sabato 14 maggio 1938.

19 Borruso 1997, 41.

in the context of the imperial religious life [...] Nobody was more gentlemanly and generous than he in supporting me and my religion".[20]

The use of a feminine icon to foster the regime's imperial policy was neither new nor exceptional. The Fascist regime often proclaimed its efforts to promote women's education and highlighted their moral role in the context of nation-building.[21] Loyalty, admiration and devotion were common *leitmotifs* of the propaganda portraying the reactions of women to Mussolini's policies, and in May 1939, just one year after the *Sceriffa*'s visit, the regime organized a large parade of women in Rome[22] during which thousands of Fascist women, who were described as an 'army', were said to have expressed "the absolute devotion and loyalty of all Italian women" to the *Duce*.[23]

The support claimed by Fascism for women's militancy in the public sphere (notwithstanding all the contradictions inherent in its conservative discourse) was not limited to the motherland: it extended overseas as well. In 1936, the Italian Government promoted Muslim women's education through the establishment of the first professional school for women in Tripoli.[24] Also, just one year after he rose to power in Italy, on the occasion of the Ninth Congress of the *International Woman Suffrage Alliance* in Rome, Mussolini declared his support for the right of women to vote.[25] Following this Congress, Huda Shaarawi (1879–1947) and Saiza Nabarawi (1897–1985), both of whom were pioneers and representatives of Egyptian radical feminism, returned to Cairo, where they removed their veils in public for the first time. This "spectacular gesture" provided Muslim women's political activism with a secularist iconography.[26] It was not shared by all feminine political figures in Muslim societies, however: in addition to Sittī ʿAlawiyya, who frequently resorted to religious discourse as a means of asserting her political activism, a well-known example of a divergent approach is the Egyptian Zaynab al-Ġazālī, who founded the Association of Muslim Women in 1936. The activities of both these women in the public and political spheres were legitimized by their aims to devote themselves completely to *daʿwa* (the Islamic mission).[27]

20 Caniglia 1940: 43.

21 Spadaro 2010: 27–52; Lombardi-Diop 2005, 146; Fraddosio 1989, 1127; De Grazia 1992.

22 Paulicelli 2002, 537–559.

23 Istituto Nazionale Luce, [1939] 'L'adunata delle donne fasciste', Istituto Luce Cinecittà Historical Archive, Rome.

24 Cresti 2000.

25 For an analysis of the national and international implications of this 1923 conference, see DuBois 2009: 1000–1021.

26 Baron 2005. Sorbera 2006: 6–10.

27 Cooke 1994: 1–20; Paciello 2002: 275–319.

"Faith" was also a key word in the political language of Fascism,[28] and according to Fascist propaganda, the outbreak of the Italo-Ethiopian war in October 1935 intensified the duty of women to be collaborators and propagandists for the regime. "The day of the wedding ring" (*la giornata della fede*) in 1935 is an illustration of the momentum generated by this propaganda. On this day, Italian couples in general, and women in particular, were asked to donate their wedding rings to support the Italian military effort and to help relieve the economic difficulties the nation was suffering as a result of the sanctions that had been imposed on it.[29] In the context of this campaign to collect gold, the press stressed the active role played by *Sceriffa Alauia el Morgani* in the Empire, in the Eritrean seaport of Massawa. Two articles published in *Corriere della Sera* and *Il Resto del Carlino* reported that she had encouraged Muslims in Eritrea to donate their gold possessions to support Italy.[30] These articles focused on the gifts as proof of loyalty rather than on the moral duty of exchange and reciprocity which, according to Marcel Mauss's famous essay, all gifts necessarily imply.[31] The propaganda intent behind this news is clear, and one would need to compare it with local written sources in order to establish whether it was actually true, but unfortunately none are available. Nevertheless, the exotic portraits of the *Sceriffa* painted by the colonial press seem to be more indicative of Italian policy and discourse than they were of her own agency. She acquired exceptional visibility in Italy in the context of the Italo-Ethiopian war, but to my knowledge, notwithstanding the remarkable proliferation of portraits in the colonial media and the fragmentary information on her activities reported in a number of colonial archives, no Arabic material on her is available.[32] Her voice is silent in the colonial archives, and her utterances are always translated into Italian (without the original version) and reported through the filter of the colonial gaze. The "silence of the colonized" and the paucity of indigenous sources force us to focus on oral sources such as oral testimonies and individual memory, and in Italian East Africa this has allowed

---

28 Gentile 1994: 127.

29 See Terhoeven 2006.

30 Perpellini 1936: 1; Barzini 1936: 1.

31 Mauss 1954.

32 The hagiographies of her family are available in the Mīrġanī family archive (the Aḥmad al-Mīrġanī Private Archive) in Cairo, to which I was granted access, and the Ḫatmīya Arabic manuscripts can be found in Rome (Archivio Storico Diplomatico del Ministero degli Affari Esteri, Archivio Eritrea, Pacco 1044), but none are about her. The only exceptions are two articles from Arabic journals in the Aḥmad al-Mīrġanī Private Archive, which I had the opportunity to copy in Cairo in 2009.

us to supplement the available documentation on the colonial experience,[33] thereby enabling us to reconstruct intermingled histories from a cross-cultural perspective by describing the complexity of the discourses circulating around colonial Islamic policy, both in Ethiopia and in Italy, through the prism of Sittī ʿAlawiyya's role. In this way, we can transcend apparently well-established dichotomies such as colonizer-colonized, Islam-Christianity, Ethiopian history-Eritrean history and colonial history-African history. Sittī ʿAlawiyya's position as a symbol and icon for a variety of actors and audiences in different contexts sheds light on the ambiguity of the Islamic policy carried out by the Italian authorities in Ethiopia. The use of oral traditions and personal memories helps explain crucial issues such as the relationship between memory and history, the researcher and his/her informant, and the transcription or translation of "oral" texts into the written word. Oral sources inevitably raise the issue of the complex relationship between the past and the present, in that memory is "a perpetually actual phenomenon [...] in permanent evolution, open to the dialectic of remembering and forgetting, unconscious of its successive deformations, vulnerable to manipulation and appropriation, susceptible to being long dormant and periodically revived".[34]

The Mosques Built in Honour of Sittī ʿAlawiyya

During the Italo-Ethiopian war, Fascist propaganda sought to co-opt the Muslim elites into presenting their government as pro-Islamic and a supporter of Muslim communities. Fascist pro-Islamic policy was politically motivated "by a strategy of exploiting Christian-Muslim antagonism and rewarding Muslims for their collaboration with the invaders. On the part of indigenous Muslims, a pro-Italian attitude was justified by their perception of the Fascists as instruments for ending religious oppression rather than by a belief in the inherent virtues of, and preference for, colonial rule".[35]

As we have seen, Italian newsreels and publications show the propaganda used to emphasize *Sceriffa Alauia el Morgani*'s support for the Italian pro-Islamic

33 Taddia 1996, 2005.

34 Nora 1989, 8.

35 Hussein Ahmed 2007b: 101. On the Fascist pro-Islamic policy in Ethiopia, see: Sbacchi 1980; Sbacchi 1985: 161–165; Alvisini 2000; Borruso 2001a, Borruso 2001b; Borruso 2002; Buonasorte 1995: 53–114.

policy, which Fascism promoted internationally.[36] During the occupation, Sittī ʿAlawiyya accepted the Italian authorities' invitation and led a delegation of Eritrean leaders and notables on a visit to Ethiopia, where she had the opportunity to meet Muslim authorities in Jimma and Harar. This group included other renowned personalities such as Ḥasan ʿAlī and Ḥasan Idrīs Kurdī.[37] Apart from Italian documents that focus on her cooperation with Italian authorities, no other written sources (such as hagiographies or Arabic writings) by or about Sittī ʿAlawiyya are available. This lack of archives that might call the colonial gaze into question is what has led me to focus on her memory, and to collect the oral and individual memories that are available in Ethiopia and among her family and descendants in Cairo, and I have chosen to report these interviews as fully as possible so as to make them available for further interpretation. Oral testimony has the ability to integrate, question, and enrich the available literature, which insists that the Italian government's goodwill towards Muslim communities in Ethiopia was closely associated with its military and political interests, and that antagonism between Christians and Muslims was instrumental to the conquest of the country.[38] The Muslim communities' desire to obtain political and religious rights and to overcome what they saw as Christian oppression was therefore seen as making a contribution towards undermining Ethiopian resistance. In this way, the Italians positioned themselves as the liberators of Muslim communities oppressed by the Ethiopian Christian state. Similarly, the literature stresses the alliance between the Oromo and the Italians during the conquest of Ethiopia, and the favours bestowed on the Oromo by the Italians during the building of the Empire. The argument of Oromo oppression under Amhara domination lay at the heart of Italian propaganda, especially under Graziani's rule.[39] In reality, after the end of the first phase of the war, which was won thanks to this military alliance, a more contradictory and conflicting relationship emerged among these actors, especially in the context of the Italian occupation. On the one hand, the Italians presented themselves as the protectors and supporters of Oromo emancipation from Amhara subjection, but on the other there was real mistrust among the Oromo people of the effects of this promise; ultimately, they seemed to realize that not much had changed in their status under Italian rule.[40] In the end, Italy lent its

---

36 See 'I mussulmani dell'Impero' (15 June 1938), *Il Giornale Italiano* (Sydney, NSW: 1932–1940). The article reports the *šarīfa's* words with which she expressed the devotion of all Muslim people to the Italian King and "Emperor of Ethiopia".

37 Puglisi 1952: 162.

38 Sbacchi 1985: 163.

39 Sbacchi 1985: 160; Calchi Novati 1994: 73.

40 Sbacchi 1985: 161.

support to local authorities who were associated with the previous regime, and never actually created an area ruled by the traditional Oromo authorities.[41] In North Shewa, the Italians were aware of the anti-Haile Selassie ambitions of the *ʿulamāʾ* and local Muslim communities; indeed, they built an authentic alliance with them. The Amhara and Christian elites' political systems of domination urged them to lead military campaigns, or so-called *ǧihād* (to use the Islamic term) with Italian support.[42] The regime rewarded the Ethiopian Muslim military and all its political supporters with land grants and funds to build mosques and Qurʾanic schools in Harar and Jimma,[43] while the Italian Government itself also built and renovated mosques in Eritrea. It financed Sayyid Hāšim al-Mīrġanī's shrine in Hetumlo in 1902 and the *Ǧāmiʿ al-Ḫulafāʾ al-Rāšidīn* in Asmara in 1900, renovating it in 1937, and funded the Friday mosque in Keren in 1896 and another one after Sayyīd Hāšim's death. They built other Friday mosques in Assab in 1892, in Tiʿo in 1907, in Adi Keyh in 1909, in Agordat in 1911 and in Mendefera in 1912, in Gindaʿ in 1933, in ʿAli Gidir in 1935, in Nakfa in 1935, in Tesseney in 1937, in Segeneiti in 1938, and in Barentu in 1938.[44] The IsIAO photographic archives provide us with rich documentation on the mosques that were built all across the country in the 1930s. Colonial photography carefully documented this mosque building and restoration activity in Eritrean cities, where the consensus of the Muslim community was considered to be particularly important, for propaganda purposes. In Ethiopia, Italian activities included the restoration of sixteen mosques and the construction of fifty stone mosques (including in Addis Ababa) and other mud-hut mosques all over the country, in Seqota, Chelga, Debaraq, Dandala, Hayq, Dessie, Metemma, Harar, Dire Dawa, Jijiga, Miʾeesso, Chiro, and Gubba.[45] Very few mosques had been built in Ethiopia before the Italian occupation because the Christian emperors had banned it. The first one built in Addis Ababa, the al-Nūr Mosque, was the result of a request for a land grant submitted to Emperor Menelik II in 1904 by a Turkish officer, with the mediation of a Swiss advisor.[46] During the Italian occupation, permission was granted for the construction of the largest

---

41 Alvisini 2000: 509, 516.

42 Ahmed Hassen Omar 2007: 7.

43 Photographic evidence of the Italian endeavours to build or renovate mosques in the 1930s is available on Asmara, Massawa, Keren, Assab, Agordat and Barentu. See 'Sezione 1 (Ex Armadi)—Eritrea—E 6 B Culto musulmano', IsIAO Archive (Rome). At the time of writing, the archives are closed, however. A precious inventory of these photographs is available in Palma 2005a.

44 Trimingham 1965: 137; Hussein Ahmed and Miran 2007.

45 Trimingham 1965: 137; Hussein Ahmed and Miran 2007; Hussein Ahmed 2007b: 104; Sbacchi 1985: 162–163.

46 Hussein Ahmed 1999: 261–268.

(as expressed by its Arabic superlative) mosque to date, *al-Anwār*. According to Mīrġanī family oral tradition,[47] the name that was given to the mosque in Addis Ababa—"Anwār"—was linked to the mosque of Sittī ʿAlawiyya's grandfather, Sayyid Muḥammad ʿUṯmān al-Mīrġanī, the founder of the Ḫatmiyya Sufi brotherhood in Khartoum. Construction of the mosque, which is the largest central mosque in Addis Ababa and the third oldest in the city, was begun during the Italian occupation and resumed in the 1950s.[48] Located at the heart of the Markato area, and named after the largest market in Ethiopia (which was originally created by the Italians during the occupation), it was intended to be a reward for all Muslims who had participated in the war to conquer Ethiopia.[49] In all the oral accounts I have collected, the mosque construction programme carried out by the Italians during the occupation, such as in the case of al-Anwar Mosque, appears to be associated with Sittī ʿAlawīyya. The interviewees all agreed that it was she who negotiated with the Italian authorities on the mosque-building question, and that she did so on behalf of the Ethiopian Muslim communities, which until then had had too few places of worship in the city.[50]

Al-Ḥāǧǧ Kāmil Šarīf, the current director of the Madrasa Abādir in Addis Ababa, described Sittī ʿAlawīyya's arrival and stay in Ethiopia in these terms:

> Sittī ʿAlawīyya al-Mīrġanī visited during the Italian occupation, sometimes in 1938, sometimes in 1937. The Italian authorities respected her. When she came to Addis Ababa, the Governor of Addis Ababa and other Italian authorities came here to ask the Muslim elders in Addis Ababa to welcome her and pay their respects to her. There was a new building in Markato that had been built by the Indians that had just been completed but had not been rented; (otherwise) there wasn't any good accommodation in Addis Ababa at that time. This Indian house was very nice, so they had her stay in it. There was a guard and all the respected people who had come with her from Massawa (Eritrea). So she used to stay there, and we were students who were instructed to go there, pay her our respects, and prepare slogans for her [...] All the elders used to go there because there was a hall [...] and they came to pay their respects: shayks and sufis.... especially Eritreans, who knew her better, Eritreans who lived in Addis

47 Interview with Aḥmad al-Mīrġanī and Šarīfa ʿAlawīyya on May 2009 in Cairo.

48 Hussein Ahmed 1999, 262–263; Hussein Ahmed 2005.

49 Sbacchi 1985: 163.

50 Interviews with Aḥmad al-Mīrġanī and Šarīfa ʿAlawīyya (Cairo, May 2009); Al-Ḥāǧǧ Kāmil Šarīf (Addis Ababa, November 2009); Ay Rawda Qallu, Ḥāǧǧi Aḥmed Kebiro and Kabīr ʿAbdu (Harar, November 2009).

> Ababa and knew her better. So they all went and offered her due respect, sitting with her and [...] practicing with her. She belonged to Sayyid Mīrġanī's family. Sayyid Mīrġanī is known as the most respected person in Sufism in Sudan. [...] He formed the Mīrġanī branch in Khartoum [...], which had a number of followers in Sudan. After the Italian occupation of Eritrea, the Mīrġanī moved to Eritrea and had a lot of followers. Then, when the Italians expanded their colony into Ethiopia and other places in East Africa, they wanted her to show her strong loyalty to the Italian government [...] so she came here to show Ethiopian Muslims that the Italian government was pro-Muslim. The Italian government came to grant them some rights or to make them free to work, free to exercise their religion. Because all the regimes of Menelik and the others did not grant any rights to Muslims to practice or to attend the mosque, most Muslims were either farmers or merchants.[51] Muslims were not allowed to be soldiers and were not allowed to hold bureaucratic positions [...] in Government offices. They were considered to be second-class citizens. And so the Italian government gave Muslims a really good chance to show and say "we are Ethiopians, but we are Muslims". To be proud of their religion, to practice their religion, and so on. In addition, Sittī ʿAlawiyya came to support this. She was really with the people and many shaykhs respected her. [...] She also played a role for Muslims by giving support not only to the Italians but also to Muslims. Muslims were denied the right to build mosques. Sittī ʿAlawiyya asked the Italian government to show its goodwill towards Muslims in Ethiopia by building a mosque in Addis Ababa. The Italians began to build the al-Anwar Mosque and an Islamic centre in that area [the area of Markato in Addis Abäba]. They began with the construction of the mosque but then the Second World War broke out and they left. When Haile Selassie came back, he just left the mosque and built a church on the rest of the grounds [...].[52]

The Italian mosque-building policy was implemented not only by the construction of the al-Anwar Mosque in Addis Ababa, but also in the Harar area,

51 On the Muslim policy of Yohannes IV and Menelik II, see Hussein Ahmed 2001.

52 I carried out and recorded my interview with Al-Ḥāǧǧ Kāmil Šarīf, the current Director of Madrasa Abādir in Addis Ababa (on November 2009), in English. I would like to thank Ibrahim Mulushewa for the contact with Al-Ḥāǧǧ Kāmil Šarīf, who was one of his main sources for his MA thesis on the Harari community in Addis Ababa, Ibrahim Mulushewa 2009. According to some sources, Sittī ʿAlawīyya's visit to Ethiopia was in 1936, while others report it as having been in 1937, 1938 and 1939. It seems that she visited the country several times, at least twice between 1936 and 1937 and at the end of 1939.

where special emphasis was placed on creating a strong alliance with Muslim elites. Here, the government granted funds to religious leaders and Islamic schools, with a project that included the creation of an Islamic University for Qur'ānic studies in Harar.[53]

> Sittī ʿAlawiyya asked the Italian government to grant permission to build mosques not only in Addis Ababa, but also in Jimma and Harar. In Harar, a mosque was built in the market square, and other mosques were built along the road by the railway line that led from Addis Ababa to Dire Dawa.[54]

Photographic evidence of the Mosque being built during the occupation in Dire Dawa is available at the Istituto Luce Cinecittà Historical Archive.[55]

> Her influence on the Italian government and Italian authorities was very powerful; everything she requested was generally granted. She visited Addis Ababa, then Dire Dawa and Harar. In Harar, an Islamic centre, she was welcomed warmly. She visited the Šayḫ Abadir shrines, the most important and largest shrines of the city, and also visited the ancient mosque of Harar and the *qādirī* centres, where she met other sufis to pray to Allāh [...]. She was very happy to see Harar because she knew how important it was as an ancient Islamic centre.[56]

Oral testimony from both Eritrea and Ethiopia confirms the statements from colonial sources on the highly-respected position that she enjoyed among the Ethiopian Muslim community. One particular narrative celebrates her role in promoting religious freedom in Ethiopia, and I was told the same story in Massawa and Cairo,[57] where interviewees reported that her visit to Harar marked a turning point for the treatment of Muslims in the area. Despite being a Christian, the city's religious leader is said to have allowed the construction of a mosque in her honour, the Mosque of Sittī ʿAlawiyya, also known as the Italian Mosque, which is located in the market square in Harär. According

53 Sbacchi 1985: 163.

54 Interview with Al-Ḥāǧǧ Kāmil Šarīf on November 2009 in Addis Ababa.

55 Reparto A.O.I—Serie H.A. Moschea [a Dire Daua]—[1938]—Moschea in costruzione a Dire Daua—campo medio—codice foto: AO00009027, Istituto Luce Cinecittà Historical Archive, Rome.

56 Interview with Al-Ḥāǧǧ Kāmil Šarīf on November 2009 in Addis Ababa.

57 Interviews with Ḥasan Muḥammad ʿAlī on August 2004 in Hetumlo and with Aḥmad al-Mīrġanī and Šarīfa ʿAlawīyya on May 2009 in Cairo.

to some Harari traditions, it was built in 1937 and inaugurated by the *šarīfa*.[58] Ḥāǧǧi Aḥmed Kebiro, a Harari teacher whom I interviewed in 2009 and who was a child at that time, described the event thus:

> When Sittīna ʿAlawiyya arrived in Harar, the Italians organized a welcome ceremony so that people would greet her on the occasion of the inauguration of the mosque. After the mosque, butchers' shops from the previous open market were inaugurated in front of it. Sittīna ʿAlawiyya stayed some months, close to the Italians' government buildings. They brought her to the historical sites of the city, such as the *awač*. She met religious people [...]. She was a great shaykha Mīrġanī, respected by the Italians. [...] In that period, people didn't go into the offices of the government; they feared it, whereas she could enter whenever she wanted with a dozen people [...] who could enter with her. [...] The Ǧāmiʿa mosque was only renovated by the Italians. She arrived with Italian and Eritrean representatives [...] Before her arrival, people in Harär didn't know about her [...].[59]

Although she appears not to have been very well known in Ethiopia prior to her visit, her family was known to the Ethiopian religious elites. In Harar, she came into contact with other Sufis, shaykhs and notables. According to these oral accounts, her religious prestige was acknowledged, and she was probably not simply perceived as a collaborator. In the memory of Ay Rawda Qallo:

> She built mosques in Harar and Dire Dawa. [...] She belonged to a rich family ... She had a big *karāma*, she built mosques in Gelemso, Badessa, Kombolcha [...] When the Italians entered a city, she arrived and inaugurated the mosque. Harari people built the Mosque in Addis Ababa [...].[60] Harӓri people, especially religious and learned people, respected and

58 I would like to thank Alessandro Gori for his advice on the evidence on Sittī ʿAlawīyya's mosque in Harar.

59 Interview with Ḥaǧǧi Aḥmed Kebiro on November 2009 in Harar.

60 Her claim that the Harari people should take the credit for building the al-Anwar mosque should be considered in the context of a number of logistical and financial problems that arose throughout the completion of the mosque project. As Hussein Ahmed has pointed out, the mosque has a long history of financial constraints and administrative obstacles (Hussein Ahmed 1999; 2005). Indeed, the Harari community had already embarked on the project to build an Islamic court and schools in Addis Ababa before the Italian occupation (Ibrahim Mulushewa 2009: 22). After the Italians departed, funds were raised to enlarge the al-Anwār Mosque through voluntary contributions (Hussein Ahmed 1999; 2005).

> knew Sittī ʿAlawiyya. There was, and still is, a network that links Sufis and erudite Muslims from different areas [...].[61]

Sittī ʿAlawiyya's commitment to promoting mosque-building is similar to that of her sister, Sittī Maryam al-Mīrġanī, who lived in Sudan under the British Protectorate,[62] which supported similar activities in Sudan, building what a British administrator described as "models of what small village mosques should look like".[63] The construction of a large number of village mosques all over the country was also promoted in Ethiopia.[64]

Muslim Attitudes towards the Italian Occupation: From Collaboration to Agency

According to my interviewees, Sittī ʿAlawiyya was also respected as a religious leader in Harar because of her powerful influence over the Italian authorities. In the city, she networked with elites such as Qādirī shaykhs. It also appears that she played a role in the promotion of a 1939 pilgrimage to Mecca that was supported by the Italians. In the context of the Italian pro-Islamic policy, special attention was paid not only to the construction of mosques and the promotion of the teaching of Arabic in schools, but also to funding pilgrimages to Mecca and Medina.[65] On the promotion of the pilgrimage, Al-Ḥāǧǧ Kāmil Šarīf recounted:

> Thanks to her influence, around 500 people were led on the pilgrimage. From Jimma, Dessie, Dire Dawa, Harar ... selected shaykhs were taken by car to Mogadishu and from there crossed the sea to Jeddah, to reach Mecca. Then, they came back. [...] I had the opportunity to be in Harar when they came back. My father was in prison in Addis Ababa at that time.[66] He had asked my aunt to bring us to Harar where we could go to

61 According to this testimony, she was credited with *karāma* (saintly marvels), a charismatic power that allowed her to build mosques. Interview with Ay Rawda Qallu on November 2009 in Harar.

62 On Sittī Maryam al-Mīrġanī, see Grandin 1988: 122–128.

63 Voll 1969: 573.

64 Hussein Ahmed 2007b: 104; Sbacchi 1985: 162–163.

65 Sbacchi 1985: 163.

66 After the attempt on Marshal Rodolfo Graziani's life in 1937, the Italians arrested a number of people, including Muslim leaders such as al-Nadil Itifaq, Šayḫ Khatima and Šayḫ Muhammad Seyyed Sadiq (sic), who were teachers at the Madrasa. Other Egyptian teachers from the same Madrasa were expelled, and the school's founder was only released

> an Islamic school to study the Qur'ān.[67] [...] My mother and sister stayed in Addis to look after my father. Therefore [in Harar], we had the opportunity to see the pilgrims [returning from Mecca], arriving from the mountains, at the entrance to Harar. Their cars paraded in front of us and people said "welcome, welcome, welcome". The streets were crowded with people, all celebrating, happy. [...] She was with this group of pilgrims, too; she entered the *Commissariato*, then went back to Addis and then to Massawa. Thanks to her, 500 people had the opportunity to go on a pilgrimage to Mecca, to do the *ḥāǧǧ*, and to come back safe and happy. Sittī ʿAlawiyya was important for Muslims' good spirits because before they had been oppressed. When she was there, on the other hand, nobody was afraid and everybody was very happy. She did positive things for Muslims.[68]

Al-Ḥāǧǧ's positive account is a clear indication of the ambivalent position of Muslim communities towards the pro-Islamic colonial policy. It was not only Christians who suffered from reprisals and imprisonment after the attempt on Graziani's life—Muslims did, too—but they also had the chance to benefit from greater freedom of worship as a result of the Islamic policy that was applied in the country. For example, in 1939, 3,585 Ethiopian and Eritrean travellers travelled to Saudi Arabia at the government's expense.[69] This connection between the pilgrimage that year and the *šarīfa's* support confirms the commitment she expressed to promoting Islam in the region.

Harar lay at the heart of the Islamic policy that was put in place by Fascism. The idea was to turn it into a flourishing Islamic centre once again, and so it is unsurprising that the *šarīfa* would have participated in promoting Islamic policy in the region. According to the oral testimonies I have collected, she was treated with great respect in Harar; she was recognized in the "City of Saints" for the spiritual power she supposedly exercised over Italian policy, which was supported by her ability to perform *karāmāt*, and to this day, people refer to her as Sittīna ʿAlawiyya (namely "our Lady" ʿAlawiyya), a term that indicates acknowledgement both of her respected status and of popular recognition of her spiritual and charismatic power. According to a Harari oral tradition:

---

after the intervention of an influential Eritrean trader, Saleh Ahmad Kekiya from Arkiko (Ibrahim Mulushewa 2009: 25). On him see also Venosa 2014: 42, 49, 83, 92, 112 and 207.

67 During the occupation, Harar was promoted as an Islamic centre of learning. The Qur'ānic school, which had 60 students under Ethiopian rule, increased in popularity, and reached 450 students in 1937/38 (Sbacchi 1985: 163).

68 Interview with Al-Ḥāǧǧ Kāmil Šarīf on November 2009 in Addis Ababa.

69 Sbacchi 1985: 163.

> People said that she was a person that could see. [...]. She saw that the Italians had cut down the coffee and *qāt*[70] plants belonging to *awliyā'*[71] to build roads and she saw the end of the Italian occupation [...].[72]

This same belief is also reported by Kabir ʿAbdu, a Harari historian and teacher, a grandson and student of Ay Rawda Qallu:

> Sittīna ʿAlawiyya saw the end of the Italian occupation and the arrival of the British. She went to Ethiopia because the Italians invited her, but when she arrived, she saw what would happen. In the final period of her life, something was broken in her relations with the Italians. We thought they wanted to imprison or kill her, we don't know very well. But in the end she died of natural causes [...].[73]

And as Ay Rawda Qallo tells it:

> Sittīna ʿAlawiyya could see [...] She foretold that the Italians would leave after five years and that the British would arrive, and that after the British, the Amhara would come. [...]. She had *karāma* and foretold this. She died with *šahāda.* [...]. She went to Ethiopia on the invitation of the Italians, but when she arrived and saw that they had cut trees, *qāt*, and coffee plants belonging to the *awliyā'* down to build roads, she predicted that after five years the British would arrive. She was not afraid to tell the truth. After she said this, the Italians wanted to kill her, but they didn't. She died a natural death shortly after. When the Italians were with her, they were warmly welcomed because she had *karāma* [...].[74]

These memories focus on her charisma ("she had *karāma*"; "she was a person that could see", etc.) and her ability to influence the occupiers' policies ("her influence on the Italian government and Italian authorities was very powerful"; "everything she requested was generally granted").[75] They also insist on her

70 *Qāt* plants are considered to have *karāma*. For a study on the past and present significance of *qāt* in Ethiopia, see Ezekiel 2004.

71 Plural form of *walī*, "he who is close to God", a Saint.

72 Interview with Al-Ḥāǧǧ Ahmed Kebīro on November 2009 in Harar.

73 Interview with Kabir ʿAbdu on November 2009 in Harar.

74 Interview with Ay Rawda Qallu on November 2009 in Harar.

75 When he returned to Italy from Ethiopia on February 1938, Italian military officer Marshal Rodolfo Graziani, a key figure in the consolidation and expansion of Italy's empire during the 1920s and 1930s in both Libya and Ethiopia, expressed his regret at not being able to see her again and say goodbye to her before he left. He therefore asked Vittorio Piola

awareness of the hypocrisy of Italian policies and the lack of respect for Harari religiosity ("she saw they had cut trees, *qāt*, and coffee plants belonging to the *awliyāʾ* down to build roads"). The oral narratives conflict with the official discourse we find in Italian propaganda regarding her unconditional support and loyalty to the Fascist regime; instead, they point out Sittī ʿAlawiyya's awareness of (and sometimes her support for) local unrest against Italian government policy, and more specifically against its land policy. According to the Harari stories I have referred to above, she predicted the end of the Italian occupation and the arrival of the British, and it is also stressed that she was not afraid to tell the truth. My interpretation is that this statement is a reference to one particular *ḥadīṯ* that argued that telling the truth to an oppressive ruler is a great *ǧihād*.

According to the oral traditions and memories collected in Harar, her prediction created a rift in the relationship she had established with the Italians, and there were suspicions that the Italian authorities wanted to arrest or kill her. While this is not supported by any written sources, it is still symbolic: the prevailing atmosphere at the time was one of disbelief at the Italians' success, and their defeat was considered inevitable. As the existing literature points out, moreover, the Fascists' pro-Islamic policy lacked effectiveness, and was marked by profound contradictions. Their alleged alliance with the Oromo people also revealed itself to be weak: during the occupation, and during the Second World War in particular, the Oromo showed a marked lack of commitment towards the colonial authorities, offered little support to the Italian army, and quickly ended up changing sides to ally with the invading British troops.[76] Contrary to the common argument of Muslim ties to the Fascist regime that is put forward in the current academic literature, religious leaders and politicians such as Muḥammad Ṣādiq (d. 1977) questioned the Italians' good intentions towards Islam, refused to recognize Italian rule, and did not collaborate with Fascist authorities, and as a result were subjected to repression and imprisonment.[77] There was widespread scepticism about an Italian victory at the time, and there were numerous cases of desertion among Eritrean and Oromo colonial soldiers. It is therefore likely that Sittī ʿAlawiyya's family and religious networks in Egypt and Sudan, as well as the acquaintances she established

Caselli, the Commissioner of Agordat, who was visiting the region, to tell her that he sent many good wishes to his (sic!) family and all Muslims in the Empire, and that he hoped to have the opportunity to see her again soon. Telegrammi: Graziani – Piola Caselli, Oggetto: Sceriffa. Agordat 10 February 1938. Piola Caselli Archive in Rome.

76 Sbacchi 1985: 161.

77 Hussein Ahmed 2006: 9.

in the region, gave her a long-term perspective of the way the conflict would develop.

In addition to underlining the general marginalization of studies on Muslim resistance to Fascism, which has previously been questioned by Hussein Ahmed, it is important to add nuance to the simplistic dichotomy between Muslim cooperation and open resistance to the Italian occupation of Ethiopia, which means looking at the negotiation and accommodation strategies pursued by Islamic leaders in their relationship with the occupying powers.[78] Life stories can offer us a deeper understanding of this complex issue, and memory and relics from the past, such as the mosques the Italian authorities built during the occupation, can help shed light on conflicts past and present. The controversial yet emblematic case of Sittī ʿAlawiyya is an illustration of a woman who stood "in the middle". It seems that her role reached well beyond the ambiguous pro-Fascist position assigned to her in the Christian-Muslim conflict; oral sources portray her as having followed her own agenda and actively promoted the Islamization campaign. Moreover, her cooperation with the colonial authorities was not offered unconditionally; it was borne of the needs imposed by particular situations, and the benefits that became available to her and Muslims.

One aspect that is worthy of note is the contrasting interpretation offered by the narratives available from oral sources, in which Sittī ʿAlawiyya's agency is highlighted. We should certainly not underestimate the complex nature of oral narratives, which are closely related both to the past and to the context in which they are produced. The past and present processes of appropriation and identification can also emerge in collective memories and personal narratives. Significantly, during my fieldwork in Harar in 2009, in response to my question on the so-called "Italian mosque", one person reacted very strongly, arguing "this is not Italian, this is Harari!". The people I interviewed underline the fact that it was she who made suggestions and influenced colonial authorities on the construction of mosques and promotion of the *ḥaǧǧ*. She is not portrayed as a mere collaborator, therefore. When we compare these oral narratives to colonial sources, it becomes clear that the available literature on the so-called pro-Islamic policy and activities fails to demonstrate how they were devised, who the real actors were, and what interests were at stake. A more profound understanding of the process must take account of the leading role played by intermediaries as actual agents of change through the dynamic of their negotiations with the occupying authorities.[79]

78 Robinson 2000; Robinson and Triaud 1997.

79 This issue is given special attention in Lawrance, Osborn and Roberts 2006.

CHAPTER 10

Conclusion: Sufi Memories

> What will be the future of the individual imagination in what is usually called the "civilization of the image"? Will the power of evoking images of things *that are not there* continue to develop in a human race increasingly inundated by a flood of prefabricated images? At one time, the visual memory of an individual was limited to the heritage of his direct experiences and to a restricted repertory of images reflected in culture. The possibility of giving form to personal myths arose from the way in which the fragments of this memory came together in unexpected and evocative combinations. We are bombarded today by such a quantity of images that we can no longer distinguish direct experience from what we have seen for a few seconds on television. (…) If I have included visibility in my list of values to be saved, it is to give warning of the danger we run in losing a basic human faculty: the power of bringing visions into focus with our eyes shut, of bringing forth forms and colors from the lines of black letters on a white page, and, in fact, of *thinking* in terms of images.
>
> ITALO CALVINO, *Six Memos for the Next Millennium, 1988, Harvard University Press,* pp. 91–92

∵

Women's Embodied Archives and Spirit Possession

The contemporary history of Eritrea and Ethiopia since 1990 has benefited greatly from a number of historical studies on photography,[1] which at the same time has become the subject of, and a tool for, highly innovative studies on social and political history. As we worked on women's history during the colonization of Eritrea and Ethiopia, we found ourselves facing a paradox that also occurs in other areas of the continent: while the voices of African women are almost absent from the colonial archives, their often anonymous bodies are constantly exposed in colonial photography. Indeed, in Northeast Africa

1 Triulzi 1995; Palma 1989: 595–609; Palma 2002: 83–148; Sohier 2011; Sohier 2012; Zaccaria 2001; Zaccaria 2012; Pankhurst and Gérard 1996.

 | DOI 10.1163/9789004356160_012

and other parts of the continent, we see the female body being over-exposed as a result of the wide-scale production of images of bodies by colonial cameras. Visual sources and the iconography of the body suddenly became vital resources that posed critical methodological and epistemological questions. Our work on visual sources such as photographs also led us to focus on the construction of ambivalences. Indeed, in the words of Carlo Ginzburg, owing to their evocative powers and their ability to generate immediate identification, images forcefully question "this interweaving of the true, the false and the fictitious that shapes the plot of our presence in the world".[2] Focusing on the false and fictitious leads us to consider the place of the imagination not only in the historical process but also in the work of historians.

As Sohier has pointed out, historical literature since the 1980s has shown us that the continent's stereotypes were not merely representations of the conquest and reflections of an asymmetrical relationship. Photographic images do not reproduce reality; rather, they give a shape to representations and interpretations of the world, and become an "intercultural" object and a complex historical source. This leads historians to attempt to interpret a physical document that has been produced, exchanged, and circulated, and that lends itself to a plurality of readings and uses, depending on its context.[3] In addition to forcing historians to consider the inner polysemous dimension of visual documents, concentrating on visuality leads us to acknowledge that photography is but one of the visual technologies, and that it is necessary to consider other ways of seeing and showing that were marginalized by the industrial technology of the 19th century. Indeed, while the Eurocentric model has historically taken a privileged, disembodied view, the African and Islamic visual cultures have the ability to challenge this disembodied and secularized gaze.[4] It is within this problematic area that the history of the *zār* as a predominantly female visual practice may be re-evaluated.

Widespread in Northeast Africa and the Middle East—most notably in Ethiopia, Eritrea, Djibouti, Somalia, Arabia, Yemen, South and South-West Iran, Egypt, and Sudan—*zār* is a multifaceted cult of spirit possession. It is not a single phenomenon, and it crosses various religious affiliations. The cult of the saints—*awliyāʾ* in the Muslim and Sufi context—has intermingled with the *zār* in various forms. Among the Oromo people in Harar, the *zār* ceremony is called *wadāja*, a word that refers back to the Oromo term for communal prayer. During the *wadāja*, people chew *qāt* and drink coffee, whereas among

2 Ginzburg 2010: 16.

3 Sohier 2012: 14.

4 Hayes 2006: 524. On visual history, see Gervereau 2000.

Somalis, the *sār* ceremony also includes dances. Some of the *zār* spirits that are invoked, not only by the Muslim Oromo but also by Christians, are Muslims.[5] We find the *zār* cult among Christian, Falashas, Muslims, and other traditional religions. It is characterized by a human body being taken over by a *zār* spirit: the ritual is a form of adorcism in which once tamed or treated with the required care, the spirit can become a source of information, an ally and a protector.

Its origins are disputed, and have not yet been resolved. Some scholars have argued that it was introduced into the Middle East during the last century by female slaves from Ethiopia, while others have suggested that the cult derives from cultural cross-pollination and the changing political, social, economic, and religious situations experienced by the Oromo in Southern Abyssinia. In fact, in Arabia, as well in Sudan and Egypt, when the cult became popularly known among outside observers, it was mainly being led by female Abyssinian slaves or women with a slave background, many of Oromo origin.[6]

The origins of the term—as well as those of the practice itself—are quite controversial, and vary depending on the linguistic area being considered. If we take the position, as Abdelsalam (1994) has suggested, that the term has Arabic etymology, it would appear to derive from *ẓahara* (to show) or *al-ẓahar* (making an appearance). According to "popular" interpretations in Sudan, the term derives from a corruption of the Arabic verb *ẓahar*, "he visited", while in Hofriyat it is pronounced *zahar*, drawing attention to the sensory, the physical, and especially the act of seeing, meaning "he became visible, perceptible, manifest".[7]

By contrast, if we consider its origin in Kushitic terms (*jar, yar*, or *daro*), the word *zār* would be borrowed from Amharic. According to Enrico Cerulli, it is a reference to the name of *jār*, the Sky-God of the Agaw people, who would later be integrated into monotheistic religions and reduced to a spirit.[8] Cerulli writes that "beliefs about evil genies (*zār*) are widespread among Christian Abyssinians, certainly from very early times. From Abyssinia, the slaves who were carried away into slavery in Arab countries also spread *zār* superstitions

5 Trimingham 1952: 258–259. In Ethiopia, as Natvig has also pointed out, smoking in the zar cult seems to have been replaced by qat-chewing and coffee-drinking (Natvig 1987: 681. See also footnote 55).

6 On this controversial issue, see Natvig 1987: 686–673.

7 Abdelsalem 1994: 73–90. See also Boddy 1989: 132. Boddy also recalls, however, that most scholars believe the word comes from Persian (Frobenious 1913; Modaressi 1968) or Amharic (Barclay 1964; Kennedy 1967; Seligman 1914, Cerulli 1936).

8 Beneduce 2002: 194.

among Muslims in Egypt and Arabia. While the idea of a genie who invades humans is commonplace among peoples of various origins, the Abyssinian belief that a *zār* can be forced to leave the body of the possessed person by the performance of specific rites is, for Christian Abyssinians, of Kushitic origin."[9]

Trance and ecstatic practices, including *zār*, have periodically been integrated into monotheistic religions, and Islam is no exception: beliefs in *ǧinn* spirits are, after all, even acknowledged in the Qur'an. In particular, Sufi orders and masters have often shown that they accept, tolerate, and even resort to ecstatic practices, but not without provoking debate and criticism from their adversaries.[10]

Anthropological literature has dealt extensively with spirit possession phenomena from different viewpoints, drawing from functionalist, psychoanalytical, psychological, biological, symbolic, and theatrical understandings.[11] While these studies have interpreted possession phenomena from a psychoanalytical perspective—for example, as a kind of hysteria—others have observed that it was mostly a feminine practice, and actually sheds light on gender dynamics. According to Lewis, spirit possession is a sort of weapon that allows women to maintain or improve their social position in the context of a "gender war". Women, who represent an important example of marginal, ill-treated individuals, challenge their social role by becoming members of "peripheral" spirit possession cults.[12] *Zār* is also considered to be a healing cult that empowers individuals—mainly women—through group therapy.[13] Janice Boddy has focused on the body of a possessed medium as the site of a struggle out of which a subaltern discourse and gender relations are expressed, and in which women have the opportunity, through trances, to claim the action space that

---

9 Cerulli, E.O. ii 35. Cit. in Trimingham 1952: 258. See Cerulli 1936.

10 In Nigeria, for example, many practices associated with the possession cult known as *bori* were closely linked to women's authority, as in the case of the Inna in Gobir, where it was controlled by aristocratic women. The *ǧihād* of ʿUṯmān Ibn Fodio made harsh attacks against the *bori*, which it considered to be a manifestation of paganism and syncretism. This attack also threatened the authority of aristocratic women, who until then had enjoyed a position of social power due to their ability to control spirits. While these women were limited to their ability to exercise their authority through the *bori* cult, some *ǧihādists* promoted girls' education in the Islamic sciences. It was in this context that Nana Asma'u, the daughter of ʿUṯmān Ibn Fodio, emerged as a writer and erudite poet who was committed to the education of women and to the feminine Muslim movement of Yan Taru, which promoted women's Islamic education.

11 See Makris and Natvig 1991: 233–282.

12 Lewis 1967.

13 Messing 1958: 1120–1126; Vecchiato 1993; Boddy 1988: 4–27; Constantinides 1972.

is otherwise denied them in their everyday lives. Concerns and anxieties about reproductive diseases that might lead to divorce or polygamy are cured or alleviated by resorting to *zār*. Collective treatment ceremonies mobilize women's support groups without threatening the accepted male social order. Through spirit possession, with the support of foreign bodies from a parallel yet separate world, women can reaffirm, criticize, and reinterpret cultural values while avoiding the shame that would otherwise be brought on them by the daily abandonment of traditional values. In this way, human conflicts are reconciled. According to the author, while possession cannot relieve the women's chronic state of subordination, it clearly can act to cultivate their own female self-awareness.[14]

The relationship between possession cults and power also deserves special attention. It has been suggested that possession cults express an embedded critique of colonial hegemonies—national or global—whose effects are felt deeply, although not exclusively, by women, and that in this sense, cults historically represent expressions of cultural resistance and counter-hegemonic narratives. Embedded in local contexts as they are, they provide a means of understanding, supporting or challenging modern life, religion, capitalism, and colonial hegemonies.[15] Another important interpretation is offered in an essay on the *zār* cult in Ethiopia by Michel Leiris, who participated in the Dakar-Djibouti mission between 1931 and 1933 under the guidance of Marcel Griaule. His work *La possession et ses aspects théâtraux chez les Ethiopiens de Gondar* is a famed point of reference for studies on possession and the *zār* cult, specifically in Ethiopia. Leiris emphasized the communicative dimension of possession, in which representation based on mimesis can stir emotions, and the possession ceremony becomes the expression of a living theatre (*théâtre vécu*). As Leiris also noted, spirit possession provokes suspicions, especially because of its theatrical formats, which are designed to stimulate the imagination and to be seductive. One aspect that has been noted is that spirit possession ceremonies can be analysed as *théâtre vécu*, in Leiris's words, or as *comédie rituelle*, according to Metraux. Performances are closely related to social memory through the contribution they make towards bringing characters and events from the past into the present. In Ethiopia, historical figures, including a number of *awliyā'* (Muslim saints) who are considered to have had a carnal existence, are also invoked during *zār* ceremonies.[16] Few historians—but quite a number of anthropologists—have focused on the relationship between spirit

14 Boddy 1989: 356.

15 Boddy 1994: 419.

16 Leiris 1958. See Beneduce 2002: 193–234.

possession and memory. Several scholars have suggested that spirit possession can be analysed as a genre of historical narrative.[17] At a narrative level, spirit possession becomes a vector for memory, in which the act of learning by heart can be viewed as a symbolic practice that leaves many narratives open to continual reformulation. It is believed that spirits can possess the bodies of a man or woman during a possession ceremony, and that spirits can manifest and express themselves through them. The possessed body can change its identity and become a vehicle for a memory. Possession becomes one of the ways in which the past can be made present and be re-presented; it can be viewed as a kind of oral history, with an emphasis on life history and social memory.[18] Gianni Dore has suggested that among the Kunama people of Eritrea, possession is a public idiom for interpreting their historical experience. He points out that "Andinne's performances and discourses could be interpreted as a system of meaning, a measure of gender conflict, an emotional and aesthetic *mise en scène* of the collective experience, the interpretation of the suffering and pain of individual biographies within a specific social context".[19]

It is remarkable to note that while colonial archives often reduce the voices of women to silence, historians have access to extensive literature on these phenomena produced by travellers and anthropologists from the colonial era.[20] As Boddy has suggested, excursions into *zār* spirit possession allow us to shed some light on women's impressions of the colonial world and certain of the figures that populated it.[21] There has been a lengthy debate about oral history and the use of memory as a source of historical knowledge, as well as the fact that memory is not merely oral, and that it is not exclusively ex-

17 Larsen 1998: 125–146; Larsen 2001: 275–296; Lambek 1998.

18 Larsen 2001: 276; Larsen 1998: 128; Lambeck 1996. According to Larsen, when a body is possessed by spirits, it acquires several identities, changes its identity, and becomes a place of re-representation of social memory (Larsen 1998: 129). See also Makris 1996: 159–182. Larsen 1998: 121. Lambek 1998. Lambek 2002.

19 Dore 2007: 45.

20 Khoury 1980; Natvig, 1998.

21 Boddy 2007: 48. Boddy also argued that: "by invoking historical (spirit) personae through *zâr*, northern Sudanese women rehearse and create *their* social memory, that which shapes experience in the present by reference to the past. In Sudan, this is a motley record of foreign invasion, slaving and warfare, peaceful and informative exchange, all captured in the ever-changing, ever-reworked figures of *zayrân*. Moreover, by taking on (rather than exorcising) exotic selves more powerful than they, and drawing them into contractual relations requiring compromise and concession, Sudanese women 'civilize' amoral, ambivalent spirits while hinting at how to cultivate human 'others' as well" (Boddy 2007: 51).

pressed through verbal communication.[22] A number of studies have shown that memory is embodied in practices, including spirit possession rituals, that can be conceptualized as an art of memory, a process of memory embodiment that allows what has disappeared to be re-presented and made current.[23] According to Boddy, women's voices, which were marginalized in colonial archives, can be heard in their embodied archives, which host the *zār* figures, the spirits who regularly appear among them and depict an imagined past.[24] For historians, attendance at these ceremonies represents a unique opportunity to enrich their archives with a lived experience, which, as we will see, can nourish their spatial imaginations. It is during these rituals, in fact, when the body itself and all its senses are engaged, that cultural memory is staged and fashioned.[25]

FIGURE 54 *Sittī ʿAlawiyya's Mosque in Harar.*
PHOTO BY SILVIA BRUZZI, HARAR 2009.

22 Severi 2004.
23 Beneduce 2002: 240.
24 Boddy 2007: 46.
25 Stoller 1992: 53–68.

Embodying Sittī ʿAlawiyya's Visit to Harar

As I followed Sittī ʿAlawiyya's tracks in Eritrea and Ethiopia, I chanced upon an embodied archive that crossed over the visual and written sources at my disposal. This was made possible by conducting oral history interviews at places of memory, not only around her residences in Keren and Massawa, where she was buried close to her father's shrines and mosque, but also near the mosques built in her honour in Addis Ababa and Harar during the Italian occupation (1935–1941). In these *lieux de mémoire*, memories crystallized, and lent further materiality to the historical evidence that has been preserved in colonial archives. My peregrinations also led me to bump into another historical narrative, one that is transmitted through the body, which turned out to be complementary to those reported in colonial accounts: my journey to Harar provided me with an occasion to attend a *zār ḥaḍra* ceremony performed by a Sufi woman who embodied the memory of Sittī ʿAlawiyya's visit to the city.

In the 1930s, during the second Italo-Ethiopian war, the Italian Government invited Sittī ʿAlawiyya to Ethiopia. She accepted, and travelled to visit Harar, "the city of the saints" (*Madinat al-awliyāʾ*), which has historically been a crossing point for learned people and mystics from all round the Muslim world. The city is marked by hundreds of shrines devoted to the memory of those figures who passed through it. Although my aim was to collect oral narratives about her visit to Harar, it soon became clear that memory is not just oral, and that it can be embodied during *zār ḥaḍra* ceremonies.

During my time there, I was also able to visit some shrines in the region that are guarded by women, such as Ummi Koda in the Harar neighbourhood. These holy places are evidence of the fact that the agency Sittī ʿAlawiyya earned around her residence in Massawa as the guardian of her father's shrine was not an exception, but rather represented a relatively well-documented example of a wider phenomenon. In Northeast Africa and beyond, the role of guardians of shrines is an acknowledged one.[26] As elsewhere, prayer groups were able to establish socio-religious and therapeutic networks around the shrines and residences of living saints. The shaykha, who in Harar is known by the title *Ay* (mother), is viewed as "medicine for the heart".[27] She represents a model of religious and moral conduct that believers should strive towards. Her residence

---

26 Shack reports the case of the cult of the Sky-God (Waq) and the Godness Damamit among the Gurage people. Waq is venerated at a shrine where the guardian is a (holy) woman known as *Yogaphacha daman*. Shack 1971: 37; Shack 1966: 77. See Böll 2003: 42.

27 Interview with Amin, Harar 2009. As Ilaria Sartori suggested to me, the term *Ay* is also employed to refer to Harari women and mothers in general.

is a destination for visits (*ziyārāt*) by locals and people passing through the city alike. Some of these women are guardians of shrines, where pilgrims come to recite *ḏikrs* under their guidance and for the *duʿā'*, the supplicatory prayer. Their place is one of solace and care, and has both a religious and a social and educational dimension. It is mainly due to their spirituality and learning that they have achieved popularity. Some of these places, which are noteworthy for the significant numbers of women in attendance, have also acquired a role in the treatment and resolution of problems relating to sexuality and fertility.[28]

Of the 356 shrines in Harar, at least 10% are dedicated to women, but there are also several mosques in the city (10 out of 82) that were built by pious women from the elites.[29] In the market square, as we saw in the previous chapter, among these material traces we found the Sittī ʿAlawiyya Mosque, or the Italian Mosque, which was built in Sittī ʿAlawiyya s honour and inaugurated by her in person during her visit in 1937.

In a coffee shop not far from the mosque, where I was interviewing a *kabīr*, a Harari teacher, and listening to his account of Sittī ʿAlawiyya's visit to the city, another man approached my interpreter and me and insisted that I go to visit Ay Rawda Qallu, who had just arrived in the city.[30] We accepted, and followed him to visit a woman who turned out to be a shaykha, a female Sufi master.[31] This encounter proved to be a pivotal moment in my investigations, because the very patchy and fragmentary written sources I had read in the archives now took on a real form through the lived experience of my visit to this woman: there was a parallel between what I was able to observe during my visit to Ay Rawda Qallu in Harar and the oral sources I had collected in Eritrea and the accounts written by Italian travellers from the 1920s and 1930s of visits people made to Sittī ʿAlawiyya's home in Massawa. During my visit, I was also able to attend a kind of play, in which Sittī ʿAlawiyya's character was placed in the context of a *zār ḥaḍra* ceremony. In the passages that follow, by moving back and

28 Some exemples are the shrines at Abu Haraz, near Wad Madani, in Sudan, and the shrines of Aw Ali Said and Ummi Koda, near Harar, in Ethiopia. On Ummi Koda, mother of ʿAbd al-Qādir al-Ǧīlānī, founder of the Qādiriyya order, see Gori 2010: 1019–1020. See also Mernissi 1977: 107; Masulovic-Marsol 1996.

29 Muna Abubeker Ibrāhīm 2007: 25.

30 They also told me that she was a nephew of Sayyid Abdullai Ṣādiq from Harar.

31 According to Hussein Ahmed "Qallu is an historical area in South-Eastern Wallo. Its name is derived from Warra Qallu, which was the name of the Oromo clan that settled from the late 16th century on in the valleys between the eastern escarpade and the western highlands of the medieval province of Amhara (…) Qallu Muslim scholars are renowned for their knowledge and for their teaching and preaching abilities, as well as for their resistance to forced conversion". Hussein Ahmed 2011. See also Leslau 1958: 194–196.

forth between these two women, written and oral sources about Sittī ʿAlawiyya alternate, are filled out, and take shape through my experience of visiting Ay Rawda Qallu. In this way, I try to express the coexistence of different temporalities that historians can experience and observe during a spirit possession ceremony.[32]

In the 1930s, the Italian journalist Martinelli began his account of his visit to Sittī ʿAlawiyya in Massawa by writing that "they told me that it would be a good idea for me to go to visit Sceriffa ʿAlawiyya. She seems to be a very interesting woman".[33] A number of colonial, oral, and visual sources have added other elements to the visits (*ziyāra*) that people from all over the Muslim world and beyond paid to Sittī ʿAlawiyya on a daily basis. "Pilgrims", wrote Caniglia, "rush from all over the Empire, driven by religious fervour and respect or impelled by a need to see her and listen to her advice".[34]

When we arrived at Ay Rawda Qallu's residence in Harar, we found that we were not the only visitors, but she welcomed us warmly and invited us to sit in a large room with others who were already there. More gradually arrived during our stay, accompanied by the incessant rhythm of prayers, stories, and blessings that were sometimes interrupted by brief exchanges with the guests. In a similar vein, Caniglia writes that Sittī ʿAlawiyya, who lived in Hetumlo, ten kilometres from Massawa, "lives a simple and austere life. She spends the day praying and receiving believers who go to see her. (…) She allows access to visitors, who are usually tribal leaders—often invited by her—who come to ask for assistance with prayers and invoke her intervention to solve issues between tribes and among their members. (…) She listens with great kindness, and gives them advice, with a word of comfort and hope to each one, inspired by the memory and work of her ancestor".[35] "When the prayers are finished, the pilgrims who needed to hear the *Sceriffa's* voice leave the place with the certainty that their prayers will be answered. (…) She loves her people, and it is with joy that she welcomes them to her house with the invitation "Sit down, and may God bless you and come to your aid", and she raises her hands to heaven, imitated by her followers, who ask God to fulfil their desires".[36] This same formula and gesture were repeated at Ay Rawda Qallu's residence after the invocations, as the visitors said "amen".

32 On the concept of the "regime of historicity", see Hartog 2002. For a study relating to the colonial context, see Bertrand 2008.

33 Martinelli 1930: 45.

34 Caniglia 1940: 36. Martinelli 1930.

35 Caniglia 1940: 33.

36 Caniglia 1940: 34.

The oral interviews I had already collected on Sittī ʿAlawiyya emphasized how people from various socio-cultural backgrounds and driven by desires and very different needs numbered among her visitors: they included local leaders, government officials, soldiers, travellers, pilgrims, and women. One oral story tells how "women worked in her house and asked her to support their marriages. She did not need money from the rich: she only received animals and donated *barakāt*, blessings".[37] One *karāmāt* story reports that a man came to her house one day to ask for her support for a marriage. She made a hole in the ground with her stick and lire (the Italian currency) came out of it. The next day, the man went to dig in the same place, but this time snakes came out.[38]

Those who come to visit Rawda Qallu include people from various socio-cultural environments: a beggar who was offered a meal, a mother seeking treatment for her sick son, a person from the Ministry of Education, to whom she gave a lesson on education, a gentleman who claimed to be her son, other believers ... and me, a researcher who was collecting memories of Sittī ʿAlawiyya's visit to Harar. The things all these visitors wished for and were seeking were very different, but everybody hoped that their desires would be fulfilled by their visit, the communal prayers and this woman's blessings.

When I had the chance to ask her about Sittī ʿAlawiyya, Ay Rawda Qallu replied: "I did not know Sittīna ʿAlawiyya (I was not born when she came), but the elders yes". Then she said: "you will find what you are looking for. There are things that one does not learn from books". Sufi spiritual and intellectual traditions often make the point that mystical knowledge (*maʿrifa*) cannot be learned from books, but only through *direct experience* and *contact* with a master. Kabīr ʿAbdu and other teachers from Harar told me later that they had "studied" with Ay Rawda Qallu because she was known to be a learned women, and especially knowledgeable about a wide repertoire of songs and *ḏikr*.[39] During my visit, her performance also proved to be an expression of social and cultural memories: one of her visitors told me he was a historian and claimed to be Ay Rawda Qallu's son. He told me he had written books after visiting her, and that she represented a source for him.

Ay Rawda Qallu's language was symbolic and metaphorical; she seemed to be speaking in tongues. In fact, a phenomenon similar to this can be found in the Pentecostal glossolalia, in which listeners try to decrypt statements simultaneously, with each offering his or her own interpretation.[40] "May Šayḫ

37 Silvia Bruzzi's interview of ʿAbd al-Raḥim ʿUṯmān Kekiya, Keren, 2009.

38 Ali Benai, Hetumlo 2009.

39 For a study on the production of Harari women's songs, see Sartori 2013.

40 Di Bella 1988: 897–907.

Hāšhim (Sittī 'Alawiyya's father) give me your tongue to communicate with you", she added. She then gave me a name and blessed me, and continued with her prayers of invocation, telling stories and engaging in cordial exchanges with her guests, mixing Arabic with Oromo. Her place, my interpreter told me—although I had begun to sense it by myself—was a *ḥaḍra*, which is a term used to identify a collective *ḏikr* session with *du'ā'* (invocations to God). Mystics use it as a synonym for *ḥuḍūr*, which means "being in the presence" (of God).[41] From that moment, I understood that the narrative on Sittī 'Alawiyya that Ay Rawda Qallu was able to communicate to me during our meeting was not merely an oral source: in actual fact, as the popular use of the term "Sittīna", meaning "Our Lady", which Harari people are accustomed to adding before 'Alawiyya's name, testifies, it was possible that her visit to Harar was profoundly integrated into a social memory that could be expressed during spirit possession ceremonies.

At Ethiopian shrines, we find a belief in certain spirits, known as *"rūḥāniya"*, which can be compared to the white *ǧinn* (*ǧinn al-abyad*) that are acknowledged as acting in the name of Muslim saints, and in the Sudanese context, the existence of Darwish spirits (*zayran*) has been especially noted.[42] Minako Ishihara has observed that as in the case of the Sudanese white *ǧinn*, Ethiopian *rūḥāniyas* can be benevolent, and are often Muslims. In particular, among the Oromo people of Ethiopia, as in the case of the Sudanese *"Darwish zayran"*, when the hosts of *rūḥāniyas* are possessed, they act like normal pious and respectable people, speaking quietly and sweetly, and intermingling Arab and Oromo terms. This way of speaking "can only be heard and achieved by a few learned men among the Muslim Oromo in this area, and it is generally unthinkable for an ordinary Oromo woman to speak in this manner. This unexpectedness and the 'gap' between the behaviour of an ordinary Oromo woman and that of the possessed is recognized by the local people as verification for the 'trustworthiness' of the phenomenon, tempting the anthropologist to 'believe'".[43] The way of speaking Ay Rawda Qallu used during my visit can be a further sign of a possession ritual. In Harar, where beliefs in *ǧinn* and *zār-ḥaḍra* ceremonies are widespread at shrines, some women—as is the case with Ay Rawda Qallu—are believed to evoke and be possessed by *awliyā'* (saints). Undoubtedly, the act of performing a possession ritual becomes a complex oral source in which the interpretations and claims made by the possessed

41 This *ḏikr* session with *du'ā'* (invocations to God) could have been a *wadaja* ceremony, as it is an Islamic and Oromo communal prayer that includes a *qāt* chewing ritual.

42 Boddy 1989: 187, 275–280. *Zayran* is the plural form of *zār* (spiritual being).

43 Ewing 1994 and Ishihara 2015.

person are not the only ones to be revealed, and those attending the ceremony also provide their own interpretations.[44] During our visit to Ay Rawda Qallu, both my interpreter and I perceived the presence of Sittī ʿAlawiyya. For me, it was as if I were attending a staging of her in the person of Ay Rawda Qallu. It was clear, however, that the communicative processes involved in this kind of performance act on the audience at an emotional level, creating a theatrical dimension in which several levels of understanding are intermingled.

As Marja Tiilikainen has observed in Somalia, outstanding female personalities are usually mentioned and praised during *sittāt* sessions. "Some of them are believed to be present among women who are performing *sittāt*. It can happen that the woman leading the session mentions to the other women that a personality is among them but they do not know who she is, so that they need to be friendly to everybody". As happened in my case, a researcher is welcomed into the group, and becomes a part of it. Eventually, according to those who attend *sittāt*, a person may obtain what she desires or hopes for after a session.[45]

Sufi Visions and Historical Imagination

Aside from the open, and as yet unanswered, questions regarding the authenticity of the possession ritual I attended at Ay Rawda Qallu's residence, what is certain is that it was effective in terms of what I was looking for, and gave me a broader understanding in several ways. During the visit that led me, as a researcher, to meet the shaykha, a number of representations and levels of interpretation emerged. First of all, it showed me a sort of staging of the written colonial sources at my disposal, which were highly fragmentary and extremely heterogeneous. The lived experience of my visit to Ay Rawda Qallu allowed me to understand, rework, and compare what I had read and what I was able to perceive on the ground as a part of the ethnographic experience, and enhanced my historical imagination. I was now in a position to visualize and give shape to the historical fragments I had collected in the archives and during my fieldwork. My visit offered me a moment that allowed me to develop the spatial imagination that historians use in their works. My challenge was to manage this intuition by moving back and forth between criticism and imagination.[46] The similarities and differences I was able to note between Ay Rawda Qallu and Sittī ʿAlawiyya from the representations Ay Rawda Qallu provided me,

44 Larsen 2001: 293.

45 Tiilikainen 2010: 209.

46 Comaroff and Comaroff 1992; Koposov 2009.

helped me gain a deeper understanding of the socio-political and religious role of the *šarīfa*; the popular meaning of the term *zār* as "making visible", which is widespread in Sudan, became particularly evocative in this sense. According to Ay Rawda Qallu, as other narratives I collected in Harar confirmed, Sittī ʿAlawiyya was a person who "could see". In the case of Sufi personalities such as Sittī ʿAlawiyya and Ay Rawda Qallu, the outside world enters their homes, and people from a variety of socio-cultural backgrounds seek their advice and place their personal or social problems in their hands. These "prophetesses" have the ability to see and to be aware of issues that the people seeking their advice do not see. On the one hand, the advice, information, and "prophecies" they provide to the people who turn to them are informed by their knowledge and awareness of society, politics and the local socio-cultural context, while on the other, by applying this knowledge, they are able to influence the perceptions of reality and the actions of those who come to them.

They follow the "index paradigm" to some extent, in that they are in contact with local and foreign informants, and are able to read clues in order to decipher reality: they have the ability to approach unknown realities on the basis of clues and signs. In the Sufi vocabulary, as Ginzburg recalls in his essay "Clues: Roots of an Evidential Paradigm", this form of knowledge is known as *firāsa*, and "designed mystical intuitions as well as forms of discernment and wisdom that were attributed to the sons of the king of Serendipity". In this sense, *firāsa* is "the instrument of conjectural knowledge",[47] a term that refers to a technique of observing external signs that permits indications and physical states to be read so as to foretell moral conditions and psychological behaviour. In religious and mystical literature, its intuitive—and almost prophetic—character is stressed in the idea of "a divine influx that assists certain privileged persons to an intuitive understanding of the secrets of men's consciences". It is represented as "a light that God causes to penetrate their hearts and tongues". As the Prophet said: "fear the intuitive eye of the true believer, for he sees with the light of God".[48]

"Sittī ʿAlawiyya was a person who could see," Ay Rawda Qallu claimed. "She had considerable *karāma*, and was not afraid to tell the truth".[49] In his writings, Aḥmad b. ʿĀṣim al-Antakī makes this recommendation: "if you converse with truthful persons, speak the truth to them, for these persons are spies (*ǧawāsīs*) of hearts; they penetrate your heart and are out again before you realize it".[50]

47 Ginzburg 1989: 125.

48 Fahad 1986 vol. 2: 916.

49 Interview with Ay Rawda Qallu in Harar on November 2009.

50 Fahad 1986 vol. 2: 916.

My visit brought about a shift in my gaze and analysis towards the bodily dimension of memory, which is a central aspect of possession rituals: looking at the body, and especially at the body's memory, must be a pivotal element of any study of a holy woman.[51] During our meeting, Ay Rawda Qallu's body and performance were revealed to be "a vehicle of history, a metaphor and metonym of being-in-time".[52]

The body in its sensual and emotional dimension, which is marginalized in the written archives, acquires a remarkable place in the character Ay Rawda Qallu plays, and also lay at the heart of the knowledge and charismatic power of Sittī ʿAlawiyya. Her embodied narrative even shed light on the rare references in written and oral sources that claimed that Sittī ʿAlawiyya "was a person who could see", and that "people needed to see her".

The emotional dimension and the issue of desire and love are highly important in Sufi mystical literature. In Harar, the term *hubbi* ("love"), which is derived from Arabic, is used in *ḏikr* with a spiritual meaning. As Ilaria Sartori has pointed out, it also describes manifestations of mystical ecstasy, including the episodes of female trance that may occur during *ḏikr*. Some *ḏikr* repertoires make reference to this inevitable mystical love that "grabs" the faithful. She also observed that oral sources report that this kind of *hubbi* may happen in a variety of situations, provided that three conditions occur simultaneously: the presence of a person—usually a woman—who is sensitive to *hubbi*; the performance of a specific *ḏikr* which increasingly stimulates dance and spiritual arousal in that person; and of course, the will of Allah (...). *Hubbi* spiritual love is considered as an accepted mystical status which brings blessings (*baraka*) to the person who receives it as well as to anyone around, and fully belongs to the sphere of Islamic religiosity.[53]

According to participants in Somali *sittāt*, a person may see his or her desires fulfilled after the session.[54] Visits to dead or living saints usually begin with the visitors' desires and the love the meeting can bring. A poem (*qaṣīda*) written by a follower of the order when Sittī ʿAlawiyya died is very revealing. It states: "you, ʿAlawiyya, you are the best of women and God takes pity on you.

---

51 Werbner and Basu 1998; Kugle 2007.

52 Comaroff and Comaroff 1992: 79.

53 See Sartori 2013. As Sartori has pointed out, the occurrence of episodes of feminine alteration of consciousness may at first suggest a connection with syncretic rituals which exist in other parts of Ethiopia, but it is important to underline that urban Harari used to take a step back from these practices, which are considered unnecessary and are attributed to rural people.

54 Tiilikainen 2010: 209.

Your tomb is of light because when you were alive you were like a medicine for people. We will not forget the good you have done for people" (Figure 55). ʿAbd al-Raḥim ʿUṯmān Kekiya recalled to me that in Keren "tigré women respected Sittī ʿAlawiyya, they gathered around her and loved her very much. They went to visit her on the occasion of the *ḥawliyya* (anniversaries of saints)".[55] "Love", "desire", "curiosity", "the need to see and listen to her", and "*karāmāt*" show how central the emotional aspect is: it is revealed by the need and desire to see the master that *muḥibbūn* (lovers or followers) feel, as with an experience of love, when they fall under the charms of the shaykha. One thing my meeting with Ay Rawda Qallu revealed is the weight of the non-verbal, physical, and emotional dimension of mystical knowledge (*maʿrifa*) that these women have mastered and transmit through their embodiment practices. This dimension, which is emphasized not only by oral sources but also in Sufi performances such as dance, music, and songs, is invisible or marginal in colonial and written archives.

Another significant discovery was the transformational process a visit can induce: indeed, visits are a moment when conversions might take place. From the colonial and missionary reports, which were noteworthy for their profound scepticism, I was not able to assess the charismatic powers of Sittī ʿAlawiyya because she was usually reduced by colonial officers and travellers simply to a "living curiosity". Even when the missionaries did recognize her power to make conversions, acknowledging that people became Muslims wherever she went, they did not recognize her value from a religious point of view, and reductively

55 Interview with ʿAbd al-Raḥim ʿUṯmān Kekiya (Keren, March 2009). During colonial times, the Kekiyas were an important family of businessmen and traders. In Addis Ababa, for example, Saleh Ahmad Kekiya di Arkiko is remembered as an influential Eritrean trader who owned a number of shops in Markato, in the capital of the AOI. According to Ibrahim Mulushewa, Italian policy at that time produced two significant consequences for the Harari community of Addis Ababa. On the one hand, they were able to acquire land and buildings for the first time, taken from the properties the Italians had confiscated from the Ras and Dejazmac, while on the other, they began to open their own shops and businesses in Markato, which had been planned by the Italians in the context of their racial segregation programme aimed at giving Ethiopians a market away from the centre in the fashion and style of a piazza. The Italians made land in the Markato area available for building shops. The Muslim Eritrean trader Ahmad Kekiya was an important investor, and it is said that he built around 480 stores. The Hararis, who up to that time had worked as employees in businesses owned by Arab and Indian traders, opened their own shops in Markato (Ibrahim Mulushewa 2009: 27–31).

classified her as a witch, using the term in a pejorative sense.[56] The scepticism of colonial settlers and travellers and their inability to fall under this woman's spiritual spell has been well described in several accounts. One traveller relates that "until recently in our Colony, there was no visitor, even in haste, who did not go to Keren to visit this person, who is a living curiosity, because certainly no Italian travellers cross the threshold of Sceriffa Alauia el Morgani's home to obtain a holy title or to make an offering to the holy descendent of the Prophet".[57] Oral narratives, on the other hand, tend to emphasize that the Italian authorities also respected her: one story in particular even reported that they recognized her as "Saint" ʿAlawiyya.[58]

At one stage in my research, I was also concerned to explore and revive her subjectivity. Also, I wanted to shed light on Sittī ʿAlawiyya's personal interests and desires. I quickly realized, however, that this was virtually impossible, and besides, to ask this last question would in a way have caused me to adopt a perspective that followed the line of colonial discourse rather than the Sufi understanding of the path. The mystical literature stresses that a perfect being must abhor Ego, the *nafs*. According to al-Shirindi, when saints return to the world to summon human beings to the Truth, their internal aspect (*bāṭin*) remains with God, while their external aspect (*ẓāhir*) stays with the humans.[59] What inspires the actions of a Sufi is internal reality (*bāṭin*), knowledge (*maʿrifa*) that is inaccessible to anyone who has failed to undertake the spiritual journey. Sufi scholars argue that Sufism cannot be understood through books, and that it can only be learned through direct contact with, and dedication to, a spiritual master. They believe that true understanding cannot be separated from direct experience and faith. This knowledge (*maʿrifa*), which is complementary to scientific knowledge (*ʿilm*), which is learned from books, is acquired intuitively through an intense cognitive experience that only those who have lived through it can understand.[60] One underlying limitation not only of my studies but also those of all scholarly analyses of Sufism is our inability to enter the sphere of *maʿarifa* and *bāṭin*, which are the central areas of mystical knowledge and the Sufi path. In the end, however, we can perhaps make the claim from a Sufi perspective that the focus of this study on Sittī ʿAlawiyya was limited to *ẓāhir*.

56 CBMC, p. 22, cit. in Da Nembro 1953: 230.

57 Massara 1921.

58 Interview with Šarīfa ʿAlawiyya on May 2009 in Cairo.

59 Ventura 1990: 70.

60 Ewing 1994: 571–84.

In my search for the traces of her figure and memory, as I followed the clues in oral and written accounts, in visual records and in material and bodily memories, I have attempted to trace the historical setting of one Sufi woman, not only in terms of a colonial encounter, but also through a slice of the period in which she lived.

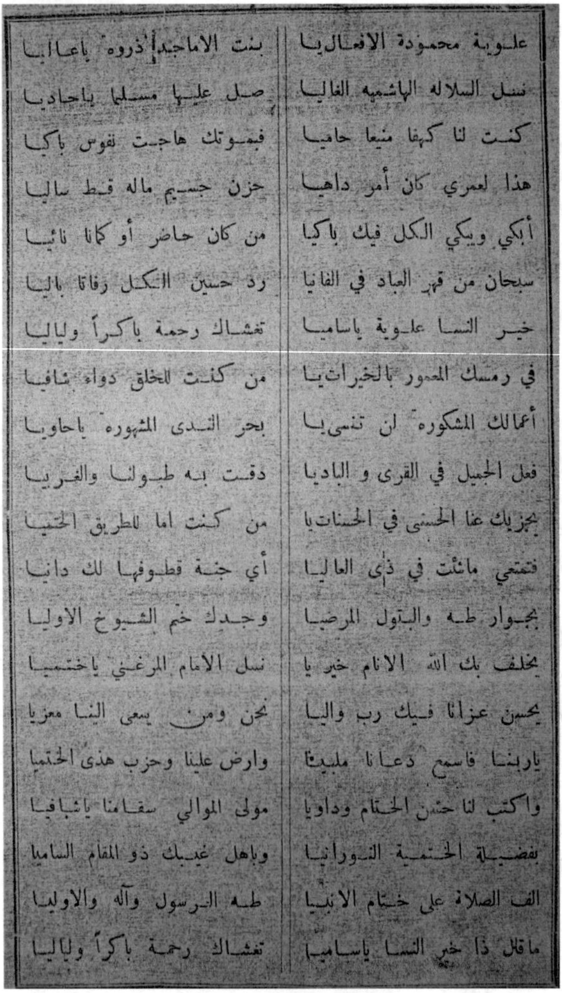

علوية محمودة الافعال يا	بنت الاماجد ذروه يا عاليا
نسل السلاله الهاشميه الغاليا	صل عليها مسلما ياحاديا
كنت لنا كهفا منيعا حاميا	فبموتك هاجت نفوس باكيا
هذا لعمري كان أمر داهيا	حزن جسيم ماله قط ساليا
أبكي ويبكي الكل فيك باكيا	من كان حاضر أو كانا نائيا
سبحان من قهر العباد في الفانيا	رد حسين الكل رفاتا باليا
خير النسا علوية ياساميا	تغشاك رحمة باكراً ولياليا
في رمسك المعمور بالخيرات يا	من كنت للخلق دواء شافيا
أعمالك المشكوره لن تنسى يا	بحر الندى المشهوره ياحاويا
فعل الجميل في القرى و الباديا	دقت به طبولنا والغربيا
يجزيك عنا الحسنى في الحسنات يا	من كنت اما للطريق الختميا
فتمتعي مانلت في ذرى العاليا	أي جنة قطوفها لك دانيا
بجوار طه والبتول المرضيا	وجدك ختم الشيوخ الاوليا
يخلف بك الله الانام خير يا	نسل الامام المرغني ياختميا
يحسن عزانا فيك رب واليا	نحن ومن يسعى الينا معزيا
ياربنا فاسمع دعانا ملبينا	وارض علينا وحزب هذى الختميا
واكتب لنا حسن الختام وداويا	مولى الموالي سقامنا ياشافيا
بفضيلة الختمية النورانيا	وباهل غيبك ذو المقام الساميا
الف الصلاة على ختام الانبيا	طه الرسول وآله والاوليا
ماقال ذا خير النسا ياساميا	تغشاك رحمة باكراً ولياليا

FIGURE 55 *Qaṣīda (poem) written at Sittī ʿAlawiyya's death.* PRIVATE COLLECTION, KEREN.

Bibliography

Abbink, Jan. 2010. 'Possession Cults'. In S. Uhlig (eds), *Encyclopaedia Aethiopica*. Vol. 4. Wiesbaden: Harrassowitz, 183–185.

Abebe, Berhanou. 2003. 'Montages et truquages photographiques dans l'Éthiopie moderne (1915–1955)'. *Annales d'Éthiopie* 19: 19–41.

Abdelsalem, S. 1994. 'L'Hôte divin: Étymologie du mot Zar'. *Nouvelle Revue d'Ethnopsychiatrie* 24: 73–90.

Abu Shouk, Ahmad Ibrahim. 1999. 'A Bibliography of the Mahdist State in the Sudan (1881–1898)'. *Sudanic Africa* 10: 133–168.

Ahmida, A.A. 1994. *The Making of Modern Libya: State Formation, Colonization & Resistance 1830–1932*. New York: State University of New York Press.

Alloula, Malek. 1981. *Le Harem colonial: Images d'un sous-érotisme*. Geneva/Paris: Slatkine.

Alvisini, Alessia. 2000. 'I rapporti politico-economici fra gli Oromo e l'Italia: Alleanze e ambiguità'. *Africa*, 56/4: 489–521.

Arielli, Nir. 2010. *Fascist Italy and the Middle East, 1933–40*. Basingstoke/New York: Palgrave Macmillan.

Arielli, Nir. 2011. 'Beyond Mare Nostrum: Ambitions and Limitations in Fascist Italy's Middle Eastern Policy'. *Geschichte und Gesellschaft* 37/3: 385–407.

Badran, Margot. 2013. *Feminism in Islam: Secular and Religious Convergences*. Oxford: Oneworld.

Baldinetti, Anna. 1997. *Orientalismo e colonialismo: La ricerca di consenso in Egitto per l'impresa di Libia*. Rome: Istituto per l'Oriente C. A. Nallino.

Baldinetti, Anna. 2009. 'Italian Colonial Rule and Muslim Elites in Libya: A Relationship of Antagonism and Collaboration'. In Meir Hatina (ed.), *Guardians of Faith in Modern Times: Ulama' in the Middle East*. (Social, Economic and Political Studies of the Middle East and Asia 105). Leiden: Brill, 91–108.

Baldinetti, Anna. 2011. 'Fascist Propaganda in the Maghrib'. *Geschichte und Gesellschaft* 37/3: 408–436.

Bancel, Nicolas, Blanchard, Pascal, Boëtsch, Gilles, et al. (eds). 2004. *Les Zoos humains: Au temps des exhibitions humaines*. Paris: La Découverte.

Bang, Anne K. 1996. *The Idrīsī State in 'Asīr 1906–1934: Politics, Religion and Personal Prestige as Statebuilding Factors in Early Twentieth-Century Arabia*. (Bergen Studies on the Middle East and Africa 1). Bergen: Centre for Middle Eastern and Islamic Studies.

Bang, Anne K. 2003. *Sufis and Scholars of the Sea: Family Networks in East Africa, 1860–1925*. London/New York: Routledge.

Baron, Beth. 2005. *Egypt as a Woman: Nationalism, Gender, and Politics*. Berkeley/Los Angeles/London: University of California Press.

Barzini, Luigi. 1936. 'Alawia la sceriffa di Otumlo e l'offerta d'oro dei musulmani di Massaua'. *Il Corriere della Sera*, 1 February.

Bashir, Shahzad. 2011. *Sufi Bodies: Religion and Society in Medieval Islam*. New York: Columbia University Press.

Basile, Cosimo. 2010. *Uebi Scebeli: Diario di tenda e cammino della spedizione del Duca degli Abruzzi in Etiopia (1928–1929)*. Bari: Stilo Editrice.

Battera, Federico. 1998. 'Le confraternite islamiche somale di fronte al colonialismo (1890–1920): Tra contrapposizione e collaborazione'. *Africa* 53/2: 155–185.

Battera, Federico. 2001. 'Islam e stato, territorio e uso del suolo in Somalia: Dal colonialismo all'età contemporanea'. *Storia Urbana* 25/95: 93–118.

Bellucci, Stefano, and Zaccaria, Massimo. 2012. 'Engine of Change: A Social History of the Car Mechanics Sector in the Horn of Africa'. In Jan-Bart Gewald, André Leliveld and Iva Peša (eds), *Transforming Innovations in Africa: Explorative Studies on Appropriation in African Societie.* (African Dynamics 11), Leiden: Brill, 237–256.

Beneduce, Roberto. 2002. *Trance e possessione in Africa: Corpi, mimesi, storia*. Torino: Bollati Boringhieri.

Ben-Ghiat, Ruth. 2008. 'The Italian Colonial Cinema: Agendas and Audiences'. In Ruth Ben-Ghiat and Mia Fuller (eds), *Italian Colonialism*. New York: Palgrave Macmillan, 179–191.

Bergstrom, Kari. 2002. *Legacies of Colonialism and Islam for Hausa Woman: An Historical Analysis, 1804 to 1960*. East Lansing: Michigan State University.

Bertrand, Romain. 2008. 'Politiques du moment colonial: Historicités indigènes et rapports vernaculaires au politique en "situation coloniale"'. *Questions de Recherche / Research in Question* 26: 2–49.

Bini, Elisabetta. 2003. 'Fonti fotografiche e storia delle donne: La rappresentazione delle donne nere nelle fotografie coloniali italiane'. http://www.sissco.it/attivita/sem-set-2003/relazioni/bini.rtf.

Blyden, Edward Wilmot. 1967 (1st ed. 1888). *Christianity, Islam and the Negro Race*. Edinburgh: Edinburgh University Press.

Boddy, Janice Patricia. 1988. 'Spirits and Selves in Northern Sudan: The Cultural Therapeutics of Possession and Trance'. *American Ethnologist* 15/1: 4–27.

Boddy, Janice Patricia. 1989. *Wombs and Alien Spirits: Women, Men, and the Zar Cult in Northern Sudan*. Madison: University of Wisconsin Press.

Boddy, Janice Patricia. 1994. 'Spirit Possession Revisited: Beyond Instrumentality'. *Annual Review of Anthropology* 23: 407–434.

Boddy, Janice Patricia. 2007. *Civilizing Women: British Crusades in Colonial Sudan*. Princeton, NJ: Princeton University Press.

Boissevain, Katia. 2006. *Sainte parmi les saints: Sayyda Mannūbiyya ou les recompositions culturelles dans la Tunisie contemporaine*. Paris: Maisonneuve & Larose/Tunis: Institut de recherche sur le Maghreb contemporain.

Böll, Verena. 2003. 'Holy Women in Ethiopia'. In Bertrand Hirsch and Manfred Kropp (eds), *Saints, Biographies and History in Africa*. Frankfurt am Main: Peter Lang, 31-45.

Bonate, Liazzat J.K. 2006. 'Matriliny, Islam and Gender in Northern Mozambique'. *Journal of Religion in Africa* 36/2: 139–166.

Boyd, Jean. 1989. *The Caliph's Sister: Nana Asma'u, 1793–1865, Teacher, Poet and Islamic Leader*. London/Totowa, NJ: F. Cass.

Boyd, Jean, and Mack, Beverly. 1997. *Collected Works of Nana Asma'u Daughter of Usman 'dan-Fodio (1793–1864)*. East Lansing: Michigan State University Press.

Boyd, Jean, and Mack, Beverly. 2000. *One Woman's Jihad: Nana Asma'u, Scholar and Scribe*. Bloomington: Indiana University Press.

Borruso, Paolo. 1997. *Il mito infranto: La fine del sogno africano negli appunti e nelle immagini di Massimo Borruso, funzionario coloniale in Etiopia (1937–46)*. Manduria: P. Lacaita.

Borruso, Paolo. 2001a. 'La crisi politica e religiosa dell'impero etiopico sotto l'occupazione fascista (1936–40)'. *Studi Piacentini* 29: 57–111.

Borruso, Paolo. 2001b, 'L'Impero etiopico e la crisi dell'identita cristiano-amarica durante l'occupazione italiana (1935–41)', *Africa* 56/1: 1–45.

Borruso, Paolo. 2002. *L'ultimo impero cristiano: Politica e religione nell'Etiopia contemporanea*. Milan: Guerini.

Braukamper, Ulrich. 2004. *Islamic History and Culture in Southern Ethiopia: Collected Essays*. Hamburg: LIT.

Brayda Gozzi, Virginia and Zangrossi Crosa, Lelia (ed.). 2012. *Irene di Targiani Giunti: La Croce Rossa Italiana nei diari e nella vita*. Mosso: Opera Pia Sella.

Bruzzi, Silvia. 2005. 'Il Colonialismo italiano e la Khatmiyya in Eritrea (1890–1941)'. *Africa* 61/3–4: 435–453.

Bruzzi, Silvia. 2011. 'Una medicina per l'Anima: Sante e confraternite sufi in Africa orientale'. In Irma Taddia, and Beatrice Nicolini (eds), *Il Corno d'Africa: Tra medicina, politica e storia*. Rome: Novalogos. Available from https://www.academia.edu/3285476/_S._Bruzzi_Una_medicina_per_lAnima_il_ruolo_delle_figure_femminili_nelle_confraternite_islamiche_in_I._Taddia_B._Nicolini_a_cura_di_Il_Corno_dAfrica_Tra_Medicina_politica_e_storia_Progetto_di_ricerca_PRIN_2007-8_Novalogos_Roma_2011._ISBN_978-88-97339-06-9 (accessed 15 October 2017).

Bruzzi, Silvia. 2012a. 'The Role of Muslim Mentors in Eritrea: Religion, Health and Politics'. *Storicamente* 8 http://storicamente.org/bruzzi.

Bruzzi, Silvia. 2012b. 'War World II: Mīrghanī Position in Eritrea within the East African Campaign'. In Nicola Melis, and Mauro Nobili (eds), *Futūḥ al-buldān. Fonti per lo studio delle società islamiche*. Rome: Aracne, 27–41.

Bruzzi, Silvia. 2013. 'Sainthood'. In Natana DeLong-Bas (ed.), *The Oxford Encyclopedia of Islam and Women*. New York/Oxford: Oxford University Press.

Bruzzi, Silvia. Forthcoming. 'Femmes, images et pouvoir en contexte colonial: Le cas de l'Érythrée dans l'entre-deux-guerres'. In Muriel Gomez-Perez, Muriel (ed.), *Femmes, génération et agency en Afrique subsaharienne: Vers de nouveaux défis*. Paris: Kharthala.

Bruzzi, Silvia, and Zeleke, Meron. 2015. 'Contested Religious Authority: Sufi Women in Ethiopia and Eritrea'. *Journal of Religion in Africa* 45/1: 37–67.

Buonasorte, Nicola. 1995. 'La politica religiosa italiana in Africa Orientale dopo la conquista (1936–1941)'. *Studi Piacentini* 17: 53–114.

Calchi Novati, Giampaolo. 1994. *Il Corno d'Africa nella storia e nella politica: Etiopia, Somalia e Eritrea fra nazionalismi, sottosviluppo e guerra*. Torino: Società Editrice Internazionale.

Campassi, Gabriella, and Sega, Maria Teresa. 1983. 'Uomo bianco, donna nera: L'immagine della donna nella fotografia coloniale'. *Rivista di Storia e Critica della Fotografia* 5: 54–62.

Caniglia, Giuseppe. 1940. *La Sceriffa di Massaua (La Tarica Katmia)*. Rome: Cremonese Libraio Editore.

Cantone, Cleo. 2012. *Making and Remaking Mosques in Senegal* (Islam in Africa 13). Leiden/Boston (Mass.): Brill.

Censoni, Domenico. 1941. *L'Italia nel Sudan orientale: La questione di Cassala*. Bologna: [s.n.].

Cerulli, Enrico. 2016. Art. 'Zār'. In *Encyclopaedia of Islam*. Brill Online, 2016. Reference. 26 March 2016 <http://referenceworks.brillonline.com/entries/encyclopaedia-of-islam-1/zar-SIM_6078>.

Cerulli, Enrico. 1971. *L'Islam di ieri e di oggi*. Rome: Istituto per l'Oriente.

Cesari, Cesare. 1913. *Contributo alla storia delle truppe indigene della Colonia Eritrea e della Somalia Italiana*. Città di Castello: Tipografia dell'Unione Arti Grafiche.

Chebel, Malek. 1995. *Dictionnaire des symboles musulmans: Rites, mystique et civilisation*. Paris: Albin Michel.

Chelati Dirar, Uoldelul. 2003. 'Church-State Relations in Colonial Eritrea: Missionaries and the Development of Colonial Strategies (1869–1911)'. *Journal of Modern Italian Studies*. 8/3: 391–410.

Chelati Dirar, Uoldelul. 2004. 'From Warriors to Urban Dwellers: Ascaris and the Military Factor in the Urban Development of Colonial Eritrea'. *Cahiers d'Études Africaines* 175: 533–574.

Chelati Dirar, Uoldelul. 2006. 'Curing Bodies to Rescue Souls: Health in Capuchin's Missionary Strategy in Eritrea (1894–1941)'. In David Hardiman (ed.), *Healing Bodies, Saving Souls: Medical Missions in Asia and Africa*. Amsterdam: Rodopi Press, 249–278.

Chelati Dirar, Uoldelul. 2007. Art. 'Truppe coloniali e l'individuazione dell'African agency: Il caso degli ascari eritrei'. *Africa e Orienti* 9/1: 41–56.

Chernetsov, Sevir. 2003. 'Bati Del Wämbära'. In S. Uhlig et al. (eds), *Encyclopaedia Aethiopica*. Vol. 1. Wiesbaden: Harrasowitz, 505.

Cifuentes, Frédérique. 2008. 'Sufi Sheikhs, Sheikhas, and Saints of the Sudan'. *African Arts* 41/2: 50–59.

Clancy-Smith, Julia Ann. 1992. 'The House of Zainab: Female Authority and Saintly Succession in Colonial Algeria'. In Nikki R. Keddie and Beth Baron (eds), *Women in Middle Eastern History*. Bloomington: Indiana University Press, 254–274.

Clancy-Smith, Julia Ann. 1994. *Rebel and Saint: Muslim Notables, Populist Protest, Colonial Encounters (Algeria and Tunisia, 1800–1904)*. Berkeley/Los Angeles/Oxford: University of California Press.

Clancy-Smith, Julia Ann, and Gouda, Francis (eds). 1998. *Domesticating the Empire: Race, Gender and Family Life in French and Dutch Colonialism*. Charlottesville: University of Virginia Press.

Coletta, Nicola. 1907. *Sulla utilizzazione a scopo d'irrigazione delle acque del fiume Gasc*. Rome: Tip. d. Camera dei Deputati.

Colin, Georges Séraphin. 1986. art. 'Baraka'. In H.A.R. Gibb, J.H. Kramers, E. Lèvi-Provençal, J. Schacht (eds), *The Encyclopaedia of Islam*. Vol. 1. Leiden: Brill, 1032.

Comaroff, John, and Comaroff, Jean. 1992. *Ethnography and the Historical Imagination*. Boulder, CO/San Francisco/Oxford: Westview Press.

Consociazione Turistica Italiana. 1938. *Africa orientale italiana*. Milan: CTI.

Constantin, François. 1987. 'Le saint et le prince'. In François Constantin (ed.), *Les Voies de l'islam en Afrique orientale*. Paris: Karthala, 85–109.

Constantin, François. 1998. 'Condition féminine et dynamique confrérique en Afrique orientale'. In Ousmane Kane and Jean-Louis Triaud (eds), *Islam et islamismes au sud du Sahara*. Paris: Karthala, 58–69.

Constantinides, Pamela. 1991. 'The History of Zar in the Sudan: Theories of Origin, Recorded Observation and Oral Tradition'. In Ioan M. Lewis, Ahmed Al-Safi, and Sayyid Hurreiz (eds), *Women's Medicine: The Zar-Bori Cult in Africa and Beyond*. Edinburgh: Edinburgh University Press for the International African Institute, 83–99.

Conti Rossini, Carlo. 1916. *Principi di diritto consuetudinario dell'Eritrea*. Rome: Tip. dell' Unione editrice.

Cooke, Miriam. 1994. 'Zaynab al-Ghazali: Saint or Subversive?'. *Die Welt des Islams* 34/1: 1–20.

Cooper, Barbara M. 1997. 'Gender, Movement, and History: Social and Spatial Transformations in 20th Century Maradi, Niger'. *Environment and Planning D: Society and Space* 15/2: 195–221.

Cooper, Barbara. 1998. 'Gender and Religion in Hausaland: Variations in Islamic Practice in Niger and Nigeria'. In Herbert L. Bodman and Nayereh Tohidi (eds), *Women in Muslim Societies: Diversity within Unity*. Boulder, CO: Lynne Rienner, 21–37.

Corbin, Alain, Courtine, Jean-Jacques, and Vigarello, Georges (eds). 2005. *Histoire du corps*. Vol. 3, Paris: Editions du Seuil.

Corriou, Morgan. 2010. 'Hourras, "hou hou" et tohu-bohu dans les cinémas de Tunisie à l'époque du protectorat'. In Omar Carlier (ed.), *Images du Maghreb, images au Maghreb (XIXe–XXe siècles): Une révolution du visuel?* Paris: L'Harmattan, 203–236.

Coulon, Christian. 1988. 'Women, Islam and Baraka'. In Donal Cruise O'Brien and Christian Coulon (eds), *Charisma and Brotherhood in African Islam*. Oxford: Clarendon Press, 113–133.

Coulon, Christian, and Reveyrand, Odile. 1990. *L'islam au féminin: Sokhna Magat Diop, cheikh de la confrérie mouride (Sénégal)*. Talence: Centre d'Étude d'Afrique Noire, Institut d'Études Politiques de Bordeaux.

Cresti, Federico. 2000. 'Per uno studio delle "élites" musulmane in Libia nel periodo coloniale: Note sulla formazione scolastica dall'epoca ottomana alla fine dell'amministrazione italiana'. *Studi Storici* 1: 121–158.

Cresti, Federico. 2011. *Non desiderare la terra d'altri: La colonizzazione italiana in Libia*. Rome: Carrocci.

Cruise O'Brien, Donal, and Coulon, Christian (eds). 1988. *Charisma and Brotherhood in African Islam*. Oxford: Clarendon Press.

Cuffel, Alexandra. 2005. 'From Practice to Polemic: Shared Saints and Festivals as "Women's Religion" in the Medieval Mediterranean'. *Bulletin of the School of Oriental and African Studies* 68/3: 401–419.

Curtin, P.D. 1961. 'The White Man's Grave: Image and Reality, 1780–1850'. *Journal of British Studies* 1/1: 94–110.

Curtin, P.D. 1998. *Disease and Empire: The Health of European Troops in the Conquest of Africa*. Cambridge: Cambridge University Press.

Daly, Martin W. 1991. *Imperial Sudan: The Anglo-Egyptian Condominium, 1934–1956*. Cambridge/New York: Cambridge University Press.

Daly, Martin W. 2012. art. 'Uthman Diqna'. In Emmanuel K. Akyeampong and Henry Louis Gates (eds), *Dictionary of African Biography*. New York: Oxford University Press, 108–110.

Da Nembro, Metodio. 1953. *La missione dei minori Cappuccini in Eritrea (1894–1952)*. Rome: Institutum Historicum Ord. Fr. Min. Cap.

De Carli, Ottavio (ed.). 2016. *In guerra per la Croce Rossa: Diari di servizio 1935–1942*. Bergamo: Edizioni Bolis.

Declich, Francesca. 1996. 'Poesia religiosa femminile: Nabi-ammaan, nel contesto rurale della Somalia'. *Africa* 51/1: 50–79.

Decker, David F. 1998. 'Females and the state in Mahdist Kordofan'. In Endre Stiansen, and Michael Kevane (eds), *Kordafan Invaded: Peripherial Incorporation and Social Transformation in Islamic Africa*. Leiden: Brill, 86–100.

Declich, Francesca. 2000. 'Sufi Experience in Rural Somali: A Focus on Women'. *Social Anthropology* 8/3: 295–318.

De Felice, Renzo. 1988. *Il Fascismo e l'Oriente: Arabi, ebrei e indiani nella politica di Mussolini*. Bologna: Il Mulino.

De Grazia, Victoria. 1992. *How Fascism Ruled Women: Italy, 1922–1945*. Berkeley: University of California Press.

Del Boca, Angelo. 1992. *Gli italiani in Africa orientale: La conquista dell'Impero*. Milan: A. Mondadori.

Dell'Osa, Pablo. 2010. *Il principe esploratore: Luigi Amedeo di Savoia, duca degli Abruzzi*. Milan: Mursia.

DeRoo, Rebecca. 2002. 'Colonial Collecting: French Women and Algerian Cartes Postales'. In Eleanor M. Hight and Gary D. Sampson (eds), *Colonialist Photography: Imag(in)ing Race and Place*. London: Routledge, 159–171.

Di Augusta Perricone, Violà. 1930. *Donne e non bambole*. Bologna: Cappelli.

Di Augusta Perricone, Violà. 1935. *Ricordi Somali*. Bologna: Cappelli.

Di Bella, M. 1988. 'Langues et possession: Le cas des pentecôtistes en Italie méridionale'. *Annales* ESC 4 (July–August): 897–907.

Di Pasquale, Francesca. 2012. 'The Spiritual Correlation: The Perception and the Response of Libyan Muslims to the Educational Fascist Policy (1931–1940)'. In *Rethinking Totalitarianism and its Arab Readings. Orient-Institut Studies* 1. http://www.perspectivia.net/content/publikationen/orient-institut-studies/1-2012/di-pasquale_correlation.

Donham, Donald, and James, Wendy (eds). 1986. *The Southern Marches of Imperial Ethiopia: Essays in History and Social Anthropology*. Cambridge: Cambridge University Press.

Dore, Gianni. 2004. *Scritture di colonia: Lettere di Pia Maria Pezzoli dall'Africa orientale a Bologna (1936–1943)*. Bologna: Pàtron.

Dore, Gianni. 2007. 'Chi non ha una parente andinna? Donne e possessione come archivio storico ed esperienza dell'alterità tra i Kunama dell'Eritrea', *Ethnorema*, 3: 45–88.

DuBois, Ellen Carol. 2009. 'Roma 1923: Il Congresso della International Woman Suffrage Alliance'. *Genesis* 2: 1000–1021.

Dunbar, Roberta Ann. 2000. 'Muslim Women in African History'. In Nehemia Levtzion and Randall L. Pouwels (eds), *The History of Islam in Africa*. Athens: Ohio University Press/Oxford: J. Currey; Cape Town: D. Philip, 397–417.

Edwards, Elizabeth. 1996. 'Postcards: Greetings from Another World'. In T. Selwyn (ed.), *The Tourist Image*. Chichester: John Wiley, 197–221.

Erlich, Haggai. 1994. *Ethiopia and the Middle East*. Boulder, CO: L. Rienner.

Esposito, John L. 1998. *Islam and Politics*. Syracuse, NY: Syracuse University Press.

Ezekiel, Gebissa. 2004. *Leaf of Allah: Khat and Agricultural Transformation in Harerge, Ethiopia 1875–1991*. Oxford: James Currey; Addis Ababa: Addis Ababa University Press; Hargeisa: Btec; Athens: Ohio University Press.

Ewing, Katherine. 1994. 'Dreams from a Saint: Anthropological Atheism and the Temptation to Believe'. *American Anthropologist* 96/3: 571–84.

Fadel, Abdallah. 1987. 'Islam, Slavery, and Racism: The Use of Strategy in the Pursuit of Human Rights'. *The American Journal of Islamic Social Sciences* 4/1: 31–50.

Fahad, T. 1986. art. 'Firasa'. In *Encyclopaedia of Islam*. Vol. 2. Leiden: Brill, 916–917.

Fair, Laura. 1998. 'Dressing Up: Clothing, Class and Gender in Post-Abolition Zanzibar'. *The Journal of African History* 39/1: 63–94.

Farid-ud-Din, 'Attar. 1976. *Le mémorial des saints*. Paris: Seuil.

Felter Sartori, Alba. 1940. *Vagabondaggi, soste, avventure negli albori dell'Impero*. Brescia: Fratelli Geroldi.

Fiaschi, Tommaso. 1986. *Da Cheren a Cassala: Note di viaggio*. Florence: Tipografia di G. Barbèra.

Ficquet, Éloi, and Smidt, Wolbert G.C. (eds). 2014. *The Life and Times of Lïj Iyasu of Ethiopia: New Insights*. Münster: LIT.

Ficquet, Éloi (ed.). Forthcoming. 'Muslims and Christians in Northeast Africa: Juxtaposed Stories, Intertwined Destinies'. *Northeast African Studies*.

Fraddosio, Maria. 1989. 'La donna e le guerra: Aspetti della militanza femminile nel fascimo-dalla mobilitazione civile alle origine del Saf nella Repubblica Sociale Italiana'. *Storia contemporanea* 6: 1105–1181.

Frede, Britta. 2014. *Die Erneuerung der Tiǧānīya in Mauretanien: Popularisierung religiöser Ideen in der Kolonialzeit*. Berlin: Schwarz-Verlag.

Frede, Britta and Hill, Joseph. 2014. 'Introduction: En-gendering Islamic Authority in West Africa'. *Islamic Africa* 5/2: 131–165.

Fusari, Valentina. 2015. 'Comboni Missionary Sisters in Eritrea (1914–2014)'. *Annales d'Éthiopie* 30: 45–69.

Gardet, L. 1997. art. 'Karāma'. In *The Encyclopaedia of Islam*. Vol. 4, Leiden: Brill, 615–616.

Gascon, Alain, and Hirsch, Bertrand. 1992. 'Les espaces sacrés comme lieux de confluence religieuse en Éthiopie'. *Cahiers d'Études Africains* 128/32: 689–704.

Gemmeke, Amber. 2009. 'Marabout Women in Dakar: Creating Authority in Islamic Knowledge'. *Africa* 79/1: 128–147.

Gentile, Emilio. 1994. *Il culto del littorio: La sacralizzazione della politica nell'Italia fascista*. Rome: Laterza.

Gervereau, Laurent. 2000. *Les Images qui mentent. Histoire du visuel au XXe siècle*. Paris: Éditions du Seuil.

Gibb, Camilla. 1999. 'Baraka without Borders: Integrating Communities in the City of Saints'. *Journal of Religion in Africa* 29/1: 88–108.

Gibb, Camilla. 2000. 'Negotiating Social and Spiritual Worlds: The Gender of Sanctity in a Muslim City in Africa'. *Journal of Feminist Studies in Religion* 16/2: 25–42.

Giglio, Carlo. 1950. *La politica africana dell'Inghilterra nel XIX secolo*. Padova: Cedam.

Ginzburg, Carlo. 1990. *Clues, Myths, and the Historical Method*. Baltimore, MD: John Hopkins University Press.

Ginzburg, Carlo. 2010. *Le fil et les traces: Vrai, faux, fictif*. Translated by Martin Rueff. Paris: Verdier.

Goglia, Luigi. 1988. 'Sulla politica coloniale fascista'. *Storia Contemporanea* 19/1: 35–53.

Goglia, Luigi. 1989. *Colonialismo e fotografia: Il caso italiano*. Messina: Sicania.

Goglia, Luigi. 1992. 'Note sul razzismo coloniale fascista'. *Storia Contemporanea* 19/6: 1223–1266.

Goglia, Luigi. 2005. 'Il falso in cartolina: Tre casi coloniali italiani'. *Mondo Contemporaneo* 2: 141–150.

Gori, Alessandro. 1995. 'Soggiorno di studi in Eritrea ed Etiopia: Brevi annotazioni bibliografiche'. *Rassegna di Studi Etiopici* 39: 81–129.

Gori, Alessandro. 2003. 'L'islam nella storia e nell'attualità dell'Etiopia'. In *Cooperazione, sviluppo e rapporti con l'islam nel Corno d'Africa*. Rome: Istituto per l'Africa e l'Oriente, 47–64.

Gori, Alessandro. 2006a. 'Contemporary and Historical Muslim Scholars as Portrayed by the Ethiopian Islamic Press in the 1990s'. *Aethiopica* 8: 72–94.

Gori, Alessandro. 2006b. *Contatti culturali nell'Oceano Indiano e nel Mar Rosso e processi di islamizzazione*. Venice: Cafoscarina.

Gori, Alessandro. 2010. 'Ummi Qoda'. In Uhlig Siegbert, Allessandro Bausi, et al. (eds), *Encyclopaedia Aethiopica*. Vol. 4. Wiesbaden: Harrassowitz, 1019–1020.

Grandin, Nicole. 1984. 'Le Shaykh Muhammad Uthman al-Mirghani (1793–1853): Une double lecture de ses hagiographies'. *Archives des Sciences Sociales des Religions* 58/1: 139–155.

Grandin, Nicole. 1988. 'La Sharifa Myriam bint al-Hashim al-Mirghani'. *Islam et Sociétés au Sud du Sahara* 2: 122–128.

Grandin, Nicole. 1989. 'Al-Sayyid Muhammad al-Hasan al-Mirghani'. *Islam et Sociétés au Sud du Sahara* 3: 107–118.

Greenstein, R.C. 1976–77. 'Shaykhs and Tariqas: The Early Muslim 'Ulama' and Tariqa Development in Malawi, c. 1885–1949'. Zomba: University of Malawi, (History seminar paper 32–33).

Grewal, Inderpal. 1996. *Home and Harem: Nation, Gender, Empire, and the Cultures of Travel*. Durham, (NC): Duke University Press.

Harrison, Christopher. 2003. *France and Islam in West Africa, 1860–1960*. Cambridge: Cambridge University Press.

Hartog, François. 2002. *Régimes d'historicité: Présentisme et expériences du temps*. Paris: Le Seuil.

Hay, M.J. Queens. 1988. 'Prostitutes and Peasants: Historical Perspectives on African Women, 1971–1986'. *Canadian Journal of African Studies* 22/3: 417–431.

Hayes, Patricia (ed.). 2006. *Visual Genders, Visual Histories. A Special issue of Gender and History*. Oxford: Blackwell.

Headrick, R.D. 1981. *The Tools of Empire: Technology and European Imperialism in the Nineteenth Century*. New York/Oxford: Oxford University Press.

Hight, Eleanor M., and Sampson, Gary D. 2002. *Colonialist Photography: Imag(in)ing Race and Place*. London/New York: Routledge.

Hill, Joseph. 2010. "All Women Are Guides": Sufi Leadership and Womanhood among Taalibe Baay in Senegal'. *Journal of Religion in Africa* 40/4: 375–412.

Hoffman, Valerie. 1996. 'Le soufisme, la femme et la sexualité'. In Alexandre Popovic and Gilles Veinstein (eds), *Les Voies d'Allah: Les ordres mystiques dans le monde musulman des origines à aujourd'hui*. Paris: Fayard, 254–260.

Hofheinz, Albrecht. 1992. 'Sons of a Hidden Imam: The Genealogy of the Mīrghanī Family'. *Sudanic Africa* 3: 9–27.

Hofheinz, Albrecht. 1995. 'A Yemeni Library in Eritrea'. *Der Islam: Zeitschrift für Geschichte und Kultur des Islamischen Orients* 72: 98–136.

Holt, Peter Malcolm. 1958. *The Mahdist State in the Sudan: 1881–1898: A Study of Its Origins, Development and Overthrow*. Oxford: Clarendon Press.

Holt, Peter Malcolm, and Daly, M.V. 1979. *A History of the Sudan: From the Coming of Islam to the Present Day*. London: Weidenfeld and Nicolson.

Hopkins, Rebecca. 2010. 'Italian Women Writers and the Fascist "Politica Islamica" in Colonial Libya'. *California Italian Studies* 1/1: 1–21.

Hussein Ahmed. 1992. 'The Historiography of Islam in Ethiopia'. *Journal of Islamic Studies* 3/1: 15–46.

Hussein Ahmed. 1999. 'Faith and Trade: The Market Stalls around the Anwar Mosque in Addis Ababa during Ramadan'. *Journal of Muslim Minority Affairs* 19/2: 261–268.

Hussein Ahmed. 2001. *Islam in Nineteenth-Century Wallo, Ethiopia: Revival, Reform, and Reaction*. Leiden: Brill.

Hussein Ahmed. 2005. art. 'Ǧāmiʿ al-Anwar'. In Uhlig Siegbert (ed.), *Encyclopaedia Aethiopica*. Vol. 2. Wiesbaden: Harrassowitz, 673–675.

Hussein Ahmed. 2006. 'Coexistence and/or Confrontation?: Towards a Reappraisal of Christian-Muslim Encounter in Contemporary Ethiopia'. *Journal of Religion in Africa* 36/1: 4–22.

Hussein Ahmed. 2007a. 'The Coming Age of Islamic Studies in Ethiopia: The Present State of Research and Publications'. Draft paper, 16th International conference of Ethiopian Studies, Trondheim, 2–7 July 2007.

Hussein Ahmed. 2007b. 'Italian Colonial Policy towards Islam in Ethiopia and the Responses of Ethiopian Muslims (1936–1941)'. In B.M. Carcangiu and Tekeste Negash, (eds), *L'Africa orientale italiana nel dibattito storico contemporaneo*. Rome: Carocci, 101–114.

Hussein Ahmed. 2011. art. 'Qallu'. In Siegbert Uhlig et al. (eds), *Encyclopaedia Aethiopica*. Vol. 4. Wiesbaden: Harrassowitz, 257–258.

Hussein Ahmed, and Miran, Jonathan. 2007. art. 'Mosques'. In S. Uhlig (eds), *Encyclopaedia Aethiopica*. Vol. 3. Wiesbaden: Harrassowitz, 1027–32.

Hutson, Alaine S. 1999. 'The Development of Women's Authority in the Kano Tijaniyya, 1894–1963'. *Africa Today* 46/3: 43–64.

Hutson, Alaine S. 2001. 'Women, Men, and Patriarchal Bargaining in an Islamic Sufi Order: The Tijaniyya in Kano, Nigeria, 1937 to the Present'. *Gender and Society* 15/5: 734–753.

Hutson, Alaine S. 2004. 'African Sufi Women and Ritual Change'. *Journal of Ritual Studies* 18/2: 61–73.

Ibn al-Ǧawzī. 1981. *Kitāb aḥkām al-nisā'iyya*. Beirut: Manshūrāt al-Maktaba al-'Arabiya.

Ishihara, Minako. 2010. 'Beyond Authenticity: Diverse Images of Muslim Awliya in Ethiopia'. *African Study Monographs* 41: 81–89.

Ishihara, Minako. 2013. 'The Formation of Trans-Religious Pilgrimage Centers in Southeast Ethiopia: Sittī Mumina and the Faraqasa Connection'. In Patrick Desplat and Terje Østebø (eds), *Muslims in Ethiopia: The Christian Legacy, Identity Politics, and Islamic Reformism*. New York: Palgrave Macmillan, 91–114.

Ishihara, Minako. 2015. 'The Role of Women in Tijāniya: From Three Oromo Religious Centers in Western Ethiopia'. *Annales d'Éthiopie* 30: 21–43.

Joseph, Suad, and Najmabadi, Afsaneh (eds). 2003. *Encyclopedia of Women and Islamic Cultures*. Vol. 1. Leiden/Boston, MA: Brill.

Kapteijns, Lidwien. 1996. 'Sittat: Somali Women's Songs for the Mothers of Believers'. In Kenneth Harrow (ed.), *The Marabout and the Muse: New Approaches to Islam in African Literature*. Portsmouth: Heinemann, 124–141.

Kapteijns, Lidwien, and Spaulding, Jay. 1996. 'Women of the Zar and Middle-Class Sensibilities in Colonial Aden, 1923–1932'. *African Languages and Cultures. Supplement*: 171–189.

Karrar, Ali Salih. 1992. *The Sufi Brotherhoods in the Sudan*. London: Hurst

Kassim, M. 1995. 'Islam and Swahili Culture on the Banadir Coast'. *Northeast African Studies* 2/3: 21–37.

Kassim, M. 2002. '"Dhikr will Echo from All Corners": Dada Masiti and the Trasmission of Islamic Knowledge'. *Bildhaan: An International Journal of Somali Studies* 2: 104–119.

Kitula King'ei. 2001. 'Aspects of Autobiography in the Classical Swahili Poetry: Problems of Identity of Authorship'. *Folklore* 16: 87–96.

Kologlu, Orhan. 2007. *500 years in Turkish-Libyan Relations*. (SAM Paper 1). Ankara: Stratejik Arastirmalar Merkezi.

Koposov, Nikolay. 2009. *De l'imagination historique*. Paris: Éditions EHESS.

Kramer, Robert S. 2010. *Holy City on the Nile: Omdurman during the Mahdiyya, 1885–1898*. Princeton, NJ: Markus Wiener.

Kugle, S.A. 2007. *Sufis and Saints' Bodies: Mysticism, Corporeality, and Sacred Power in Islam*. Chapel Hill: University of North Carolina Press.

Labanca, Nicola (ed.). 1992. *L'Africa in vetrina: Storie di musei e di esposizioni coloniali in Italia*. Paese (TV): Pagus.

Lambek, Michael. 1998. 'The Sakalava Poiesis of History: Realizing the Past through Spirit Possession in Madagascar'. *American Ethnologist* 25/2: 106–127.

Lambek, Michael. 2002. 'Fantasy in Practice: Projection and Introjection, or the Witch and the Spirit-Medium'. *Social Analysis* 46: 198–214.

Larsen, Kjersti. 1998. 'Spirit Possession as Historical Narratives: The Production of Identity and Locality in Zanzibar Town'. In N. Lovell (ed.), *Locality and Belonging*. London: Routledge, 121–146.

Larsen, Kjersti. 2001. 'Spirit Possession as Oral History: Negotiating Islam and Social Status. The case of Zanzibar'. In Biancamaria Scarcia Amoretti (ed.), *Islam in East Africa: New Sources*. Rome: Herder, 275–296.

Last, Murray. 1988. 'Charisma and Medicine in Northern Nigeria'. In C. O'Brien and C. Coulon (eds), *Charisma and Brotherhood in African Islam*. Oxford: Clarendon Press.

Laura, G. Ernesto. 2000. *Le stagioni dell'Aquila: Storia dell'Istituto Luce*. Rome: Ente dello Spettacolo.

Lazreg, Marnia. 1988. 'Feminism and Difference: The Perils of Writing as a Woman on Women in Algeria'. *Feminist Studies* 14/1: 81–107.

Le Gall, Michel. 1989. 'The Ottoman Government and the Sanūsīya: A Reappraisal'. *International Journal of Middle East Studies* 21/1: 91–106.

Leiris, Michel. 1958. *La possession et ses aspects théâtraux chez les Éthiopiens de Gondar*. Paris: Plon.

Leiris, Michel. 1988. *La possessione e i suoi aspetti teatrali tra gli etiopi di Gondar*. Milan: Ubulibri.

Leslau, Wolf. 1958. 'The Arabic Origin of the Ethiopic Qollē Spirit'. *Arabica* 5/2: 194–196.

Lewis, Geoffrey. 1975. 'The Ottoman Proclamation of Jihad in 1914'. *Islamic Quarterly* 19/3: 157–163.

Lewis, Ioan. M. 1967. 'Spirit Possession and the Sex War'. Paper presented at a meeting of social research fieldworkers in northeastern Africa at Haile Selassie I University, Institute of Ethiopian Studies, Addis Ababa, 20–23 April 1967.

Lewis, Ioan M. 1989. *Ecstatic Religion: An Anthropological Study of Spirit Possession and Shamanism*. London: Routledge.

Lewis, Ioan M., Al-Safi, Ahmed, and Hurreiz, Sayyid (eds). 1991. *Women's Medicine: The Zar-Bori Cult in Africa and Beyond*. Edinburgh: Edinburgh University Press for the International African Institute.

Locatelli, Francesca. 2009. 'Beyond the Campo Cintato: Prostitutes, Migrants and "Criminals" in Colonial Asmara (Eritrea), 1890–1941'. In Francesca Locatelli, and P. Nugent (eds), *African Cities: Competing Claims on Urban Spaces*. Boston, MA/ Leiden: Brill, 220–240.

Lombardi-Diop, Cristina. 2005. 'Fascist Women in Colonial Africa'. In R. Ben-Ghiat and M. Fuller (eds), *Italian Colonialism*. New York: Palgrave, 145–154.

MacDonald, C.A. 1977. 'Radio Bari: Italian Wireless Propaganda in the Middle East and British Countermeasures 1934–38'. *Middle Eastern Studies* 13/2: 195–207.

Madelung, Wilferd. 1971. art. 'Imāma'. In *The Encyclopaedia of Islam*. Vol. 3. Leiden: Brill, 1163–1169.

Mahmood, Saba. 2001. 'Feminist Theory, Embodiment, and the Docile Agent: Some Reflections on the Egyptian Islamic Revival'. *Cultural Anthropology* 16/2: 202–236.

Makris, Gerasimos P. 1996. 'Slavery, Possession and History: The Construction of the Self among Slave Descendants in the Sudan'. *Africa* 66/2: 159–182.

Makris, G.P., and R.J. Natvig. 1991. 'The Zar, Tumbura and Bori Cults: A Select Annotated Bibliography'. In I.M. Lewis and A. al-Safi, S. Hurreiz (eds), *Women's Medicine: The Zar-Bori Cult in Africa and Beyond*. Edinburgh: Edinburgh University Press for the International African Institute, 233–282.

Marongiu Buonaiuti, Fabrizio. 1982. *Politica e religioni nel colonialismo italiano (1882–1941)*. Milan: Giuffrè Editore.

Martin, B.G. 1992. 'Shaykh Zayla'i and the nineteenth-century Somali Qadiriyya'. In Said S. Samatar (ed.), *In the Shadow of Conquest: Islam in Colonial Northeast Africa*. Trenton, NJ: Red Sea Press, 11–32.

Martinelli, Renzo. 1930. *Sud: Rapporto di un viaggio in Eritrea ed in Etiopia*. Florence: Vallecchi.

Massara, Ercole. 1921. 'Islamismo e confraternite in Eritrea. I Morgani'. *L'Illustrazione Coloniale* 3/8: 306–7.

Masud, Muhammad Khalid, Salvatore, Armando, and van Bruinessen, Martin (eds). 2009. *Islam and Modernity: Key Issues and Debates*. Edinburgh: Edinburgh University Press.

Mašulović-Marsol, Liliane. 1996. 'Tombes de saints musulmans et guérison: Une approche anthropologique'. In J. L. Bacqué-Grammont and A. Tibet (eds), *Cimetières et traditions funéraires dans le monde islamique* 2. Actes du Colloque International du Centre National de la Recherche Scientifique. İstanbul, 28–30 septembre 1991. Ankara: Türk Tarih Kurumu Basimevi, 125–134.

Mecca, Selamawit. 2009. 'Women in Ethiopic Hagiographies'. In Svein Ege, Harald Aspen, Birhanu Teferra and Shiferaw Bekele (eds), *Proceedings of the 16th International Conference of Ethiopian Studies*. Trondheim: NTNU, 1365–1374.

Melis, Nicola. 2006. 'Il concetto di ǧihād'. In Manduchi, Patrizia (ed.), *Dalla penna al mouse: Gli strumenti di diffusione del concetto di ǧihād.* Milan: Franco Angeli, 23–55.

Melis, Nicola. 2012. 'The "Talking Machine" Affair in Ottoman Yemen (1907)'. In Nicola Melis and Mauro Nobili (eds), *Futūḥ al-Buldān: Fonti per lo studio delle società islamiche*. Rome: Aracne, 107–151.

Mernissi, Fatima. 1977. 'Women, Saints, and Sanctuaries'. In *Women and National Development: The Complexities of Change*. Special issue of Signs: *Journal of Women in Culture and Society* 3/1: 101–112.

Mernissi, Fatima. 1992. *Le sultane dimenticate: Donne capi di stato nell'Islam*. Genoa: Marietti.

Mernissi, Fatima. 1994. *The Forgotten Queens of Islam.* Cambridge: Polity Press.

Messing, S.D. 1958. 'Group Therapy and Social Status in the Zar Cult of Ethiopia'. *American Anthropologist*. New Series 60/1: 1120–1126.

Mignemi, Adolfo (ed.). 1984. *Immagine coordinata per un impero: Etiopia 1935–1936.* Torino: Gruppo editoriale Forma.

Miran, Jonathan. 2005. 'A Historical Overview of Islam in Eritrea'. *Die Welt des Islams* 45/2: 177–215.

Miran, Jonathan. 2009. *Red Sea Citizens: Cosmopolitan Society and Cultural Change in Massawa*. Bloomington: Indiana University Press.

Miran, Jonathan. 2010. 'Constructing and Deconstructing the Tigre Frontier Space in the Long Nineteenth Century'. In Gianfrancesco Lusini (ed.), *History and Language of the Tigre-Speaking Peoples*: *Proceedings of the International Workshop, Naples, February 7–8, 2008*, (Studi Africanistici. Serie Etiopica 8). Naples: Università di Napoli 'L'Orientale', 33–50.

Miran, Jonathan. 2014. art. 'Hashim al-Mīrġanī'. In A. Bausi (ed.), *Encyclopaedia Aethiopica*. Vol. 5. Wiesbaden: Harrassowitz, 342–343.

Mondaini, Gennaro. 1927. *Manuale di storia e legislazione coloniale del Regno d'Italia.* Vol. 1. *Storia coloniale*. Rome: s.n.

Moosa, Ebrahim. 2003. 'Sub-Saharan Africa: Early 20th Century to Present'. In *Encyclopedia of Women & Islamic Cultures*. Vol. 1. Leiden/Boston, MA: Brill, 286–293.

Morin, Didier. 2003. art. 'Beni 'Amer'. In Uhlig Siegbert (ed.), *Encyclopaedia Aethiopica*. Vol. 1. Wiesbaden: Harrassowitz, 527–529.

Motadel, David (ed.). 2014. *Islam and the European Empires*. Oxford: Oxford University Press.

al-Munajjid and, Salah al-Din, Khuri, Yusuf Q. 1970. *Fatāwā al-Imām Muḥammad Rašīd Riḍā*. Beirut: Dār al-Kutub al-Ǧadīd.

Nadel, Siegfried Frederick. 1945. 'Notes on Beni Amer Society'. *Sudan Notes and Records* 26/1: 51–94.

Natvig, Richard Johan. 1987. 'Oromos, Slaves, and the Zar Spirits: A Contribution to the History of the Zar Cult'. *International Journal of African Historical Studies* 20/4: 686–673.

Natvig, Richard Johan. 1991. 'Some Notes on the History of the Zar cult in Egypt'. In I. M. Lewis, Ahmed al-Safi and Sayyid Hurreiz (eds), *Women's Medicine: The Zar-Bori Cult in Africa and Beyond*. Edinburgh: Edinburgh University Press for the International African Institute, 178–188.

Natvig, Richard Johan. 1998. 'Arab Writings on Zar from 1880 to the Present'. *Sudanic Africa* 9: 163–178.

Negash, Tekeste. 1986. *No Medicine for the Bite of a White Snake: Notes on Nationalism and Resistance in Eritrea, 1890–1940*. Uppsala: University of Uppsala.

Negash, Tekeste. 1987. *Italian Colonialism in Eritrea, 1882–1941: Policies, Praxis and Impact*. Uppsala: University of Uppsala.

Negash, Tekeste. 2008 (first edition 2005). 'Educational Policy and Praxis in Eritrea'. In Ben-Ghiat R. and Fuller M. (eds), *Italian Colonialism*. New York: Palgrave Macmillan. 109–120.

Nelson, Cynthia. 1974. 'Public and Private Politics: Women in the Middle Eastern Word'. *American Ethnologist* 1/3: 551–563.

Nettler, Ronald L., Mahmoud, Mohamed, and Cooper, John. 1998. *Islam and Modernity: Muslim Intellectuals Respond*. London: I.B. Tauris.

Nora, Pierre. 1989. 'Between Memory and History: Les lieux de mémoire'. *Representations* 26: 7–24.

Odorizzi, Dante. 1916. *Note storiche sulla religione mussulmana e sulle divisioni dell'Islam, con appunti speciali relativi all'Islam in Eritrea*. Asmara: Stabilimento Tipografico Coloniale M. Fioretti.

O'Fahey, Rex Seán. 1990. *Enigmatic Saint: Ahmed ibn Idris and the Idrisi Tradition*. London: Hurst / Evanston: Northwestern University Press.

O'Fahey, Rex Seán. 1994. *Arabic Literature of Africa*. Vol. 1: *The Writings of Eastern Sudanic Africa to c. 1900*. Leiden/New York/Köln: E.J. Brill.

O'Fahey, Rex Seán, and Radtke, Bernd. 1993. 'Neo-Sufism Reconsidered'. *Der Islam* 70/1: 52–87.

O'Fahey, Rex Seán, Hofheinz, Albrecht, and Radkte, Bernd. 1994. 'The Khtamiyya Tradition'. In R.S. O'Fahey (ed.), *Arabic Literature of Africa*. Vol. 1. *The Writings of Eastern Sudanic Africa to c. 1900*. Leiden/New York/Köln: E.J. Brill, 178–227.

Omer Beshir, Mohamed. 1977. *Revolution and Nationalism in the Sudan*. London: Rex Collings.

Østebø, Terje. 2008. *Localizing Salafism: Religious Change among Oromo Muslims in Bale, Ethiopia*. Stockholm: Stockholm University.

Paciello, Maria Cristina. 2002. 'Zaynab al-Ġazālī al-Ǧabīlī, Militante Islamica Egiziana: Un Modello Islamico di Emancipazione Femminile'. *Oriente Moderno* 21/2: 275–319.

Palma, Silvana. 1999. *L'Italia coloniale*. Rome: Editori Riuniti.

Palma, Silvana. 2002. 'Fotografia di una colonia: L'Eritrea di Luigi Naretti (1885–1900)'. *Quaderni Storici* 37/1: 83–148.

Palma, Silvana. 2005a. *L'Africa nella collezione fotografica dell'IsIAO: Il fondo Eritrea-Etiopia.* Rome: Istituto italiano per l'Africa e l'Oriente.

Palma, Silvana. 2005b. 'The Seen, the Unseen, the Invented'. *Cahiers d'Études Africaines* 1: 39–69.

Pankhurst, Rita. 2009. 'Taytu's Foremothers Queen Ələni, Queen Säblä Wängel and Bati Dəl Wämbära'. In Svein Ege, Harald Aspen, Birhanu Teferra and Shiferaw Bekele (eds), *Proceedings of the 16th International Conference of Ethiopian Studies.* Trondheim, 51–63.

Pankhurst, Richard. 1974. 'The History of Prostitution in Ethiopia'. *Journal of Ethiopian Studies* 2: 159–179.

Pankhurst, Richard. 1987. 'The Development of Racism in Fascist Italy's Colonial Empire (1935–1941)'. *Ethiopian Journal of African Studies*, 4/2: 32–51.

Pankhurst, Richard. 1992. 'The Political Image: The Impact of the Camera in an Ancient Independent African State'. In E. Edwards (ed.), *Anthropology and Photography, 1860–1920.* New Haven, CT/London: Yale University Press, 234–41.

Pankhurst, Richard, and Gérard, Denis. 1996. *Ethiopia Photographed: Historic Photographs of the Country and Its People Taken between 1867 and 1935.* London: Kegan Paul International.

Passerini, Luisa. 2000. 'Transforming Biography: From the Claim of Objectivity to Intersubjective Plurality'. *Rethinking History: The Journal of Theory and Practice* 4/3: 413–416.

Passerini, Luisa. 2003. *Memoria e utopia: Il primato dell'intersoggettività.* Turin: Bollati Boringhieri.

Paul, Andrew. 1954. *A History of the Beja Tribes of the Sudan.* Cambridge: Cambridge University Press.

Paulicelli, Eugenia. 2002. 'Fashion, the Politics of Style and National Identity in Pre-Fascist and Fascist Italy'. *Gender and History* 14/3: 537–559.

Perbellini, A.M. 1936. 'Fedeltà degli eritrei all'Italia'. *Il Resto del Carlino*, 7 February, 1.

Peters, Rudolph. 1979. *Islam and Colonialism: The Doctrine of Jihad in Modern History.* The Hague: Mouton.

Pickering Iazzi, Robin. 2000. 'Feminine Fantasy and Italian Empire Building, 1930–40'. *Italica* 77/3: 400–417.

Pinkus, Karen. 1995. 'Selling the Black Body: Advertising and the African Campaigns'. In Karen Pinkus, *Bodily Regimes: Italian Advertising under Fascism.* Minneapolis/London: University of Minnesota Press: 22–81.

Piga, Adriana. 2004. 'Colonialismo francese e saperi islamici nell' AOF fra marginalizzazione e creazione di nuove identita' (1900–1950)'. *Sociologia e Ricerca Sociale* 73: 1–34.

Pollera, Alberto. 1913. *I Baria e i Cunama.* Rome: Reale Società Geografica.

Pollera, Alberto. 1935. *Le popolazioni indigene dell'Eritrea.* Bologna: Cappelli.

Ponzanesi, Sandra. 2005. 'Beyond the Black Venus: Colonial Sexual Politics and Contemporary Visual Practices'. In Jacqueline Andall and Derek Duncan (eds), *Italian Colonialism: Legacy and Memory*. Bern: Peter Lang, 165–189.

Ponzanesi, Sandra. 2012. 'The Color of Love: Madamismo and Interracial Relationships in the Italian Colonies'. *Research in African Literatures* 43/2: 155–172.

Puglisi, Giuseppe. 1952. *Il Chi è? dell'Eritrea: Dizionario biografico*. Asmara: Agenzia Regina.

Reese, Scott Steven. 1999. 'Urban Woes and Pious Remedies: Sufism in Nineteenth-Century Benaadir (Somalia)'. *Africa Today* 46/3–4: 169–192.

Reese, Scott Steven. 2012. 'Salafi Transformations: Aden and the Changing Voices of Religious Reform in the Interwar Indian Ocean'. *International Journal of Middle East Studies* 44/1: 71–92.

Reeves, Edward B. 1995. 'Power, Resistance, and the Cult of Muslim Saints in a Northern Egyptian Town'. *American Ethnologist* 22/2: 306–323.

Renard, Michel. 2013. 'L'armée française et la religion musulmane durant la Grande Guerre (1914–1920)'. Paper presented at the international conference *'Les troupes coloniales et la Grande Guerre'*, Rheims, 7–8 November 2013. *Études-Coloniales* 15: 'Le monde colonial en métropole'. http://etudescoloniales.canalblog.com/archives/2014/08/23/30279901.html.

Reynolds, Jonathan. 2001. 'Good and Bad Muslims: Islam and Indirect Rule in Northern Nigeria'. *The International Journal of African Historical Studies* 34/3: 601–618.

Rieker, Martina (ed.), 2007. *Pioneering Feminist Anthropology in Egypt: Selected Writings from Cynthia Nelson*. Cairo: American University in Cairo Press.

Robinson, David. 1988. 'French 'Islamic' Policy and Practice in Late Nineteenth-Century Senegal'. *Journal of African History* 29/3: 415–36.

Robinson, David. 1991. 'Beyond Resistance and Collaboration: Amadu Bamba and the Murids of Senegal'. *Journal of Religion in Africa* 21/2: 149–171.

Robinson, David. 1997. 'An Emerging Pattern of Cooperation between Colonial Authorities and Muslim Societies in Senegal and Mauritania'. In D. Robinson and J.-L. Triaud (eds), *Le Temps des marabouts: Itinéraires et stratégies islamiques en Afrique occidentale française 1880–1960*. Paris: Karthala, 155–180.

Robinson, David. 1999. 'France as a Muslim Power in West Africa'. *Africa Today* 46/3–4: 105–127.

Robinson, David. 2000. *Paths of Accommodation*. Athens: Ohio University Press; Oxford: J. Currey.

Robinson, David, and Triaud, Jean-Louis (eds). 1997. *Le temps des marabouts: Itinéraires et stratégies islamiques en Afrique occidentale française, v. 1880–1960*. Paris: Karthala.

Rochefort, Florence (ed.). 2007. *Le pouvoir du genre: Laïcités et religions 1905–2005*. Toulouse: PUM.

Romandini, Massimo. 1984. 'Politica musulmana in Eritrea durante il governatorato Martini'. *Islam, Storia e Civiltà*. Rome: Unione Islamica in Occidente, Accademia di Cultura islamica, 3/2: 127–131.

Romandini, Massimo. 1985. 'Personaggi Musulmani nelle pagine di F. Martini'. *Islam, Storia e Civiltà* 4/1: 57–72.

Romani, Cesare. 2008. 'Il corpo dell'esotismo: Cartografia, fotografia, cinema'. *Le Globe: Revue Genevoise de Géographie* 148/1: 107–128.

Rosenwein, Barbara H. 2010. 'Problems and Methods in the History of Emotions'. *Passions in Context* 1/1: 1–32.

Saler, Michael. 2006. 'Modernity and Enchantment: A Historiographic Review'. *The American Historical Review* 111/3: 692–716.

Samatar, Said S. (ed.). 1992. *In the Shadow of Conquest: Islam in Colonial Northeast Africa*. Trenton, NJ: Red Sea Press.

Sartori, Ilaria. 2013. 'Lo dhikr e le donne nella città dei santi'. In G. De Zorzi (ed.), *Con i dervisci: Otto incontri sul campo*. Milan-Udine: Mimesis.

Sbacchi, Alberto. 1980. *Il colonialismo italiano in Etiopia: 1936–1940*. Milan: Mursia.

Sbacchi, Alberto. 1985. *Ethiopia under Mussolini: Fascism and the Colonial Experience*. London: Zed Books.

Sbacchi, Alberto. 1997. *Legacy of Bitterness: Ethiopia and Fascist Italy 1935–1941*. Trenton: NJ: Red Sea Press.

Scardigli, Marco. 1996. *Il braccio indigeno: Ascari, irregolari e bande nella conquista dell'Eritrea, 1885–1911*. Milan: F. Angeli.

Scattolin, Giuseppe. 1993. 'Women in Islamic Mysticism'. *Encounter* 198: 3–26.

Schimmel, Annemarie. 2003. *My Soul is a Woman: The Feminine in Islam*. New York: Continuum.

Scott, Joan W. 1986. 'Gender: A Useful Category of Historical Analysis'. *The American Historical Review* 91/5: 1053–1075.

Searcy, Kim. 2010. *The Formation of the Sudanese Mahdist State*. Leiden: Brill.

Serra, Enrico. 1966. *La questione di Cassala e di Adua nelle nuove fonti documentarie*. Milan: A. Giuffrè.

Severi, Carlo. 2004. *Il percorso e la voce: Un'antropologia della memoria*. Turin: Einaudi.

Shack, William A. 1971. 'Hunger, Anxiety, and Ritual: Deprivation and Spirit Possession Among the Gurage of Ethiopia'. *Man*. New series 6: 30–43.

Al-Shahi, Ahmad. 1981. 'A Noah's Ark: The Continuity of the Khatmiyya Order in Northern Sudan'. *Bulletin of the British Society for Middle Eastern Studies* 8/1: 13–29.

Shankar, Shobana. 2007. 'Medical Missionaries and Modernizing Emirs in Colonial Hausaland: Leprosy Control and Native Authority in the 1930s'. *Journal of African History* 48/1: 45–68.

Sheldon, Kathleen. 2005. 'Writing about Women: Approaches to a Gendered Perspective in African History'. In John E. Philips (ed.), *Writing African History*. Rochester, NY: University of Rochester Press, 465–489.

Smidt, Wolbert G.C. 2003. 'Bilin History [History of the ethnic group and the Bogos land]'. In Siegbert Uhlig (ed.), *Encyclopaedia Aethiopica*. Vol. 1 Wiesbaden: Harrassowitz, 586–588.

Sohier, Estelle. 2011. *Portraits controversés d'un prince éthiopien: Iyasu (1897–1935)*. Montpellier: L'Archange Minotaure.

Sohier, Estelle. 2012. *Le Roi des rois et la photographie: Politiques de l'image et pouvoir royal en Éthiopie sous le règne de Ménélik II*. Paris: Publications de la Sorbonne.

Sontag, Susan. 1992. *Sulla fotografia: Realtà e immagine nella nostra società*. Turin: Einaudi.

Sorbera, Lucia. 2006. 'Viaggiare e svelarsi alle origini del femminismo egiziano'. In Anna Rosa Scrittori (ed.), *Margini e confini: Studi sulla cultura delle donne nell'età contemporanea*. Venice: Editrice Cafoscarina, 6–10.

Sorgoni, Barbara. 1998. *Parole e corpi: Antropologia, discorso giuridico e politiche sessuali interrazziali nella colonia Eritrea (1890–1941)*. Naples: Liguori.

Sorgoni, Barbara. 2002. 'Contraddizioni coloniali: Comprensione etnografica ed esigenze politiche negli scritti di Alberto Pollera'. *Antropologia* 2/2: 66–90.

Soulé, Aramis Houmed. 2005. *Deux vies dans l'histoire de la corne de l'Afrique: Mahamad Hanfare (1861–1902) et Ali Mirah Hanfare (1944–), sultans Afars*. Addis Ababa: Centre Français des Études Éthiopiennes.

Soulé, Aramis Houmed, and Piguet, François. 2009. 'La région Afar dans la première moitié du XXe siècle de l'autonomie au démembrement'. *Annales d'Éthiopie* 24: 251–280.

Spadaro, Barbara. 2010. 'Intrepide massaie: Genere, imperialismo e totalitarismo nella preparazione coloniale femminile durante il fascismo (1937–1943)'. *Contemporanea* 1: 27–52

Spadaro, Barbara. 2013. *Una colonia italiana: Incontri, memorie e rappresentazioni tra Italia e Libia*. Florence: Le Monnier.

Stefani, Giulietta. 2007. *Colonia per maschi: Italiani in Africa orientale, una storia di genere*. Verona: Ombre corte.

Stockreiter, Elke. 2015. *Islamic Law, Gender and Social Change in Post-Abolition Zanzibar*. Cambridge: Cambridge University Press.

Stoller, Paul. 1992. 'Embodying Cultural Memory in Songhay Spirit Possession'. *Archives de Sciences Sociales des Religions* 79: 53–68.

Streets, Heather. 2004. *Martial Races: The Military, Race and Masculinity in British Imperial Culture, 1857–1914*. Manchester: Manchester University Press.

Taddia, Irma. 1996. *Autobiografie africane: Il colonialismo nelle memorie orali*. Milan: F. Angeli.

Taddia, Irma. 2005. 'Italian Memories/African Memories of Colonialism'. In R. Ben Ghiat and M. Fuller (eds), *Italian Colonialism*. New York: Palgrave, 209–220.

Taddia, Irma. 2012. 'Riflessioni sull'Islam moderno nel Corno d'Africa: Un ricordo di Ottavia Schmidt di Friedberg'. *Ethnorêma* 8/8: 51–65. http://www.ethnorema.it/rivista-presentazione-link/numero-8-2012.

Tanvir, Anjum. 2014. 'Mediational Role of the Sufis in the Islamicate South Asia: A Conceptual and Empirical Study'. *Journal of the Research Society of Pakistan* 51/1: 157–77.

Taraud, Christelle. 2012. *Amour interdit: Marginalité, prostitution, colonialisme (Maghreb, 1830–1962)*. Paris: Payot & Rivages.

Terhoeven, Petra. 2006. *Oro alla patria: Donne, guerra e propaganda nella giornata della Fede fascista*. Bologna: Il Mulino.

Thomassen, Einar, and Radtke, Bernd. 1993. *The Letters of Ahmad ibn Idris*. London: Hurst.

Tiilikainen, Marja. 2010. 'Sitaat as Part of Somali Women's Everyday Religion'. In Marja-Liisa Keinänen (ed.), *Perspectives on Women's Everyday Religion*. Stockholm: Acta Universitatis Stockholmiensis, 203–218.

Topan, Farouk. 2004. 'From Mwana Kupona to Mwamvita: Female Representations in Swahili Literature'. In Pat Caplan and Farouk Topan (eds), *Swahili Modernities*. Trenton, NJ: Africa World Press, 213–227.

Trento, Giovanna. 2012. 'From Marinetti to Pasolini: Massawa, the Red Sea, and the Construction of "Mediterranean Africa" in Italian Literature and Cinema'. *Northeast African Studies* 12/1: 273–307.

Triaud, Jean-Louis. 1995. *La légende noire de la Sanûsiyya: Une confrérie musulmane saharienne sous le regard français, 1840–1930*. Paris: Maison des Sciences de l'Homme.

Triaud, Jean-Louis and Robinson, David (eds). 2000. *La Tijâniyya: Une confrérie musulmane à la conquête de l'Afrique*. Paris: Karthala.

Trimingham, John Spencer. 1952. *Islam in Ethiopia*. London/New York/Oxford: Oxford University Press.

Trimingham, John Spencer. 1965. *Islam in the Sudan*. London: Frank Cass.

Trimingham, John Spencer. 1971. *The Sufi Orders in Islam*. Oxford: Clarendon Press.

Trimingham, John Spencer. 1980. *The Influence of Islam upon Africa*. London/New York: Longman/Beirut: Librairie du Liban.

Triulzi, Alessandro (ed.). 1995. *Fotografia e storia dell'Africa*. Naples: Istituto Universitario Orientale.

van Bruinessen, Martin. 2009. 'Sufism, "Popular" Islam and the Encounter with Modernity'. In Muhammad Khalid Masud, Armando Salvatore and Martin van Bruinessen (eds), *Islam and Modernity: Key Issues and Debates*. Edinburgh: Edinburgh University Press, 125–157.

van Bruinessen, Martin and Howell Julia Day, (eds). 2007. *Sufism and the 'Modern' in Islam*. London/New York: I.B. Tauris.

Vaughan, Megan. 1994. 'Healing and Curing: Issues in the Social History and Anthropology of Medicine in Africa'. *Social History of Medicine* 7/2: 283–295.

Vecchiato, Norbert L. 1993. 'Illness, Therapy, and Change in Ethiopian Possession Cults'. *Africa* 63/2: 176–196.

Venosa, Joseph. 2013. 'Adapting to the New Path: Khatmiyya Sufi Authority, the al-Mirghani Family, and Eritrean Nationalism during British Occupation, 1941–1949'. *Journal of Eastern African Studies* 7/3: 413–431.

Venosa, Joseph. 2014. *Paths toward the Nation: Islam, Community, and Early Nationalist Mobilization in Eritrea, 1941–1961*. Athens: Ohio University Press.

Ventura, Alberto. 1990. *Profezia e santità secondo Shofez Ahmad Sirhindi*. Cagliari: Istituto di Studi Africani e Orientali.

Vikør, Knut S. 1995. *Sufi and Scholar on the Desert Edge*. London: Hurst.

Vikør, Knut S. 2000. 'Sufi Brotherhoods in Africa'. In Nehemia Levtzion and Randall Pouwels (eds), *The History of Islam in Africa*. Athens: Ohio University Press; Oxford: J. Currey, 441–476.

Voll, John O. 1979. 'The Sudanese Mahdī: Frontier Fundamentalist'. *International Journal of Middle East Studies* 10/2: 145–166.

Voll, John O. 2000. 'The Eastern Sudan, 1822 to the Present'. In Nehemia Levtzion, and Randall Pouwels (eds), *The History of Islam in Africa*. Athens: Ohio University Press; Oxford: J. Currey, 153–167

Voll, John O. art. 'al-Ahdal Family'. *Encyclopaedia of Islam, Three*. Brill Online, 2014. Available from http://dx.doi.org/10.1163/1573-3912_ei3_COM_23488 (accessed 15 October 2017).

Volterra, Alessandro. 2005. *Sudditi coloniali: Ascari eritrei 1935–1941*. Milan: F. Angeli.

Warburg, Gabriel. 2003. *Islam, Sectarianism and Politics in the Sudan since the Mahdiyya*. London: Hurst.

Warburg, Gabriel. 2013. 'Islam in Sudan under the Funj and the Ottomans'. In David J. Wasserstein, and Ami Ayalon (eds), *Mamluks and Ottomans: Studies in Honour of Michael Winter*. London: Routledge, 206–225.

Werbner, Pnina. 2003. *Pilgrims of Love: The Anthropology of a Global Sufi Cult*. Bloomington: Indiana University Press.

Werbner, Pnina. 2016. 'Between Ethnography and Hagiography: Allegorical Truths and Representational Dilemmas in Narratives of South Asian Muslim Saints'. *History and Anthropology* 27/2: 135–153.

Werbner, Pnina, and Basu H. (eds). 1998. *Embodying Charisma: Modernity, Locality and the Performance of Emotion in Sufi Cults*. London: Routledge.

Wright, John. 2005. 'Mussolini, Libya, and the "Sword of Islam"'. In Ruth Ben-Ghiat and Mia Fuller (eds), *Italian Colonialism*. New York: Palgrave Macmillan, 121–130.

Yarber, Angela M. 2011. *Embodying the Feminine in the Dances of the World's Religions* (Liturgical Studies 1). New York: Peter Lang.

Yeğenoğlu, Meyda. 1998. *Colonial Fantasies: Towards a Feminist Reading of Orientalism*. Cambridge: Cambridge University Press.

Zaccaria, Massimo (ed.). 2001. *Photography and African Studies: A Bibliography*. Pavia: University of Pavia, Department of Political and Social Studies.

Zaccaria, Massimo. 2005. 'Il Sudan e gli esordi del colonialismo italiano'. In Gianpaolo Romanato (ed.), *Giovanni Miani e il contributo veneto alla conoscenza dell'Africa: Esploratori, missionari, imprenditori, scienziati, avventurieri, giornalisti. Atti del XXVII Convegno di Studi Storici, Rovigo 14–16 novembre 2003*. Rovigo: Minelliana, 305–315.

Zaccaria, Massimo. 2012. *Anch'io per la tua bandiera: Il V battaglione ascari in missione sul fronte libico (1912)*. Ravenna: Giorgio Pozzi Editore.

Zaccaria, Massimo. 2013. 'Writing Letters from the Libyan Front'. In Lars Berge and Irma Taddia (eds), *Themes in Modern African History and Culture: Festschrift for Tekeste Negash*. Padova: Libreriauniversitaria.it.edizioni, 223–240.

Zaghi, Carlo. 1940. 'Il problema di Cassala e l'Italia: Le trattative italo-britanniche del 1890 alla luce del carteggio dal Verme-Crispi'. *Storia e Politica Internazionale* 2: 412–464.

Zeleke, Meron. 2010. 'Ye Shakoch Chilot (the Court of the Sheikhs): A Traditional Institution of Conflict Resolution in Oromiya Zone of Amhara Regional State, Ethiopia'. *African Journal of Conflict Resolution* 10/1: 63–84.

Zeleke, Meron. 2010. 'Teru Sina'. In Siegbert Uhlig (ed.), *Encyclopaedia Aethiopica*. Vol. 4. Wiesbaden: Harrassowitz, 924–925.

Zeleke, Meron. 2013. 'The Gendering Discourse in the Debates of Religious Orthodoxy'. In Patrick Desplat and Terje Østebø (eds), *Muslims in Ethiopia: The Christian Legacy, Identity Politics, and Islamic Reformism*. New York: Palgrave Macmillan, 115–137.

Zeleke, Meron. 2015. *Faith at the Crossroads: Religious Syncretism and Dispute Settlement in Northern Ethiopia*. Wiesbaden: Harrasowitz.

Zürcher, Erik-Jan (ed.). 2016. *Jihad and Islam in World War I: Studies on the Ottoman Jihad on the Centenary of Snouck Hurgronje's 'Holy War Made in Germany'*. Leiden: Leiden University Press.

Unpublished Theses, Papers and Researches

Abubeker Ibrahim, Muna. 2007. *Gender Issues in the Diwan (Court) and Sijil (Register) of the City of Harar during the 19th Century*. MA diss, Institute of Language Studies, Addis Ababa University.

Barrera, Giulia. 1996. *Dangerous Liaisons: Colonial Concubinage in Eritrea, 1890–1941*. Doctoral diss. Evanston, IL: Northwestern University, Program of African Studies.

Bruzzi, Silvia. 2005. *Colonialismo italiano e Islam in Eritrea (1890–1941)*. Tesi di Laurea in Storia orientale. Università di Bologna.

Bruzzi, Silvia. 2013. 'Corps et images en contexte colonial: Imaginer le genre, le genre en images'. Unpublished paper presented at EHESS (Paris).

Constantinides, Pamela. 1972. *Sickness and the Spirits: A Study of the Zaar Spirit-Possession Cult in Northern Sudan*. PhD diss. University of London.

Di Barbora, Monica. *Colonisatrices et colonisées: Les femmes dans l'Éthiopie de 1936 à travers les écrits et les photos de Ciro Poggiali*, Paper presented at the international conference "Femmes et genre en contexte colonial, XIXe–XXe siècles", Paris, 19–21 January 2012. http://genrecol.hypotheses.org/146 (accessed 31 March 2016).

Gazzini, Claudia Anna. 2004. *Jihad in Exile: Aḥmad al-šarīf al-Sanusi 1918–1933*. MA diss. in, Near-Eastern Studies. Princeton University.

Gemechu Jemal Geda. 2007. *The Faraqasa Indigenous Pilgrimage Center: History and Ritual Practices*. MA diss. University of Tromso.

Gibb, Camilla. 1997. *In the City of Saints: Religion, Politics and Gender in Harar, Ethiopia*. PhD diss. University of Oxford.

Hutson, Alaine S. 1997. *We Are Many: Women Sufis and Islamic Scholars in Twentieth Century Kano, Nigeria*. PhD diss. Indiana University.

Lamothe, Ronald M. 2010. *Slaves of Fortune: Sudanese Soldiers and the River War, 1896–1898*. PhD diss. Boston University.

Matzke, Christine. 2003. *En-gendering Theatre in Eritrea: The Roles and Representations of Women in the Performing Arts*. PhD diss. University of Leeds.

Mulushewa, Ibrahim. 2009. *A History of the Harari Community in Addis Ababa (1917–1991)*. MA diss. Addis Ababa University, Department of History and Heritage Management.

Ryan, Eileen. 2012. *Italy and the Sanusiyya: Negotiating Authority in Colonial Libya, 1911–1931*. PhD diss. Colombia University.

Sartu, Shemsuddin. 2013. *The Harro Šayḫs' Collection, with Annotated Translation of Astronomy Manuscript*. MA diss. in Atabic Philology. Addis Ababa University.

Voll, John O. 1969. *A History of the Khatmiyyah Tariqah in the Sudan*. PhD diss. Harvard University.

Archives and Private Collections

Accademia dei Lincei in Rome

Archivio Generale dei Cappuccini (AGCR) in Rome

Archivio Storico Diplomatico del Ministero degli Affari Esteri (ASDMAE), Archivio Eritrea (AE) in Rome

Archivio Storico Diplomatico del Ministero degli Affari Esteri (ASDMAE), Archivio Storico del Ministero dell'Africa Italiana (ASMAI) in Rome
Biblioteca Africana, Private Collection in Fusignano
Biblioteca dell'Archiginnasio in Bologna
Biblioteca Istituto Parri in Bologna
Celsio Bragli's Private Collection in Modena
Ḫatmiyya Private Collection in Asmara
ISIAO (Istituto Italiano per l'Africa e l'Oriente) in Rome
Istituto Luce Cinecittà Historical Archive in Rome
Ottavio de Carli's Private Collection in Brescia
Pavoni Social Centre in Asmara
Piola Caselli Archive in Rome
Research and Documentation Centre (RDC) in Asmara
The Institute of Ethiopian Studies (IES) in Addis Ababa
The Mahmoud Salih and SMI Collection in Bergen
The Mīrġanī family Private Collection in Cairo

Informants

Šarīfa ʿAlawiyya al-Mīrġanī, daughter of Ǧaʿfar al-Mīrġanī, namesake granddaughter of Šarīfa ʿAlawiyya bint Hāšim al-Mīrġanī (Cairo, May 2009).
Aḥmad al-Mīrġanī, son of Šarīfa ʿAlawiyya bint Sīdī Ǧaʿfar (Cairo, May 2009).
Al-Hāǧǧ Kamīl Šarīf, Director of the Madrasa Abadīr of Addis Ababa (Addis Ababa, November 2009).
Ay Rawda Qallo, shaykha Qādirī of Harar, granddaughter of Sayyid ʿAbdullai Ṣādiq (Harar, November 2009).
Ḥāǧǧī Aḥmed Kebiro, Harari teacher (Harar, November 2009).
Kabīr ʿAbdu, Harari historian and teacher (Harar, November 2009).
Ḫalīfa Aḥmad, *ḫalīfat al-ḫulafāʾ* of the Ḫatmiyya in Keren (Keren, September 2004).
ʿAbd al-Raḥim ʿUṯmān Kekiya (Keren, Mars 2009).
Hāšim Muḥammad ʿAlī Blenaī, 102 years old, Ḫatmiyya fellow (Massawa, Mars 2009).
Muḥammad Ṣāliḥ, *ḫalīfa* of the Ḫatmiyya in Massawa, nephew of Šayḫ ʿAlī Efendi Yahya (Massawa, March 2009).

Index

ʿAbd al-Qādir al-Ǧīlānī 13, 63 n. 2, 213 n. 28
ʿAbd al-Raḥīm 77 n. 47, 102 n. 45, 104 n. 50, 160 n. 44, 215 n. 37, 220
ʿAd Šayḫ 45, 144–145
Addis Ababa 129–130, 185, 187–188, 189 n. 11, 195–196, 198–201, 212, 220 n. 55
ʿAfar 34, 65, 162 n. 51, 167
Agordat 32, 144–145, 150, 152 n. 32, 182 n. 52, 182 n. 52, 183, 186 n. 70, 188 n. 5, 195, 203 n. 75
Aḥmad al-Mīrġanī 30 n. 21, 32 n. 27, 55 n. 42, 56 n. 46, 57 n. 48, 73 n. 32, 77 n. 49, 115 n. 8, 116 n. 12, 133 n. 35, 135 n. 43, 137 n. 44, 145 n. 18, 160 n. 45, 161 n. 49, 182 n. 52, 183 n. 57, 192 n. 32, 196 nn. 47, 50, 198 n. 57
Aḥmad ibn Idrīs 17, 19–22, 83, 140
Al-Azhar 27, 98
Al-Ġazālī (Persian Mystic) 54
Al-Ġazālī, Zaynab 191
Al-Hudaydah 29, 141
ʿAlī al-Mīrġanī 26–27, 57, 72, 152, 179, 181, 184–185
ʿAlī Muḥammad (*ḫalīfa*) 168
ʿAlīm, ʿulamāʾ 17, 20–22, 27, 29, 48, 98, 141–142, 162, 164, 195
Anglo-Egyptian Sudan 27–29, 34, 45, 97–98, 167 n. 7
Anwar Mosque 196–197, 199 n. 60
Arabic 8–9, 15, 19–20, 29, 49 n. 23, 51 n. 26, 63–64, 67, 74, 91, 96 n. 24, 101, 103, 107, 115, 116 n. 11, 129, 135, 149–150, 167, 176, 179, 181–182, 185, 187–188, 192, 194, 196, 200, 207, 216, 219
Army 25, 30, 31 n. 24, 32–33, 44, 95, 162, 166, 168–169, 175, 177, 184, 188, 191, 203
Artega 28–29
Askari, askaris 57 n. 51, 162, 166–167, 170, 175–179
Asmara 56, 58, 65 n. 7, 78, 82, 86, 95, 103, 115, 129, 149 n. 20, 150, 152 n. 30, 153 n. 33, 160 n. 43, 168–169, 170 n. 21, 177 n. 37, 187, 188 n. 5, 195
Ašrāf 19, 66–67, 70
Assab 30, 65, 82, 160, 188 n. 5, 195
Axum 12
Ay Rawda Qallo 129 n. 30, 145 n. 18, 196 n. 50, 199–200, 202, 213–220

Bakrī al-Mīrġanī 27–28
Barentu 82, 145, 172, 188 n. 5, 195
Bashi-bazouk 166
Batī Del Wambara 12, 64
Baṭin 221
Battle of Adwa 35
Battle of Agordat 32, 35
Battle of Keren 3, 183
Beni ʿAmer 23, 30–34, 44, 66, 72, 84, 94, 100 n. 41, 167, 186
Bidʿa 50
Bilen 89, 92, 94–96, 98, 100–101
Blessings 4, 39, 55, 77, 94, 97, 104, 151, 153, 214–215, 219
Body, embodiment 3, 7–9, 39 n. 53, 40–41, 53, 55, 70, 78, 87, 89, 91, 96, 105, 107, 113, 116–117, 134–135, 138, 142, 166, 206–208, 210–212, 219–220
British 1 n. 3, 3, 15, 19, 25, 27–28, 30–36, 45, 72, 82 n. 53, 97 n. 27, 98, 145, 151–152, 165–166, 174–175, 176 n. 30, 178 n. 40, 181–186, 200, 202–203

Cairo 27, 30 n. 21, 32 n. 27, 36 n. 42, 41, 55 n. 42, 56 n. 46, 57 n. 48, 73 n. 32, 77 n. 49, 97–98, 102 n. 45, 115–116, 119, 129 n. 31, 133, 135 n. 42, 137 n. 44, 145 n. 18, 150 n. 21, 151 n. 26, 153 n. 33, 160 n. 43, 161 n. 49, 168 n. 12, 181, 183 n. 57, 184 n. 60, 185 n. 69, 191, 192 n. 32, 194, 196 n. 47, 198, 221 n. 58
Caniglia, Giuseppe 35 n. 35, 74 n. 38, 75, 77, 103–105, 111, 120, 190, 214
Catholic mission 94
Ceremony 1, 6, 57, 66, 72, 91, 96–97, 104–105, 107, 110, 121–122, 125, 128–131, 150–151, 153, 156–157, 175, 177–178, 187–189, 199, 206–207, 209–214, 216–217
Charisma 6–7, 39, 71, 74, 137, 143, 156, 202
Charity 70, 77–78
Christian 12, 14–15, 25, 33, 55–56, 64, 68, 75, 78, 82–83, 86, 94–95, 102, 107, 132–135, 137, 149, 153, 165–166, 177–178, 189, 193–195, 198, 201, 204, 207–208
Cinema, cinematography 111, 113, 117, 120–122, 129, 138
Citizen, citizenship 59, 188, 197
Coletta, Nicola (Italian engineer) 152
Community 5, 12–13, 21, 36, 38, 41, 47–49, 52, 55, 57–59, 76–78, 102, 108, 125, 129, 143 n. 9, 167, 179, 195, 197 n. 52, 198, 199 n. 60, 220 n. 55

Conflict 2, 4, 6, 11–12, 16–17, 20–22, 26, 28, 31–34, 41, 45, 47–49, 56–59, 65, 68, 72, 76, 83–84, 86, 104 nn. 51–52, 134–135, 140–141, 143, 151–152, 159–161, 166, 169, 171–172, 179, 181, 184–186, 203–204, 209–210
Cotton 105, 152

Dada Masiti 67–68
Dam 152–153
Danakil 160–161, 188
Dance, dancing 70, 89, 91, 94, 96–98, 100–101, 108, 111, 113 n. 5, 142, 207, 219–220
Dār al-Islam 14, 16, 165
Daʿwa (call) 17, 56, 191
De Feo, Vincenzo (Governor of Eritrea) 117, 122, 125, 128
Desire 40, 45, 67, 77, 88, 90–91, 104, 107, 120, 134, 194, 214–215, 217, 219–221
Ḏikr 68, 70–72, 94, 96–97, 142, 213, 215–216, 219
Dire Dawa 195, 198–200
Djibouti 74, 206, 209
Dress 4, 55, 100, 105, 107, 110, 118 n. 16, 131, 133, 135
Duce (see also Mussolini, Benito) 120, 125, 130, 187, 190–191
Duke of the Abruzzi, Prince Luigi Amedeo of Savoy-Aosta 111, 117, 119, 121
Duʿā' (invocation) 213, 216

East Africa 1, 35, 41, 66, 71, 73 n. 34, 88–89, 91, 95, 98, 107, 117, 122, 130, 179, 183, 186, 189–190, 192, 197
Education 5, 15–17, 51, 66–67, 71–72, 82, 117, 120, 145, 149, 151, 167, 188, 191, 208 n. 10, 213, 215
Egypt 4, 13–14, 17, 19, 21–23, 26, 28, 36, 58 n. 51, 74–76, 97–98, 145, 166, 176–177, 179–180, 181 n. 52, 188 n. 6, 203, 206–208
Elena Pesenti 58 n. 53, 78, 104, 110 n. 61, 153,
Emancipation 1, 43, 138, 190, 194
Emotion 7–8, 209–210, 217, 219–220
Entertainment 70, 102, 142
Eritrea 2–4, 8, 10, 13, 19, 21, 23, 28–36, 38 n. 44, 40 n. 54, 41, 44–46, 47 n. 15, 49, 50 n. 25, 51 n. 26, 52 n. 30, 53, 54 n. 35, 55–58, 65 n. 7, 68, 71, 73–74, 77, 82–84, 85 n. 61, 86 n. 62, 91, 95 n. 20, 96 n. 24, 101 n. 42, 102–103, 104 n. 51, 117, 120 n. 18, 122, 129, 133–135, 141 n. 2, 142, 144–145, 149 n. 20, 150–152, 157, 160–162, 165, 166 n. 6, 167 n. 10, 168–169, 170 n. 22, 171 n. 22, 172–173, 175–181, 183–184, 186–187, 190, 192, 195–198, 205–206, 210, 212–213
Ethiopia 2–3, 7–8, 11–14, 19, 43, 53, 64, 68, 72, 74–75, 89, 91, 95–98, 104 n. 52, 112, 119, 121–122, 129–130, 133, 137–138, 145, 159 n. 42, 162, 184, 187, 189–190, 193–200, 202, 204–207, 209, 212, 213 n. 28, 216, 219 n. 53
Ethiopian Christian Empire 14
European travellers 6, 34, 56, 77, 97, 102–105, 110, 120, 210, 213, 220–221

Faith 7, 13, 25, 48, 64, 66, 77, 82, 84, 98, 165, 178, 192, 221
Family 3–5, 8, 10, 19–23, 26–29, 31–32, 36 n. 43, 38, 44–45, 51, 53–54, 56, 58–59, 65–68, 70 n. 22, 72–73, 76–77, 92, 103, 116, 129 n. 31, 135 n. 42, 143–144, 149–150, 160, 162, 177, 179, 181 n. 52, 185, 192 n. 32, 194, 196–197, 199, 203, 220 n. 55
Fantasia, fantasy 88–92, 95–96, 97 n. 25, 98, 101, 107–108, 111–112, 113 n. 5, 142 n. 7
Fascism, Fascist regime 1, 35 n. 35, 56, 59, 89, 117, 121–122, 125, 128–130, 132, 181–183, 187–194, 201, 203–204
Fascists' racial policy 181
Fashion 92, 101–102, 104, 107, 119, 128, 132, 220 n. 55
Fāṭima, al-Mīrġanī 27, 58, 68, 74
Fatwā (*plur: fatāwā*) 98
Felter Sartori 59 n. 58
Female religious practices 2
Festival 142–143
Fioccardi (*Commissario*) 48, 53, 83–86, 95–96, 97 n. 25, 98, 120 n. 18, 168–169, 172
First World War 1, 27, 57 n. 51, 68, 88, 174, 178–180
Fitna 26, 58
France 14–15, 189

Gasparini, Jacopo (Governor of Eritrea) 152, 157, 168
Ǧaʿfar al-Mīrġanī 8, 32 n. 27, 44–47, 49–50, 52–54, 57–58, 73, 102 n. 45, 115, 117, 122, 133 n. 35, 135 n. 43, 137 n. 44, 149–152, 156–157, 161 n. 49, 167–173, 175, 177–178, 180–183, 184 n. 60, 186
Gender 2–6, 9, 43, 48, 53, 55, 58, 67 n. 15, 92 n. 16, 95, 100, 116, 133, 208, 210
Gift 38, 75, 77–78, 103–104, 110, 116 n. 11, 151, 156–157, 160–161, 166, 192
Ǧihād 12, 17, 26, 73, 179, 180 n. 45, 195, 203, 208 n. 10
Ǧinn 39, 78, 208, 216
Great Britain (see also British and England) 14, 180

Habab 23, 29, 31, 41, 45 n. 9, 72
Ḥadīṯ 20, 22, 50, 52, 54, 67, 72, 135, 182, 203

Ḥaḍra 46–47, 94, 97, 150, 212–213, 216
Ḫalīfa, (plur.) *ḫulafā'* 6, 22–23, 26–27, 32–33, 36 n. 43, 44, 46–47, 49–51, 53, 57–58, 66, 104, 115 n. 8, 133 n. 35, 135 n. 43, 137 n. 44, 149–151, 156–157, 167–169, 171–172, 175, 177, 183 n. 58, 185, 195
ḥalwa 71–72, 149
Ḥanafī 20, 23, 30 n. 21
Harar 13, 35 n. 35, 64, 67, 70, 105 n. 55, 129, 145 n. 18, 164, 187, 194–195, 196 n. 50, 197–201, 202 n. 72, 203–204, 206, 212–216, 218–219
Ḥasan al-Mīrġanī 21–23, 28, 31, 68, 184
Hāšim al-Mīrġanī 8, 26, 28–30, 32, 34, 36, 38–41, 44–47, 58, 66, 71, 73, 77–78, 92, 94, 102, 157, 166, 168, 195
Ḫatmī, Ḫatmiyya 2–4, 8, 10, 13, 18–20, 22–23, 26–27, 30–36, 38, 40 n. 56, 45–46, 49, 52, 68, 71–72, 74, 76, 102 n. 45, 103–104, 115 n. 8, 133 n. 35, 135 n. 43, 137 n. 44, 140–145, 151–152, 159, 161, 166–169, 172 n. 24, 175, 177, 179, 181, 182 n. 56, 183–184, 185 n. 66, 186, 192 n. 32, 196
Ḥawliyya 70, 77, 94, 220
Health 39, 41, 78, 82, 84–85, 157
Hejaz 4, 12, 17, 19–23, 27, 36, 76, 164
Heresy, heretical (see also Unorthodox) 22, 50, 56
Hetumlo 40–41, 58, 73, 76, 103, 105, 161, 195, 198 n. 57, 214, 215 n. 38
Ḥiǧāb 55–56, 58
Hiǧra 12
Horn of Africa 10, 12–14, 63, 70, 83, 129
Huda Shaarawi 191

Idrīsī Tradition 140
Image (see also Picture) 9, 31, 39 n. 53, 55–56, 59, 68, 88–91, 92 n. 16, 102, 107, 112–113, 115, 117, 119–120, 122, 125, 128–135, 137–138, 175, 205–206
Imagination 9, 11, 88, 91, 95–96, 111, 113 n. 5, 121, 144, 205–206, 209, 211, 217
Imām (imamate) 12, 49–52, 57, 64, 101, 141, 156, 167
Inauguration 41, 125, 128, 130, 151–153, 187, 199, 213
India 20, 76, 107, 177, 196, 220 n. 55
Intermediary, intermediaries (see also Mediator) 3, 11, 14, 16, 28, 32–33, 41, 44, 74, 103, 132–134, 157, 159, 162, 165, 174–175, 181, 204
Interpreter, interpreters 107, 110, 145, 213, 216–217
Islamic revivalist movements 1
Italian colonialism 2, 4, 9–10–11, 14, 16 n. 14, 19, 30, 34–35, 44, 56, 59, 65, 89, 112 n. 2, 125, 160, 165, 168, 176–177, 181, 188
Italo-Arabic school in Massawa 187
Italo-Ethiopian war 1, 11, 59, 160, 162, 189, 192–193, 212

Jabarti 13, 21, 64, 169
Jeddah 200
Journalist 103–104, 107, 110–111, 214

Karāma, (plur.) *karāmāt* (see also Marvel) 6, 22, 29–30, 67, 70, 76, 133, 140, 143–145, 159–161, 164, 184–185, 199–200 n. 61, 201–202, 215, 218, 220
Kassala 22, 26–27, 31–33, 35, 45–46, 58, 68, 75–76, 167, 171–173, 175, 183–185
Keren 3, 8, 10, 21, 28, 31–32, 35, 41, 45–46, 48–49, 52–53, 57, 76, 77 n. 47, 83–85, 92, 94–96, 97 n. 25, 98, 100–103, 104 nn. 50–51, 115–116, 133 n. 35, 135 n. 43, 137 n. 44, 144 n. 15, 145, 150, 151 nn. 25, 27, 156–157, 159, 160 n. 44, 167–169, 170 n. 20, 171, 177, 183–185, 187, 188 n. 5, 195, 212, 215 n. 37, 220–221
Khartoum 68 n. 21, 152, 168, 185, 196–197

Lalla Zaynab 5
Leadership, leader 1–2, 4–6, 11, 14, 16, 19, 21, 22 n. 35, 25–28, 31, 33–35, 39, 41, 44, 46–47, 49, 51–52, 55–57, 64, 70, 72–73, 82 n. 53, 86, 96–97, 101–102, 104 n. 51, 112, 116, 130, 140–141, 151, 160, 168–169, 172–173, 175, 179–181, 184, 185 n. 66, 189, 194, 198, 200, 203–204, 214–215
Leisure 95–96, 102
Liberation 3, 33
Libya 1, 2 n. 8, 11, 16, 22, 58 n. 51, 72, 88, 91, 130, 168–169, 175–181, 187–189, 202 n. 75
Love 40, 55, 133, 219–220
Luce Institute 116–117, 119–122, 129–130, 152, 162 n. 51, 190, 191 n. 23, 198

Madama 88–89, 95
Madrasa 196, 197 n. 52, 200 n. 66
Maghreb (see also North Africa) 13–14, 17, 20, 48, 74, 83, 91
Mahdī, Mahdiyya 25–27, 29, 34, 98, 179
Maḥmūd Ibrāhīm Muḥammad 168–169
Manāqib 30 n. 21
Mancini, Pasquale Stanislao 10
Marriage (see also Wedding) 21, 28–29, 32, 55, 63 n. 2, 65–66, 73, 76–77, 94, 151, 215
Martinelli, Renzo 40 n. 54, 72 n. 29, 103–105, 110–111, 120, 214
Martini, Ferdinando (Governor of Eritrea) 35, 40 n. 57, 41, 45, 102, 144, 187
Maryam al-Mīrġanī 26, 28–30, 38, 44, 55, 57–58, 68, 70–73, 75, 145, 151, 152 n. 28, 185–186, 200

Massawa 3–4, 8, 10, 13, 26, 28, 30–31, 35–36, 38, 40–41, 44–47, 51 n. 27, 58, 65, 68, 71–72, 74–77, 82, 92, 96, 97 n. 25, 102–103, 105, 117, 121–122, 125, 129–130, 135, 144 n. 14, 150, 153, 161, 166–167, 171, 175, 177–178, 183, 184 n. 61, 187, 188 n. 5, 190, 192, 195 n. 43, 196, 198, 201, 212–214
Maʿrifa 215, 220–221
Mecca 12, 17, 19–22, 28, 40, 58, 73, 75, 83, 116, 179, 182 n. 54, 200–201
Media (Colonial media) 3, 57, 102, 111, 113, 117, 120–121, 129–130, 132–134, 137–138, 162 n. 51, 176–177, 192
Mediator (see also Intermediary) 48, 56, 71, 133, 137, 141, 151–152, 159, 162
Medicine 38–39, 70, 78, 82 n. 53, 85, 157, 161, 212, 220
Mediterranean region 1, 10, 75, 91, 121, 129, 187, 190
Memory, memories 4, 7–9, 11, 63, 70, 104, 110 n. 61, 121, 142 n. 7, 179, 181 n. 51, 189, 192–194, 199, 204–205, 209–212, 214–216, 219, 222
Menelik 137 n. 47, 195, 197
Middle East 1, 15, 43, 97, 121, 132, 187 n. 3, 189–190, 206–207
Mīrġanī, Mīrġaniyya 3–4, 8–10, 19–23, 26–33, 36 n. 43, 38, 44–48, 54 n. 35, 55–58, 66, 68, 70 n. 22, 71–73, 75–76, 78, 82, 86, 129 n. 31, 135 n. 42, 141, 143–144, 150, 153, 156–157, 159, 160 n. 43, 165–167, 169–172, 174–176, 179, 181, 184–186, 192 n. 32, 196–197, 199
Missionary 16, 78, 82–83, 86, 220
Modern, modernity, modernization 2, 14, 23, 82 n. 53, 110–111, 140–141, 143–145, 149, 151, 153, 156–157, 159, 161–162, 209
Momina (Sittī) 68, 75
Mosque 4, 6, 8, 11, 17, 27, 31, 33, 40–41, 45–47, 49–50, 52–53, 58, 70–71, 75, 98, 101, 103, 104 n. 51, 105, 117, 125, 128–130, 144–145, 153, 156, 167, 176, 187–189, 195–200, 204, 212–213
Muftī 36, 40–41
Muḥammad Aberra Hagos 168–169
Muḥammad Hanfare (Sultan) 65, 160–161
Muḥammad Nūr Sirāǧ 40
Muḥammad Sadiq (Shaykh) 200 n. 66, 203
Muḥammad Ṣāliḥ 45–46, 58, 73
Muḥammad Sirr al-Ḫatm, al-Mīrġanī 22–23, 26–27, 29–30, 31 n. 24
Muḥammad ʿUṯmān, al-Mīrġanī 18–23, 26, 30, 31 n. 24, 38, 68, 73, 184, 196
Muslim 1–2, 4–5, 10, 12–17, 19–20, 25, 32–33, 35–36, 38–41, 43–52, 55–58, 63–66, 68, 70–72, 74–75, 78, 82–83, 86, 94, 96, 98, 101–103, 105, 107–108, 116, 120, 122, 125, 128–130, 132–133, 137–138, 140, 142–145, 149–153, 157, 159, 162, 164–167, 171, 175–180, 182 n. 54, 183, 185–198, 200–201, 203–204, 206–209, 212, 213 n. 31, 214, 216, 220
Muslim Policy (see also Pro-Islamic policy) 41, 187–188, 197 n. 51
Mussolini, Benito (see also Duce) 1, 35 n. 35, 59, 104, 116 n. 11, 117, 125, 128–131, 133, 157, 162, 168, 187–191
Mussolini, Edda 111, 120
Muwalat—collaborazione

Nāfisa, al-Mīrġanī 27, 58, 68, 73
Nafs 67, 221
Nana Asma'u 5, 83, 208 n. 10
Naqšbandī, Naqšbandiyya 20, 56, 142
Networks 5, 10, 16, 23, 48, 53–54, 67, 70–73, 76–77, 83–84, 107, 141, 143, 162, 167, 175, 200, 203, 212
North
Africa
(see also Maghreb) 7, 15, 89 n. 5, 91, 113 n. 5, 189
Nurse, nurses 64, 77–78, 104, 107, 153

Offerings 36, 38, 77–78, 84, 87, 102, 170–171, 176, 215, 221
Orality, oral history 5, 7–9, 11, 28, 32–34, 38 n. 38, 40, 56–58, 66 n. 10, 67, 70–71, 74, 103–104, 116, 122, 132–133, 140, 145, 160, 175, 181 n. 51, 183, 192–194, 196, 198–199, 201, 203–204, 210, 212–216, 219–222
Oromo 159 n. 42, 188, 189 n. 11, 194–195, 203, 206–207, 213 n. 31, 216
Orthodox Church 153, 177
Ottoman Empire 1, 14, 19–20, 22–23, 25–26, 28, 33–34, 58 n. 51, 97, 119, 140–141, 166, 177–179, 180 n. 45

Performance 91–92, 95–96, 98, 100–102, 111, 142, 208–210, 215, 217, 219–220
Phonograph 140–141
Photographs, photography 8–9, 55, 68, 88–89, 91–92, 95–96, 98, 101–102, 110–113, 115–117, 119, 121, 129, 131, 133–135, 137–138, 145, 151–152, 156–157, 166, 170, 187, 190, 195, 198, 205–206
Picture (see also Image) 89, 91–92, 96 n. 25, 100, 112, 117, 120, 128, 134, 151
Poem 8–9, 67, 142, 151, 219
Popular 7, 11, 17, 20–21, 23, 29, 35 n. 35, 39, 41, 47–48, 55, 64, 67–68, 70–71, 73–75, 94–98, 101–102, 111–112, 117, 119–120, 129,

132, 140–141, 143, 166, 168, 175–177, 184, 201, 207, 216, 218
Possession, possessed 47, 94–98, 112–113, 206, 208–211, 214, 216–217, 219
Press 1, 74, 88, 102, 105, 111, 131, 137–138, 189–190, 192
Prince Umberto of Piemonte 152
Pro-Islamic policy (see also Muslim policy) 1, 128–129, 178, 193, 200–201, 203–204
Propaganda 1, 26, 117, 119–121, 128–130, 132, 151, 176–178, 180, 181 n. 52, 187–195, 203
Prostitution 25, 44, 95, 100, 176

Qāḍī 36 n. 43, 41, 67, 162, 167, 176–177, 188
Qādirī, Qādiriyya 13, 16, 20, 39, 67–68, 165, 198, 200, 213 n. 28

Rābiʿa al-ʿAdawiyya 54
Red Cross 77, 104, 107, 153
Red Sea 4, 10–14, 18–19, 21–23, 26, 28, 30–31, 34, 66, 68, 71, 75–76, 120, 140–142, 176
Rome 1, 3, 30 n. 21, 117, 120, 130, 162, 168, 187, 189–191, 192 n. 32

Saint 5, 7–8, 39, 47, 54–56, 63 n. 2, 73–74, 94, 97, 121, 134, 140–143, 151, 159, 201, 202 n. 71, 206, 209, 212, 216, 219–221
Saiza Nabarawi 191
Salafi 142, 143
Salary 35, 36, 40, 45, 57
Saleh Ahmad Kekiya (Eritrean family) 201 n. 66, 220 n. 55
Ṣāliḥiyya 16, 18
Salvago Raggi School 145, 150, 167, 169, 187
Sanūsī, Sanūsiyya 16, 18, 21–23, 172 n. 24, 176, 179–181, 188
Second World War 3, 68, 72, 159, 181, 182 n. 56, 183, 186, 197, 203
Selassie, Haile 162, 164, 195, 197
Sex, sexuality 51, 53–55, 59, 89–90, 92 n. 16, 95–96, 112–113, 134, 213
Shrine, shrines 4, 6, 8, 31, 39–41, 45, 48, 53, 58, 63 n. 2, 67–68, 70–71, 73, 75, 94–95, 97–98, 103–105, 117, 142–143, 167, 176, 195, 198, 212–213, 216
Sinkat 26, 29, 70, 72, 75
Sittāt 74, 217, 219
Slave, slavery 25, 33, 64–65, 67, 76, 94, 97, 118 n. 16, 167 n. 7, 207
Sokhna Magat Diop 6
Soldiers (see also Askaris) 1, 30, 33, 56, 89, 95, 102, 166, 167 n. 7, 168–169, 175, 178, 180, 187–188, 197, 203, 215
Somalia 2 n. 8, 14 n. 10, 16, 35 n. 35, 39, 67, 74, 91, 117, 165, 168, 206, 217
Suakin 21, 26–31, 44, 57–58, 68, 71–72, 75, 102 n. 46, 151
Sub-Saharan Africa 1, 16, 63
Sudan 4, 13, 19, 21–23, 26–31, 33–36, 41, 45–46, 57–58, 68, 71–74, 75 n. 38, 76, 92, 97–98, 144–145, 150–152, 166, 167 n. 7, 173–175, 179–181, 182 n. 56, 183–184, 185 n. 66, 186, 197, 200, 203, 206–207, 210 n. 21, 213 n. 28, 218
Sword (of Islam) 1, 115–116, 128, 135, 187

Tancredi Saletta (Italian General) 30
Ṭarīqa, (plur.) *ṭuruq* 13, 16, 19–20, 23, 28, 49–51, 56, 68, 70–73, 103, 151 n. 26, 167, 175, 177, 180, 186, 190
Tax, taxes (see also Tributes) 23, 33–34, 145, 151, 166
Taytu 137 n. 47, 138
Tiru Sina 75 n. 39, 97 n. 30, 104 n. 52
Tesseney 145, 152–153, 159, 183, 195
Ṭibb 39
Trade, trader 13, 16, 25, 28, 31–32, 34, 35 n. 35, 65–66, 75–76, 151, 161, 168–169, 201 n. 66, 220 n. 55
Travel, Travellers 6, 8–9, 13, 17–22, 26, 34, 54, 56, 58–59, 74–75, 77, 82–84, 86, 89, 91, 95–97, 100, 102–105, 107, 110–111, 117, 120–121, 144, 161, 168, 201, 210, 212–213, 215, 220–221
Tributes (see also Tax) 84, 119, 121, 166, 170
Turks 58 n. 51, 176–180, 195

ʿUmar al-Muḫtār 181
Unorthodox (see also Heresy, heretical) 2, 15, 47, 115
ʿUṯmān Tāǧ al-Sirr 26, 28–30, 38, 39 n. 48, 71–73, 167

Veil, veiling 4, 21, 25, 50, 56, 58, 90, 100–101, 105, 107, 115–117, 118 n. 16, 119, 128, 131, 133–135, 137, 156, 191
Visit (see also *Ziyāra*) 1, 4, 19–21, 27–28, 31–33, 35 n. 35, 39, 48, 51, 56, 67, 71, 75, 77–78, 82, 87, 94–95, 97, 101–105, 107, 111, 119–121, 125, 130, 142 n. 7, 144, 151–152, 157, 159, 166, 168, 187, 190–191, 194, 196, 197 n. 52, 198–199, 203 n. 75, 207, 212–217, 219–221
Voice 87, 89, 122, 130, 132, 134, 141, 176, 192, 205, 210–211, 214

Wahhābiyya 17
Walī, (plur.) *awliyāʾ* 22, 39, 52–54, 74, 133, 202–203, 206, 209, 212, 216
Wedding (See also marriage) 25, 77, 150–151, 192

West Africa 14, 43 n. 3, 53, 83, 189
Women 1–8, 11–13, 22, 25–26, 28–29, 32–34, 38, 43–44, 46–56, 59, 63–68, 70–75, 77, 82–83, 85–86, 89–92, 94–98, 100–103, 104 n. 52, 105, 107–108, 111–113, 115–116, 119, 128, 130, 133–135, 138, 142, 151, 156, 161, 164, 176, 190–192, 204–205, 207–217, 219–222

Yayyo of Awsa (Sultan) 160–162
Yemen 4, 19, 21–23, 29, 73, 140, 168, 179, 206

Ẓāhir 221
Zār, zār-ḥaḍra 47, 94, 96–98, 111, 142, 206–213, 216, 218
Zāwiya, zāwiyyat, (plur.) *zawāyā* 22, 46, 181
Zaylaʿ 12–13, 64
Ziyāra, (plur.) *ziyārāt* 39, 52, 63 n. 2, 66–68, 70–71, 75, 94, 120, 143, 213–214
Zoli, Corrado (Governor of Eritrea) 120